AF837220

The Military as a Separate Society

The Military as a Separate Society

Consequences for Discipline in the United States and Australia

Pauline Collins

LEXINGTON BOOKS
Lanham • Boulder • New York • London

Published by Lexington Books
An imprint of The Rowman & Littlefield Publishing Group, Inc.
4501 Forbes Boulevard, Suite 200, Lanham, Maryland 20706
www.rowman.com

6 Tinworth Street, London SE11 5AL, United Kingdom

Copyright © 2019 by The Rowman & Littlefield Publishing Group, Inc.

All rights reserved. No part of this book may be reproduced in any form or by any electronic or mechanical means, including information storage and retrieval systems, without written permission from the publisher, except by a reviewer who may quote passages in a review.

British Library Cataloguing in Publication Information Available

Library of Congress Cataloging-in-Publication Data

ISBN 978-1-4985-5704-7 (cloth)
ISBN 978-1-4985-5705-4 (electronic)

Contents

Chapter One

The Military: A Separate Society and Its Morality

UNITED STATES AND AUSTRALIAN MILITARY

The operation of the military in Western countries has transformed. This has occurred on three fronts, all of which concern the nature of the civil-military relationship. First, the legislation governing military discipline has gone through considerable review in countries such as Australia and the United States of America, in response to concerns about fairness and legitimacy in the treatment of service persons, both in the realm of criminal and civil law, and in response to human rights. Second, the nature of standing militaries is changing. They are different from the World War II civilian or conscript armies, as they are now not only volunteer professional military, but they are increasingly becoming outsourced or privatized. Third, war today is largely conducted by multinational forces rather than a single state military. Each of these three aspects brings a continuing tension around the military treatment of its personnel, which relates to the historical differences in the civil and military systems for punishing aberrant behavior and the inherent purpose and values of discipline systems.

The alleged requirements of the military mission have been given a great deal of prominence in the US and Australia. George Washington's justification for a separate discipline system in 1759, namely that "[d]iscipline is the soul of an army. It makes small numbers formidable; procures success to the weak, and esteem to all,"[1] requires reconsideration. Changes bring a new breed of militarianism, labelled by some as a "Revolution in Military Affairs" (RMA). Andrew Marshall, a Cold War warrior and nuclear intellectual, has been accredited with the idea behind the RMA and he advocated the expenditure of billions of dollars to provide military hardware and technology in order to fight wars in a new way, remote from the battlefield, through altered strategic and organizational changes:

> . . . in 1997, the Clinton administration's National Defense Panel recommended spending between $5 billion and $10 billion annually to implement the doctrine . . . the following year, Secretary of Defense William Cohen said that the Pentagon's "willingness to embrace the Revolution in Military Affairs—to harness technology to ultimately bring about fundamental conceptual and organizational change—is critical" to meeting future national security challenges.[2]

This ushered in a new way in which war is conducted that embraces technology and is characterized by a flattened networking structure. Combined with the introduction of private military contractors (PMCs) into technologically advanced militaries, it requires justifications for the need for a system of discipline that is separate from the mainstream civilian system to be reviewed afresh.[3] The arguments do not accommodate that the military is an all-volunteer force assuming workplace rights, or that PMCs now act in combat roles that may fall outside the military discipline system. The quality of military work-life balance may seem a mundane matter but it is fundamental to the entire military enterprise. Any professional can only fully deliver at an expected performance level if they have a secure and satisfying workplace. This in turn has consequences for recruiting, retaining, and career development of military employees.

One aspect perhaps highlights these dilemmas of the workplace more than any other. The ongoing reports of sexual and other misconduct in the military of Western states not only damages the esteem of the institution, but diminishes the experience of employees and undermines the credibility of arguments in favor of maintaining a separate system from civilian justice. However, little has been done to unpack the arguments that sustain a separate military discipline. Rowe has referred to the justifications as the "dead hand of 'tradition'"[4] and as such, it stops any consideration of whether the reality does in fact demand that a military person be treated differently in order to be able to undertake their employment obligations.

Courts-martial, as generally ad hoc courts, are convened to deal with military offences, which include civilian criminal offences as and when a commanding officer considers such a level of punishment necessary or an alleged offender chooses such a method. This covers military members or those defined as coming within jurisdiction.[5] In the US[6] and Australia[7] courts-martial are not controlled by tenured judges and the panel, sometimes seen as the "jury," is comprised of other military personnel often less in number than a 12-member civilian jury.[8] This panel determines guilt or innocence as well as punishment on a non-unanimous basis. The system sits outside the normal civilian courts established under Chapter III of the Constitution in Australia and Article III courts in the US Constitution. These legislative "courts" combine with a delegation of authority to the executive, which enables rules to be promulgated by the executive arm for their operations: the Governor General as Commander in Chief of the Australian Defence Force, and the President as Commander in Chief in the US.[9] The legislature establishes the courts-martial in order to try specific military offences, as well as all general criminal offences, and apply a range of penalties as well as enforcing the outcomes. This system is very different to the civilian justice system. As then Australian High Court Justice Kirby pointed out in *White v. Director of Military Prosecution*:

> . . . [t]he lack of the necessity (or actuality) of universal legal training; the *ad hoc* constitution of the tribunal; the lack of tenure of members; and the requirement to select persons who must be associated with the Force (and therefore necessarily interested in the conduct of the accused), all represent very serious departures from the normal features of Ch III courts.[10]

These legislative courts remain distinct even though they have undergone reform to civilianize, and more closely resemble the civilian courts. Nevertheless, significant differences remain and these include being heard by "judges" of limited tenure; commanders deciding whether a matter will be referred to discipline and deciding on which process, currently subject to some rights for the accused to choose the level of dealing; limited rights to object to panel members; different processes than the committal hearing in Australia or grand jury process in the US; a non-unanimous panel decision; the panel deciding punishment and the possibility of having this process overridden by a military member outside the "court" or a mandatory review body.[11] The military "judges" may have limited legal training, and likewise for the prosecuting and defense counsel who also may have less experience than their civilian equivalents.

The executive and legislative arms of military control support this system, to this day particularly the command control element. A court-martial, unlike a civilian criminal trial, includes the ability of the panel of "jurors," who are fellow workers, to directly question witnesses and only two-thirds of their votes are needed for a conviction.[12] Panels can also be comprised of fewer members than would be the case in a civilian jury and they are involved in deciding the sentence.[13] A "military judge" presides over a court-martial, which proceeds by using rules of evidence and procedure as in a civilian criminal trial, but there are distinct differences. In the US plea agreements are distinctive, enabling changes in charges and agreements to lesser sentences, and although the judge is not bound by the agreement, it is nevertheless binding on a convening authority. Unlike in a civilian case, a military judge is not made aware of any lower sentence agreement made with the convening authority and the accused has the benefit of receiving whichever is the lower—the court-martial sentence or the sentence pre-agreed with the convening authority. Any findings and sentence are not final until the convening authority has given approval. This power has had some curtailment due to a serious sexual offending case in 2014.[14]

The military system has evolved very slowly from Roman times and is wholly focused on discipline. Much debate has occurred along the tension lines of discipline and the need for a system that evinces justice. As Schlueter explains:

> The military justice system has been described as a "rough form of justice," a system providing more rights than its civilian counterparts, a system of "drumhead," a system incapable of dispensing justice, an evolving system, a system that has been civilianized, a system in need of modernization, and a system in search of respect. However one describes or views the system, there has always been, and will always be, a debate over the exact purpose and function of the military justice system.[15]

The term military discipline, rather than justice system, is preferred in this work as a reminder that the principle justification for a separate system remains the threat of punishment to ensure discipline as the *raison d'etre* for that system. This is very different to civilian justice administered under Art III/Ch III courts of justice. It highlights that the preponderance of the punishment's focus is on discipline. Any civilianizing has served the purpose of making it more agreeable to both military members and civilian society. For instance, the *U.S. Manual for Courts-Martial* (*MCM*) cloaks its purpose by placing the word "justice" before "maintaining good order" when defining the purpose of the military system:

> The purpose of military law is to promote justice, to assist in maintaining good order and discipline in the armed forces, to promote efficiency and effectiveness in the military establishment, and thereby to strengthen the national security of the United States.[16]

The line between administrative workplace discipline and criminal offending becomes blurred in the military domain, which leads to a corresponding failure to appreciate the difference between the two. The reality is that most matters, irrespective of which end of the spectrum they fall—serious criminal behavior or workplace indiscretions—are often dealt with at the less administrative end. Confusion exists around the options commanders have in enforcing discipline,[17] including administrative actions such as separation from the military, or a non-judicial punishment (NJP) option under the Uniform Code of Military Justice (UCMJ) art 15, and in Australia the Discipline

Officer Scheme. Non-judicial punishment enables a commander to impose a direct punishment as opposed to a sentence. The courts-martial range from summary, to special and general courts-martial hearing matters, which may be as serious as the criminal offence of murder, leading to potential capital punishment in the US. The lack of refinement in discussing these very different options has been described as an "apple and oranges problem."[18]

In civilian workplaces, there has been a shift from adversarial discipline to tribunal processes and internal Codes of Conduct that are enforced through administrative procedures. These processes commence in the workplace but have outside appellate body options. The approach is designed to overcome legal constraints and the more onerous "beyond reasonable doubt" burden of proof in preference for a "balance of probabilities" burden. At the same time, it aims to provide a process that ensures fairness and protection of rights. Sanctions, however, are not painless and can include significant financial penalties, rank reduction, and employment termination.[19] Workplace law is used to keep order in the workplace and a sense of discipline, and it operates in the civil law, as opposed to the criminal law, domain within the civilian system. Criminal offending is an offence against the state and requires all the trappings developed over centuries to ensure that the conviction and sentencing of an offender is done with justice and that the offender is the true perpetrator of the offence.

When the civilian courts refuse, in military matters, to consider arguments relating to rights to a fair hearing by an independent and impartial tribunal,[20] access to an effective remedy for breach,[21] protection of the law,[22] as well as constitutional rights to due process and equal treatment before the law, the very clear question arises: "who guards the guardians?"[23] A deferent approach by the civilian courts enables allegations of impunity when it comes to the military.

Militaries have existed long before democracies. It has been universally claimed that for a military apparatus to function, it must have exceptional discipline in the form of the unquestioning obedience of personnel bought about by a rigid hierarchical command structure. This is particularly so in the battlefield where there is no time for hesitation or debate. However, mercifully, the battlefield is generally the exception and much of the time military personnel are working in a peacetime environment. Discipline however, as Chief Judge Baker of the United States Court of Appeals for the Armed Forces (CAAF) points out, is best achieved in ways other than through punishment:

> . . . discipline is principally a matter of leadership and culture. The most effective form of leadership is leadership by example, not leadership by court-martial. Most matters of military discipline are addressed through counseling, leadership, and command, not military justice.[24]

Historically, looking at the UK, from which the US and Australian military systems grew, military courts could not operate in peacetime when civilian courts were open and functioning. This reflects the principle that the civilian domain takes precedence over the military in democracies. Democracies have claimed the upper hand, realizing the need to keep the military under control so it does not become a danger to the democratic state, while still acknowledging it is a useful tool to maintain power. The US Supreme Court decisions of *Milligan*[25] and *Duncan*[26] support this understanding of the US Constitution. In order for civilian control to prevail, where civilian courts were operating, martial law courts were not permitted, even in wartime.[27]

Unfortunately, despite the claimed need for greater discipline of military members, the exercise of public power by the military in civilian Western democracies such as Australia and the US demonstrates a tendency toward failure in moral discipline. As a total institution,[28] one in which the people work and often live together as members who are subject to special policies and laws separate from the civilian system, a distinct culture arises that demands total loyalty to the institution and seeks to prevent external interference.[29] In this work I make a normative value claim that the justifications for separateness, which enables the military to operate a different system of criminal punishment outside the civilian justice system, no longer stand and can lead to a failure in maintaining civilian institutional control. This has unacknowledged potential consequences for the civil-military relationship, operational functioning of the military, and human rights. The normative claim is that being subject to a secondary and alternative system of criminal law imposed internally by a separate coterie on its members leads to moral decline. Members ought to, and may well, improve in discipline if criminal offending is removed to the primary civilian justice system.

Coterie is a term that signifies a separate group that feels some elite allegiance to each other as members but not necessarily the same allegiance to the broader citizenry. Membership of the group gives entitlement to special treatment, which is reinforced by being subject to different rules or laws, and being segregated by dress, code, and even physical location. A coterie mentality can range across many groupings in society, from private schooling institutions and universities, to clergy, prisons, police, and the military. The effect of a coterie is the members' mental separatism, which is of great significance when it comes to matters of behavior and discipline. History reveals when a group is subject to different laws and treatment, one of the first failings is in the area of morality, including behavior towards others, for example, in the form of bullying and explicitly sexual conduct. The Royal Commission into Institutional Responses to Child Sexual Abuse in Australia (Royal Commission) referred to sexualized bullying, normalizing aggressive and dominant behavior, and cultures that tolerate this, as evidence of masculine domains.[30] Such behavior is aided where institutions have total authority and discretionary influence over how bad conduct is addressed: "the danger of institutional adjudications of sexual assault is own self-interest: . . . institutions . . . directly affected by the outcomes of a case . . . may be willing to sacrifice individual rights for an outcome beneficial to the organization."[31]

Historical cultural understandings provide a backdrop for comprehending the temperament of such coteries. For instance, when considering the church as one such coterie and its response to sexual abuse, the phrase *la bella figura* has arisen.[32] Literally meaning the beautiful figure, this is a concept derived from Italian culture and refers to a preference for always projecting your best image, particularly regarding reputation. Such desire means that the opposite, *la brutta figura* (the bad figure), or matters that damage one's image in general, remain hidden. Denial of failings and suppression of wrongs enables a disavowal that ensures these aspects of an organization are never aired, understood, or addressed. A concept derived from Italian culture, it has been noted that this "reverence is consistent with a pervasive elitism within Italian society."[33] Secrecy is an inherent need where *la bella figura* operates. The Royal Commission heard retired Bishop Geoffrey Robinson explain how this concept develops a culture of secrecy that adds to a pervasiveness of hidden sexual abuse:

> Secrecy is a very, very big thing in Italy. I am told it actually goes back to Roman times. So it has been around for 2000 years and so is not easily changed. Every Italian knows the two phrases, "*bella figura*" and "*brutta figura.*" . . . What they mean is keeping up appearances. You tell others—you appear in the best light possible. You keep secret anything that would put you in a bad light . . .[34]

Akin to the spread of Italian cuisine, this concept has become ubiquitous in many organizations. It has been observed that "Italians prefer to identify themselves as members of smaller units, especially families, towns, or regions."[35] The concept of a coterie develops a worldview that makes members feel they are somehow special, elite, and differentiated from the remainder of society. The Royal Commission heard evidence of this belief in the priesthood:

> There's a phrase in the Letter to the Hebrews, and it was a mistranslation, the Greek original simply says "taken from among human beings," whereas the Latin translation done by St Jerome says "taken up," *ex hominibus assumptus* . . . and that became this idea that the priest is taken up, he's up above somehow . . . all sorts of unhealthy things developed out of it. It's still around. In fact, some . . . very young priests, just ordained . . . will talk about the ontological difference between a priest and a layperson . . . part of it means you have to be perfect, and if you can't be perfect, you have got to appear to be perfect . . .[36]

Claims of "blue-ribbon" panels being comprised of military members with higher education levels than civilian juries, as a reason to keep the military discipline system, is an example of this elitist attitude.[37] The military is an organization in which *la bella figura* plays a significant role. The military codes have a long history, some argue buried in antiquity, and many refer to the Roman military as a starting place for borrowed concepts of discipline and military societies.[38] These are explored in this book. It is all about power and in a closed system this ultimately favors an environment ripe for abuse. The belief that ". . . the human body [is] a source of temptation, a source of leading you astray. [That] It's not the beautiful thing that God created; [that] it's a dangerous thing [means that] sex becomes dark and troublesome and a negative force in life."[39]

This coterie aspect is pervasive in the military in Australia and the United States, both advanced Western democracies. They have a common heritage in their approach to military discipline and maintain a separate system of punishment. These countries present two types of democratic political systems, the parliamentary and the presidential respectively. Australia has an executive and legislative authority combined in a Westminster-style system of responsible government.[40] This presents more as a two-way separation of power, with the legislature and executive on one side, making the independence of the courts all the more important. The presidential style operates in the US where separation of the executive, the legislature, and the judiciary is more distinct. Democratic governance systems maintain connections through the political franchise of members who remain able to vote. This is compulsory in Australia and a matter of choice in the US, but it is the key factor in both systems. The representatives of the people are held accountable to the people through a process of regular and fair elections. It is through this process of election by the people that a state's military is directly accountable to the citizenry it protects.

Claims that the legislature and executive alone are responsible for the containment of the military on the basis that they are elected by, and representatives for and on behalf of, the citizens is diminished when considering the degree of representation the political system actually provides. While voting is compulsory in Australia and non-compulsory in the US, in each state segments of the community are disenfranchised,[41] and if they can and do vote their choice is generally limited to the ideologies of two parties that are becoming more closely aligned.[42] Furthermore, the growth of the power of the executive in Australia and the US places the judicial arm in contention with the executive more often, as the judiciary is to uphold the protection of the individual's liberty and sanctity of the person by observing rule by law.[43]

The growing consumption of civilian areas of governance from the primary democratic society by the secondary military coterie results in provision of an internal, parallel, but different hierarchical governance. This secondary society operates a separate system for criminal discipline, prisons, health, and other areas, thereby challenging the concept of the military being under the governance of the civilian democratic structure. Greater integration rather than separation would support individual military members, the sustaining of the standing military, the civil-military principle, and the maintenance of the primary democratic polity.[44]

The military, particularly in the US, has grown far beyond what was envisaged by the founders of the Constitution. While it may well protect the US, it can also operate as a threat, perhaps not overtly as the Anti-federalists claimed it may,[45] but through a process of general militarization in which over 1.3 million serving personnel and many millions more as veterans of the US citizenry are now subject to non-democratic internal governance by a secondary society.[46] Any social cost from this is impossible to quantify. Jefferson was one amongst many to see a separate military as an anathema to the idea of a free and fair republican system. Turley describes this secondary society as a "pocket republic" that "was clearly understood by the Framers in their almost universal rejection of a large standing army and a separate military caste or society [as one that] raises fundamental questions of citizenship and population stratification that are distinct from its univocal function of preserving the political system."[47] Despite this, the separation is advanced by factors such as the Supreme Court's jurisprudence, the powerful coterie protecting its own interests, and the move to an all-volunteer professional force engaging non-citizens and private military contractors of many nationalities that operate from diverse bases across the world.

Sir Samuel Warren described military law as ". . . emanat[ing] wholly from the civil power, and may properly be regarded, like the ecclesiastical law, as a distinct division of the civil laws of the realm."[48] The parallel with ecclesiastical law and military law in development and operation is instructive. When canon law was at its height in the thirteenth century, the church was extremely influential, not only over the individual but also in relation to the political leadership, and as such it was an institution with enormous power and wealth.[49] The separate ecclesiastical law or canon law enabled the church to claim subject matter jurisdiction, using law as its medium for promoting its values, such as the embedded mores of *la bella figura*. Not unlike the military law today, with its separate system of "courts," the church also maintained a separate system of "ecclesiastical courts." Again, like military discipline appropriating from civilian law, the ecclesiastical law borrowed heavily from its counterpart at the time, the Roman law, but it also expanded its influence through legislation and case law. This continued to such an extent that, according to Seidman, by "the thirteenth century, 'canon law began to . . . give herself airs of superiority.'"[50] When one makes the comparison with current military practice in the US and Australia, the similarity is evident. In its time the church's

> ability to operate a separate system of law and courts by claiming a specialist area of expertise, along with its resources, meant it became "a major political actor, power broker in European politics, and significant property owner across the continent, the church found itself in a position to challenge the great secular authorities."[51]

The claim today that the military is entitled to maintain a separate system of discipline, along with its powerful position within the governmental structure, sees shadowy echoes from the height of ecclesiastical historical times. The early church courts operated alongside the royal courts and a lay member of the church, on arrest, had the option of choosing to be dealt with by a church court. The church courts tended to hand down penalties that were more lenient and they could not impose the death penalty. This meant lay clerical members committing murder could potentially walk away without a death penalty. Attempts by Henry II to change this resulted in The Constitutions of Clarendon presented to the bishops at the 1164 Council of Clarendon.[52] The document sought to define the relationship between the King's courts and the cannon law in sixteen clauses. The church strongly protested, claiming ancient privileges, which underpinned the rift between Henry II and Thomas Becket.[53] It took Henry VIII and Thomas Cromwell to provide a definite break with the Pope and Rome in favor of the Parliament and King.[54]

Bringing the church to heel in the period of Henry VIII did not ultimately "destroy" the church, which has continued to operate until today in a generally more settled role within the political structure, which still enables the individual to exercise spiritual freedom. Despite the demand by the church for special treatment having been significantly curtailed, vestiges of remaining separation still present issues regarding certain entitlements that are claimed to exist for purely internal church matters.[55] This perception of entitlement under remnant separate law has seen churches embroiled in sexual abuse scandals in many countries, including Australia and the US. Like the churches, the military's assertion that without special treatment they will fail to operate appropriately, also cannot be sustained. Indeed, as this work and others', such as Turley's, suggest, abandoning the separate coterie as regards criminal punishment, may well increase the military's ability to sustain its core functional role in providing security.

The US system provides a constitutional framework that enabled Congress to establish by legislation the UCMJ on May 5, 1950;[56] also relevant is the

Manual for Courts-Martial (MCM) incorporating all executive (Presidential) orders, including the rules for trial by court-martial.[57] These replaced the long-standing Articles of War in operation since 1775.[58] Those Articles of War provided only for offences unique to the military, with no corresponding civilian offence. They included matters such as mutiny, desertion, disrespect, and failure to obey a commander. Civilian dominance was maintained with provisions requiring all capital crimes in peacetime, such as murder or rape, to be processed in the civilian courts. This was enforced by imposing obligations on the commanding officer to refer certain matters to the civilian authorities, backed up by a punishable offence if the commanding officer failed in this duty.[59] There is no reason therefore that a similar approach could not be reinstituted.

The UCMJ was the greatest change in military discipline in the US. Introduced after WWII it provided one discipline code that for the first time incorporated the whole of the civilian criminal law, along with specific military offences applicable to all service areas. It was claimed, at the time, to contain protections not available for civilians, as a Court of Military appeals managed by civilian judges was established, along with greater roles for legal advisors.[60] Australia followed some thirty-two years later, with the *Defence Force Discipline Act*, 1982 (DFDA). Along the same lines, this legislation incorporated the whole of the criminal law of the Jervois Bay territory. The explanation for inclusion was that it would cover offences committed outside Australia. It was specifically noted: "[w]ith two minor exceptions, similar offences committed within Australia will be left to be dealt with by the civil courts."[61] Notwithstanding the explanations, the DFDA claimed that "[r]efusing to deliver to the civil power a member accused by the civil authorities of a civil offence . . . [was] unnecessary," to include as an offence itself.[62] As a result, subject to the Constitution, civilian courts do not have jurisdiction to try civilian criminal offences if they are ancillary to service offences.[63]

Post-WWII the UCMJ and DFDA reforms aimed to address the tsunami of criticisms of the discipline experienced by citizen soldiers during that war. Little explanation justifying incorporating the whole of civilian criminal law into the military discipline system was given. Commander control was maintained in both states but some recognition of the need for due process was attempted with the introduction of the concept of "justice," not just "discipline." In a process of swings and roundabouts, amendments of these military disciplinary laws have continually sought to balance demands for effective enforcement of discipline alongside the prosecution of offences. At other times these have provided more justice with due process protections to the accused, and more recently, with the sexual assault claims, also to the victims of offenders.[64]

The challenge to democratic notions of the rule of law that encapsulate the idea of "one law for all" remain constant. Each of the developments has been in response to the belief that military discipline required fairness, and that, at the very minimum, justice needs to be seen to be done for military discipline to prevail. In other words, society would not tolerate a discipline system that relied on fear. The UCMJ was said to bring ". . . a distinct evolution in philosophy. Its drafters recognized that justice and fairness were an integral component of the disciplinary process."[65] This clouded the view of military discipline with the need for due process or "justice" in applying discipline, and failed to recognize that the introduction of the whole of the civilian criminal law further removed military personnel from the due process accorded the ordinary citizen.[66]

Rule of law is a concept that also encapsulates certainty in the law. The person must know in advance whether their actions will attract a penalty. The law must clearly spell this out. The UCMJ and DFDA, through vague provisions such as disciplining conduct unbecoming of an officer and a gentleman, or prejudicial conduct, and through enabling commanders to determine when to apply disciplinary provisions, offend this core precept.[67]

In Australia, these changes ultimately brought with them the attempts to introduce a specialized military court that essentially was the same as a federal court exercising criminal jurisdiction, but that remained outside the Constitutional construct for Ch III courts. The Australian Military Court (AMC) was declared unconstitutional after two years of operation by the High Court in *Lane v Morrison* in 2009.[68] The legislation provided for the same general principles as in the Criminal Code (Commonwealth) to be applied in the AMC. The accused had the ability to elect a trial by the AMC, while a presumption of innocence and the burden of proof beyond reasonable doubt rested on the prosecution. Provision was made for an independent office of the Director of Military Prosecutions and the Director of Defence Counsel Services, with appeal rights to the Defence Force Discipline Appeals Tribunal (DFDAT), an administrative body presided over by tribunal members who may be federal, state or territory justices or judges. The AMC was a court of record. This went too far for the Australian High Court, giving the AMC, a legislative court, the judicial power of the Commonwealth, which can only reside in a court created under Ch III. As French CJ and Gummow J stated, "[t]he upshot is that while the Parliament has given to the AMC some of the attributes of a court which may be created by the Parliament for the exercise of the judicial power of the Commonwealth, it has not created such a body."[69] A further problem was that the appeal rights from the AMC were to the administrative tribunal, known as the DFDAT, and the judges observed the following:

> The creation of an "appeal" from a federal court, were the AMC to have that character, to an administrative body such as the Appeal Tribunal, would be repugnant to Ch III of the Constitution, in particular to s 73(ii) which provides for the appellate jurisdiction of this Court.[70]

While both the US and Australia have made some attempts to grapple with the problem of physical and sexual abuse through suggested legislative changes, or referral to various complaint bodies, such as in Australia the Defence Ombudsman or the Army Inspector General, or in the US in the form of a UCMJ art 138 complaint against a commanding officer, they seem never to address the fundamental underlying problem.[71] Two factors contribute to this. One goes to a cultural belief, transposed down through the ages, regarding the elite and special reputation of the coterie's military members. The second relates to the enabling by the civilian courts of the development of a separate and powerful second society, a secretive and undemocratic one. The financial cost of this is one thing, but the costs to people's lives and the broader community is far more substantial and the consequences are hard to identify fully. The normative value proposition in this work offers a straightforward policy solution. The separate military society must be brought within the mainstream justice system so all members of that society are subject to equal treatment and the same set of values as the entire civilian population. Granted, the civilian criminal system will always have opportunity for improvement in its handling and prosecuting of sexual assault crimes, the fact remains that it sits at the forefront in following current civilian society norms and provides for a transparent and public equality of treatment. The money saved in removing a duplicate system could go some way toward improving the one civilian system to address any outstanding issues. An organization able to investigate its own fails to operate under a rule of law that sees equal treatment for all, which ultimately results in injustice, and cover-ups lending itself to a proliferation of immoral behavior.

In uncovering the misalliance of military values and legal democratic values, a focus on their purpose and field of operation may assist in understanding why ongoing scandals and eternal reviews seem to make little progress. As Turley aptly states, "the inconsistency between military values and legal values reflects the difference between an institution designed for combat and an institution designed for governance."[72] Some in the military hierarchy may read this argument as being antithetical to the military operation. As a coterie, the military would be expected to argue that it is a family that places the lives of its members at the pinnacle of its concerns. No doubt for many that is the experience. However, it should not be used to deflect inquiring observations. Bringing into the light concepts such as *la bella figura* and *la brutta figura* may ultimately assist the military and protect its reputation better than current practices.

The consequences of the almost continual internal and external reviews conducted on, and most often by, the military organizations within Australia and the United States are observed in this work. Where appropriate, parallels are drawn from other states and coteries, such as the church. The normative claim is that the justification for separate treatment is no longer valid, leading to moral decline, and that the time is now for an understanding of the degree of civilian control required for military organizations to operate within a democratic society. A pivotal proposition is that the justification for separate treatment outside the civilian courts and civilian rule of law weakens both the military's standing and the practice of civilian control of the military. The central aspect of the rule of law, equality of treatment for all, is altered by a system that applies a specialized and different option for imposing criminal law on members of the society, dependent on their membership within a coterie.[73]

The very different military society has not seen a corresponding pace of change in the way discipline is administered. The literature, often written by military members, rehearses a standardized conception of the history, along with phrases repeating certain beliefs like a mantra. Many seem to tinker at the edges, looking at minutiae, without any genuine attempt to dissect these claims or engage with the fundamental overall structure and system of military governance and in particular military discipline.[74] Military members working in the field have authority and first-hand knowledge, but what they lack is an outsider perspective that is not imbued with a preferred history and a set of claims that become enculturated among those operating from within. Civilian researchers can help to provide this broader, less constrained perspective, and as the civilian in the civil-military relationship, they have every right to do so. This work attempts to explore this space from a legal normative perspective, by observing, through a lens focused on abuse and sexual crime, whether claims of higher discipline and thus separateness are justified.[75] How this separate society operates and responds to the many reviews and inquiries, in a manner that seems to favor myopic inward-looking protection of the secret coterie, is observed.

The mantra enlisted in support for a separate system claims a number of grounds. First, the essential nature of the military occupation and the legality of killing another human being make it historically exceptional to all other professions. Second, it is argued that the need for a separate military system is supported by the existence of offences known as disciplinary offences, which are unique to military personnel and are not found in civilian criminal law. The third argument is known as command control and requires that decisions made on battlefields require instant obedience, as the superior officer must decide a matter that the group is obliged not to question, or debate, but to follow faithfully. A final argument concerns the protection of military personnel from being tried in foreign courts and subjected to foreign punishment and imprisonment. These arguments are explored in this work, which seeks to reveal that not only do they not withstand scrutiny, but they have led to the expansive development of standing military forces as separate secret coteries that can impose their own criminal sanctions and thus threaten the fundamental principles of democratic governance. Consideration of each of the key arguments for the maintenance of a traditional separation from the main civilian legal system is now introduced.

JUSTIFICATIONS FOR SEPARATENESS

Argument 1—The Exceptional Profession

The first argument by which the historical development of the military system is referred to in a self-perpetuating and sustaining way maintains that the needs of the military are unique. Essential to this understanding is the ability of a soldier to kill another, an act that is normally illegal. The argument is maintained without consideration of the impact of the revolution in military affairs, the introduction of private military contractors, and a technologically advanced military fighting new types of conflict.[76] The argument persists that the nature of the military sets it apart because there is no parallel in other civilian areas whereby employers can insist their employees perform tasks that may be unpleasant or endanger life. *The Profession of Arms*, an army white paper, makes the following claim: ". . . a self-policing Ethic is an absolute necessity, especially for the Profession of Arms, given the lethality inherent in what we do."[77] It is argued:

> No civilian parallel may be drawn to explain the need for enforcing discipline. Civilian employers cannot legally compel their subordinates to come to work on time, much less induce them to perform a task resulting in substantial likelihood of death.[78]

The argument ignores both the requirements of employment law generally and many situations where employees may be required to kill another, such as police work, and risk their lives on a daily basis. Many employment situations have risks with potentially higher injury and death rates than the risk adverse operation of today's military combat. For instance, police officers can face situations of death, as can prison guards, fire and rescue workers, and even deep-sea fishermen. Commercial fishermen, if the number of deaths is any indication, have been in one of the most dangerous jobs for decades in the US, but this has never justified a separate discipline system to compel fishermen to go to sea.[79] That discipline is practiced within professional contexts without the need to establish a "system" outside the civil domain receives little mention in military literature. Medical practitioners hold lives in their hands and lawyers, accountants, and financial planners can seriously affect the rights of individuals and their lives in significant ways. Many of these professions have added responsibilities over and above a citizen working for instance as an administrator in an office, which calls for their professional regulation, but this does not fall outside the civil justice system.[80] The separate prosecution of normal crimes by the military stamps the claim of a privileged separate society on its members. However, it is not obvious why referral, even by a commander, of criminal behavior to the civilian justice system, along with internal administrative actions that many professional organizations, including the public service, observe for workplace breaches, would undermine a soldier's responsiveness to their commander.

Many see the separate courts-martial as an unfair differentiation. Evidence that this separate discipline system creates better-behaved soldiers, or even an "officer and gentlemen" of superior quality to the ordinary citizen, is contested by the many instances of sexual and other abuse operating within this society. Turley makes the point that "[a] rapist may conduct himself in . . . carrying out his duties, [as]an exemplary soldier. A rape is a violent assault on another individual and only tangentially can be viewed as an assault on the military system."[81] However, such offending breaches the heart of the claim that a separate system delivers a stronger and more effective discipline, as trust among the members is destroyed and the group cohesion required for effective functioning is lost. The potential for any greater deterrence, detection, or harsher sentencing is not discernible, particularly given the costs that this separate system incurs. It appears, on closer investigation, that a tendency to deal with crimes as administrative workplace disciplinary matters keeps the rate of offending in the military hidden and the sentences far less harsh than civilian criminal courts' sentencing.

The military and civilian world differ substantially. A crime in the civilian society is a crime against the state. It represents disorder that the state punishes in order to maintain and support a civil society. This tends to be forgotten in the focus on survivors as victims. However, it remains that in civil criminal matters the survivor is a witness and at the end of the day, whether the matter proceeds or not is not up to them. The deference to survivors puts them in jeopardy of further threats from the perpetrator and gives them a power that is actually not theirs. The criminal law has evidentiary rules to accommodate reluctant or "hostile" witnesses, and support and protect such witnesses through the process. In the civilian system, the public criminal law exists independently from the civil administrative workplace laws that enable discipline of employees for conduct that breaches ethical and obligatory workplace standards and that attract privacy law protections.

Many seem to have lost sight of the uniqueness of the military coterie as a community that combines criminal law with workplace discipline in a seamless merging, with the commander having the say internally where on this line an individual matter sits. As courts-martial are demanding of time, effort, and money, and the more of these occur the more the potential for reputational damage, there is a strong natural incentive to punish offending by using the lower order administrative dealings as more efficient and private. Unfortunately, such a system sends a message to perpetrators that this is a place, which can protect their inclination to criminal behavior.[82]

This is evident when considering the more widely reported events and how the military organization responds to them. That many matters, including criminal offences, end up being dealt with administratively is acknowledged by Judge Baker of CAAF who states, "where military justice is invoked, most dispositions are non-judicial in nature. By quantifiable example, in 2013 the Army had 42,407 NJP, compared to 380 summary courts-martial, 373 special courts-martial, and 714 general courts-martial."[83] NJP, such as rank reduction and forfeiture of pay, can be devastating to individuals, but they are not a criminal charge resulting in a criminal conviction. Disincentives for a military person wishing to contest the facts in a NJP include having to resort to having the matter being dealt with as a criminal matter by court-martial. Pressure not to go down this path, taking up time and resources invoking the ire of superiors and facing an uncertain outcome, can be intense.

In order to deter criminal behavior, theory indicates four requirements must be satisfied,[84] all of which are related to punishment. In order of impact, the first is the integrity of the system. Generally, a criminal will only respond when they witness the law enforced. Second, only if there is a belief that one can be caught and punished does the severity of the punishment become relevant.[85] Therefore, severity is relevant only if there is integrity. Third, the speed of enforcement of punishment is a contested factor in deterrence, but some claim there is a relationship when punishment follows the action without delay.[86] Fourth, deterrence may be encouraged where the punishment attracts additional collateral penalties such as loss of registration, work rights, or rank.[87] Some have suggested that perceived unfairness in treatment will adversely affect deterrence from offending.[88]

Ghiotto claims that the UCMJ in its attempts to balance discipline with due process created obstacles that have led to an ineffective discipline system, which is unable to deliver on its claims for supporting a functional military. He verifies this by reference to commander's preference to enforce discipline in both the Korean and Vietnam wars, through methods other than courts-martial:

> Statistics reflect the fact that commanders rarely utilize the court-martial to preserve good order and discipline within their units . . . In 1953, a congressional committee consisting of military commanders . . . concluded that "professional standards have been permitted to deteriorate through lack of disciplinary control. The adoption of the [UCMJ], with its unwieldy legal procedure, has made the effective administration of military discipline within the Armed Forces more difficult." Commanders in Vietnam expressed similar dissatisfaction with the UCMJ . . . Consequently, commanders often accepted favorable pretrial agreements or dismissed charges to avoid the laborious court-martial process.[89]

Despite this, the US Supreme Court and Australian High Court have maintained the historical importance of the military as a separate society that has developed specialized laws and traditions of its own.[90] Lichtman's research confirms that the US Supreme Court decisions demonstrate that where the military is concerned, there is a peculiar blindness:

> The Supreme Court's promilitary decisions are . . . the *affirmative product of an intellectual perspective that the Court unabashedly promotes* . . . the *military often gets the benefit of the doubt from* the Supreme Court *precisely because the Supreme Court wants to give them the benefit of the doubt.*[91]

The different standard for the military is incompatible with the rule of law, the legality principle,[92] and the civilianization of the military, which recognize individual rights. The court's historical obsession yokes its arguments to a specific time in the 1800s when conscripts fought conflicts and the focus was on punishment in order to keep troops at the front line of combat. This historical bent obscures consideration of the civilian concerns of the anti-federalists who were anxious to keep the military as a whole under strict control in order to limit its invasion of the civilian domain. The broader concern was with protection of the democratic ideals and institutions to which the military is an anathema.[93] Madison and other federalists also shared the anti-federalists concerns that the character of military institutions are antithetical to democracies, which seek the greatest liberty and freedom of individual expression. The framers of the American Constitution looked to Roman antiquities but perhaps not with the clearest of views, mixing the Spartan experience with the Athenian. The Athenians integrated the military society within the civilian and kept training to a minimum while maximizing the freedom and independence of the citizens. The Spartans on the other hand insisted on a separate warrior culture.[94] The Athenian approach would better accommodate military personnel as they transition back into civil society. Currently this is not well done. It has been described as an experience in which

> [t]heir sense of identity, tribal connection and purpose disappears in one moment. This can easily lead to alienation and isolation from family and civilian society which can predispose the veteran to more acutely experience trauma than if surrounded by strong social networks.[95]

This ignites the civil-military relationship that has two tenets. The first is the functional tenet, namely that militaries must be strong enough to defend their country and many military necessity arguments rely on this creed. However, the civil-military principle also has to work in harmony with a second tenet that is often neglected. This second tenet is structural. It demands that the military must not be so tough as to threaten the society it exists to protect. It has two branches. The first is consideration of the society's values and ideology: this includes rights and behavioral expectations. The second branch in democracies, organized according to the doctrine of separation of powers, requires that the three institutions of government: the executive, legislature, and courts, operate within a constitutional pact that respects the separation of powers as a check on each, in order to avoid arbitrary abuses.[96] Luban argues cogently that "misunderstanding the theory may lead to a larger deformation in our political culture: an erosion of popular commitment to the rule of law in favor of militarism and militarist fantasy,"[97] particularly when considering executive power and the role of commander in chief.[98] The justifications for keeping the military in check are not addressed by the highest civilian courts. Rather the emphasis is on military necessity and leaving it for the elected arms of government to control the military.

That the two systems operate by applying unequal law is supported by the CAAF, the highest appellate body within the US military structure, which chooses to follow the Supreme Court or not, as it seemingly pleases. The CAAF has been happy to adopt the Supreme Court's separate society jurisprudence,[99] justifying this by arguing that while military members are not excluded from the Constitution's First Amendment protections, these will be applied differently given the separate military mission and different military community. In some circumstances, the CAAF departs from the civilian law and provides protections unavailable in the civilian jurisdiction to military members.[100] Conversely, this military court can also choose to follow the UCMJ in preference to the Constitution and the Supreme Court rulings where the two are at odds. For instance in *United States v. Easton,*[101] the CAAF considered the double jeopardy UCMJ art 44, which is different to the Constitution's 5th Amendment Double Jeopardy Clause. Under the UCMJ it is only after introduction of evidence that double jeopardy is considered whereas the

Constitution requires this to be attached at the time a jury is empaneled. The Supreme Court refused a *writ of certiorari* to address the CAAFs decision not to follow Supreme Court rulings as the highest civil court bound to interpret Constitutional rights.[102] The well-worn argument of military necessity becomes a catchall phrase, which perpetuates the myth that it can be the only manner in which obedience and discipline is possible. Yet research has established that this is not the case and in reality such an argument, if maintained, could actually undermine obedience.[103]

The revolution in military affairs, a flatter structure that includes civilians, and increasing use of new technologies, provides evidence that the military is a changing organization that does not operate on the same principles as in the past. For this reason alone, it is dangerous for courts to cling to precedents based on a historical vision that no longer applies. The military as a separate entity with different values, like a secondary society, does not sit well within democracies, as it creates an inherent tension of competing values. The democratic notion of debate and transparency with majority rule under the law does not find favor with the necessities of the military, particularly in battle where instantaneous decisions are called for. Subjecting these decisions to later legal review can be inherently difficult and is argued to be unfair. However, this does not accommodate the majority of the military experience, which occurs in a peacetime environment.

Claims of elitism challenge fundamental rule of law concepts like the need for justice "to be seen to be done." In the Australian High Court case of *White v. Director of Military Prosecutions*[104] a criminal offence, indecent assault, was allegedly committed by an off-duty military person in civilian clothing during peacetime on Australian soil in a suburban hotel. The public that fund both the civilian criminal and military disciplinary system via their taxes have a right to know what happens to such an offender. This extends to knowledge that military persons are receiving equivalent punishments as civilians for the same crimes. Because *White* proceeded in the military system, it was subject to overriding privacy protections for the individual involved as it related to their workplace.[105] The military system merges the line between workplace administrative law and criminal law. This meant the public could not see justice being done in relation to this criminal behavior in their community. A Freedom of Information application would have been required if a member of the public was determined to know the outcome.

It is interesting how this protection can vary as two Australian cases, involving navy personnel being charged and heard in ordinary civilian criminal courts, were not accorded the attendant considerations of military protection because one was a cadet and the other was a veteran. One in Victoria[106] involved a trainee at HMAS Cerberus being found guilty by jury trial of two counts of rape and not guilty on another rape charge and indecent assault charges. Another case, involving a former lieutenant commander in the Royal Australian Navy, was heard by the civil Supreme Court in Queensland. This was made possible by the extraterritorial criminal jurisdiction that covers Australian citizens who engage in sexual activity with children under the age of sixteen while overseas. The accused was convicted of child sex offences that occurred in the late 1990s in Kiribati.[107] Both cases assist the primary society by informing it of the actions of military persons as, it is contended, they ought to be. This also allowed the offenders to more closely observe the current civilian values and standards regarding crime and punishment and the manner in which such matters are regarded by the primary society. The civilian system could handle both efficiently, including the fact that the latter involved out of normal jurisdiction offending. The trust placed in the legislature by the courts, and by the legislature in the military, is misplaced, as reliance on a closed secret coterie that prioritizes institutional loyalty and reputation over individuals' experiences in addressing abuse within its ranks has rebounded on the organization. Inevitably, the institution is damaged by lack of transparency.

Argument 2—Military Necessity

Military necessity has become a vague and undefined catchall relied on in numerous ways to enable the military to evade duties and legal requirements that would otherwise be applicable. In the US, this includes overriding Constitutional obligations based on assertions of public policy interests. Caruço has conducted a study of CAAF decisions that address military necessity claims and found four rather circular but dominating themes. These have enabled avoidance of the application of Constitutional rights where the matter is considered to be: 1) essential to mission accomplishment, 2) necessary to prevent grave danger to society, 3) likely to manifest injury to the military,[108] or 4) for good order and discipline. On this last aspect, Caruço makes the following point:

> CAAF's jurisprudence also demonstrates that the military community is different. . . . It exists for a singular purpose—to wage war—though, the rationale for this fact as a basis to limit service members' constitutional rights has been called into question. That said, the military community existed before there was a United States and has developed its own laws and traditions. At the core of this community is good order and discipline. Good order and discipline, however, is often quoted, yet rarely, if ever, defined.[109]

The arguments for a separate military system in part are claimed by the existence of special offences, known as disciplinary offences, which are unique to military personnel and not found in civilian criminal law. These offences include desertion, absence without leave, disobeying orders, disrespect, dereliction of duty, and behavior unbecoming of an officer and a gentleman. They are to ensure soldiers do their job by following orders, irrespective of difficult circumstances. This is required in order to achieve the military's objective or ultimate functional imperative to protect the state and its citizens. Caruço's findings support that in the category of "essential to military mission," cases involving disobeying orders are regular.[110] This book addresses this specific argument under the category of command obedience in the next section. The argument of military necessity in its other guises is a rather vague all-encompassing and circular one, but the argument is that: "[d]iscipline for the sake of good order is not an objective of our civilian society, but is a necessary requirement of our military justice system."[111] While "good order and discipline" is repeated as a sacred mantra and commanders have considerable influence over the legal processes permissible to try to achieve this, what it actually means is never clearly articulated or explored.[112] The argument would also appear to ignore the corollary, namely that the state requires criminal law to play a key role in the state's provision of law and order thought necessary to avoid becoming an anarchical or failed state. Good order therefore is of equal importance to a well-functioning democratic state.

Crime mandatorily must be reported, and not to do so can result in offences such as conspiracy or obstruction of justice. The difference for military members is that the crime is reported to one's employer superiors before the civilian police, or perhaps never to the police. The focus is on the military coterie's needs and not on unqualified criminal law precepts.[113] In the military, the commander decides what level of inquiry will take place. This is dependent on the allegations made in relation to the member. It could be the commander's own investigation, or be given to other members internally, or the military or civilian police. These are broader options than arise in the civilian domain. Commanders have this role, even though they may have had limited or no training in investigations or prosecutions. When determining and weighing factors, such as whether there is sufficient evidence, its probity and admissibility, the character of the alleged offender, or the desires of the victim, and whether military necessity requires the matter to be dealt with via one of the many different options, such as NJP, the commander has immense personal power.

The claimed need to deal with peculiarly military offences in a separate system provides no evidence as to why these types of offences cannot be addressed within the general criminal law. It is claimed, in a rather circular fashion, that since persons other than those subject to military discipline cannot commit military offences, they cannot be tried in the ordinary courts of the land and can only be tried in a military court. However, criminal law can specifically apply to a class of persons who satisfy the elements of a particular offence. For instance, the Australian Criminal Code[114] has offences that apply only to corporations, or directors of corporations, or only to members of certain organizations, for example, a prescribed terrorist organization.[115] Why specific criminal offences cannot apply to all those who fall within a prescribed category, such as military, that is specified as part of the element of the offence, along with its associated actions, is not clear. After all, one has a choice as to whether one belongs to a category such as company director, terrorist organization, or volunteer military. Like other European states, the Czech Republic has subsumed military offences into their general criminal code without issue and it provides a working example of how this is done, including providing for particular sentencing options.[116] Civilian judges and juries regularly decide facts without any specialist knowledge of the field, for example where professionals, such as doctors and accountants, are tried. Yet this is never a justification by the courts for not deciding a matter.

The reliance for support on protection from grave danger and manifest injury or damage to the military highlights the secret coteries demand for sustained protection as a separate organization. Protection of individual members through constitutional or other human rights legislation is curtailed, ultimately to protect the reputation of the organization. Just what is required for manifest injury to the organization however, is never fully articulated. Examples such as disobeying a lawful order as the basis for arguing manifest injury, which is then extended by such vague arguments as military necessity, occur in a very circular and anesthetizing manner.

A court-martial involving Staff Sergeant Amos A. Womack highlights the merging of justifications.[117] Womack was ordered to inform sexual partners of his HIV status in order to protect others from harm. In relation to an action of forcible sodomy, he was court-martialed for willful disobedience of a lawful order. He challenged his punishment before the CAAF, who found that "[t]he military and society at large, have a compelling interest in having those who defend the nation remain healthy and capable of performing their duty."[118] Consequently, the order served a valid military purpose: "to preserve unit readiness and to protect and safeguard the health of Air Force members."[119] Protection from harm by others is a fundamental principle underlying much of the law in democracies. How this need is any different from the civil law domain requirement to ensure its population, including its working population, remain healthy is not established. One could simply restate it as "society at large, have a compelling interest in . . . the nation remain[ing] healthy," and therefore this requires one citizen not to harm another. The harm principle applies across the broad spectrum of the primary society and has no particular specificity to protecting the military from grave danger. The claim of "compelling interest" by its very nature becomes redundant as almost every eventuality can be said to affect the military function no matter how remotely connected to military employees. A disconnect exists in how this sits when it comes to harm, with the US military being protected from tort claims for negligence when it harms its members. This is due to the case of *Feres v. United States,*[120] and subsequent legislation which is discussed later in this work and which seems to conflict with this claim for a compelling interest in maintaining a healthy fighting force.

The Defence Abuse Response Taskforce (DART) has reported the difficulties in Australia when the military is not subject to a civilian justice system. These include that in the military discipline system no criminal record occurs when one is convicted, as no register of sex offenders or exposure to civilian sentencing sanctions exists. There is thus a lack of concern for survivors. They do not have the choice to present victim impact statements, or access compensation schemes available in the civilian realm. Programs for perpetrator rehabilitation are minimal. Furthermore, the DFDA prosecutions are subject to a statutory limit of five years, which is not applicable to a civilian criminal prosecution for the same offence.[121]

The US Texas incident surrounding the ex-military member Devin Kelley's massacre of twenty-six victims, and wounding another twenty in 2017, showed the possibilities for failure when running two separate systems. In this case, it appears that the Air Force omitted entering Kelley's previous court-martial for domestic violence offending in the federal criminal database used by gun sellers to check his eligibility to purchase weapons.[122] Notwithstanding the normalizing of military discipline such that in the US a conviction in a military matter should result in similar outcomes as in the civilian domain, including registration on the National Crime Information database, sex offender registration, and denial of the right to vote or possess firearms, the separate system can and does lead to failures.

Lack of transparency impacts the primary society, as the public cannot easily see justice done with courts-martial held on military bases, making public access challenging.[123] This ignores the germane requirement of the court system—serving an essential aspect of accountability by ensuring the public maintenance of law and order in a state. The public cannot access military trial outcomes or documents without Freedom of Information requests that are a time-consuming obstacle. Military case reporting is generally restricted to appellate-level decisions.

Criminal actions ought to be in the criminal law courts. For instance, assault occurring in a military context can be addressed as an assault in the civil courts, with the military context creating an aggravating factor that the judge can take into account when sentencing. Once the higher civil judicial standards are applied and the person is found guilty, they can then be processed for professional misconduct like any other profession that has internal professional standards to uphold, such as police, lawyers, doctors, and accountants.[124] This is where the peculiar penalties of the military, such as reduction in rank and withholding of pay, or dismissal, can occur. There is nothing preventing these matters being dealt with in the same manner as any other professional disciplinary board deals with an employee's workplace misconduct or professional's misbehavior within the civil domain.

The extent of rights denied due to military status lack any supporting theoretical basis. Many of the curtailed rights of military persons would seem to bear little relation to their ability to perform their job accurately.[125] The demands of "military necessity" applied to military personnel, without even distinguishing between their rank and role within the military, reaches too broadly.[126] Notwithstanding that military experience is predominately a peacetime one, as already noted in relation to the exceptional profession argument, the need for immediate discipline of troops in conflict is attended to largely by administrative actions, not a justice system as such, and so few courts-martial occur.[127] Those that do have usually occurred many years after the event and on home soil. This does not justify the removal of serious criminal offences from the civil system into a parallel, but separate, military system. Even in WWI, when technology and fast planes were not so readily present, soldiers were sent home to be court-martialed many months after the event. This applied even in cases of alleged dereliction of duty on the front line where the demand for immediate discipline due to military necessity stands strongest. Private Kelliher subsequently returned to the front and was awarded the Victoria Cross, but not before he was sent back to Australia to be court-martialed during WWII

> On 12 November 1942 . . . under enemy fire, Kelliher moved back to Coy HQ saying he had been sent back by his Platoon Commander . . . [who] was killed before he could confirm . . . Despite Kelliher's vigorous defence of his actions . . . Kelliher was returned to Queensland, on 19 January 1943 . . . a District Court-martial found him guilty of misbehaving before the enemy in such a manner as to show cowardice, and sentenced [him] to 12 months detention. Both the finding and the sentence was quashed on 31 May 1943, by the Audit General.[128]

Given the serious allegations in both the US and Australia of abusive sexual conduct and drug misuse within the military, the question arises whether separate treatment may contribute in any way to this behavior or, at the very least, prove that justifications for a separate discipline no longer hold.[129] Whether civil disciplinary procedures operating in tandem with a civil criminal law result in less disciplined professions, for instance within the public service, police force, medical and accounting professions, compared to the military, is not evinced at all. It may be that civil society is not as unruly as is inferred. With volunteer professional forces, the incentives to stay and do a good job are different from conscript militaries. The desire to please and be promoted in a professional military surely holds a similar degree of will to act professionally as in any other bureaucratic organization, and this influence on behavior should be considered.[130]

The privatization of militaries also damages the argument for loyalty to command, which is relevant to "civilian armies" in which authority to control possibly reluctant soldiers is more essential. With professional soldiers, this is less likely to be a problem. Private military actors are not so easily subject to the chain of command, and therefore to orders and discipline. They are employed by other non-military organizations with a goal to make a profit. *United States v. Alaa Mohammad Ali*[131] presented this interesting dilemma. The case involved a dual Canadian Iraqi citizen born in Baghdad but having lived in Canada from 1992. He was contracted with L-3 Titan Communications ('L3 Corp') to act as an interpreter for the Department of Defense (DoD). His contract made no mention of duties or responsibilities to the US military or the applicability of the UCMJ. Under the contract, Ali could refuse to participate in missions.[132] However, the military required Ali in order to train and advise the local police force. Ali assaulted another civilian employee of L3 Corp and was charged under UCMJ art 128, and held in pre-trial confinement for 115 days at the US Victory Base, Camp Iraq. He was court-martialed on June 22, 2008, in Baghdad, despite flights being made daily from Baghdad to the US. Another PMC, at the same time as Ali was held, was flown to the US within a month of his arrest to face charges in a civilian court under the *Military Extraterritorial Jurisdiction Act* (*MEJA*)[133] for possession of child pornography.[134] *Ali* raised the question for the CAAF of how to control and discipline the activities of such actors. The CAAF came up with some rather odd and circular claims in order to justify military punishment of Ali, in the end acknowledging that "[a] deployed military unit without discipline is nothing more than an armed mob roaming a foreign country."[135]

The rule of law principle, requiring certainty and clarity of the law for an individual to be able to plan and make informed choices when conducting their lives, is challenged.[136] This is not satisfied by civil courts avoiding provision of clear guidelines as to which rights do, or do not apply, to military personnel. The demand that all be treated equally under the law fails when applied to military persons, and in some cases infiltrates the civilian world to affect civilians when concepts such as institutional necessity are used to justify incorporating individuals beyond the military community.

Argument 3—Command Obedience

The military strongly defends the perceived need that the commander should always have the power to decide whether, and if, a matter should result in discipline and therefore the nature of the likely punishment. Caruço notes:

> The most general of explanations, that "[n]o question can be left open as to the right to command in the officer, or the duty of obedience in the soldier," appears inadequate in many areas of the modern military. That is certainly the case for the war fighter, when discipline is put to the test under hostile fire, but it becomes less adequate an explanation for the much larger number of personnel that support the war fighter in the relative safety of large, hardened bases, or stateside garrisons. Beyond agreeing with the Court that, due to these needs, "the rights of men in the armed forces must perforce be conditioned to meet certain overriding demands of discipline and duty," CAAF has provided little in the way of examples.[137]

The need for speedy justice is often unmet by the reality, even in war zones. In the heat of conflict, the commanding officer needs freedom to focus on essential tasks such as combat. It is onerous holding a court-martial and imposing detention punishments in a battle zone where it will create distraction from the primary fighting purpose, and the facilities to conduct such trials and punishment are not readily available. UCMJ art 10 provides for immediate steps to be taken when an accused is in pre-trial confinement to charge or release them.[138] Military cases indicate that this can result in dismissal of charges where the observance of a speedy trial has not occurred.[139] Ghiotto has documented general courts-martial in the Air Force averaging around 400 days from the discovery of the offence until the convening authority has taken action.[140] Examples taking longer exist, such as in *United States v. Cooley.*[141] The accused was confined in December 2012 and tried in 2014; just under 700 days after the matter arose. A tendency for justice in ensuring punishment is imposed fairly and adequately can be abandoned in favor of expediency.[142] Reliance on administrative separation in preference to even NJP appear to have become more commonplace from the 1980s:

> . . . commanders have either failed to address allegations of misconduct, or, more likely, have increasingly relied upon administrative discharges. Within the military leadership . . . the commonly held viewpoint became "[a]dministrative separations could eliminate service members quickly and quietly."[143]

In cases where courts-martial have occurred on the battlefield, the inherent problems in doing this in a war zone have become apparent. One incident resulted in an outcry in the Australian community during the Vietnam War. It involved a soldier handcuffed to a star picket in the weapon's pit by day and to a stretcher in a tent by night for failure to attend a punishment parade. The Battery Commander (BC), Major Tedder, was court-martialed for treating the soldier in this manner. However, after an inquiry into the incident the charge was dismissed.[144] As Major Tedder's combat unit had been in constant active combat operations and had no detention facility available, it was considered operationally wise not to remove him. The defense of "condonation" was successfully raised, alleging the Australian Defence Force (ADF) had condoned or accepted his actions in punishing Gunner O'Neill.[145] The issue of impossibility of holding a soldier in detention while on the front line of combat was sidestepped. The public outcry caused a review of the practice of using restraints, resulting in the banning of its use as a means of field punishment for the future.[146]

These difficulties were experienced in Afghanistan's long war.[147] Rosenblatt undertook an important study in 2010 of the operation of the US court-martial system in recent conflicts. This study of military discipline confirmed the inability of the system to function effectively in a conflict, undermining the very justifications for it continuing as a separate system. Rosenblatt reinforced the absence of empirical evidence to support the regular assertions made.[148] His study supported an opposing view, perhaps most concerning of which was his overall observation that ". . . it cannot be said that the American court-martial system functioned effectively in Afghanistan or Iraq . . . this court-martial frailty is consequential and bears directly on the success or failure of our national military efforts."[149] The study measured numerous instruments including judge advocates reports, case numbers, types of cases, punishments and concluded that despite

> . . . the conventional wisdom [there was] . . . a nearly unanimous recognition that the full-bore application of military justice was impossible in the combat zone. In practice, deployed commanders and judge advocates exercised all possible alternatives to avoid the crushing burdens of conducting courts-martial, from sending misconduct back to the home station, to granting leniency, to a more frequent use of administrative discharge procedures. By any measure . . . deterrence of other would-be offenders, contribution to good order and discipline, justice, or the provision of a meaningful forum for those accused of crimes to assert their innocence or present a defense . . . are inadequate.[150]

Despite this, others such as Behan hold contrary views. Behan refers to Borch's description of three general courts-martial, one special court-martial and six summary courts conducted over the four months of Operation Desert Shield and Desert Storm.[151] A general court-martial occurred the night before the Iraqi assault, with proceedings held in Saudi Arabia, Iraq, and

Kuwait in *United States v. Presbury*.[152] While such an operation may reinforce the importance of discipline, it is not apparent why a less demanding approach, such as referral to the civilian criminal system and flying the offender to home soil for this to take place, would be any less conducive to discipline. It certainly would be less arduous on the commander during such a high-pressured time, and it would entail less diversion of resources such as the use of a helicopter to bring the counsel and judge to the field, along with power generators, tents, and other required personnel as described by Borch.[153] Such a process would, in short, still be supportive of the functional imperative at the same time as it would uphold the structural imperative. Notwithstanding Behan's support for the military system he still noted that the rate of court-martial convictions was proof that the system was "biased against the accused and thus essentially unjust."[154]

One of the significant problems with military discipline as outlined here is the control the commander and convening authority have over various aspects of the court-martial procedure. The role of the commanding officer gives rise to suspicions of bias in the discipline process, as the commander is an embedded component of the hierarchical organization. The requirement for checks and balances to remove power from a single internal authority has resulted in some changes in military discipline.[155] A need to separate the prosecution from the defense, and from the decision makers in a particular matter, is an essential aspect for fairness and justice. This, along with decisions by commanders arbitrarily determining when to take action, or not, in disciplining breaches of law, further challenges the rule of law principle of certainty. As Sherrill recognized, "[o]ne favored method of conditioning a man into docility is to make trial and punishment not only arbitrary but unpredictable."[156] Arbitrariness as explicit as in *United States v. Sadinsky*[157] demonstrated the US Court of Military Appeals supporting the concept that conduct could be prohibited by the military, notwithstanding the fact that the UCMJ did not proscribe such conduct.[158] This uncertainty would not be tolerated in the civilian domain.

While commanders are themselves becoming subject to being overridden through changes in the legislation, as a consequence of moving towards the demands for fairness resulting from recent reviews, it also must be noted that many "leaders" have no convening authority ability.[159] Nevertheless, these leaders and commanders remain in control of the cultural climate under their command and have influence and power, including the ability to activate non-judicial discipline. A commander's leadership and behavior involves the risk that subordinates will act in a fashion consistent with what they think the commander wants. The desire ordinarily to please one's boss is a constant. In the military, it is no less absent and arguably even stronger, given the powers of command. This has the unsatisfactory outcome of limiting the supreme commanders from making what would be expected comments from leaders about sexual abuse. Obama, as commander in chief, in stating sexual offenders in the military should be "prosecuted, stripped of their positions, court-martialed, fired, dishonorably discharged" in 2013, was criticized for the command influence risk these statements held when attempting to successfully prosecute court-martial offences.[160] Likewise, in Australia, then General David Morrison attracted condemnation for statements made regarding the Jedi Council sex scandal and more broadly decrying sexual abuse within the military.[161]

Commanders have many other resources than the threat of discipline by which to lead and command members who would be loyal to their demands. History has seen good commanders who looked after their troops being revered. Positive rewards once included providing a share in the plunder of war, but fortunately, these can now come in the form of recognition such as awards and promotions. A 1973 study found "the primary factor in ensuring the will to fight is identification with the direct commanding officer."[162] In this study, respected and established commanders were able to gain compliance from soldiers in combat much more effectively than disrespected leaders. Enabling commanders to refer discipline matters to the civilian authorities would relieve them of the burden and distraction from their main duty and assist in maintaining a good relationship with their members. The civilian authorities would carry the burden of the bogeyman. The argument for loyalty to command is relevant to "civilian armies" in which authority may have been necessary to force reluctant citizen-soldiers to obey, but it is less essential for professional soldiers. The threat of the commander's referral to a civilian investigation has never been proven to diminish the overall discipline and good order of troops, because it has never been given a chance to be trialed or studied in the US or Australia.

Another concern with the claim for command obedience is that decisions made on battlefields happen in exceptional circumstances in which the commander has to make a decision that the group is obliged to follow. The argument for instant obedience and the necessity for a hierarchical structure is perhaps not so essential during a peacetime situation. It is clear that difficulties have existed in the foggy interface, creating an uncertainty gap over jurisdiction demarcation for those operating in the civilian and military system. Deference accorded both ways, between the military and the civilian authorities, can result in failures to follow-up matters referred to the civilian police or any administrative action taken by the military.[163]

A 2009 independent review, before the Australian Military Court (AMC) was ruled unconstitutional by the High Court, noted that despite an increased transparency and greater independence from the chain of command under the AMC, difficulties were still observed. These primarily related to delays in investigations and the AMC's ability to deliver outcomes.[164] A subsequent review by the Australian Inspector General of the Australian Defence Force (IGADF)[165] looked into the complaints management system and treatment of survivors of sexual abuse by focusing on transparency and the interaction between military and civilian criminal punishment systems. The Inspector General was inclined to look favorably on the Australian system when comparing it to like jurisdictions such as Canada and New Zealand where similar courts-martial processes operate.[166] Still, room for improvement in clarification and implementation of certain policies was observed,[167] and the much feted Australian Fairness and Resolution Database of Unacceptable Behaviour was not seen to be maintained to an expected standard.[168] On the other hand, a more independent review by an appointed law firm, DLA Piper,[169] made a number of observations about the military handling of sexual abuse complaints. These included a history of under-reporting, seemingly contributed to by the culture and the military discipline system: "a 'substantial number of people' have been 'dissatisfied and disillusioned with the ADF's application of military [discipline] processes and approach to complaint handling.'"[170]

Despite the effectiveness of the military being said to depend on the discipline of the force requiring obedience to commanders' lawful orders, observance of the applicable law, and a high degree of self-control, more and more examples of lapses in discipline are occurring.[171] It is not appropriate to continue to label these as aberrations or just a few rotten apples. Responsibility in the military is hierarchical and held by command so it should follow all the way up the line. Yet in the Abu Ghraib incident, no senior military or civilian figures carried accountability.[172] As this work documents in subsequent chapters, many senior personnel have shown themselves guilty of lapses in discipline and capable of immoral behavior when they feel untouchable and beyond the law's reach. The private military contractors (PMC) who were heavily involved in the Abu Ghraib incident also escaped consequences for their actions. The US court-martial of a PMC, *United States v. Alaa Mohammad Ali* ("*Ali*"),[173] as noted above, provides one of the only examples of a court-martial conducted on foreign soil in which a civilian PMC was tried. This unusual example demonstrates the challenges when PMCs operate alongside military personnel in foreign jurisdictions and raises the concerns addressed in the next section regarding jurisdiction and authority over members.

Argument 4—State's Exclusivity over Military Members

A final argument in support of the maintenance of the current discipline system is that military discipline must be widely and readily available, for instance in the theatre of a conflict, which is most likely to be in a foreign jurisdiction. The contention is that a civilian justice system is not set up to handle this reach of jurisdiction or the different physical conflict locations. States tend to require that their military personnel be subject to their own disciplinary system, be that military or civilian, and not the foreign jurisdiction where the incident may occur. The argument is made that "[i]f the military justice system did not exist, our military members would have their cases tried in foreign courts and be imprisoned in foreign jails."[174] Although it is rarely voiced, this argument implies the risk that military personnel held in foreign prisons may face torture to extract highly sensitive military information. This is a more logical reason not to want to subject these persons to foreign jurisdictions. Generally, however, this is unlikely to occur given that in war-torn states the civilian apparatus for judicial proceedings and prosecution is most often not operating, or operating ineffectively. International agreements and Status of Forces Agreements (SOFA) that provide for military personnel to be punished by their own countries' laws, overcome the issue. However, this does not mean the law to be applied has to be military as opposed to civilian. An example is the US in Iraq, and the Coalitional Provisional Authority agreement that stated that all US citizens would be dealt with under US law.[175] Little thought appears to have been given to the creation of specialized civilian Ch III /Art III courts that could travel with the military to war zones just like other professional civilians, such as medical and training personnel. DFDADT has the power for the civilian judges to sit in theatre although this has never occured. In any event, as noted previously, the spectacle of courts-martial hastily convened in the field of battle appear very infrequent and prohibitive in battlefield circumstances. Rosenblatt,[176] like others,[177] demonstrates that a court-martial in a conflict zone is too taxing on the war-fighting effort and is not suitably undertaken in such a location. The determination of a charge, the constitution of a court-martial, and the prosecution of a charge necessarily take time. During that time, a military member can be transferred to a civilian court in the home country or, in urgent cases, face a hearing by video link with such a court. The use of resources in this manner is not only more cost-efficient but likely to satisfy the requirement that a soldier not be subject to a foreign jurisdiction, as well as being less demanding on a commander, and therefore ultimately supportive of military functionality.

Frequent use of PMC in conflicts, when they are not subject to military discipline and command, undermines the argument for a separate treatment. In current times, those exceptionally enabled to take another's life in a combat zone are just as likely to be civilian operators of drone and other unmanned technologies far from the battlefield.[178] These operators can suffer many of the same traumatic effects, such as PTSD, as combat soldiers,[179] yet they may not be subject to the military discipline code argued to be necessary to keep regular soldiers at their station doing their job. While PMCs have been charged, tried, and imprisoned in foreign jurisdictions, the question might be asked why PMCs are treated differently—does this represent an equal treatment before the law? A PMC from Australia suffered this very fate, being sentenced to death for murder in the local Afghanistan courts. He was subjected to the local law of Afghanistan.[180] Can this difference in treatment of military members and PMCs be a justification for allegations of discrimination? The Australian position leaves these questions hanging in the balance.

PMCs and soldiers dealt with in civilian courts of their home territory also indicate that extraterritorial jurisdiction issues can be overcome and civilian courts are able to deal with matters occurring in conflict. Legislative ability exists to cover citizens' criminal activity on foreign soil. The demands of respect for sovereign state boundaries are challenged by global demands for respect for human rights and a new value set, in which the individual, rather than the state, is sovereign. The US *MEJA*[181] and *Criminal Code* 1995 (Cth) in Australia show that jurisdiction may extend to cover the activities of citizens beyond the territory of the state and that they be dealt with in civilian courts. While this may be a case of civilian courts operating in a foreign state, extradition treaties and SOFAs are able to deal with the peculiarity of the need to protect military members.[182]

Beyond this, the state alone does not have total control over the discipline of its military. The international domain makes particular demands, including that states do not exonerate their soldiers of human rights abuse nor subject their military to unfair treatment.[183] The Human Rights Committee has noted that "[t]he trial, by military tribunals, of members of the armed forces . . . accused of serious human rights violations that constitute crimes is a current practice in many countries. It is frequently a source of impunity."[184] Many states have now disbanded specialized military courts—at least for crimes committed by their soldiers within the state's bounds. These include countries like Argentina, the Czech Republic, Denmark, Finland, France, Germany, Italy, the Netherlands, Norway, Spain, and Sweden to name a few.[185]

It was for purely military offences and for soldiers operating in foreign jurisdictions, out of reach of the civil courts of their state, that the exception for military jurisdiction was first established.[186] However, this vision belongs to a different world and should not be clung to for history's sake. As "out of reach" is no longer a relevant argument. Technology, for instance, is used by some to claim flexibility that enables deployed battlefield commanders to continue to conduct their command duties over non-deployed personnel at home:

> . . . as a practical matter the vast majority of legal work conducted by judge advocates and military paralegals can be supervised and migrated across space and time without regard to the actual location of the players. The key enabler is

> technology, combined with sound business practices and properly empowered people who know how to use it.[187]

As then Justice Kirby of the Australian High Court, a dissenter when it comes to deferential treatment of the military, noted:

> The advent of fast air travel, including (perhaps especially) to and from theatres of war, armed conflict, peace-keeping and like operations, has changed the content of what is necessary and obvious for the effective achievement of service discipline today.[188]

History has shown that even when technology for video court linkups and fast planes was not available, military members were still flown home for their court-martial, even during WWII.[189] The argument of exclusivity justifying a special discipline in the field has been superseded by the modern technologically advanced world that renders it no longer justifiable for any trials to be occurring in conflict zones because they are "out of reach." The reasoning for a separate military system that argues that civilian courts cannot operate on foreign soil, nor "resolve misconduct with the speed and flexibility required by the military,"[190] is no longer sustainable.

Conducting courts-martial in combat is a drain on needed personnel's time and distracts from the main objective of combat forces. It is more effective to use the facilities of a standing court with a jury, if necessary comprised of defense personnel or civilians, in the home country so as not to diminish the fighting forces' effort.

Notwithstanding the US flurry of changes to the UCMJ in response to the sexual assault claims, it remains that a special court-martial may still comprise only three members and a general court-martial five members, and only a two-thirds guilty vote is required for conviction and a three-quarters vote for a sentence involving confinement.[191] As it stands, a military panel in Australia is comprised of an officer or senior warrant officer rank, and they range in number from two to twelve, the latter for more serious matters.[192] A majority of panel members is required to answer any question before the panel,[193] and if there is an equal vote on whether a member is guilty or not, then the finding shall be not guilty.[194]

The military has flagged a number of times the difficulty in finding suitable panel members within the services, as court-martials draw members away from their core duties, particularly if this is a matter to be heard in the field. One of the objections of the Australian government to establishing a Ch III court has been the Constitutional requirement that indictable offences receive a jury trial.[195] A court-martial panel is not the same thing, as it is smaller in number, is selected from a limited pool of superiors rather than peers or even a selection of diverse members, and is permitted to bring in a non-unanimous verdict.[196] In Australia the Registrar of Military Justice, who is a member of the military outside the chain of command and is an enrolled legal practitioner for at least five years, selects the panel.[197] A panel decision does not need to be unanimous if after eight hours they have failed to reach a decision, a majority verdict of five-sixths will stand.[198] The US Supreme Court has also confirmed that court-martial panels have no equivalence to civilian juries:

> We find nothing in history or constitutional treatment of military tribunals which entitles them to rank along with Article III courts as adjudicators of the guilt or innocence of people charged with offenses for which they can be deprived of their life, liberty or property.[199]

Many of the features of the curial process have been especially created to maintain and reinforce the citizen's right to demand accountable institutions. Juries have played a significant role in criminal matters because of their essential importance to a liberal democracy. The jury system settled in the eighteenth century when concerns around due process were being embraced. The jury performed the role of acting as a check against government institutional abuse.[200] Ironically, their function was a major factor in having to establish separate trial systems when soldiers were on foreign soil. The absence of an available jury from the accused's community was the reasoning behind not hearing matters arising beyond the realm. As foreign juries could not be called upon in common law courts, the courts could not decide the factual dispute.[201] Importantly, the need for impartiality, while still maintaining a representative nature, was reinforced as early as 1705, when selecting jury members from the accused's immediate neighborhood was abolished so personal knowledge could not influence the decision.[202] This significant safeguard is undermined when in the military context the jury is diminished, if not removed altogether, and replaced with members of the accused's workforce as a panel.[203] This potential for unfair bias in a panel taking into account extraneous factors is long overdue for an update in the twenty-first-century military world.

The claim that those trying a matter should have distinct knowledge related to the military situation has never been substantiated by strong empirical evidence. Aside from the fact that many of the matters tried are actually normal criminal offences, such as fraud or drug crimes, this argument does not apply to any other profession. A jury comprised of the normal citizenry with no specialized knowledge determines factual matters relating to doctors, lawyers, and police charged with criminal offences. The need to understand the context of a military matter surely can only be argued, if at all, in cases where offences have occurred in the heat of combat, such as where allegations of murder or other criminal conduct have occurred on the battlefield. Yet even this is a weak argument as demonstrated by *United States v. Green.*[204] In that case the crime of murder and rape was committed in a combat zone but one offending soldier, Green, was tried in a civilian court because he had left the military by the time the offence was uncovered. In these circumstances obviously aggravating factors arise, which a jury or judge can address. There is no reason why a special amicus curia or friend of the court could not provide relevant contextualizing information to the court and the jury.[205] Juries and judges, since time immemorial, have been trusted to act appropriately in every other situation although they may have no specialized experience or knowledge of the field. This is what makes them arbiters of the facts. If the argument put by the military was valid then why are trials of surgeons or actuaries not entitled to a jury of superior professional peers?[206]

The justifications for a separate military discipline, given the escalating claims of physical and sexual abuse, are open to challenge, although few seem to be doing so. In a changed technological world, it is time the arguments were studied afresh. They need to be addressed in the context of overall changes occurring in institutions that take account of the challenges of globalization as well as demands for respect for individual rights.

Why Is This Important

Many reasons exist to justify the need for a totally new approach to this societal problem. When hazing, physical and sexual abuse occur, not only is the individual damaged, often for life, making it impossible to contribute to their full potential, but it also extends to the wider family and frequently affects in an intergenerational manner.[207] Service personnel have indicated that, once abused, their loss of career or, if they stay on, their inability to perform at full potential, or worse, adding to a dysfunctional work environment by becoming an abuser, sustains the wrong. The personal impacts are unfathomable and the economic consequences alone can never be fully determined. The cost of training defense personnel to high standards is a loss to taxpayers when they can no longer operate as expected. This does not bode well for civil-military relations, at least in Australia, where one of the least popular areas among civilians for more government expenditure is in the area of defense.[208]

The early military discipline, such as that contained in the Articles of War 1775–1776, showed a limited military jurisdiction, which applied only to unique military offending and respected the authority of the civilian domain. This protected military member rights such as a right to trial by jury. Civilian court authority existed by ensuring "at least a primary power to proceed against military offenders violating the civil law, although the same acts were concurrently within the jurisdiction of the military courts."[209] Pragmatism during the US Civil War, 1863, when civilian courts were prevented from operating at the time, saw the gradual erosion of the limited military jurisdiction. This resulted in all crimes, except for murder and rape, being drawn into the military domain by 1916, and the completion of this process with the introduction of the UCMJ in 1950.

Yet, to continue the current discipline system is to go against the trend demanded internationally, namely to bring military discipline within the domain of the civil courts. In 2006 the Draft Principles Governing the Administration of Justice through Military Tribunals[210] were presented at the 66th session of the Commission on Human Rights. The Decaux principles, as they became known, were designed to reinforce the integrity of the justice system by situating "military justice" within an overall framework, and requiring the containment of military tribunals so they are not "outside the scope of ordinary law or above the law."[211] A major concern is the use of military tribunals in prosecuting breaches of human rights by soldiers as it is alleged this "is in many countries undertaken by military courts for the purpose of avoiding the accountability of perpetrators of such acts. It is therefore significant that the UN Special Rapporteur has reaffirmed that the jurisdiction of ordinary courts should prevail in such cases."[212]

In an evolutionary environment where the military largely no longer exist solely to fight defensive wars, but rather operate in a multinational military in a globally connected world, differences in employment conditions and the practice of discipline are highlighted. Relying on volunteer-only forces in a resource-constrained environment, the conditions of employment of national military members affects the ability to recruit good candidates. These conditions demand a legitimate and justifiable discipline system that respects individual rights. As Caruço correctly notes, "[c]itizens who are confident that the military will only infringe on their freedoms to the minimum extent necessary to protect the Nation are more likely to sign up and stay in the armed forces."[213]

Incorporating the normal civilian criminal law into the UCMJ and DFDA, with little debate or commentary to justify it, is a significant move that has resulted in a blurring of the line between criminal offences and workplace indiscretions. This has in turn resulted in general confusion and a perpetual tension between fairness and punishment, justice and discipline. Rustico agrees, "[t]hat is why both a system of complete commander control and one of complete prosecutor control are equally unsatisfying."[214] The confusion has led to specialized legislative appellate bodies designed to support the military mission, such as the CAAF in the US, or the DFDAT in Australia, interpreting their respective Constitutions and case law. Such bodies decide whether to follow the highest civilian courts as regards constitutional or human rights or the specialist military discipline legislation, such as the UCMJ or DFDA.[215]

These arguments must be revisited, given the different military world now in operation. The changes by the US Supreme court made under Chief Justice Rehnquist's influence in *Solorio v United States*[216] have led to the status test that removed the previous limitation contained in *O'Callahan,*[217] requiring matters to have a service connection before they could be removed from the civilian courts. The status test no.w gives the UCMJ a broadening reach. It covers an increasing number of citizens, including retired members entitled to pay or hospitalized in military hospitals, military and other detainees, and members of any organization required to serve with the military, which may now encompass PMCs due to changes in the UCMJ and *United States v. Alaa Mohammad Ali* ("*Ali*").[218] The deference of the Supreme Court is to functional arguments, such as military necessity for force readiness, over any structural concerns that denial of individual rights may have:

> The practice of judicial abstention in regard to misconduct by and within the military is so longstanding and deeply entrenched that it successfully has been deployed to justify even the most egregious institutional limitations on individual, constitutional rights.[219]

The Rehnquist line follows the Huntington drive to focus on the functional imperative of a strong fighting force. This may partly be because Huntington gave little attention to the structural imperative, perhaps in the hope that the US democratic structure would look after itself. This approach sees the court along with military figures place the separateness of the coterie above all other considerations. However, the structural imperative is essential for a healthy functioning military and looks to the primary cultural values, as well as the vital recognition of the separation of powers underpinning the function of democratic governance. Janowitz[220] alternatively considers that the military should more closely observe civilian values, and keeping pace with these would occur by bringing discipline under the civilian domain to support the structural imperative. Dr Scally, in his submission to the Foreign Affairs, Defence and Trade References Committee, entitled "The Constant Battle: Suicide by Veterans," described the Spartan separation from civilian life and family concerns as a primary emphasis in the Australian military:

> The often quoted Army phrase of "You were not issued with a family" was commonly used to harden those who struggled to maintain a balance between the overriding needs of the military, and the veteran's commitments towards his/her family. The defence force mandate is to make military the individual's family itself, and to override other commitments. Family disengagement and divorce are consequentially likely outcomes.[221]

Hierarchical Coteries

Causes for bullying and abusive behavior are often sought through understanding the psychology of the individual and groups. This approach can offer a good insight into some of the motivators behind such behavior. However, there is also a separate point of view for assessing behavior and that is through organizational sociology. This approach looks at institutionally supported bullying and poor behavior usually occurring within structures of hierarchical power.[222] Bully cohorts work as a shadow or unofficial organization, coexisting and feeding off the structure of the main institutional apparatus. The shadow organization has its own unofficial code, sometimes ritualistic and tribal, and it often turns upside down normal social expectations. The system is sustained by the promise that loyalty to the coterie, if proven, eventually is rewarded with privileges such as a social promotion within the shadow organization. The abused can be enticed by claims they may one day graduate to become the abuser and do unto others as was done to them. The activities of this shadow structure have a preference for shaded times and locations, such as out of hours, off-duty, out of country, or when the survivor is vulnerable—sleeping or attending to their personal hygiene.

The type and extent of abuse can vary. Often the extremes are applied to those who are "different" from the coteries' attributes, or worse, those who break loyalty to the coterie. Consider some of the common practices with the terms used to describe such activity, which are designed to humiliate, subjugate and control, and have been utilized particularly during the abuse process of initiation and other tribal hazing rituals. Examples include:

a. "Blackballing" or "Nuggeting"—a practice that involves being held down by others while substances such as boot polish and toothpaste are forcibly applied, sometimes with a hard brush to the genital or anal area;
b. "Royal flush"—pushing a person's head into either a flushed or unflushed toilet bowl and flushing;
c. "Running the gauntlet"—the gauntlet involves members forming a human corridor that the survivor must run through while being beaten by heavy objects or otherwise assaulted and humiliated;
d. "Gotcha"—involves grabbing or pinching of the genitals, often while naked in the shower.[223]

Assault and sexual abuse, ranging from masturbation, oral sex, anal and vaginal penetration by a penis or an object occur alongside the examples described above. Particularly in the case of male survivors, these activities are often accompanied by violent physical assault incurring serious injury. In the case of females, often positions of power and dominance suffice to overpower the survivor. The Australian Royal Commission heard evidence from survivors that the impact of these assaults and the institution's (non)responsiveness had both significant short- and long-term consequences for them.[224] These included not only the panoply of depression, anxiety, suicidal tendencies, drug and alcohol ingestion, and post-traumatic stress disorder (PTSD), but also relationship failures, inability to work, and homelessness.[225] The inability to assess the cost of this to society is often a factor that goes unaddressed when considering the suitability of the military discipline system.

A new element to add to the arsenal of means in the shadow organization is the opportunities provided by technology. Rituals can develop incorporating contemporary dimensions to old activities. Filming sexual acts, live Skyping acts of bullying, and recording of violence and sharing it with a wider group can extend the reach of bullying behavior and sexual predators and thus ultimately their power and damage. Examples are provided in the following chapters—the US marine's sex video scandal, the Jedi Council sex scandal in Australia, and the ADF Academy Skype sex scandal are just some instances of these behaviors whereby technology functioned to aid the pervasiveness of the crime.

Organizations such as the military are ideal for fostering this type of shadow organization, as the central organization relies on ranked hierarchical power, command obedience, loyalty, toughness, and group cohesiveness. It is therefore the perfect environment for breeding such shadow behavior. Why an individual will honor an institution even if it is harming the individual involves a mix of *la bella figura*, anti-dobbing, and the repercussions a whistleblower can attract when seen as a disloyal outsider to the coterie.[226] This is fostered by keeping the discipline system internal and less than transparent to the members, let alone the broader society. Survivors frequently complain that they are not informed. Attempts to overcome this in the military system have presented further issues and an added cost burden that victim support in the civil system could best address.

Understanding the operation of a secret coterie provides even more grounds to justify separating military discipline from the institution's control and placing it back in the hands of the civil society. Fraternity and sorority groups practice the same principles and operate within total institutional structures, that is, educational institutions.[227] A person voluntarily joining an organization will often become enculturated and protective of the subculture's norms.[228] Like an entrapment, the more invested in the organization one becomes the harder it is to criticize or resist the overriding norms "as individuals move up through the hierarchy of their organization and therefore have greater potential to effect change, the greater the pressures they experience to incorporate the dominant cultures' values."[229] Bullying is integral to group control and a tool for maintaining power. It has operated throughout human history but that is not a valid reason to maintain it in today's world. Concepts such as *la bella figura* become normalized in the human psyche and take considerable education and training to overcome. The structures of our institutions of democracy aim to work as a counterbalance to the inevitability of human behavior. As Banner notes:

> Sociological justifications for retention of inefficient or even biased cultural practices range from "functional necessity," a fear the organizational structure will collapse if entrenched and expected practices do not continue, to inertia to greed. Perhaps the most common hypothesis regarding the persistence of harmful cultural norms is simply normalization, a person "does what he has to do."[230]

A class description of the ethos underpinning the type of training provided to military cadets is described in the Supreme Court decision of *United States v. Virginia:*

> VMI produces its "citizen-soldiers" through "an adversative, or doubting, model of education" which features "[p]hysical rigor, mental stress, absolute equality of treatment, absence of privacy, minute regulation of behavior, and indoctrination in desirable values." As one Commandant of Cadets described it, the adversative method "dissects the young student," and makes him aware of his "limits and capabilities," so that he knows "how far he can go with his anger, . . . how much he can take under stress, . . . exactly what he can do when he is physically exhausted." (Quoting Col. N. Bissell).
>
> VMI cadets live in Spartan barracks where surveillance is constant and privacy non-existent; they wear uniforms, eat together in the mess hall, and regularly participate in drills. Entering students are incessantly exposed to the rat line, "an extreme form of the adversative model," comparable in intensity to Marine Corps boot camp. Tormenting and punishing, the rat line bonds new cadets to their fellow sufferers and, when they have completed the 7-month experience, to their former tormentors.
>
> VMI's "adversative model" is further characterized by a hierarchical "class system" of privileges and responsibilities, a "dyke system" for assigning a senior class mentor to each entering class "rat," and a stringently enforced "honor code," which prescribes that a cadet "does not lie, cheat, steal nor tolerate those who do."[231]

Problems such as bias will always exist as long as an institution can discipline its own in an exclusive manner.[232] Survivors commonly indicate that if they attempted to complain they were either not believed, told that the abuse was "a rite of passage," or that no action would be taken.[233] Another common experience is the survivor receiving punishment for the activity involving their victimization including being threatened with, or actually receiving, a dishonorable discharge.[234] The military seems to have a pervasive misunderstanding around consent in a hierarchical organization, with age and rank associated with command obedience creating strong power differentials.

Conclusion

This work investigates the implications of the inadequacies of, and difficulties with, the current discipline system. It does this through a normative legal analysis investigating the four justifications outlined in this chapter for maintaining a separate discipline system. These justifications are considered against the evidence provided in cases, reports, legislation, and academic writing through the lens of just one type of offending, namely sexual offending. The normative value position outlines the claim for what the government policy ought to be and that it is vital to imagine suitable alternative futures. The UN Sub-Commission on the Promotion and Protection of Human Rights[235] noted that the trial of military personnel accused of serious human rights violations still occurs in military tribunals in many states. However, the situation is changing around the world with military discipline increasingly conducted within the civil justice system. Countries outside the US and Australia have often led the way by adopting legislation, or even constitutions, that limit their military discipline, particularly where serious violations of human rights have occurred.[236] Countries such as France, Germany, and the Czech Republic, to name only a few, have abolished the use of military courts during peacetime, including trial of military offences and the trial of breaches of ordinary criminal offences committed by military persons. This is the exclusive province of civilian judges, as was the historical position in the UK. Military courts sometimes operate when military personnel are serving in time of war in foreign states although this is also subject to civilian court review.[237]

This compares with the US and Australia where trial by military courts-martial of civil criminal matters, with no distinction between peacetime and war, and now potentially encompassing civilians in the US, is supported by the highest civil domestic courts. The continued demand of the military and executive branches in the US and Australia that, due to historically claimed needs of expediency and command control, the military discipline exceptionally needs a separate system to the civil system of justice challenges the concept of the democratic notions of the rule of law.[238]

The refrain by the military that a state ". . . can't simply abolish its entire military justice system and rely upon civilian courts and existing civilian criminal laws to handle misconduct committed by military members"[239] is not a claim supported by evidence. Civilian society still demands order to function and uses coercion such as criminal punishment and workplace discipline to maintain this.[240] The justification that military discipline includes offences not contained in the civil criminal system is solvable. Offences that apply to specific conduct, or specific types of activity or categories of person, exist throughout criminal laws. It becomes merely an element of the offence that the individual belongs to a certain class of persons engaged in the particular category of activity at the time of the offence.

The claim that a separate discipline system is necessary to address misconduct expeditiously regardless of where it happens is also a myth long unquestioned. The acknowledgment that the court-martial system does not work in conflict zones or in disciplining ordinary criminal offences such as assaults, including sexual assaults, is clear, particularly after each major conflict, including again in the Iraq and Afghanistan conflicts.[241]

The common assertion in the fourth argument, that military personnel deserve their own military discipline for offences committed on foreign soil also holds no substance upon investigation.[242] When PMCs can be subject to local host state's punishment, it is accepted that they be dealt with and imprisoned according to the local law of the country in which they have offended.[243] This is the same as civilians travelling overseas who commit crimes on foreign soil. They can expect to be subject to the local law.[244] With the increasing use of PMCs, who are often retired military, who may or may not be subject to court-martial in the field, at least within the US, the claim that a separate system is required to keep discipline in the field is undermined. If PMCs cannot be subject to this discipline system, yet are placed in conflict zones, then the civil system must be considered sufficient. In addition, cases involving military persons tried in civilian courts, as discussed in this work, indicate that the argument that the civilian courts are not capable of dealing with criminal offences, even when they do occur in a conflict zone, is redundant.

Addressing the ongoing claims of abuse within the military requires more than ad hoc band-aid solutions. The tinkering by the legislatures with existing military discipline laws is more often an attempt to be seen as responding without actually attacking the fundamental nature of the issue. This work explores the arguments and suggests a simple and swifter resolution ought to remove the separate discipline system that appears not to achieve its stated justifications, and bring military personnel within the mainstream justice system. If a desire to end the impunity is genuine, this course of action is the only obvious way forward. It does not mean sexual assault and drug taking will stop, but it does mean claims of impunity that are damaging the function and reputation of the military may. No longer will a soldier be able to believe in their own impunity, protected within the military coterie, and no longer can they say to a civilian police officer, "I am your worst nightmare. I can do anything and you can't touch me."

NOTES

1. Peter Tsouras (ed), *Warriors' Words: A Dictionary of Military Quotations* (Arms and Armour Press: A Cassell Imprint, 1994): 139.

2. Ken Silverstein, *Private Warriors* (Verso, 2000): 17.

3. William A. Moorman, "Fifty Years of Military Justice: Does the Uniform Code of Military Justice Need to Be Changed?" *The Air Force Law Review* 48 (2000): 185.

4. Peter Rowe, "The Soldier as a Citizen in Uniform: A Reappra isal" *N.Z. Armed Forces Law Review* 7 (2007): 1, 7.

5. *Defence Force Discipline Act* (Cth) 1982 (DFDA) s107; *Uniform Code of Military Justice* (UCMJ) US 1950: art 2.

6. Uniform Code of Military Justice (UCMJ); 10 U.S.C. art 16, The three kinds of courts-martial in each of the armed forces—(1) general courts-martial, (2) special courts-martial, and (3) summary courts-martial, consisting of one commissioned officer.

7. *DFDA* 1987 s114 (1) A court-martial shall be either a general court-martial or a restricted court-martial.

8. Marc Edward Rosenthal, "Where Is the Justice? The Sexual Assault Crisis Plaguing the Military and a Lack of Meaningful Justice" *University of Miami National Security & Armed Conflict Law Review* 41 (2013): 295, 306; Jeremy Stephens, "Factually Insufficient: A Response to the Military Justice Review Group's Appellate Review Proposal" *Army Lawyer* (2016): 32.

9. David Luban, "On the Commander in Chief Power" *Southern California Law Review* 81 (2008): 477; Lindsy Nicole Alleman, "Who Is in Charge, and Who Should Be? The Disciplinary Role of the Commander in Military Justice Systems" *Duke Journal of Comparative & International Law*16 (2006): 169.

10. *White v. Director of Military Prosecution* [2007] HCA 29, [92] (Kirby J).

11. Stephens, "Factually Insufficient": 35–36; Andrew S. Williams, "Safeguarding the Commander's Authority to Review the Findings of a Court-Martial" *BYU Journal of Public Law* 28 (2014): 471.

12. See *U.S. ex rel. Quirin v. Cox*, 63 S.Ct. 22 (1942); Jeremy D. Broussard, "Restoring Balance to the Scales: Higher Panel Quorums and Voting Requirement in Light of Article 60 Restrictions" *Army Lawyer* (2016): 5; James T. Hill, "Achieving Transparency in the Military Panel Selection Process with the Preselection Method" *Military Law Review* 205 (2010): 117.

13. Dru Brennerbecka, "Assessing Guidelines and Disparity in Military Sentencing: Vive la Différence!" *Federal Sentencing Reporter* 27(2) (2014):108; Megan N. Schmid, "This Court-Martial Hereby (Arbitrarily) Sentences You: Problems with Court Member Sentencing in the Military and Proposed Solutions" *Air Force Law Review* 67 (2011): 245; Bradley Huestis, "Anatomy of a Random Court-Martial Panel" *Army Lawyer* (2006): 22.

14. *National Defense Authorization Act for Fiscal Year* 2014, Pub. L. 113-66 [FY14 NDAA], § 1705 1702(b). See Elizabeth Holtzman et al., "Statistical Data Regarding Military Adjudication of Sexual Assault Offenses for Fiscal Year 2015" (Judicial Proceedings Panel, Septemeber 15, 2017): 19–20.

15. David A. Schlueter, "The Military Justice Conundrum: Justice or Discipline?" *Military Law Review* 215 (2013): 4, 5 (footnotes omitted).

16. Manual for Courts-Martial, United States, (2012) cited in Schlueter "The Military Justice Conundrum": 11.

17. Greg Rustico, "Overcoming Overcorrection: Towards Holistic Military Sexual Assault Reform" *Virginia Law Review* 102 (2016): 2027, 2036–37.

18. James E. Baker, "Is Military Justice Sentencing on the March? Should It Be? And If So, Where Should It Head? Court-martial Sentencing Process, Practice, and Issues" *Federal Sentencing Reporter* 27, no. 2 (2014): 72, 75.

19. Mark Cunliffe, Geoffrey Brown, and Gerard Fogarty "Re-Thinking Systems of Inquiry, Investigation, Review and Audit in Defence, Annex G: Specialist Roles and Processes" (2014): [6.2.1.], 31 "For example, in the past both the Australian Federal Police (AFP) (prior to 2007) and the APS (prior to 1999) used tribunal-based disciplinary systems. In the case of the AFP, the report of Justice Fisher found the AFP's tribunal processes to be unduly legalistic and slow. Both organizations now have flexible, values-based Codes of Conduct that allow the imposition of sanctions against an individual if they are found by a delegate to be in breach of the relevant code. APS Code of Conduct decisions are administrative decisions, based on any relevant information (regardless of the process used to collect it)."

20. See e.g., *Weiss v. United States,* 510 U.S. 174; *White* [2007] HCA 29.

21. See e.g., *Chappell* 462 US 296 (1983).

22. See e.g., *US v. Stanley* 483 US 669 (1987); *White* [2007] HCA 29.

23. See e.g., *US v. Green* US Court of Appeals Sixth Circuit Nos. 09-6108/6123; *US v. Nazario*, No. ED CR 07-127-SGL (C.D. Cal 2007); *Parker v. Levy* 417 US 733 (1974); *White* [2007] HCA 29; Christopher Waters, "Beyond Lawfare: Juridical Oversight of Western Militaries" *Alberta Law Review* 46 (2009): 855; Jonathan Turley, "The Military Pocket Republic" *Northwestern University Law Review* 97 (2002): 1.

24. Baker, "Is Military Justice Sentencing on the March?": 75.

25. *Ex parte Milligan* 71 US 2 (1886).

26. *Duncan v. Kahanamoku* 327 US 304 (1946).

27. Timothy C. MacDonnell, "Military Commissions and Courts-Martial: A Brief Discussion of the Constitutional and Jurisdictional Distinctions between the Two Courts" *Army Lawyer* (2015): 6, 21.

28. Erving Goffman, *The Characteristics of Total Institutions*, in *Organization and Society* (January) (1961): 312, 314.

29. Hannah Brenner, Kathleen Darcy, and Sheryl Kubiak, "Sexual Violence as an Occupational Hazard and Condition of Confinement in the Closed Institutional Systems of the Military and Detention" *Pepperdine Law Review* 44 (2017): 881.

30. Peter McClellan, Robert Fitzgerald, and Helen Milroy, "Royal Commission into Institutional Responses to Child Sexual Abuse" (December 15 2017) https://www.childabuseroyalcommission.gov.au/final-report: 370–371, 375: "Research suggests that some institutional cultures tolerate and even value bullying as an appropriate expression of masculinity."

31. Graci Bozarth, “Strange Bedfellows: The Military, the University, and Sexual Assault” *University of Missouri-Kansas City Law Review* 84 (2016): 1003, 1007.

32. Adam DeVille, “Kenosis vs. La Bella Figura” *The Canadian Journal of Orthodox Christianity* 2(3) (2007): 94.

33. Anita Bernstein and Paul Fanning, “Heirs of Leonardo: Cultural Obstacles to Strict Products Liability in Italy” *Vanderbilt Journal of Transnational Law* 27 (1994): 1, 10.

34. McClellan, “Royal Commission” Transcript produced by DTI 24/08/2015 (156) 16088.

35. Bernstein and Fanning, “Heirs of Leonardo”: 19.

36. McClellan, “Royal Commission” Transcript produced by DTI 24/08/2015 (156) 16094.

37. Christopher W. Behan, “Don’t Tug on Superman’s Cape: In Defense of Convening Authority Selection and Appointment of Court-Martial Panel Members” *Military Law Review* 176 (2003): 190, 300.

38. See e.g., Turley, “The Military Pocket”: 1; William R. Hagan, “Overlooked Textbooks Jettison Some Durable Military Law Legends” *Military Law Review* 113 (1986): 163, 198; Cullen Murphy, *The New Rome? The Fall of an Empire and the Fate of America* (Scribe Publications Ltd, 2007); C. Quince Hopkins, “Rank Matters but Should Marriage?: Adultery, Fraternization, and Honor in the Military” *UCLA Women’s Law Journal* 9 no. 2 (1999): 177.

39. “Royal Commission” Transcript produced by DTI 24/08/2015 (156) 16083.

40. Robert S French, “The Executive Power” (Paper presented at the Inaugural George Winterton Lecture, Sydney Law School, The University of Sydney, February 18, 2010); Andre Kaiser, “Parliamentary Opposition in Westminster Democracies: Britian, Canada, Australia and New Zealand” *The Journal of Legislative Studies* 14 no. 1 (2008): 20.

41. David Held, *Models of Democracy* (Polity Press, 2nd ed, 1996); Major General H. Kujat, “The Role of the Military in a Democracy” *NATO Information Seminar* (July 2–3, 1998) http://www.nato.int/docu/speech/1998/s980702h.htm; Kent Freiderich, “Strange Bedfellows: The American Public and Its Military in the Aftermath of September 11th” (U.S. Army War College Carlisle Barracks, July 4, 2003).

42. Peter Irons, “The Constitution Is Just a Scrap of Paper”: Empire versus Democracy” *University of Cincinnati Law Review* 73 (2005): 1081; Ronald R Krebs, “One Nation under Arms? Military Participation Policy and the Politics of Identity” *Security Studies* 14 no. 3 (2005): 529.

43. D Heydon, “Judicial Activism and the Death of the Rule of Law” *Quadrant* 47 no. 1 (2003): 9.

44. See Turley, “The Military Pocket”: 1, 101; Richard Kohn, “How Democracies Control the Military” *Journal of Democracy* 8 no. 4 (1997): 140.

45. Luban, “On the Commander in Chief ”: 81.

46. See Defense Manpower Data Center, DoD Personnel, Workforce Reports and Publications https://www.dmdc.osd.mil/appj/dwp/dwp_reports.jsp; See, for the US, “Veterans and Military Families” *Substance Abuse and Mental Health Services Administration* (SAMHSA) (2017) https://www.samhsa.gov/veterans-military-families:

23.4 million veterans, approximately 2.2 million military service members, and 3.1 million immediate family; Military Bases.com: approximately 324 military bases on US soil and approximately 800 in other countries: https://militarybases.com/by-state/.

47. Turley, "The Military Pocket": 1, 101–2.

48. Samuel Warren, *Blackstone's Commentaries Systematically Abridged and Adapted to the Existing State of the Law and Constitution* (W Maxwell, Bell Yard, Lincoln's Inn., 1855): 323–24.

49. Guy I. Seidman, "The Origins of Accountability: Everything I Know about the Sovereign's Immunity, I Learned from King Henry III" *Saint Louis University Law Journal* 49 (2005): 393, 403. See also, Frederick Pollock and Frederic William Maitland, *The History of English Law. Before the Time of Edward I.* (Cambridge University Press, 2nd ed, 1968).

50. Seidman, "The Origins of Accountability": 49.

51. Ibid., 49.

52. Ernest F. Henderson, *Select Historical Documents of the Middle Ages* London: George Bell and Sons, 1896, available on the Yale Law School Avalon Project Documents in Law History and Diplomacy http://avalon.law.yale.edu/medieval/constcla.asp.

53. C. R. Cheney, *From Becket to Langton: English Church Government* (Manchester University Press, 1956): 1170–1213.

54. *Act of Submission of the Clergy* 1533, 25 Henry VIII c 19; *R v Millis* (1844) 8 English Reports 641, 898: "The canon law of Europe does not, *and never did,* as a body of laws, form part of the law of England."

55. See e.g., G. W. Bernard, *The King's Reformation: Henry VIII and the Remaking of the English Church* (Yale University Press, 2005).

56. President Truman signed into law the UCMJ on May 5, 1950. The code became effective during the Korean War, on May 31, 1951.

57. The MCM incorporates the Preamble, the Rules for Courts-Martial, the Military Rules of Evidence, the punitive articles, and non-judicial punishment.

58. *American Articles of War*, enacted June 30, 1775.

59. *American Articles of War*, § 18, art. 5 of 1776; *American Articles of War,* § 33 of 1806; *American Articles of War,* § 59 of 1874; Andrew S Effron et al., "Report of the Military Justice Review Group. Part I UCMJ Recommendations" (December 22, 2015): 44.

60. See, James B Roan and Cynthia Buxton, "The American Military Justice System in the New Millennium" *Air Force Law Review* 52 (2002): 185, 188–89.

61. Commonwealth, "Defence Force Disciplinary Code: Report of the 1973 Working Party" (1974): 133.

62. Clause 17, 350.

63. DFDA (Cth) 1982–s 190.

64. David A. Schlueter, "The Military Justice Conundrum: Justice or Discipline?" *Military Law Review* 215 (2013): 1, 4.

65. Roan and Buxton, "The American Military Justice System": 188.

66. Schlueter, "The Military Justice Conundrum": 74.

67. UCMJ art. 133; DFDA s 60 prejudicial conduct. See also, Sherrill, *Military Justice Is to Justice as Military Music*: 74–75.

68. (2009) 239 CLR 230.

69. (French CJ and Gummow J) [36].

70. (French CJ and Gummow J) [35]; See e.g., James Stellios, "The Dismantling of the Australian Military Court: Lane v Morrison" *The Australian Centre for Military Law and Justice* 2 (2010): 3.

71. Caitlyn Gribbin, "Defence Abuse Response Taskforce Reverses Call for Royal Commission into Sex Abuse at ADFA" *ABC News* August 2, 2016 http://www.abc.net.au/news/2016-09-02/taskforce-reverses-call-for-commission-into-sex-abuse-at-adfa/7811136.

72. Turley, "The Military Pocket": 1, 96.

73. Irene Zubaida Khan, "The Rule of Law and the Politics of Fear: Human Rights in the Twenty-First Century" *Buffalo Human Rights Law Review* 14 (2008): 1.

74. John W. Brooker, "Improving Uniform Code of Military Justice Reform" *Military Law Review* 222 (2014): 1, 24.

75. Effron et al., "Report of the Military": 17.

76. David Schmidtchen, *The Rise of the Strategic Private. Technology, Control and Change in a Network-Enabled Military*, The General Sir Brunenell White Series (Commonwealth of Australia, Land Warfare Studies Centre, 2006).

77. Army White Paper, *The Profession of Arms* December 8, 2010: 3; John S. Cooke, "Manual for Courts-Martial 20X," in *Evolving Military Justice*, Eugene R. Fidell and Dwight H. Sullivan eds. (Naval Institute Press, 2002): 173, 182 cited in Brooker, "Improving Uniform": 6.

78. Roan and Buxton, "The American Military Justice System": 190.

79. US Census 2000 shows that between 1980 and 1999 there were a total of 563 hostile deaths, the highest in 1984 (276) and 1991 (148) this amounts to 0.1 percent per 100,000 582. U.S. Active Duty Military Deaths, by Manner of Death http://www.allcountries.org/uscensus/582_u_s_active_duty_military_deaths.html; This compares with commercial fishermen rating 1 as the mostly deadly jobs in the US at 116 deaths per 100,000 in 2010; 129 deaths and 61 injuries per 100,000 for 2008 with a total of 27 percent of deaths per 100,000 population for farming, fishing and forestry http://www.bls.gov/iif/oshwc/cfoi/cfoi_revised10.pdf; See also, Matthew Goldberg, "Death and Injury Rates of U.S. Military Personnel in Iraq" *Military Medicine* 175 (2010): 220, indicating the degree of difficulty in extracting exact figures for death in combat.

80. Tomas Kucera, *The Military and Liberal Society. Societal-Military Relations in Western Europe* (Routledge, 2018): 103.

81. Turley, "The Military Pocket": 1, 128 ". . . it is not clear that the ability to prosecute criminal acts increases either legal compliance or, conversely, adds to deterrence for would-be violators."

82. Peter T. Kilborn, "Sex Abuse Cases Sting Pentagon, but the Problem Has Deep Roots" *New York Times* February 10, 1997 http://www.nytimes.com/1997/02/10/us/sex-abuse-cases-sting-pentagon-but-the-problem-has-deep-roots.html.

83. Baker, "Is Military Justice Sentencing on the March?": 75.

84. Anthony J. Ghiotto, "Back to the Future with the Uniform Code of Military Justice: The Need to Recalibrate the Relationship between the Military Justice Sys-

tem, Due Process, and Good Order and Discipline" *North Dakota Law Review* 90 (2014): 485, 529.

85. Ibid.: 528–529; See further, Lana Friesen, "Certainty of Punishment versus Severity of Punishment: An Experimental Investigation" *Southern Economic Journal* 79 no. 2 (2012): 399.

86. Daniel S. Nagin and Greg Pogarsky, "Time and Punishment: Delayed Consequences and Criminal Behavior" *Journal of Quantitative Criminology* 20(4) (2004): 295.

87. Ghiotto, "Back to the Future": 528.

88. Alex R. Piquero, Zenta Gomez-Smith and Lynn Langton, "Discerning Unfairness Where Others May Not: Low Self-Control and Unfair Sanction Perceptions" *Criminology* 42 (2004): 699.

89. Ghiotto, "Back to the Future": 513 (footnotes omitted).

90. *Parker v. Levy,* 417 U.S. 733, 743 (1974); *White* [2007] HCA 29 [9] (Gleeson CJ).

91. Steven B. Lichtman, "The Justices and the Generals: A Critical Examination of the U.S. Supreme Court's Tradition of Deference to the Military, 1918–2004" *Maryland Law Review* 65 (2006): 907, 945 (emphasis added).

92. Steven Churches, "The Shield of the Crown in England and Australia: The Need for Statutory Interpretation that Applies the Principle of Legality" *Public Law Review* 22 (2011): 182.

93. James M. Hirschhorn, "The Separate Community: Military Uniqueness and Servicemen's Constitutional Rights" *North Carolina Law Review* 62 (1983–84): 177; See further, Kucera, *The Military and Liberal Society*: 83.

94. See Kucera, *The Military and Liberal Society:* 55; Turley, "The Military Pocket": 1.104.

95. Alex Gallacher et al., "The Constant Battle: Suicide by Veterans" (Foreign Affairs, Defence and Trade References Committee, August 2017) https://www.aph.gov.au/Parliamentary_Business/Committees/Senate/Foreign_Affairs_Defence_and_Trade/VeteranSuicide/Report: 115 [6.5].

96. Pauline Collins, *Civil-military "Legal" Relations: Where to from Here? The Civilian Courts and the Military in the United Kingdom, United States and Australia.* (Leiden: Brill Nijhoff, 2018): 6–7.

97. Luban, "On the Commander in Chief."

98. See further, Edward Sherman, "Legal Inadequacies and Doctrinal Restraints in Controlling the Military" *Indiana Law Journal* 49 (1974): 539.

99. See, *Parker* 417 U.S. 733 (1974).

100. H. F. "Sparky" Gierke, "The Use of Article III Case Law in Military Jurisprudence" *Army Lawyer* August (2005): 25, 38. See *United* States *v. Tulloch*, 47 MJ 283, 285 (1997) varied from the Supreme Court regarding discrimination based on race in jury selection *Batson v. Kentucky*, 476 U.S. 79 (1986).

101. *United States v. Easton* 71 M.J. 168, 177 (C.A.A.F. 2012).

102. *Easton v. United States*, 133 S.Ct. 930 (2013). See further, Robert D. Merrill, "The Military's Dilution of Double Jeopardy: Why United States v. Easton Should Be Overturned" *Military Law Review* 219 (2014): 176; Rodrigo M. Caruço,

"Treating Members of the Military at Least as Well as Inmates and Students: Determining When Military Necessity Requires Infringing upon Constitutional Rights in Cases before the Court of Appeals for the Armed Forces" *University of Memphis Law Review* 46 (2015): 61.

103. See Dean Lusher, Peter Kremer, and Garry Robins, "Cooperative and Competitive Structures of Trust Relations in Teams" *Small Group Research* 45 no. 1 (2014): 3; Piquero, Gomez-Smith, and Langton, "Discerning Unfairness."

104. 231 CLR 570 [2007] HCA 29.

105. DFDA (Cth) 1982 ss 190A, 190B (3) "The convicted person is not required to disclose to any person, for any purpose (other than a service purpose), the fact that the person has been convicted of the offence."

106. Michelle Draper, "A Royal Australian Navy Sailor Has Broken Down after Being Found Guilty of Raping a Female Defence Force Colleague" *The Sydney Morning Herald*, August 10, 2011 https://www.smh.com.au/national/navy-sailor-guilty-of-rape-20110810-1ilxd.html.

107. Amelia Bentley, "Ex-Naval Officer Faces Child Sex Trial," *Brisbane Times*, July 26, 2011 http://www.brisbanetimes.com.au/queensland/exnaval-officer-faces-child-sex-trial-20110726-1hxwp.html.

108. Caruço, "Treating Members of the Military": 19.

109. Ibid., 124–125 (footnotes omitted); See also Jeremy S. Weber, "The Disorderly, Undisciplined State of the 'Good Order and Discipline' Term." *Air War College* Thesis Publication, February 16, 2016.

110. See e.g., *United States v. Milldebrandt* 8 U.S.C.M.A. 635, 638 (1958); *United States v. Robinson* 6 U.S.C.M.A. 347, 352–3 (1955); mentioned in Caruço "Treating Members of the Military": 106–107 "On a separate occasion, CAAF recognized that military necessity is an 'amorphous term,' but it knew it when it saw it. Members of CAAF have also criticized the majority at times for citing military necessity as a basis to ignore a constitutional rule without proper justification."

111. Roan and Buxton, "The American Military": 190.

112. Ghiotto, "Back to the Future."

113. Brooker, "Improving Uniform": 31.

114. See e.g., *Australian Criminal Code Act* 1995 (Cth) 4.1 (1) "A physical element of an offence may be: (a) conduct; or (b) a result of conduct; or (c) *a circumstance in which conduct, or a result of conduct, occurs*." (emphasis added).

115. See e.g., *Australian Criminal Code Act* 1995 (Cth) Division 12.

116. Tomas Zipfel, "The Politics and Finance of Civil-Military Reform in the Czech Republic" *Journal of Communist Studies and Transition Politics* 17 no. 1 (2001): 96.

117. Caruço, "Treating Members of the Military": 122–23.

118. *United States v. Womack*, 29 M.J.88 (C.M.A 1989) 90.

119. Ibid.

120. 340 U.S. 146 (1950).

121. Robert Cornall, "Defence Abuse Response Taskforce" Final Report "DART" (Commonwealth of Australia, March 2016) https://www.defenceabusetaskforce.gov.au/reports/Documents/dart-final-report.pdf: 43.

122. Melissa Jeltsen, "Air Force Failed to Enter Church Shooter's Domestic Violence Record in U.S. Database" *Huffington Post,* November 7, 2017 http://www.huffingtonpost.com.au/entry/texas-church-shooting-domestic-violence-record_us_5a00d8c0e4b066c2c039ace8; Sig Christenson, "After Killings, Pentagon Added Thousands of Dishonorable Discharge Cases to FBI Database" *San Antonio Express-News,* February 12, 2018 https://www.mysanantonio.com/news/local/article/After-killings-Pentagon-added-thousands-of-12608025.php.

123. DFDA (Cth) 1982–s 140 provides for public hearings but notes the need to address the issue of access to a base.

124. See e.g., *Disciplinary Tribunal Health Practitioner Regulation National Law* Act (Cth) 2009; *Police (Complaints and Disciplinary Proceedings) Act* (Sth Aust.) 1985.

125. See, *Goldman v. Weinberger* 475 US 503 (1986) (*Goldman*); *US v. Stanley* 483 US 669 (1987).

126. Peter Rowe, *The Impact of Human Rights Law on Armed Forces* (Cambridge: Cambridge University Press, 2006); Caruco, "Treating Members of the Military": 61.

127. See Eugene Fidell, "A World-Wide Perspective on Change in Military Justice" *The Air Force Law Review* 48 (2000): 195.

128. Harry Willey, "Kelliher VC" (2002) *Digger History: An Unofficial History of the Australian and New Zealand Armed Forces* www.Keliher VC_ From Court-martial to VC.mht.

129. Kathryn Quinn, "Sexual Harassment in the Australian Defence Force" (Commonwealth of Australia, 1996) http://www.defence.gov.au/fr/reports/shinadf.pdf; Department of Defense, "US Department of Defense Sexual Assault Prevention and Response Program" http://www.sapr.mil/; Angela Snell, "The Absence of Justice: Private Military Contractors, Sexual Assault, and the U.S. Government's Policy of Indifference" *University of Illinois Law Review* (2011): 1125.

130. See e.g., W Niskanen, *A Bureaucracy and Representative Government* (Aldine-Atherton, 1971).

131. 71 M.J. 256 (C.A.A.F. 2012).

132. *Ali*, Final Brief on Behalf of the Appellant Crim App. No 20080559 USCA Dkt No 12-0008/AR: 5.7; See also, Antenor Hallo de Wolf, "Modern Condottieri in Iraq: Privatizing War from the Perspective of International and Human Rights Law" *Indiana Journal of Global Legal Studies* 13 (2006): 315, 323.

133. *Military Extraterritorial Jurisdiction Act* H.R. 3380—116th Congress (1999–2000) (*MEJA*).

134. *US v. Waltrip,* No 1:08-CR-283, Dkt. 19 (E.D.Va July 22, 2008); See also *Ali* 70 M.J. 514 brief of Amici Curiae: 11–12.

135. *Ali* 70 M.J. 256, 276 (Baker CJ); See Eugene Fidell, "Criminal Prosecution of Civilian Contractors by Military Courts" *South Texas Law Review* 50 (2009): 845.

136. See, Joseph Raz, "The Rule of Law and Its Virtue" *Law Quarterly Review* 93 (1977): 193.

137. Caruço, "Treating Members of the Military": 125 (footnotes removed).

138. See also, R.C.M. 707 euphemistically known as the 120-day speedy trial rule; The DFDA (Cth) 1982 s129D requires the trial of a charge commence "as soon as

practicable within the period of 3 months after the accused person is charged with the service offence."

139. *United States v. Cooley*, 75 M.J. 247 (C.A.A.F. May 6, 2016) (confinement on December 20, 2012; trial on October 3, 2014).

140. Ghiotto, "Back to the Future": 514, 516.

141. *United States v. Cooley*, 75 M.J. 247 (C.A.A.F. May 6, 2016).

142. Takashi Kagawa, "Soldier's First Offense: Article 15 or Summary Court-Martial?" *Army Lawyer* January (2014): 33.

143. Ghiotto, "Back to the Future": 517 (footnotes removed).

144. NAA, Department of External Affairs, A1209, 1966/7194, File 66/7/94 PM Dept; Note DFDA (Cth) 1982 s143 Condonation is now no bar to discipline.

145. NAA, Department of External Affairs; But *cf Military Court of Australia Bill* 2010 s 66 "Condonation of service offence not to prevent institution of proceeding."

146. Antony Buckingham, "A Brief History of Australian Military Law" Australian MP History Website, www.home.iprimus.com.au/buckomp/BriefHistAustralian-MilLaw.htm.

147. Eric Hanson, "Know Your Ground: The Military Justice Terrain of Afghanistan" *Army Lawyer* November (2009): 36.

148. Franklin D. Rosenblatt, "Non-Deployable: The Court-martial System in Combat from 2001 to 2009" *Creighton Law Review* 44 (2011): 1045.

149. Ibid., 1046.

150. Ibid., 1046.

151. Frederic L. Borch, *Judge Advocates in Combat. Army Lawyers in Military Operations from Vietnam to Haiti* (U.S. Government Printing Office, 2001), 188 cited in Behan, "Don't Tug on Superman's Cape": 297.

152. Ibid., 189.

153. Ibid., 188.

154. Ibid., 298.

155. R. Peter Masterton, "Recent Developments in Military Justice" *Federal Lawyer* 63 (2016): 8; Michael I. Spak and Jonathan P. Tomes, "Sexual Harassment in the Military: Time for a Change of Forum" *Cleveland State Law Review* 47 (1999): 335; Jonathan P. Tomes and Michael I. Spak, "Practical Problems with Modifying the Military Justice System to Better Handle Sexual Assault Cases" *Wisconsin Journal of Law, Gender & Society* 29 (2014): 377.

156. Sherrill, *Military Justice Is to Justice as Military Music*: 63.

157. *United States v. Sadinsky,* 14 U.S.C.M.A. 563, 34 C.M.R. 343, 345 (1964) cited in *Parker* "art 134 does not make 'every irregular, mischievous, or improper act a court-martial offense,' but its reach is limited to conduct that is 'directly and palpably—as distinguished from indirectly and remotely—prejudicial to good order and discipline.'"

158. *United States v. Sadinsky,* 14 U.S.C.M.A. 563, C.M.R. 343 (1964) supported the belief that conduct does not have to be specifically prohibited in the UCMJ for it to be impermissible in the military.

159. Rosenthal, "Where Is the Justice?"

160. Jennifer Steinhauer, "Remark by Obama Complicates Military Sexual Assault Trials" *New York Times,* July 14, 2013, A1; Jonathan Drew, "Bergdahl Lawyers: Trump's Criticism Prevents Fair Trial" *The Navy Times*, January 20, 2017 https://www.navytimes.com/news/your-army/2017/01/20/bergdahl-lawyers-trump-s-criticism-prevents-fair-trial/; see further, Luban, "On the Commander in Chief."

161. David Morrison, Lt. General Chief of the Australian Army, "Address to the Closing Plenary Session at the Global Summit to End Sexual Violence in Conflict" (2014); Alex Gallacher et al., "Matters Raised by NSW Police Strike Force Civet" (Foreign Affairs, Defence and Trade Refeerences Committee, 2017); Alex McDonald, "'Jedi Council' Ringleader Hastings Fredrickson Who Shared Photos of Sex Acts Facing Correction Order," *ABC News*, February 9, 2015 http://www.abc.net.au/news/2015-02-09/jedi-council-ringleader-hastings-fredrickson-jailed/6081028.

162. Dave Grossman, *On Killing: The Psychological Cost of Learning to Kill in War and Society* (Back Bay Books, 2009) 144–45 cited in Ghiotto, "Back to the Future": 527.

163. Gary Rumble, Melanie McKean, and Dennis Pearce, "Report of the Review of Allegations of Sexual and Other Abuse in Defence. Facing the Problems of the Past" *DLA Piper Review* (October 2011) Volume 1: 106.

164. Laurence Street and Les Fischer, "Report of the Independent Review on the Health of the Reformed Military Justice System" (January 23, 2009): 9, 16–17; Alexander Street, "Australian Military Justice and Chapter III Where to Next?" (Paper presented at the APCML/CCSJoint Seminar, October 6, 2009).

165. Geoff Earley, "Review of the Management of Incidents and Complaints in Defence Including Civil and Military Jurisdiction" (Department of Defence, September 6, 2011) http://www.defence.gov.au/Publications/Reviews/SystemsInquiry/.

166. Ibid., 33.

167. Ibid., 49.

168. Rumble et al., *DLA Piper Review*: 135.

169. Alan Eggleston et al., "Report of the DLA Piper Review and the Government's Response" (Foreign Affairs, Defence and Trade References Committee, June 2013).

170. Ibid., 106.

171. Kathryn Quinn, "Sexual Harassment in the Australian Defence Force" (Commonwealth of Australia, 1996) http://www.defence.gov.au/fr/reports/shinadf.pdf: 44; Defence and Trade Senate Standing Committee on Foreign Affairs, "Sexual Harassment in the Australian Defence Force" (August 1994) http://www.aph.gov.au/senate/committee/fadt_ctte/completed_inquiries/pre1996/harassment/report.pdf; Department of Defense, "US Department of Defense Sexual Assault Prevention and Response Program" http://www.sapr.mil/; Snell, "The Absence of Justice."

172. James Ross, "Black Letter Abuse: The US Legal Response to Torture Since 9/11" *International Review of the Red Cross* 89 no. 867 (2007): 561; Bradley Graham and Josh White, "Top Pentagon Leaders Faulted in Prison Abuse Oversight by Rumsfeld and Others Inadequate, Panel Says," *Washington Post*, August 25, 2004.

173. 71 MJ 256 (CAAF 2012).

174. Roan and Buxton, "The American Military Justice": 191.

175. Paul Bremer, "Coalition Provisional Authority Order Number 17 (Revised)" (2004); Ian Wexler, "A Comfortable SOFA: The Need for an Equitable Foreign Criminal Jurisdiction Agreement with Iraq" *Naval Law Review* 56 (2008): 43.

176. See, Rosenblatt, "Non-Deployable."

177. Richard Weiland, "Court-Martial Charges for Australian Commandos Dismissed" (May 2011) http://www.nimjblog.org/2011/05/court-martial-charges-for-australian.html; Ian Westwood, "Australian Military Court Report" (Department of Defence, 2009): 9.

178. Michael W. Lewis, "Drones and the Boundaries of the Battlefield" *Texas International Law Journal* 47 no. 2 (2012): 293; Jean L. Otto and Bryant J. Webber, "Mental Health Diagnoses and Counseling among Pilots of Remotely Piloted Aircraft in the United States Air Force" *Medicial Surveillance Monthly Report* 20 no. 3 (2013): 3; Presenter: Natasha Mitchell and Guest: Brandon Bryant, "Drone Warfare and the Psyche: An Insider Speaks" *Radio National Broadcast*, August 19, 2017 http://www.abc.net.au/radionational/programs/sciencefriction/drone-warfare-and-the-psyche-an-insider-speaks/8817340.

179. See e.g., Otto and Webber, "Mental Health Diagnoses."

180. Michael Edwards, "Robert Langdon: Last Western Prisoner Held in Afghanistan Pardoned, Flown Home to Australia" *ABC News,* August 10, 2016 http://www.abc.net.au/news/2016-08-09/australian-prisoner-robert-langdon-leaves-afghanistan/7711308.

181. *Military Extraterritorial Jurisdiction Act* H.R. 3380—116th Congress (1999–2000).

182. See e.g., *The North Atlantic Treaty Organisation Status of Forces Agreement*, art 7 outlines jurisdiction for sending and receiving states in relation to discipline and criminal matters https://www.nato.int/cps/en/natohq/official_texts_17265.htm.

183. Gabriela Knaul, "Report of the Special Rapporteur on the Independence of Judges and Lawyers" (United Nations General Assembly, August 7, 2013): [15].

184. Ibid., [10]: "The State party should prohibit, and punish effectively, any conduct by military personnel, whether in peacetime or wartime, that is contrary to human rights, in particular the conduct set forth in articles 6 and 7 of the *Covenant*"; Human Rights Committee Eighty-first session, "Concluding observations of the Human Rights Committee" (CCPR/CO/81/BEL, 2004) http://daccess-dds-ny.un.org/doc/UNDOC/GEN/G04/432/21/PDF/G0443221.pdf?OpenElement; Decaux, Emmanuel, "Draft Principles Governing the Administration of Justice through Military Tribunals," UN Commission on Human Rights 62nd Sess., U.N. Doc. E/CN.4/2006/58 (January 13, 2006).

185. See e.g., Edward F. Sherman, "Military Justice without Military Control" *The Yale Law Journal* 82 no. 7 (1973) (June): 1398.

186. Stephen Payne Adye, *A Treatise on Courts-martial, to Which Is Added an Essay on Military Punishments and Rewards* (J Murray, 3 ed, 1786); J E A Jolliffe, *The Constitutional History of Medieval England from the English Settlement to 1485* (W W Norton and Company Inc, 1961); Pollock and Maitland, *The History of English Law.*

187. George R. Smawley, "Making Justice Flat: A Challenge to the View That Deploying Commanders Must Relinquish Command and General Court-Martial Convening Authority over Non-Deploying Forces" *Army Lawyer* (2013): 29, 31.

188. *White* [2007] HCA 29 [157] (Kirby, J).

189. Willey, "Kelliher VC."

190. Moorman, "Fifty Years of Military Justice": 191; Theo Farrell, *Norms of War: Cultural Belief and Modern Conflict* (Lynne Rienner, 2005).

191. Broussard, "Restoring Balance": 5 "Under the *Military Justice Act* 2016 a general court-martial will have a standard sized panel of eight members, and a special court-martial will have a standard sized panel of four panel members. . . . Every court-marital panel will consist of this set number of members, no more and no less. Even when the vote was and is 2/3 to convict, if the panel size happened to be 8 members, the prosecution still needed 6 out of 8 members to convict" https://www.ucmj-defender.com/new-standard-sized-panels-military-justice-act-2016/; Jonathan Choa, "Civilians, Service-Members, and the Death Penalty: The Failure of Article 25a to Require Twelve-Member Panels in Capital Trials for Non-Military Crimes" *Fordham Law Review* 70 (2002): 2065.

192. See above DFDA (Cth) 1987 s 114–A general court-martial comprises a president not below the rank of Colonel, and at least four other members. A restricted court-martial comprises a president, not below the rank of Lieutenant Colonel, and at least two other members.

193. DFDA (Cth) 1987 s 133 (2).

194. DFDA (Cth) 1987 s 133 (4).

195. Len Roberts-Smith, "A Nettle Grasped Lightly: The Introduction of the Australian Military Court" (Paper presented at the 2007 Judicial Conference, Washington DC, May 17, 2007): 23 "The other sting associated with making the court compliant with Chapter III of the Constitution involved Chapter III's guarantees to trial by jury, similar to the guarantee offered by section 2, Article III of the American constitution."

196. Ibid., 23 ". . . the military jury fell short of the common law jury requirements implicit in section 80, Chapter III"; See Alexander Street, "Submission No 2 of Alexander Street SC" *Inquiry into the Military Court of Australia Bill 2012 and Military Court of Australia (Transition Provisions and Consequential Amendments) Bill 2012*, no. July 11 (2012): 21 http://www.aph.gov.au/DocumentStore.ashx?id=3846db08-d509-42cd-8c36-e3eb12fb9157.

197. DFDA (Cth) 1987 s 119 convening order.

198. DFDA (Cth) 1987 s 133; Roberts-Smith, "A Nettle Grasped Lightly": 27 "Given the size and operational tempo of our Defence force I believe that it will be difficult in practice to obtain the numbers of officers and senior warrant officers required to sit as jury members, especially seeing that the Registrar is currently encountering difficulties panelling courts-martial that only require three"; See Broussard, "Restoring Balance": 6 "These early courts-martial required thirteen panel members, and the Articles of War were silent regarding the number of votes required for a conviction. . . . Because some units were unable to provide the sufficient number of officers to convene thirteen-member panels, Congress authorized court-martial panels reduced to as few as five members. . . . The need to address these articles is timely, considering the recent changes Congress has made to the convening authority's abilities under Article 60."

199. Williams "Safeguarding the Commander's Authority": 472.

200. Stephan Landsman, "A Brief Survey of the Development of the Adversary System" *Ohio State Law Journal* 44 (1983): 713, 725 "Cases like the famous New

York trial of John Peter Zenger on charges of seditious libel in 1734 and *Bushell's Case* illustrate this trend. In both cases jurors resisted government efforts to use the judicial mechanism as a means of punishing political opponents."

201. Charles S. Cumming, "The English High Court of Admiralty" *Tulane Maritime Law Journal* 17 (1993): 209, 216 "Common-law tribunals could not entertain causes of action arising outside of the realm because by law issues of fact had to be tried by a jury from the place where they were 'laid.'"

202. Ibid., 216.

203. See e.g., *United States v. Rivera*, 6 M.J. 535, 537 (N.C.M.R. 1978) "Court-martial panels aren't juries. If they were, they couldn't have only five members or reach non-unanimous verdicts when they have six members"; But *cf R v Stillman*, 2019 SCC 40 in which the SCC unfortunately denied the claim of the right by military members, in relation to certain crimes, to a civilian jury trial.

204. *United States v. Green* US Court of Appeals Sixth Circuit Nos. 09-6108/6123.

205. See e.g., *Attorney-General (Cth) v. Alinta Limited* [2008] HCA 2, "the High Court granted the Attorney-General leave to appoint counsel as amici curiae. . . . This precedent raises the prospect of amici being used in wider circumstances than they are currently, with the potential for the court to appoint its own amicus curiae or perhaps to invite arguments from interested persons."

206. See e.g., *Jayant Mukundray Patel v. The Queen* [2012] HCA 29.

207. Robert Cornall, "DART": 51 "participation bought home the wider impact on families. Several generations are often affected, not only the serving member"; Gadi Zerach, "Coping Strategies of Former Prisoners of War Mediate the Intergenerational Transmission of Post-traumatic Stress Symptoms" *Anxiety, Stress, & Coping* 31(2) (2018): 175.

208. Social Research Centre, "Public Opinion towards Governance: Results from the Inaugural ANU Poll" Melbourne, April 16, 2008 publicpolicy.anu.edu.au/anupoll/.../2008-04-16_ANUpoll_governance_report.pdf: 12, other unpopular areas include culture and the arts, and unemployment benefits; Social Research Centre, "Attitudes to Government and Government Services, 2011 http://csrm.cass.anu.edu.au/research/publications/attitudes-government-and-government-services.

209. *Caldwell v. Parker*, 252 U.S. 376, 382 (1920) cited in Williams, "Safeguarding the Commander's Authority": 482.

210. *Decaux Principles,* U.N. Doc. E/CN. 4/2006/58; Knaul, "Report of the Special Rapporteur."

211. *Decaux Principles,* Principle 1 [14].

212. Alex Conte, "ICJ Welcomes UN Expert Report on Military Tribunals" *press release* October 29, 2013 https://www.icj.org/icj-welcomes-un-expert-report-on-military-tribunals/.

213. Caruço, "Treating Members of the Military": 23.

214. Rustico, "Overcoming Overcorrection": 2065.

215. See e.g., *Miranda v. Arizona* 384 U.S. 436 (1966). See further Caruço, "Treating Members of the Military"; *Chief of the Defence Force v. Gaynor* [2017] FCAFC 41 (8 March 2017).

216. 107 S. Ct 2924 (1987).

217. *O'Callahan v. Parker,* 395 U.S. 258 (1969).
218. 71 MJ 256 (CAAF 2012); Rosenthal, "Where Is the Justice?": 127.
219. Francine Banner, "Institutional Sexual Assault and the Rights/Trust Dilemma" *Cardozo Public Law, Policy and Ethics Journal* 13 (2014): 97, 117.
220. Morris J. Janowitz, *The Professional Soldier: A Social and Political Portrait* (Free Press, 1960).
221. Gallacher, "The Constant Battle": Submission 59, 3.
222. Turley, "The Military Pocket": 1.
223. McClellan "Royal Commission" Case Study 40: [59]–[60].
224. Ibid., 10–11, 32–33, 55, 62.
225. Ibid., 48, 115–117; Gallacher, "The Constant Battle": 23–24.
226. Margaret Thornton, "Sexual Harrasment Losing Sight of Sex Discrimination" *Melbourne University Law Review* 26 (2002): 422.
227. Sherrill, *Military Justice Is to Justice as Military Music.*
228. Banner, "Institutional Sexual Assault": 108 "if a person has chosen to join an activity or organization, often at the expense of discounting other activities, in fact, she may be even *more* likely to support even dubious cultural norms and expectations. The member becomes particularly protective of an organization which she is aware she voluntarily—and not without self-sacrifice—has agreed to constitute. Further, the longer the individual belongs to the organization, the more she is likely to be invested in replicating and reinforcing norms, especially those that are considered essential to institutional viability."
229. Elizabeth Parsons and Vincenza Priola, "Agents for Change and Changed Agents: The Micro-politics of Change and Feminism in the Academy" *Gender, Work and Organization* 20 no. 5 (2013): 580, 583 cited in Banner, Institutional Sexual Assault."
230. Ibid., 583 (footnotes omitted).
231. 518 U.S. 515, 522 (1996) (Ginsberg J) (footnotes omitted).
232. Borch, *Judge Advocates in Combat.*
233. McClellan "Royal Commission" Case Study 40, 9, 34–36.
234. Ibid., 33–34.
235. Louis Joinet, "Issue of the Administration of Justice through Military Tribunals'" (E/CN.4/Sub.2/2002/4, UN Sub-Commission on the Promotion and Protection of Human Rights 54th session, July 9, 2002).
236. Ibid., 12.
237. Joinet, "Issue of the Administration of Justice": 15.
238. *Decaux Principles*: [11].
239. See Moorman, "Fifty Years of Military Justice."
240. See e.g., *Australian Federal Police Act 1979* (Cth) (AFP Act) and the *Australian Federal Police Categories of Conduct Determination 2006* (Cth) establish the disciplinary regime relevant to AFP appointees, category 3 conduct, the investigator may recommend any one or more of the following: termination; remedial action; training and development action; or any other action that the Commissioner can take in relation to the AFP appointee; See *Public Service Act* 1999 (Cth) s15 Breaches of the Code of Conduct (1) An Agency Head may impose the following sanctions on

an APS employee in the Agency who is found (under procedures established under subsection (3)) to have breached the Code of Conduct:

(a) termination of employment;
(b) reduction in classification;
(c) re-assignment of duties;
(d) reduction in salary;
(e) deductions from salary, by way of fine;
(f) a reprimand.

241. Rosenblatt, "Non-Deployable."

242. Moorman, "Fifty Years of Military Justice."

243. Jeremy Kelly, "Ex-Digger Robert William Langdon Gets Death Sentence in Afghanistan," *NewsCore,* January 27, 2010: 56–57.

244. Colman Lynch, "Indonesia's Use of Capital Punishment for Drug-Trafficking Crimes: Legal Obligations, Extralegal Factors, and the Bali Nine Case" *Columbia Human Rights Law Review* 40 (2008): 523; Anthony Lambert, "Mediating Crime, Mediating Culture: Nationality, Femininity, Corporeality and Territory in the Schapelle Corby Drugs Case" *Crime, Media, Culture* 4 no. 2 (2008): 237.

Chapter Two

The US Military Experience—Discipline and Sexual Offending

BACKGROUND

Sexual assault in the military has since at least the 1980s become a mounting concern. Much of this is linked to the Supreme Court jurisprudence arising around this time. Before the change of jurisprudence, many sexual matters were tried in the civilian courts.[1] Chapter three outlines these changes, but first this chapter will provide some evidence of the cases and the issues. The attempts to reform the treatment of people of homosexual orientation within the US military provides a salient lesson in the military society's intransigence to change. The Joint Chiefs of Staff, members of Congress, and a portion of military members, at the time, opposed the change campaign initiated by former US President Bill Clinton. The outcome was a rather hypocritical compromise, encapsulated in the "Don't Ask Don't Tell" (DADT) policy, as the best Clinton was able to achieve in 1993 to overcome the ban on homosexuals that had been in place since WWII.[2] DADT enabled homosexual people to enlist but at the same time homosexuality remained a ground for discharge with consensual sodomy remaining an offence.[3] Resistance to the change continued and over the next fifteen years around 12,000 military personnel were discharged based on their sexual orientation.[4] It took until 2014 for the UCMJ article 125 prohibition on consensual sodomy to be removed.

The courts played a role in overturning the discrimination. The District Court of California found that DADT appeared to violate the First and Fifth Amendments in *Log Cabin Republicans v. United States*.[5] Judge Phillips urged Congress and the executive to abandon DADT and the military to halt any discharges based on the policy. As Banner notes in going behind the rhetorical claims,

> Judge Phillips . . . found that copious empirical research demonstrated no connection between the DADT policy and the "task cohesion" essential to military readiness . . . rather . . . factors such as the negative effect of DADT on military recruiting, actually served "not to advance the Government's interests of military readiness and unit cohesion, much less to do so significantly, but to harm that interest." In other words, Judge Phillips read the advancement of individual rights of sexual autonomy as consonant with the development of institutional trust and loyalty.[6]

President Obama finally repealed DADT in 2010 but even then, it took another nine months for the regulatory changes to be implemented.[7] The change has not assisted others. Notably, President Trump, by tweet, in 2017 declared that there is no place in the military for transgender people and he has found subsequent procedural support in the Supreme Court.[8] Discrimination such as this is claimed to rely on the costs to the military of medical support for gender change, despite claimed expenditures in the millions being permitted for members' erectile dysfunction.[9] However, the RAND Corporation found in a 2016 study[10] that being transgender has no effect on military functionality in the military of at least 18 other countries.

Given the larger numbers of males in the military, inevitably men account for a larger number of assault survivors. This is so notwithstanding that men are less likely to report.[11] A significant factor is that reporting abuse can result in the survivor being dishonorably discharged. This intolerable position means the military society can sweep the abuse out of sight in an attempt to protect its brand reputation.

In the meantime, the people suffer. An occupation in the military can be a tough one and the aim should not be to make it worse. With many people affected, beyond the over 1.3 million military service members and estimated 23.4 million veterans in the United States, there are also around 3.1 million immediate family members to consider.[12] Estimates of high post-traumatic stress (PTSD) and depression (around 18.5 percent of US members serving in Iraq or Afghanistan) and high rates of death by suicide are also troubling.[13] The data on suicide is inherently difficult to obtain. However, estimates by some in the US report around one suicide every 36 hours by military personnel. This translates to approximately 1,100 lives during the period between 2005 and 2009, with army suicides reaching a high point in 2012.[14] Others indicate an 80 percent increase in the suicide rate in the army from 2004–2008.[15]

The statistics in Australia appear to reflect a similarity with the US.[16] While military survivors and family members remain eligible for care, many do not take the option for fear of repercussions on their career. The story is repeatedly one of survivors not wanting to tell their version of events for fear of retribution, fear of non-belief, and fear of losing their career. Many survivors say the institution's response is often more damaging than the assault. Service members reporting sexual assaults in 2015 perceived retribution in the form of reprisals, ostracism, or maltreatment in 58 percent (women) and 60 percent (men) of cases.[17] In submission number 51 to the Australian Foreign Affairs, Defence and Trade References Committee: "The Constant Battle: Suicide by Veterans," Mr. Birt explained:

> The final trigger may not be to do with the incident but a build-up, a LOT of the anxiety, depressive disorders, and attempted or successful suicide attempts are not necessarily caused by the "initial" injury but:
>
> a) By the feelings of injustice or abandonment;
> b) Being made to feel you are asking for something you don't need;
> c) The feeling you are malingering; and
> d) The pain, loss of income resulting in family, work and social breakdown.[18]

The case of Emily Vorland, a survivor reporting sexual harassment and receiving a dishonorable discharge for her efforts is just one instructive US example.[19] Vorland, a lesbian, reported her assault when the DADT policy was still current and she then became a target for further abuse. When removed by dishonorable discharge Vorland went through an environment contaminated by unconscious bias, before the Board for the Correction of Military Records, when she sought to change the dishonorable discharge in order to overcome the difficulties of getting work that such a discharge entails. Congress created these boards in 1946 to consider decisions made by commanders, under the pressure of the frontline environments, which removed personnel from the force with a dishonorable discharge. This was to provide a mechanism for some fairness in the military. In the civilian world, fairness encompasses the ability to bring dismissal before the courts for review. It appears that the boards, staffed by civilians, have been largely permeated by "'military staff who do all the decision-making for the boards' rubber stamp."[20] While an appeal option from the boards' decisions to federal courts exist, in practice few veterans have the emotional stamina and financial ability to choose this option. For instance, in the five years from 2008–2013, out of the thousands of board decisions, only 56 matters were appealed and of these only 12 saw the courts reverse decisions and some only in part.[21] The boards can feel impunity in their power as they face negligible effective review.

Non-reporting by survivors is said to be high for a number of reasons including emotions such as embarrassment, fear of retaliation, or loss of career progression, as well as other potential consequences such as punishment.

Belief in being able to brush it off or handle it, that the commander is unlikely to respond or, if they do, respond negatively, the stress associated with subsequent proceedings, and working in small tight-knit teams are all known justifications for non-reporting. Incidents where survivors are required to leave their workplace and offenders remain without punishment are not uncommon.[22] Perhaps somewhat surprisingly is a lack of reporting due to the survivor wanting to forget and move on, or perceiving the event as not significant. Some of this reflects a culture in which a tolerance level for bad behavior is accommodated. It certainly would not be reflective of a culture where zero tolerance is practiced.[23] Hazing is often written off as a tradition one has to endure. Men can fail to identify an assault as rape when it occurs as part of a hazing event, and acquaintance rape is also often not identified as part of the rape narrative.[24]

The lack of superintendence is a bigger problem for the military, which stands outside the mainstream justice system applicable to all citizens, forming its own separate coterie. Sexual assaults are classically civilian crimes that appear to have no connection to the military discipline offences such as desertion, disobeying an order, or aiding an enemy. However, they do undermine the support for claims that the military has to have a stronger and more disciplined outlook in order to function, and claims around the level of trust needed for the operative functional imperative to be effective. Such offences go to the heart of this aspect, and when they are not contained they destroy this imperative. Discussion would not be complete without reference to some statistics. However, the soundness of the data, and the interpretation of the data are always subject to the confirmation bias of the interpreter and so in this work it is only touched on.

The Statistics

Statistical comparisons are never an exact science as many surveys rely on self-reporting, are conducted by different organizations, and often cannot provide exact comparisons of oranges with oranges due to different definitions of terms used, different cohorts covered, and other variations.[25] Nevertheless, while such data can lead to crude perceptions, they can give a general idea of the level and the nature of the problem and perhaps whether it is an increasing or decreasing scenario. Statistics also paint a picture that may evidence some areas that require further investigation to advance our understanding. Keeping that in mind, this section delves into some of the statistical reporting.[26]

The US military screens for evidence of sexual harassment and behavior, sexual violence, and discrimination through the Defense Research, Surveys, and Statistics Center (RSSC) and the Defense Manpower Data Centre (DMDC).[27] The Workplace and Gender Relations Survey of Active Duty

Members (WGRS) started in 1988. Data is collected via a confidential online survey that provides self-reporting information on the prevalence of sexual assault, sexual harassment, sexist behavior, discrimination, perceptions of related support services, and training and policy practices in the preceding 12 months. Historically, the surveys in 2006, 2008, 2010, and 2012 used a measure of unwanted sexual contact (a term used to cover the range of sexual activity prohibited under the UCMJ), despite this actual term not being used in the UCMJ. Criticism of this resulted in Congress asking for an independent assessment by RAND in 2014[28] of active and reserve forces.

A further limitation of the data gathering is that it is disaggregated across the services. The WGRS survey comprises different components of the military, active duty, academy and reservists. In the 2010 survey of active duty members, 4.4 percent of women and 0.9 percent of men reported that they had experienced unwanted sexual contact. This was a lower rate than in 2006 (6.8 percent women and. 1.8 percent men).[29] In 2012, this survey covered 22,792 active duty members from all branches, and 6.1 percent of women and 1.2 percent of men responding alleged that they had been sexually assaulted in the preceding 12 months. This indicated an increase of 1.7 percent for women, and 0.3 percent for men since 2010.[30] Viewing it from an alternative perspective, 66 percent of females and 81 percent of males did not report an incident. The surveys, which measure by anonymous self-reporting of experiences, do not provide evidence of levels of actual reporting, investigation, or successful prosecution outcomes.

Due to the introduction of a new definition of sexual assault for 2014 and 2016, direct comparisons with survey data prior to 2014 are not viable. Congress in 2014 requested that the WGRS survey reflect more accurately the types of crimes experienced by military members. The DoD contracted RAND to conduct the survey of both active duty and reserve personnel. The definition of sexual assault was aligned with the UCMJ language and the elements of sexual assault in articles 80 and 120. RAND used two surveys: one using the unwanted sexual contact question (WGRS 2014) and the other using a newly constructed crime victimization measure aligned with the legal definitions contained in the UCMJ. The essential estimates between the new definition and the WGRS 2014 measure was found by the RAND Corporation's 2014 study to be statistically similar, but different categories of people and crimes arose.[31] Reporting of experiences that were more closely aligned to a crime still did not mean the matter had been investigated. The DoD survey data since 2014 has sought to benchmark the impact of the changes the military has made.[32]

There are now two sources of data, the official annual Sexual Assault Prevention and Response Office (SAPRO) reports and the bi-annual self-report survey data from the Office of People Analytics (OPA) and RAND. SAPRO arose from the 2004 former Secretary of Defense Rumsfeld's direction for a review into military care for sexual assault survivors, and the office was established in 2005.[33] There is a significant variation in the data from the various sources. While indicating an improvement in reporting between 2012 and 2014, the official data indicated a much lower incidence of assault. In 2014, 1,080 men and 3,690 women made official reports of sexual assault, compared to self-report data of 10,400 men and 8,500 women.[34] The SAPRO data collection has attracted criticism from the Judicial Proceedings Panel. This included the absence of a standardized collection process and a need for greater tracking of the legal disposition of matters. Specifically, lack of collection of intimate partner or spousal assaults was of concern, and that

> . . . SAPRO information on case adjudication is deficient because it cannot be used to thoroughly assess how sexual assault crimes are resolved through the military justice system. Despite recent improvements in the amount of case information collected, DSAID omits several important case characteristics. It does not include details on all sexual assault offenses alleged and charged, the outcome of each charge, the pleas of the accused, whether the accused was tried by a military judge or jury, the specific findings and sentence adjudged, and the convening authority action taken on the case in accordance with plea agreement terms or clemency requests.[35]

In 2016, the surveys conducted by the Defense Research, Surveys, and Statistics Center within the Defense Manpower Data Center (DMDC) were taken over and conducted by the newly established OPA. The new sexual assault measure was used in the survey, taking account of a response rate of 24 percent (representing 151,010 active duty members across the Army, Navy, Marine Corps, Air Force, and Coast Guard who were below flag rank and had five months on active duty), it indicated that approximately one in 23 women (4.3 percent) and one in 167 men (0.6 percent) had experienced unwanted sexual contact in the preceding 12 months.[36] The survey indicated an unchanged statistic on attempted and actual penetrative sexual assault of males since 2014, but a slight decline in assault that was non-penetrative.[37] The statistics for males must be read with the caution that men experiencing sexual assault tend to pass it off as hazing and not report abuse at all.[38]

There are differences in the nature of the attacks on men and women. The RAND studies found that men are often assaulted by multiple offenders and over multiple incidents during work time. This abuse is often referred to as hazing, singling out difference, and is designed to humiliate, creating some form of "hen pecking" order. Men are likely to keep these types of attacks to themselves for long periods.[39] Assaults on women tend to involve alcohol or other drugs and occur out of work hours. The rates vary between the services with the air force seeing lower assaults than the army and navy overall.[40]

RAND incorporated questions that would uncover the Military Equal Opportunity infringements. Evidence shows that harassment and discrimination often accompany sexual assault as part of the process, in that "[s]ervice members who experienced sexual harassment or gender discrimination in the past year also experienced higher rates of sexual assault, and approximately one-third of service members who are sexually assaulted stated the offender sexually harassed them before the assault."[41] Despite this, the DoD has housed responsibility in different bodies—harassment is with the Office of Diversity Management and Equal Opportunity while SAPRO deals with sexual assaults. The Defense Advisory Committee on Women in the Services recommended in 2013 to combine these into one program.[42]

Many argue that the UCMJ covers a wider range of conduct and therefore is better equipped than the civilian system to deal with abuse.[43] However, this fails to recognize the distinction made in the civil domain between crimes and workplace wrongs. Harassment is not dealt with as a specific offence in the UCMJ but falls under the general article 134 as an indecent act. In the civilian arena harassment falls within workplace legislation. Examples of matters treated as a crime, even though this is generally no longer so in the civilian world, such as adultery, still exist under the UCMJ. This raises a further consideration that although the UCMJ may cover many matters, it means nothing if there is no enforcement, or if offences that would correctly be identified as rape are instead charged as adultery.

Of significance in the 2014 RAND survey was the reserve forces' indication of a decreased risk of assault, but one that increased when they were associated with a military space or military personnel.[44] Military personnel (81 percent) often perpetrated the abuse experienced by the reservists, with the majority of the assaults happening in a military setting (63 percent).[45] An inference may be that a sense of protection exists, and that the military space shrouds the perpetrators in a place of difference and impunity or entitlement, a place where military discipline will protect perpetrators. Research evidence from perpetrators would be of assistance here.[46] The notion of impunity sees some support when considering that around 60 percent of the reported abusers were in positions of authority and control as supervisors or unit leaders.[47] As the RAND 2017 survey indicated,

> (1) people are more likely to engage in problematic behaviors, such as sexual harassment, if that person perceives that peers and leaders condone those actions; and (2) some organizations responsible for addressing unlawful discrimination

> and sexual harassment lack adequate policies, plans, information systems, and resources needed to establish a departmental approach to certain behavioral issues, inform senior leadership about these problems, and ensure that leadership's decisions about problematic behaviors are uniformly enforced.[48]

The 2018 SAPRO report found "5,277 Service members made a report of sexual assault in fiscal year 2017 for an incident that occurred sometime during military service, an increase of 10 percent from the 4,794 reports from Service members received last year."[49] The overall story claimed in this report was one of increased reporting but declining prevalence of sexual assault since 2006. This claim was made even though the report indicated, "[d]ue to the lack of the *Workplace and Gender Relations Survey of Active Duty Members* this fiscal year, the Department is unable to make any assumptions with regard to prevalence of sexual assault and its relationship to reporting."[50] The increase was taken as a positive indication that survivors were feeling more confidence in reporting although the report still acknowledged that only a fraction of the reality is likely to be reported.

When survivors feel disbelieved they will not report and when this occurs, a culture of impunity develops, which enables some perpetrators to become serial offenders.[51] When the military deals with offences by discharging perpetrators into the civil society, there is no accountability for the consequences that such offenders can unleash on the community.[52] The failure to reflect on the larger consequence, focusing instead on containment of damage to reputation by describing such events as "isolated" or "aberrant behavior," leads to repetition without really addressing the causes and the consequences.[53] It also fails to consider the effect of dismissing perpetrators to become civilian society's problem. As, perhaps surprisingly, data on offenders in the civilian sphere and any past military service is hard to come by, if recorded at all, then evidence of this consequence is not available. However, it must be kept in mind that we know that a small number of perpetrators can be accountable for a large number of offences. That this occurs was supported by Lisak and Miller's research sampling of a general male population, mostly university students, over seven years in relation to a study described as "childhood experiences and adult functioning."[54] From this survey, 120 participants self-reported 483 acts of rape for which there had never been any criminal prosecution. Within this cohort, 44 of the 120 had raped once and the remaining 76 had committed rape more than once, accounting for 439 of the total 483 rapes.[55] The 120 individuals also indicated committing a further 1,225 incidents of interpersonal violence.[56] This study indicated the importance of appropriately prosecuting individual acts of violence.

Special consideration in the statistics category must apply to the academies as training institutions in which young people are receiving tutelage, often from superiors perhaps only a few years older. The Service Academy Gender Relations Survey[57] showed a decline in the reporting of unwanted sexual contact in the academies from 2012 to 2013. In 2012, 12.4 percent of academy women and 2.0 percent of academy men reported unwanted sexual contact, compared to a rate of 8.2 percent of academy women and 1.1 percent of academy men experiencing unwanted sexual contact during the year 2013 to 2014.[58] In the academic program year 2013–2014, there were 61 reports of sexual assault, which was a decrease from the 70 reports received in academic program year 2012 to 2013.[59] This follows a trend of declining reports since 2011. Unfortunately, this does not indicate whether there is a decline in the number of incidents or a decline in reporting due to the various factors that can contribute to this. That the academies need to strengthen and maintain their efforts to ensure the reporting of these events is clear.

During the academic program year 2013 to 2014, the academies received 20 complaints of sexual harassment, involving only one formal complaint in the United States Military Academy, but 19 informal complaints, 15 from the Naval Academy and four from the Air Force Academy.[60] This represented an overall increase in reporting of sexual harassment complaints from 2012 to 2013, when 11 informal complaints were made in the academies. Rough and Amor highlight that across the year ranges for which data is available, and commencing in 2008, the academies show a higher sexual assault rate for women than in the wider military. This ranges between rounded percentages of 9 to 13.[61] Although it is noted that, compared to sexual harassment reporting, there was an increase in sexual assault reporting in the active force in fiscal years 2013 and 2014, this was not so in the Military Service Academies during the year 2013 to 2014.[62]

With accounts of up to 80 percent of sexual assaults being unreported in the military, it is clear exact numbers will never be known. Dishearteningly, Rough and Amor report analyzing the available data since 2006, which shows no clear answer as to whether sexual assault in the military is rising, decreasing, or remaining constant.[63] Comparisons with the civilian statistics provide little help. What is available indicates that in 2000 a nationwide survey had 1.7 percent of female college students reporting a rape, compared to a survey report in 2002 of 7.4 percent female military academy students reporting rape or attempted rape, and 18.8 percent sexual assault.[64] In such a climate, one would expect convictions and incarcerations for the crime of rape but up to 2003 it is alleged no such incarcerations for academy cadets occurred in the military courts-martial.[65]

Lohman suggests that rape prosecutions of around 17 percent in the military contrasts to the national average of 37 percent of rapes prosecuted in civilian society.[66] Notwithstanding these considerations, as an example, the FBI Uniform Crime Reporting of rape/attempted rape for 2002, was 64.8 percent per 100,000 population, and the reported rate of sexual assaults in the services in 2002 was 69.1 percent per 100,000 population.[67] The FBI Uniform Crime Reporting (UCR) rates are useful as they rely on similar definitions as the military when reporting UCR rates. However, in 2015–2016 the civilian criminal law revised the definition of rape from "carnal knowledge of a female forcibly and against her will" to "penetration, no matter how slight, of the vagina or anus with any body part or object, or oral penetration by a sex organ of another person, without the consent of the victim."[68] This change varied the statistics, showing a civilian rate of 3.5 percent based on the new definition and 4.4 percent on the old definition.[69]

Looking to evidence of the comfort of individuals intervening as bystanders to prevent the targeted activities indicate organizational climate change is slow or not substantiated. Assertions in the 2016 WGRS survey show that while there was a statistical increase in women and men in the army and air force, indicating a greater likelihood of reporting as a bystander,[70] men in the other services were still significantly less likely to intervene by reporting or recommending counselling.[71] Furthermore, women viewed the recognition and correction of sexual harassment when and where it occurs, across all ranks, less favorably.[72] The survey approached this concern with how well members at different pay grades made clear that sexual assault would not be tolerated.[73]

Military whistle-blower legislation was introduced in 1988, but it has had to go through a number of amendments[74] and still in 2015, a damning report was produced on the administration and observation of the legislation by the military.[75] Anti-dobbing is paramount in a closed culture in which "telling" is seen as traitor behavior in breach of group loyalty. Woldoff and Weiss note:

> As part of their training and socialization, soldiers are exposed to explicit and implicit messages about what they can and cannot share with the general public . . . To members of the military, violating a code of silence is more than abuse of trust; it is an affront to the honored code of brotherhood and respect for the chain of command. A military snitch is a traitor not just to his brothers-in arms, but to the institution charged with protecting the ideals, rights, and culture of the country.[76]

While comparisons with the general civilian population's rates of harassment and abuse are never as clear-cut as one would like, statistics exist that paint a general picture of the civilian and the military societies. Indicators of higher sexual activity, and therefore promiscuity, in the military compared to the civilian population are corroborated by statistics on the level of sexually transmitted infections.[77] The Center for Disease Control provides this point of comparison and in 2010 this showed the civilian rate for sexual assault to be at 3.8 percent compared to the DoD official rate of 4.1 percent.[78] This indicates a generally higher level of STD in the military population. STD transmission is intuitively likely to be higher where alcohol and drug consumption is greater, multiple partners are available, mental health issues arise, and where non-safe sex practices, such as non-use of condoms, occur.[79] Schenck notes that despite many thousands of pages in DoD annual reports, little attention is paid in a holistic manner to the role of alcohol.[80] Still, the 2014 RAND report indicated a significant connection between alcohol and sexual abuse.[81]

Other findings of concern by the US Government Accountability Office included failure to meet statutory notification deadlines in around 50 percent of investigations into allegations of reprisal in the 2013 fiscal year, and long delays of up to 526 days and high average investigation times in 2013–2014, over three times longer than the DoD internal 180 day limit.[82] Reviewed again in 2016, some further improvements were noted but room for more was still identified.[83] This specific internal and government review process, at considerable taxpayer cost, would not be required if a civilian system with its required public reporting was operating from the beginning. Carson and Carson report that:

> Remarkably, even though required by Congress since 2005, there is currently no reliable, uniform source of military justice data available anywhere within the Department. The work of the Judicial Proceedings Panel is the first ever to collect uniform, military-wide sexual assault case disposition data directly from case documents, and it has met significant challenges.[84]

This position was disturbingly reinforced through the Judicial Proceedings Panel in their attempt to undertake congressional tasks. They found a lack of reliable data and concluded that the DoD should "collect and analyze case adjudication data using a standardized, document-based collection model similar to . . . the U.S. Sentencing Commission."[85] Surprisingly, the DoD has chosen not to implement this recommendation, instead claiming that "new requirements set forth in the *National Defense Authorization Act* for Fiscal Year 2017 pertaining to the collection and analysis of military justice data will influence our way forward on these recommendations."[86]

Where does this statistical conundrum leave everyone? Clearly aligning collection and surveys as much as possible with the crime statistics collection in the civilian domain, while taking account of unique jurisdictions, would make the understandings and comparisons clearer. Why a holistic approach to do this simply and effectively has not occurred is unclear. Claims are made on both sides to support strongly held beliefs that either the sexual abuse in the military is at crisis point or, conversely, that there is no issue with placing military behavior in any different position to the civilian population.

Mechanisms such as *la bella figura*, supported by groupthink and confirmation bias, lead to data and information being used to support each side's beliefs. All of the actions reflect a legal tension in the concern over survivors' and perpetrators' rights within a criminal law system that operates alongside the primary society's criminal system. What all this misses is the bigger picture. That bigger picture includes consideration of the operation of a secondary secret hierarchical society, encompassing significant proportions of the primary society, while operating within the primary democratic society, which claims observance of concepts such as the rule of law, equality before the law, individual rights, and a three-way system of separation of powers. It should not be a question of whether the military or the civilian society has worse statistics for sexual and other abuse. Rather it is about the military institution and its claims for the need for a separate system of criminal discipline, and the institutional response to sexual abuse as one area for focus, when considering the grounds justifying the institution's claims. It is argued here that these justifications for maintaining a separate criminal discipline system such as higher discipline in the military have failed to be substantiated when investigated. The cases of abuse are just one example, irrespective of whether the statistics portray more or less, or even the same level, of abuse as in the primary society. Running a costly parallel but different system of discipline and then holding multiple reviews and inquiries at ongoing taxpayers' expense is unsustainable when it fails to achieve what it claims. Viewing the operation of the military discipline system from both the perpetrators' and the survivors' perspectives shows it cuts both ways, when addressing concerns for individual rights. Sexual and other abuse will always occur in the military, just as it does in the primary society, but taking the resources and focusing allocation on improving one civilian justice system applicable to all can only result in far better outcomes for the whole of society. That this is possible is demonstrated by many other countries' militaries having demonstrated when they have devolved criminal matters to the civilian authorities the sky has not fallen in, thus showing that the shift is absolutely possible.

THE CASES

Unfortunately, when looking at the incidents and scandals one can choose from many. However, just a few discussed here are sufficient to detail the history and nature, over nearly three decades, of the cases that have reached the media, which provide some idea of the range of issues. The significance of these examples is not only in highlighting their almost perennial nature, and therefore the failure to significantly change the culture and address the issues, but also the details of the common responses by the military as an institution, and problems that have arisen for survivors and perpetrators since the 1990s.

Tailhook

The now familiar pattern was played out very publically in one of the first of the modern military scandals when a number of woman dared to make known their experiences at the aviator's convention in 1991. It became labelled as the now infamous Tailhook scandal,[87] and involved 83 women complaining of a gauntlet-groping event.[88] Tailhook is a group that started in 1957 and educates on aircraft carrier aviation. However, a darker component of sex, alcohol, and male tribal behavior had also evolved.[89] Lieutenant Paula Coughlin was the first to persist when her complaint was waved away by her chain of command. She went around and above to Vice Admiral Dunleavy, the head of the navy.[90] Despite her persistence, the outcome was defeating as the Marine Corp determined there was insufficient evidence to prosecute the alleged captain perpetrator.[91] Although Coughlin was adamant she could identify her assailant, no corroborating witnesses came forward and the judge dismissed the court-martial when a photo of the accused in different clothing could not be identified.

Two navy investigations, one by the Naval Investigative Service (NIS) and then an Inspector General (IO) investigation, the latter costing around $40,000, left only two people identified as carrying responsibility, both admirals, who both resigned.[92] The investigation did not provide for lessons learned or solving the problem of a military culture based on hierarchy and violence, with a discipline system ineffectual in providing and maintaining discipline. The response was an abject failure and has been criticized from all sides, leaving no one impressed with the outcome.[93] Coughlin pursued a civilian tort claim for failure to provide security against the Las Vegas Hilton Hotel and the Tailhook Association, for which she and six others were awarded significant damages.[94] Coughlin reportedly received over five million dollars, but this was unlikely to make up for the loss of a promising and exciting career as a helicopter pilot and an admiral's aide. Like many of those involved, on both sides, she resigned in 1995 with her military career ended.[95]

Internally, many were subject to workplace discipline, ranging from three admirals receiving censures for not intervening and preventing the conduct, to another thirty receiving cautions placed on their permanent records. Around another forty navy captains, commanders and marine corp colonels were issued with either discipline letters of censure or reprimand, or they were fined.[96] All of this occurred through administrative discipline processes available at the choice of the command. While not public, nor criminal sanctions, they can have lasting repercussions for the careers of those involved. A letter of reprimand can cover anything that reflects on integrity or trustworthiness of the person and can be placed on their file.[97] Secretary of Navy, Garrett, resigned after allegations of involvement and coverup, and chief of Naval Operations, Frank Kelso, retired early after his court-martial was dismissed. He only just managed to keep his four stars in retirement.[98] Admirals Williams (NIS) and Gordon (JAG) also resigned and Coughlin's boss, Snyder, was relieved of his duty given his dismissive reaction to Coughlin's initial complaint.[99] Due to the command-interference issue in Tailhook, among other issues, not a single court-martial prosecution resulted in an outcome of accountability. This effectively endorsed support for the internal culture and resulted in the dismissal of the last three cases in the matter. Potential witnesses evaporated, while hundreds interviewed developed a faded memory, often blamed on their alcohol consumption.[100]

In a demonstration of an inability to rely on a separate society to prosecute its own, allegations arose of bias and command interference from the navy judge, Captain William T. Vest Jr. His one hundred and eleven-page judgment illustrated the military discipline system's malfunctions.[101] Admiral Kelso, who oversaw the investigation and prosecutions, despite his denials, was found by Judge Vest to be present at the infamous gauntlet, and therefore his position in the hierarchy, along with alleged lies and shielding of his own position, tainted the prosecutions.[102] In the court-martial of navy Lt., Cole Cowden the matter was discontinued when the judge stated that Captain Jeffrey Williams, the senior legal officer, had become personally involved to the extent that he "exceeded the permissible bounds of his official role as legal advisor."[103] Three navy prosecutors also lost their positions because of the scathing condemnation of the investigation and the conduct of the military prosecutors. Judge Vest described the probe as a "novice approach to criminal investigation" and the Military Court of Appeals referred to it as a "curiously careless and amateurish approach [that] raises the possibility of a shadiness in respecting the rights of military members."[104]

Interestingly, two civilian women made the first complaint to the Hilton Hotel regarding the behaviors of the navy personnel. As Coletti notes "[t]he fact that civilian culture spoke against this behavior shows a split between military culture and . . . civilian culture had moved on enough from the gender stereotypes the military drew on and new (sic) to question."[105] On the other side, the anger concerning what was described as hysteria, double standards, and a "witch hunt" still remains.[106]

Whatever the claims made, the effects linger, as if a bomb had exploded internally and the military was left depleted by the losses. One would think that was lesson enough to ensure a major change in processes, given the systems failure for all involved. The contention of political involvement and backlash speaks directly to the civil-military relationship. Political arms of government, such as the executive and legislature, are sensitive to media reporting and consequent political repercussions become one of the few levers for public interest to push for maintaining civilian control of the military. The legislature and executive are the ones seen as responsible for what happens in the military and for the superintendence of its discipline. The third arm of the triangle of government, the non-elected US Supreme Court, has taken a hands-off approach ever since Chief Justice Rehnquist opened up the possibility. The "separate society jurisprudence"[107] accommodated by this ex-military judge means the court abdicates its role when it comes to military matters. If the civilian Supreme Court had upheld its part in the three-way power balance, being the non-elected arm, it would have aided the legislature and executive in controlling the military.[108] Gageler draws attention to an important distinction when considering deference, particularly for courts in arbitrating on the limits of constitutional power:

> [t]he standard dictionary definition of deference includes two alternative meanings. One meaning is respectful regard for the judgment or opinion of another. Another meaning is respectful acknowledgment of the authority of another. The two meanings point to two different forms of deference. Neither meaning equates deference to servility, much less to an abdication of duty.[109]

What lessons come from this? Whistle-blowers suffer, many personnel lose their career, some their life, the military coterie closes ranks, some may be picked out to be scapegoated, and many may suffer financially, including the military with its loss of talented, trained personnel and loss of reputation, but in the end business goes on as usual. In other words, the true lesson from Tailhook is a separate military coterie is not capable of enforcing and disciplining bad behavior and prosecuting criminal conduct. The only system that is equipped, the civilian justice system, is the one that ought to be operating. None of the problems occurring in Tailhook would have been likely to transpire to the degree they did if independent civilian police investigators, criminal prosecutors, and civilian juries and judges had been involved. To take the risk of institutional failure and interference out of the equation, the solution is simple. These matters need to be addressed in the appropriate forum—the civilian criminal prosecution system. Clearly delineating this system from internal workplace discipline and organizational employment law, and the ability for military employees to have administrative sanctions for breaches imposed, are vital.

Tailhook sent a significant message to survivors that if they do say something the outcomes are not likely to be helpful to them and, worse, are likely to damage them and others. Coletti has described a navy lieutenant's portrayal of the regular convention event as a forum in which men were enabled to be ". . . so masculine—they're beastlike."[110] The sense of enabling men to let off steam because they are soldiers, privileging their needs above the law's domain, provides a space for a condoned perverted elite masculinity in which the "differentiated," including females, become mere playthings.[111] This sense of entitlement will be seen again in many of the incidents, including in the navy photo scandal. The voluminous investigations and subsequent changes in policy have not avoided things going wrong with scandals remaining a perennial problem. Meanwhile the Senate Armed Forces Committee, peopled by ex-military figures, shakes its head and demands that military leaders address the problems without understanding the fundamental underlying issue.

Aberdeen and Other Events in the 1990s

Five years after Tailhook, in 1996, it was the army's turn as stories of assaults at the Aberdeen Proving Ground became public. This just happened to be the same year as the Supreme Court, in *United States v. Virginia*,[112] found that the Virginia Military Institute's all-male policy breached the Article 14 Equal Protection Amendment as a publically funded educational institution. That problems for female cadets had been going on for many years was becoming clear.[113] In this case, eleven drill sergeants stood accused of multiple counts of rape and sexual misconduct. This event has a number of salient lessons seemingly yet to be addressed. Many of the complainants claimed that the system that required internal reporting to commanders was fraught with the possibility of furthering criminal misconduct. In the Aberdeen case, a company commander, Captain Robertson, pleaded guilty to adultery[114] and sodomy[115] with a female trainee after she had sought him out for help concerning a drill sergeant who was sexually harassing her.[116] Robertson's charges were less than the original potential rape charges. The consequence was that the hierarchy-enabled leadership provided impunity for one particular drill sergeant, Delmar G. Simpson, to perpetrate his serial offending in the form of raping at least ten women, and five on more than one occasion, in a protected enabling environment. Ultimately, drill sergeant Simpson was charged with 58 offences, including 19 counts of rape, involving 21 victims. He was convicted by court-martial,[117] and received a sentence of twenty-five years imprisonment, amounting to an average of nearly one and a half years per rape (compared to a penalty of life imprisonment which was available), a dishonorable discharge, total forfeitures, and a reduction in rank.[118]

Further outcomes from the army scandal included the opening of a hotline to which thousands of complainants from around the globe responded.[119] The army won a public relations award for its quick response in setting up the Senior Review Panel on Sexual Harassment within two weeks of the complaints arising.[120] The panel questioned the military's resolve to address the issues and was critical of the leadership in gaining trust, given the level of sex discrimination and sexual harassment, and the military commitment to equal opportunity. It went on to make forty recommendations, including incorporating ethics and values training, updating equal opportunity training, and improving standards for drill sergeant selection.[121] Unfortunately, the haste in setting up the panel was perhaps ill advised as it produced its own initial scandal.

The problem of leadership and chain of command in this protective environment was no better demonstrated than when Sergeant Major Gene McKinney, as the army's highest-ranking enlisted member, with multiple decorations and honors, was appointed to head the task force to investigate the problem of sexual abuse and harassment post the Aberdeen incidents. The appointment of McKinney caused women who had never previously reported assaults to come out with allegations of McKinney's own misconduct.[122] Holster, as one of six women who went through what she considered an ordeal in speaking out, felt she suffered immensely as a result.[123] McKinney was court-martialed, his wife gave evidence on his behalf, and a panel of four officers and four enlisted soldiers acquitted him of all charges, except one of obstructing justice. He received a reduction in rank to master sergeant and a reprimand as punishment, but kept his pension for his more than 29 years of service, including in Vietnam.[124] The good soldier character evidence prevailed, based on his many commendations and decorations, which are particularly persuasive in a hierarchical world with a panel comprised of fellow members of the institution.[125] To add further insult and deterrence to survivors, McKinney, although unsuccessful, pursued a civil damages claim against Holster, who, as a retired military figure, was open to civilian suit.[126] The use of good character as a defense was altered in 2015 to restrict its application to offences related to military service, such as larceny or drug taking. Its use for a broader range of offences, including sexual assaults, rape, robbery, and related crimes, has been removed.[127]

Around the same time, other army bases such as Fort Leonard Wood had seventeen instructors and drill sergeants convicted of sexual offences, and Fort Jackson had sixty-four members investigated for sexual offences.[128] Following the Aberdeen incident, the Criminal Investigation Command was also tasked to interview every female member stationed at Aberdeen over the previous two years.[129] Then Secretary of Defense Cohen set up the Federal Advisory Committee on Gender-Integrated Training and Related Issues in 1997, chaired by Senator Nancy Kassebaum-Baker. The committee comprised five retired military members and six civilians, including Condoleezza Rice. The committee produced a report six months after the Panel report in 1997 with some thirty recommendations including the re-segregation of the sexes, improving values training, eliminating the "no talk, no touch" policy, enforcing policies addressing disparaging gender reference, consistency in fraternization rules, enforcing tough punishments for false accusations, and improved screening of trainers.[130] Despite the added expense of this report, it seemed to add little more than the very thorough Panel review, repeating similar themes. Further, then Defense Secretary Cohen somewhat controversially rejected the committee's recommendation on segregation, except in relation to accommodation, maintaining the need for integration of the sexes.[131]

Subsequent allegations of sexual abuse and consequent court-martials have continued.[132] These particular events demonstrate a hierarchical power system the effects of which are not understood, by survivors, perpetrators, or the broader system. Crime occurs because those in power turn a blind eye or abuse their power and status. It is particularly a problem in a closed coterie in which the members are the ones who determine who is punished and who sits in judgment of the outcomes.[133] Chamallas added as far back as 1998 that one of the key concerns was the extra factors a commander may take into account when deciding whether an act is worthy of punishment. These included the degree of privacy of the conduct, the status of the parties and their spouses, the time delay between the event and reporting of it, most importantly, whether it affects the member's ability to perform their role, and the degree of damage to the military's reputation.[134] These factors are a constant problem. In the Senate Armed Services Committee's Subcommittee on Personnel, in March 2013, Anu Bhagwati stated, "[c]ommanding officers cannot make truly impartial decisions because of their professional affiliation with the accused, and often times with the victim as well."[135]

The system fails all. Perpetrators often never have to address their conduct, even when they are caught, but they do have to live with what they have done. Those few who are caught and punished have seen unhappy outcomes such as Sergeant Simpson, who continued to claim he never received a fair and just trial due to the surrounding publicity and command influence.[136] This shows a failure to understand the implications of the rule of law.

A further problem in the military setting is the survivors fearing punishment themselves for their part in the sexual activity. Often this can pervert their testimony unless immunity is offered. Some alleged survivors came forward in the Aberdeen incident to say they were forced to make statements that they were coerced into sexual encounters, which they really had consented to willingly.[137] This naturally resulted in nil prosecution outcomes. Others were dismissed with or without further administrative punishments that the civilian population remain unaware of, and are still then at the mercy of these persons, some of whom have been serial abusers. Often the focus on the special military coterie means the unequal treatment for civilians charged with criminal offending, who do not have the luxury of opting for a discharge in order to avoid a trial and punishment, goes unaddressed.[138] The following scenarios emanate from the academies, which the statistics report as being less abusive than the regular military forces.

Air Force Academy Scandals

The air force, of the four military branches, is allegedly the least affected by sexual assaults. However, it has not escaped the profile of abuse claims. It took two brave woman coming forward in 2002 to attract public interest and encourage many other women to tell their stories throughout 2003. A number of these women, Sharon Fullilove, Kira Mountjoy-Pepka, Beth Davis, Lisa Bellas, and Jessica Brakey, were prepared to forego anonymity, recounting sexual assaults and rape occurring from 1999 to 2003.[139] The public airing resulted in the uncovering of earlier allegations made over many years. A Colorado Springs rape crisis center finally came forward in 2003 admitting that 22 cadets had contacted the center seeking confidential help over the prior 15 years.[140]

To add to the injury, a common claim was that the reporting survivors were often subjected to more severe punishment than the alleged offenders. People lost their jobs.[141] Again, a high-level body was appointed to report. This commission included three retired military personnel and Republican Senator Tillie K. Fowler.[142] The chronology of events within the air force from 1993 to 2003 was detailed in the report.[143]

An internal US Air Force general counsel working group, known as the Walker Review, also investigated and released its findings ahead of the Fowler inquiry.[144] No prizes for guessing that one of the outcomes of the Walker Review was the exoneration of academy leaders and their superiors, resolving that there was "no systemic acceptance of sexual assault at the academy [or] institutional avoidance of responsibility."[145] The review did note that issues with confidentiality and privacy concerns for survivors had resulted in limited information being available for successful prosecution of matters.[146] It also addressed the usual problem of fear of retribution inhibiting any reporting. Ironically, the privacy protection was a reform introduced in 1993, after Tailhook, to encourage survivors to feel safe in reporting. The Fowler-led commission reported three months after the internal Walker Review in 2003.

The Fowler Commission was critical of the Walker Review exonerating leaders and their superiors, indicating there was clear evidence, as early as 1993, of problems.[147] While specific individuals came in for criticism, there was a more general concern with the failure to respond to the problem for at least a decade. This was attributed to leadership changes and a general potential for confusion. The commission, however, described a "chasm" in air force leadership who were aware of the serious sexual misconduct, and attributed the issues to a breakdown in values that permissibly enabled an omnipresence of assaults.[148] In all, 21 recommendations were made, some of them repeating previous recommendations that had remained unaddressed and others urging a closer alignment with the civilian experience, such as access to psychological and crisis counselling.[149] However, the recommendations never went as far as suggesting the broken military discipline system be entirely overhauled by separating criminal offending from workplace discipline.

Placing a new leader in charge of an "Agenda for Change" resulted in adjustments to at least 43 areas where improvement was considered possible, with the proposals designed to eliminate the problem.[150] One clear change was moving to mandatory reporting with a complainant required to provide evidence. Further changes included better supervision of dormitories, with this being removed from junior cadets to ranking officers, and generally, alcohol, as an ingredient in many assaults, was now made a ground for expulsion if given to an underage cadet.[151] This however, did not address the issues.

While all cadets are subject to the UCMJ,[152] few are dealt with via a courts-martial process.[153] Douglas Meester was the first cadet to be charged out of the 2003 scandal. His most serious charges were for offences of rape, sodomy, and conduct unbecoming of an officer. The offences were alleged to have occurred in 2002, when, in an all too common scenario, on a date in which both parties had been consuming alcohol. The case was a difficult one to prosecute, with Meester denying the charges and the complainant indicating she never said "no." The investigating officer decided there was no case but the legal authority overturned this. The case ended with a settlement plea to lesser charges of indecent acts, dereliction of duty, and conduct unbecoming of an officer involving a fine and reprimand.[154] The charges were seen as a showcase in order for Defense to been seen to be doing something, but they chose a case that was doomed to fail and in the process, young lives, already fragile in the circumstances, were further affected. Interestingly by comparison a cadet on a rape charge in Australia was dealt with by a civilian Supreme Court before a civilian jury. Notwithstanding it resulted in an acquittal, this case demonstrates there is no threat to discipline by having matters bought before the civilian courts, and justice can be observed taking place in the public arena.[155]

The air force events led to Congress requesting then Secretary of Defense, Donald Rumsfeld, establish a Defense Task Force on Sexual Harassment and Violence at the Military Services Academies to encompass all military academies. This body was comprised of six civilians and six members from four of the service areas. One of the significant recommendations of this task force was a review of the legislation and the sexual offences in the UCMJ. The Service Academy Task Force (SATF) issued its first report on June 30, 2005.[156] The task force observed that the "sexual harassment and assault prevention program execution and management is fragmented and inadequate . . . the two Academies, much like the record of the Department of Defense, is one of sporadic and incomplete attempts to eliminate sexual harassment and assault."[157] There was an observed need for closer relations with the civilian community, taking account of the reality that "the insight from years of sexual assault reform in the civilian community is that permanent solutions must be community solutions,"[158] and counselling and victim services in the civilian domain should be utilized. Perhaps most astounding was the finding that academy discipline had not established any formal agreements or arrangements with civilian law enforcement agencies regarding criminal offending such as sexual assaults.

Rumsfeld was also required to establish a second task force to address concerns coming out of sexual assaults in the Operation Iraqi Freedom campaign. This Task Force on Care for Victims of Sexual Assault held investigations over three months, leading to some of the first policy development on sexual assault and clarification of essential terms.[159] The task force recommended at least a single point of accountability for policy relating to sexual assault be established. This became the Joint Task Force on Sexual Assault Prevention and Response (JTF-SAPR) in October 2004 as a temporary point of accountability to implement the *National Defense Authorization Act* for Fiscal Year 2005.[160] This act also initiated a review of the UCMJ and MCM to be conducted by the Defense Joint Services Committee on Military Justice (JSC), a body essentially comprised of senior judge advocates from the services.[161] The committee reported:

> After a thorough review, the subcommittee members were unable to identify any sexual conduct (that the military has an interest in prosecuting) that cannot be prosecuted under the current UCMJ and MCM. Based on this determination, the subcommittee unanimously concluded that change is not required.[162]

However, while favoring no change (other than some changes to the MCM) and suggesting the UCMJ operated efficiently in relation to all types of sexual offences, the JSC did put forward six options for change. Congress chose to follow option five and substantially amended the UCMJ article 120 to incorporate fourteen distinct sex offences across a spectrum from the most serious, forcible rape, to the least serious of indecent exposure, and included for the first time "sexual assault."[163] The amendment also controversially changed the burden of proof, requiring the accused to raise consent as a defense before the prosecution take on the burden of disproving consent. Signifying the road to hell may be paved with good intentions, this amendment was removed within five years[164] due to the CAAF decision in *United States v. Prather*,[165] which considered that the change in burden was unconstitutional and a legal impossibility. Still, sexual intercourse without consent or where force is not involved proved difficult to address and the scandals kept coming.

Lackland Air Force Trainee's 2009/2012

Notwithstanding the investigation and changes made by the Agenda for Change to avoid future such activities in the Air Force Academy, the air force experienced one of its most publicly damming episodes through what became known as the Lackland incident.[166] This ranged over a period from 2009 to 2012 and involved 32 instructors implicated in sexual assaults on 62 trainees. Yet another review was set up, this time the Woodward report, with twenty-two findings and another forty-six recommendations. Unsurprisingly the findings yet again revolved around leadership oversight, selection and training of instructors, reporting and detection, and policy guidance.[167]

Major General Leonard A. Patrick, who was in charge of enlisted training for the air force at the time, conceded supervision of trainees was minimal and that leadership and accountability had increased since the incident. A buddy system was developed.[168] However, the fundamental problem of in-house criminal punishment being still in the hands of commanders remained, with the hierarchical chain being responsible for the abuse. Not one of the survivors of the Lackland event reported it. It was only uncovered by a by-stander female trainee who had not been assaulted, but reported what she knew.[169] Thirty-five instructors were court-martialed. Two received 20-year sentences; the next most serious punishment was thirty months for one, with fourteen receiving less than three months.[170] A number had their cases overturned on appeal. Leadership accountability was considered addressed by having a group commander and one squadron commander relieved from command, while six other commanders received administrative discipline, two received letters of reprimand, and four letters of admonishment.[171]

This event highlighted a lack of understanding of "consent" in the context of power and work relationships, particularly where trainees are members of a society in which obeying orders of those above one is ubiquitous.[172] Defense counsel attempted to argue the trainees had consented. Allegations surfaced after the event of unfair outcomes for both survivors and the accused. Some alleged the air force investigations put political considerations and notions of *la bella figura* before consideration of due process rights of individuals. In an effort to redeem reputation, inappropriate prosecutions involving adding the array of charges against an accused encouraged the adoption of plea deals.

At the heart of the problem is a conflict for commanders when they have to consider functionality and the need to have a ready, capable, and willing fighting force at all times. If prosecuting an individual would influence this, then priority is given to the functional needs and not the discipline needs. The catch-22 in this tension is that discipline is said to underpin a strong fighting force. However, the failure to grasp the fundamental flaw in a system of internal criminal punishment by one's own means the functional ability of the military is under threat.[173]

The Navy Marines Photo Scandal

In 2013, Congresswoman Speier wrote to the Secretary of Defense, General Hagel, Commandant of the Marine Corp, General Amos and Principal Deputy Director, Halbrooks with explicit reference to websites such as "F'N Wook," and included images taken from the websites stating:

> It is my understanding that not only is the Marine Corps Inspector aware of this page and monitoring it, but they have been doing so for over three years. . . . Last year General Amos admitted that the reported number of sexual assaults in the Marine Corps showed that "we have been ineffective at addressing and eliminating" this problem. . . . This year's [2013] Sexual Assault [Prevention] and Response Office (SAPRO) report indicates the rate of sexual assault has increased in the past year, and that the reforms adopted this far have been woefully insufficient. The military cannot eradicate this problem without fundamentally changing its approach . . .[174]

In early 2017, the not-for-profit investigative journalist website the Warhorse, dedicated to matters of defense and veterans, reported a new scandal. This story uncovered that the Marines United Facebook website with around 30,000 members, limited to male-only marines, navy corpsmen and British Royal Marines, included a link to postings of intimate sexual images of woman, both civilian and military, without their consent. Links to a website,

AnonIB, dating back to May 2016 were found. Many of the men and women in the photos were identified by name, rank, and service location.[175]

A formal investigation by the Naval Criminal Investigative Service was launched. Another congressional hearing ensued.[176] The Commandant of the Marines, General Robert Neller, appeared before the Senate Armed Services Committee. The general openly admitted to being at a loss, but agreed more was needed and that included a significant cultural change, stating "we are going to change and can change."[177] As Senator Kirsten Gillibrand stated the use of these well-worn statements "rings hollow."[178] Senator Gillibrand went on to make the poignant point that "[i]f we can't crack Facebook, how are we supposed to be able to confront Russian aggression and cyber-hacking throughout our military?"[179]

Unfortunately, the impunity provided in a coterie means that the protagonists feel able to continue their activity. A cultural mentality unfortunately can taint a person for life, as both this scandal and the photo sex scandal in Australia (described in chapter 4) indicate. Veterans or reservists who became civilian employees of private contractors initiated both scandals. However, both received repercussions. The US ensured the initiator lost his private job. This, however, is not the same as prosecution for a criminal offence. In Australia, the ringleader of the sex photo scandal, as an ex-ADF member and reservist employed by a private contractor, received from a civilian court a jail sentence of 15 months served as a non-custodial intensive correction community order, after pleading guilty to three offences related to using a carriage service to send offensive material.[180] In an endless game of cat and mouse, subsequent sites can be opened continuing such activity as appeared to be the case in the US.[181]

The posts include revenge porn, as it has become known, whereby intimate photos taken consensually during a relationship are shared with others after the relationship has ended, without the consent of the original participant. Law is playing catch up with the technology that enables sharing of photos in a manner that broadens the breach of privacy.[182] More than 2,500 comments, including from the site's administrators and ranging across service members stationed around the world, were posted about the photos. That members felt no fear of wrongdoing is underlined by the use of their personal Facebook accounts disclosing their identity.[183] This does not speak of a group that feel they are perpetrating any wrongdoing, moral or legal, or are controlled by fear of command discipline. It speaks of a feeling of elite privilege and loyalty to the coterie. Banner says the "longstanding Marine slogan *Semper Fidelis*, meaning 'always loyal,' further highlights this ideal."[184]

Perhaps some of this mentality is displayed in the comments made by the Facebook site's administrators as justifying behavior on a site originally intended as a support place for marines suffering PTSD. The administrator allegedly said "[a]t worst, [the photos are] juvenile, but exactly what you would expect from the kind of men who have experienced what less than one tenth of one percent of the population has experienced. . . . We do not wish to make any further efforts to censor our members."[185] This form of justification is telling as to the nature of the culture and the long way it has to return from the underlying sense of entitlement, due to difference, that extends to being exempt from behavioral constraints.

The marines are a male-dominated domain, with less than 10 percent being women, compared to nearly double that percentage in the wider military community. The photo scandals occurred alongside the assigning of women to marine units for the first time in January 2017.[186] In that sense, the websites can be perceived to be places for sanctuary of the male bastion. This activity has led to some female survivors countering the behavior with their own naming and shaming websites, in which matters not criminally prosecuted nevertheless see survivors outing the names of their alleged rapists. Women have described resorting to this when they feel the system has failed them.[187] This entire process develops a slippery slope in which the state loses its hold on controlling criminal conduct within society as individuals take justice into their own hands.

In this Facebook scandal, the military responded about a month after it was disclosed in what was considered a speedy response. The Navy Regulations, article 1168 was amended to prohibit "non-consensual distribution or broadcasting of an image."[188] However, again the enforcement was reliant on the chain of command and the commander's call in gauging whether the action was substantiated and whether it called for removing of the perpetrator.[189] Over twelve months later, it was still ineffective at eliminating the behavior.[190] The Government Accountability Office produced a report at the end of 2017 detailing a lag in response by the military organization in adopting legislative measures, such as those introduced in the *National Defense Authorization Act* for Fiscal Year 2017.[191] This included updating policy to incorporate the new definition of sexual harassment, ensuring anonymized reporting, and streamlining the collection of harassment data to incorporate the Center for Disease Control and prevention guidelines on addressing risk of sexual harassment.[192] Definitional and other issues in proving a breach of the navy regulations were eventually addressed by the National *Defense Authorization Act* for the Fiscal Year 2018, which inserted a new article 117a as a punitive provision covering wrongful broadcast or distribution of intimate visual images.[193]

The internal inquiry in the Navy Photo Scandal produced only one early prosecution. The director of the Naval Criminal Investigative Service NCIS,

Andrew Traver, suggested identifying perpetrators is difficult due to the anonymity of the internet and the many thousands of images. However, six months after the incident sixteen suspects were identified, including nine active duty marines, two reservists, three navy members, one navy reservist, and a civilian. Suspected crimes included extortion, stalking, threats, and theft of photos, with maximum penalties in the range of seven years' incarceration. A further 55 members are alleged to have received some form of punitive action over the following twelve months. This concerned approximately 200 websites with potentially 20,000 inappropriate images that were military related.[194]

Many saw the incident as a continuation of the similar sexualized and degrading activities towards women in the past. This signifies that attempts to change the institution have not delivered and the reality remains that these events of abuse and degradation of others continue.[195] Unlike the original Marines United Facebook site, in which members used their own names, there has been an effort to continue the practices but in a more underground and evasive manner, with postings now generally using fictional identities to gain anonymity and hosting of the sites outside of jurisdiction.

A significant change is that the means of carrying out the abuse is aided by the introduction of technology. This brings two important differences. First, the abuse can be far greater in its reach and extent because of the technology's ability to cover the globe with the ease of a button push from the secrecy of one's private location. For instance, British Royal Marines were also on the Marines United Facebook. The second change is the ability to do this with considerable anonymity. This slippery slope from abuse to sexualized abuse and lack of clarity of purpose and roles, as well as respect for the law is clear in the following examples.

Other High-Profile Cases

We cannot leave this discussion without looking at the leaders who are often but not always protected by the separate society ethos. Major General Hale[196] was the deputy inspector general and Commanding General of the US Army forces in Southeastern Europe, Deputy Commanding General and Chief of Staff of US Army Forces in the Pacific, Assistant Division Commander, and Deputy Director for Politico-Military Affairs, Joint Chiefs of Staff. He is a veteran of Vietnam and Desert Storm and was awarded the Silver Star and Purple Heart. Despite allegations of sexual assault, Hale retired with honor in 1998, after only four months in his command position in Europe. However, he was eventually court-martialed for his adulterous affairs with four wives of subordinate military personnel. Adultery committed with lower-ranked personnel's partners is an abuse that relies on the hierarchy and fear of job or rank loss. Partners may be aware of the liaison but may have to suffer it for fear of retaliation.[197]

Hale became the second only army general at that time to face a court-martial since the inception of the UMCJ in 1951. Criticized heavily for double standards, Congress required the army to change its policy to prevent retirement before misconduct was dealt with. Unusually, the military did court-martial the retired general and he pleaded guilty to eight counts of misconduct. He was demoted to a one-star brigadier general resulting in a pay reduction. The Secretary of the Army, Louis Caldera, still convened a three-person panel to consider the one rank reduction before he agreed to accept this punishment. General Hale, not unlike other high-ranking offenders, first reacted by attempting a civil suit against the survivors for defamation. Hale accused Ms. Carpino, one of the wives, of stalking him. While he subsequently dropped the action, Ms. Carpino sought reimbursement from the army for her $26,000 costs in defending the matter.[198]

In a not dissimilar move on November 17, 1999, Secretary of the Army Louis Caldera, having learned from the experience with Hale, imposed another reduction, this time by two ranks, on Major General John J. Maher 3rd, a vice director for the Joint Chiefs of Staff. His behavior involved sexual liaisons with two officers' wives and an enlisted soldier. Maher also was not allowed to retire before he was dealt with in an administrative hearing for conduct unbecoming of an officer, for which he received, in addition to the rank reduction, a pay deduction and a letter of reprimand. He escaped a court-martial with possible heavy penalties in a manner that attracted criticism.[199]

In 2012 Brigadier General Jeffrey Sinclair, former deputy commander of the 82nd Airborne Division, became the third general in sixty years to face a court-martial.[200] He faced multiple charges in relation to an affair with a captain under his command and 17 years his junior. The offences included allegations of non-consensual sex, wrongful sexual conduct, violating an order, and inappropriate incidences with two other female military personnel.[201] The charges held the possibility of life imprisonment. However, in a plea deal the charges were discontinued when he pleaded guilty to adultery, inappropriate conduct when asking the women for their nude photograph, and conversing inappropriately through explicit sexual emails. The plea agreement suggested Sinclair receive no more than eighteen months imprisonment, but Colonel Pohl, as the judge in the matter, issued an even lighter reprimand and a fine of $20,000 only.[202] He could have imprisoned Sinclair for up to 20 years on the matters to which a guilty plea was entered, and he could have dismissed the Brigadier General, leaving him without health care and military retirement benefits. Eventually Sinclair was reduced to Lieutenant General and retired.[203]

The case had all the ingredients that indicate the military is not the appropriate place to be addressing criminal conduct, particularly sexual crimes. The prosecution had been ongoing for nearly two years. The survivor was young and under the hierarchy of the perpetrator. She prevaricated in her evidence as the conduct had occurred over three years earlier. While said to be consensual conduct this was a situation of authority over a young woman who wanted to believe it was love and only reported the matter when discovering emails to the general's wife and other female military members that indicated it was otherwise. The concern that she could be disciplined was again at play and immunity had to be given to ensure her evidence would hold in the internal prosecution.

Not unlike Tailhook, interference also came from the politicization of military sexual offending and the need for the legislative and executive arms to be seen to be doing something. Given the executive arm is the president, who is also the commander in chief, as the most senior figure in the military hierarchy, anything the president or other generals and commanders say can be also be seen as hierarchical command influence, which would prejudice a court-martial. For instance, comments made by General Amos, in what has now become known as the infamous Heritage Brief tour, were designed to raise awareness of the issue of sexual and other abuse, but this backfired with court-martials falling apart because of defense arguing successfully that there was unlawful command influence.[204] General Amos, in his Heritage Brief tour, included comments that "80 percent of sexual assault accusations are legitimate;" "the 'buyer's remorse' defense in sexual assault cases as 'bullsh-;" and "condemn[ing] immoral actions by Marines . . . and press[ing] for aggressive responses when they were discovered."[205] He was subsequently required to draw back from his forceful statements with a letter to all marine commanders clarifying "I am not directing or suggesting specific administrative or military justice actions be taken absent compliance with established law."[206] General Amos and the Heritage Brief demonstrates just another reason the military discipline system needs to be rethought.

Colonel Pohl ruled in Sinclair's case that there was evidence the army had allowed external political considerations to influence the handling of the matter, which also induced the acceptance of a plea deal. A further aspect of this, and the publicity attending such matters, is the opportunity of empaneling a group from within the military that could bring an unbiased and fearless mind to assessing the guilt or innocence in the matter, given they are all part of the hierarchical structure and subject to work reviews and career progression. All of these issues aided in undoing the successful prosecution and a plea deal with the general being retired two grades lower in rank.[207] If the matters were dealt with in the civilian criminal justice system, none of this would be an issue, as Senator Gillibrand clearly noted: "[you] want justice to be blind. That's the whole point."[208] Commanders trying to lead and encourage their military members to do the right thing would not feel trapped or damned for either doing so, or not doing so.[209] Senator Gillibrand, who had been unsuccessful in her attempt at the time to remove prosecution decisions from commanders into the hands of military lawyers, said Sinclair's case

> . . . has illustrated a military justice system in dire need of independence from the chain of command. . . . It's not only the right thing to do for our men and women in uniform, but would also mitigate issues of undue command influence that we have seen in many trials. . . .[210]

On the same day as Sinclair was sentenced, another high-profile case of sexual assault was to unravel. The case involved a navy member who had allegedly sexually assaulted a female military class member at a party in 2012. The military judge found the accused not guilty. Two other midshipmen had been originally charged but were later cleared as the evidence was found insufficient.[211]

Another very senior military figure to fall prey to allegations of inappropriate sexual conduct was the four-star Commander of the International Security Assistance Force (ISAF) and Commander, U.S. Forces Afghanistan (USFOR-A). General David Petraeus had served in many senior leadership roles in his 37 years in the army, including as Commander, U.S. Central Command (USCENTCOM) and Commanding General, Multi-National Force—Iraq (MNF-I), before taking over as Director of the CIA in 2011. Petraeus retired from the U.S. Army on August 31, 2011, and resigned as Director of the CIA on November 9, 2012, referring to his extramarital affair with his biographer Paula Broadwell, which was exposed by an FBI investigation. The affair allegedly commenced after he left the army in 2011 and ended in the summer of 2012. Petraeus pleaded guilty to a misdemeanor charge of mishandling classified information, although Justice Department prosecutors had recommended felony charges for allegedly providing classified information to his biographer while he was Director of the CIA.[212] In 2015, a federal court judge sentenced Petraeus to two years' probation plus a fine of $100,000. Despite Petraeus' new civilian status, the military considered demoting Petraeus, given that a military member can be retired at the last rank at which they are deemed to have served honorably. However, then Secretary of the Army, John M. McHugh, recommended no further action be taken before he left office himself in October 2015.[213]

This differs from the treatment of Major General Wayne Grigsby, Commander of the First Infantry Division, who was retired at the lesser rank of brigadier general and reprimanded after an Inspector General of the Army investigation concluded that he had engaged in an inappropriate relationship with another military member in 2016. Occurring just before he was deployed to Iraq, Grisby was the first division commander to be relieved of duty in around 45 years.[214] Other high-level members that have received penalties for immoral conduct include Lieutenant General Ron Lewis, senior military adviser to the Defense Secretary, for using his government-issued credit card at strip clubs, and Major General David Haight, both in 2016.[215] Haight had done a number of tours of Iraq and Afghanistan and had been Director for operations at U.S. European Command in Germany. He was demoted three levels to the rank of lieutenant colonel for his "swinger lifestyle" and affair that had continued over ten years, conducted using government-issued phones.[216]

Lieutenant Colonel Joseph Morse, chief of the Trial Counsel Assistance Program at Fort Belvoir, his office also being responsible for training army prosecutors where he supervised over twenty-five prosecutors specializing in sexual and domestic violence matters, was alleged to have made unwanted sexual advances while on a conference dedicated to the topic of sexual assaults in the military. The female captain made the allegations some three years after the alleged event, and the evidence was insufficient for a criminal case. Morse was reassigned duties before resigning in 2015.[217] Peculiar things happened during this matter, including interference in his defense by a commander forbidding he speak with a potential witness in constructing his defense. The Army Court of Criminal Appeals was involved and in the end the army reneged on the order.[218]

Lieutenant Colonel James Wilkerson presents as a high-water-mark example. Wilkerson was a well-regarded F-16 fighter pilot and Aviano's inspector general. He held a private party at which a civilian stayed after the party ended, as she did not have the means to travel home. She did not know her hosts prior to the party. She awoke during the night allegedly to find Wilkerson in her bed sexually assaulting her. Wilkerson's wife allegedly removed her from the house.[219] The matter was heard by court-martial, comprised of a panel of five colonels. Commander General Franklin from the Ramstein Air Base in Germany ordered the court-martial as the convening authority. However, a verdict of guilty delivered by the five panel members, due largely to inconsistency in Wilkerson's wife's evidence, was overturned by the commander without reason or justification being provided.[220] There should not be any shock in this, as he was perfectly entitled as the convening authority, according to the military law that existed at the time, to overturn the outcome of a court-martial or change the sentence.[221] Both operational necessity, as a war situation may have meant the accused was needed for battle, and a desire to overcome due process concerns in the military discipline system, enabled this. However, as neither applied in this situation, the exercise of this power left many shocked and the response was punitive for the commander. The commander's decision meant Wilkerson was released from prison and reinstated at full rank. Consequences flowed. These included Wilkerson being later required to retire and reduced in rank, due to a further investigation revealing he had committed adultery and fathered a child outside of marriage.[222] Commander General Franklin was reduced from a three- to a two-star general and retired. He was not the only one to incur an adverse result. Even Christensen, the military prosecutor in the matter, suffered in his annual performance review.[223] While grants of clemency or reversal of court-martial panel verdicts was rare, they were not unheard of. Following Franklin was LTG Susan Helms, who likewise had overturned a conviction for sexual assault by general court-martial. As a result, her career ended, despite having been nominated by President Obama for consideration as a four-star general.[224]

Changes were made to the UCMJ article 60 in 2014. These included preventing commanders overturning the court-martial verdict.[225] Prior to this, the broad power of the convening authority to change a court-martial result had found support in the CAAF.[226] Other changes have included the introduction of special victim counsels, ability for an accuser to move work location, and the dishonorable discharge or dismissal of a perpetrator convicted of rape.[227] Some military writers have expressed considerable disquiet regarding the changes to article 60. They are seen as undermining command discipline power. However, when one looks at the historical justification for such power, neither the need for the commander to consider operational ability nor to balance individual rights against harsh punishment prevail to the required extent. With the much larger military numbers than in the early historical times, there is no longer a pressing need for a commander to decide whether to court-martial, or provide clemency. The concept has been held onto, much like the number of panel members that was established early, for similar pragmatic reasons giving consideration to the effect on the war-fighting effort. Now, both panel sizes and commander's freedom to determine discipline outcomes are likely to have little effect on operational ability, thus removing these justifications.

Unfortunately one could really continue endlessly with case examples of leaders committing sexual abuse and dishonesty offences, such as Major General Ralph Baker, Combined Joint Task Force-Horn of Africa commander, who was dismissed for alcohol and sexual offences.[228] These examples reinforce the lack of suitability for the military to be enforcing the criminal law, and conversely, the capability of the civilian system to operate effectively. The matter of Colonel Jeffrey Krusinski, a former Air Force Sexual Assault Prevention and Response Office director, is an example that shows that the civilian courts are perfectly capable of fairly dealing with military offenders.

There is no solid justification to explain why all such matters could not proceed in a similar way. A civilian jury found Krusinski not guilty for assault and battery in 2013 in regards to a butt-grabbing incident involving a civilian. It seems the civilian involved had not hesitated in responding with force.[229] Krusinski subsequently received a letter of reprimand as an administrative workplace punishment.

CONCLUSION

Aberdeen, Tailhook, Lackland, the navy military academy and marine corp, to name just a few, have seen senior leaders attend congressional and other hearings. Often they repeat the same desire for change, and implementation of some changes may occur, but the repetition of this process means it is starting to wear thin as Senators note "each time hold [a] hearing [and] bring the brass up here to say right words and then we go about our business."[230]

Many writers bring a fresh perspective and many writing from within the institution risk an unconscious bias when commenting on the UCMJ. However, listening to the varied voices requires a discernment to ensure groupthink does not become a blind path on which real problems become hidden like *la brutta figura*. Little tracking and care is taken when the military discharges perpetrators into the civilian realm without appropriate punishment or opportunity for rehabilitation. It is claimed such individuals do not reach the high standards expected for discipline and order in the military, but they are willingly ousted into the civilian community. This is not only highly disrespectful to the primary society but it speaks of an elitist coterie that has lost sight of its purpose and meaning, and one that poses danger to the civilian population and democracy itself.

Some suggest the answer is more leadership training,[231] or thinking slow,[232] or getting the balance between discipline and justice just right.[233] Some wrench their hair asking, "Why are problems so bad these days? They're worse . . . because military actions in the last decades have been so fruitless, so purposeless, and so frustrating."[234] Not unlike Lewis Carroll's Alice; when asking "where should I go?" she was provided with good advice by the Cheshire Cat answering "that depends on where you want to end up."[235] Each new scandal reinforces the inadequacy of the military discipline system and therefore the impunity felt by perpetrators and observed by survivors. The answer is simple: if this is not what the military and civil society want any longer then the only way to address the issues is like Jesus did in the temple: turn over the table and start afresh. A different system of punishment administered outside the primary society risks generating a feeling of being untouchable that enables more than just sexual offences but enables a basic abuse of power within a protected coterie.

NOTES

1. Julie K. Carson and Brad R. Carson, "The Historical Roots and Future Directions for Military Law and Policies on Rape and Sexual Assault" *Military Psychology* (2017): 1.

2. Fred L. Borch III, "The History of 'Don't Ask, Don't Tell' In the Army: How We Got to It and Why It Is What It Is" *Military Law Review* 203 (2010): 189; Sherilyn A. Bunn, "Straight Talk: The Implications of Repealing 'Don't Ask, Don't Tell' Preserving Aspects of the Current Policy"' *Military Law Review* 203 (2010): 207.

3. *National Defense Authorization Act for the Fiscal Year* 2014 (Pub. L. No.113-66): s 125; John W. Brooker, "Improving Uniform Code of Military Justice Reform" *Military Law Review* 222 (2014): 1.

4. Mark Thompson, "'Don't Ask, Don't Tell' Turns 15" *Time*, January 28, 2008 http://content.time.com/time/nation/article/0,8599,1707545,00.html.

5. 716 F. Supp. 2d 884 (C.D. Cal. 2009).

6. Francine Banner, "Institutional Sexual Assault and the Rights/Trust Dilemma" *Cardozo Public Law, Policy and Ethics Journal* 13 (2014): 97, 122 (footnotes removed); See further, Bernard D. Rostker, Susan Hosek, and John D Winkler, *Sexual Orientation and U.S. Military Personnel Policy: An Update of RAND's 1993 Study* (RAND Corporation, 2010).

7. Barack Obama signed the legislation on December 22, 2010. The policy ended officially on September 20, 2011; *Don't Ask, Don't Tell Repeal Act* of 2010 (H.R. 2965, S. 4023). In 2010, two federal courts ruled the ban on openly gay, lesbian, and bisexual service personnel unconstitutional and on July 6, 2011, a federal appeals court suspended the DADT policy.

8. Agnes Gereben Schaefer et al., "Assessing the Implications of Allowing Transgender Personnel to Serve Openly" (RAND Corporation, 2016) https://www.rand.org/pubs/research_reports/RR1530.html; German Lopez, "Trump: Allowing Transgender Military Service Would Hurt Combat Readiness. Actual Research: Nope" *Vox Media*, July 26, 2017. https://www.vox.com/identities/2017/7/26/16034040/trump-transgender-military-study. On July 26, 2017, President Donald Trump announced the reinstatement of the ban on service by transgender individuals through Twitter. The ban has not been officially reinstated; The Supreme Court on January 22, 2019 granted stays of two district court preliminary injunctions to enable the lifting of the injunctions on Trump's proposed ban while the cases proceed through the U.S Court of Appeals for the Ninth Circuit in *Trump v. Karnoski* January 22, 2019, Supreme Court of the US. No. 18-676 and *Trump v. Stockman* January 22, 2019, Supreme Court of the U.S. No. 18A627.

9. Schaefer et al., "Assessing the Implications": 34. Covering gender-reassignment surgery would cost the military "between $2.4 million and $8.4 million annually,

representing a 0.04 to 0.13 percent increase in active-component health care expenditures"; Patricia Kime, "DoD Spends $84M a Year on Viagra, Similar Meds" *The Military Times* February 13, 2015 https://www.militarytimes.com/pay-benefits/military-benefits/health-care/2015/02/13/dod-spends-84m-a-year-on-viagra-similar-meds/.

10. Schaefer et al., "Assessing the Implications": 50.

11. Jessica Turchik and Susan Wilson, "Sexual Assault in the U.S. Military: A Review of the Literature and Recommendations for the Future" *Aggression and Violent Behavior* 15 (2010): 267.

12. Substance Abuse and Mental Health Services Administration (SAMHSA), "Veterans and Military Families" (2017) https://www.samhsa.gov/veterans-military-families; David A. Schlueter, "The Military Justice Conundrum: Justice or Discipline?" *Military Law Review* 215 (2013): 1.

13. SAMHSA, "Veterans and Military Families."

14. SAMHSA, "Veterans and Military Families."

15. Timothy W. Lineberry and Stephen S. O'Connor, "Suicide in the US Army" *Mayo Clinic Proceedings* 87 no. 9 (2012): 871.

16. Alex Gallacher et al., "The Constant Battle: Suicide by Veterans" (Foreign Affairs, Defence and Trade References Committee, August 2017) https://www.aph.gov.au/Parliamentary_Business/Committees/Senate/Foreign_Affairs_Defence_and_Trade/VeteranSuicide/Report Some reports from ex-service organizations suggest that the number of veterans who have committed suicide may be more than 280 since 1999; "The Incidence of Suicide among Serving and Ex-serving Australian Defence Force Personnel 2001–2014," AIHW, November 30, 2016, cited in Gallacher et. al., "The Constant Battle": 15–16 found that between "2001 and 2014, there were 292 certified suicide deaths among people with at least one day of ADF service since 2001. Of these:

- 84 occurred in the serving full-time population;
- 66 occurred in the reserve population;
- 142 occurred in the ex-serving population; and
- 272 were men and 20 were women.

In particular, the AIHW study found that after adjusting for age, when compared with all Australian men, that men serving full-time and in the reserve had a lower suicide rate (53 per cent and 46 per cent). However, the suicide rate for ex-serving men was 13 per cent higher. In 2002–2014, younger ex-serving men were at higher risk of suicide death compared with all Australian men of the same age. Among ex-serving men, those aged 18–24 accounted for . . . a suicide rate almost 2 times as high as Australian men of the same age." 11.

17. Lisa Davis et al., "Workplace and Gender Relations Survey of Active Duty Members" (Defense Research, Surveys, and Statistics Center, 2016) xv.

18. Gallacher et al., "The Constant Battle": Witness 51.

19. Mark Thompson, "Military Sexual Assault Victims Discharged after Filing Complaints" May 18, 2016 *Time* http://time.com/4340321/sexual-assault-military-discharge-women/.

20. Sara Darehshori, "Booted. Lack of Recourse for Wrongfully Discharged US Military Rape Survivors" Human Rights Watch Report, May 19, 2016 https://www.hrw.org/report/2016/05/19/booted/lack-recourse-wrongfully-discharged-us-military-rape-survivors. See also, Sara Darehshori, "Embattled. Retaliation against Sexual Assault Survivors in the US Military" Human Rights Watch Report, May 18, 2015 https://www.hrw.org/report/2015/05/18/embattled/retaliation-against-sexual-assault-survivors-us-military:1.

21. Darehshori, "Booted."

22. Thompson, "Military Sexual Assault."

23. Jill A. Rough and David J. Armor, "Sexual Assault in the U.S. Military: Trends and Responses" *World Medical & Health Policy* 9 no. 2 (2017): 206, 207.

24. Banner, "Institutional Sexual Assault": 157–58: "men—particularly young men—may not themselves frame experiences of sexual assault as rape. Both acquaintance rape and male-on-male sexual assaults generally fall outside this traditional narrative. As Elizabeth J. Allen, Director of the University of Maine Hazing Project observes, 'When we ask students to define hazing . . . there's this disconnect between defining it and recognizing it when it happens to them. . . .'"

25. See Alexandra Lohman, "Silence of the Lambs: Giving Voice to the Problem of Rape and Sexual Assault in the United States Armed Forces" *Northwestern Journal of Law & Social Policy* 10 no.1 (2015): 230; Stav Ziv, "Report on Sexual Assault in the Military Draws Criticism," *Newsweek*, December 8, 2014 http://www.newsweek.com/report-sexualassault-military-draws-criticism-290173; "Military Sex Assault Reports Up 8 Percent," *Chicago Sun Times*, December 4, 2014 http://politics.suntimes.com/article/washington/ap-sources-military-sex-assaultreports-8-percent/thu-12042014-726a: 2.

26. Rough and Armor, "Sexual Assault."

27. *National Defense Authorization Act* for Fiscal Year 1997 (Pub. L. No. 104-201); Davis, "Workplace and Gender Relations Survey" administered in 1988, 1995, 2002, 2006, 2008, 2010, 2012, 2016: US Defense Manpower Data Center, "2012 Workplace and Gender Relations Survey of Active Duty Members: Survey Note and Briefing," Defense Technical Information Center, 2013; "Department of Defense Annual Report on Sexual Assault in the Military: Fiscal Year 2012," US Department of Defense, 2012, Volume 1: 7–8; Elizabeth P. Van Winkle et al., "Workplace and Gender Relations Survey of Active Duty" (Defense Research, Surveys, and Statistics Center, 2016); Megan Bastick, "Integrating a Gender Perspective into Internal Oversight within Armed Forces" The Geneva Centre for the Democratic Control of Armed Forces, 2014 http://www.osce.org/odihr/118325?download=true; Alexandra Iorfino, "Military Justice: Whether a Systematic Overhaul of the Uniform Code of Military Justice is Required to Combat the Sexual Assault "Epidemic" *Chapman's Journal of Law & Policy* 20 (2014–2015): 45.

28. Andrew R. Morral, Kristie L. Gore, and Terry L. Schell, "Sexual Assault and Sexual Harrasment in the U.S. Military" (RAND Corporation, 2014).

29. Lindsay M. Rock et al., "Workplace and Gender Relations Survey of Active Duty Members: Overview Report on Sexual Assault" (2010) http://www.sapr.mil/

public/docs/research/DMDC_2010_WGRA_Overview_Report_of_Sexual_Assault .pdf; Rachel N. Lipari et al., "Gender Relations Survey of Active Duty Members" (2006) http://www.sapr.mil/public/docs/research/WGRA_OverviewReport.pdf: In 2010 the Department of Defense's Sexual Assault Prevention and Response Office reported 3,158 sexual assaults, although the Pentagon indicated this figure of 13.5 percent was likely to represent only a small portion of the more probable estimate of 19,000 assaults in the last year.

30. Rough and Armor, "Sexual Assault": 210.

31. "Report to the President of the United States on Sexual Assault Prevention and Response" Department of Defense, 2014: 57; Morral et al., "Sexual Assault and Sexual Harrasment—Top-Line Estimates for Active-Duty Service Members from the RAND Military Workplace Study" (2014): 23, ix–x—This included sexual assault that is penetrative, non-penetrative, and attempted, and sexual harassment encompassing unwanted persistent, offensive or severe sexual advances, and conduct, use of power to coerce sexual favors, and gender discrimination or unequal treatment.

32. Elizabeth P. Van Winkle et al., "2014 Survivor Experience Survey Report on Preliminary Results Fiscal Year 2014, Quarter 4" (Defense Manpower Data Center, October 2014).

33. "Sexual Assault Prevention and Response Office, Mission and History" http://www.sapr.mil/index.php/about/mission-and-history.

34. Rough and Armor, "Sexual Assault": 209.

35. Holtzman et al., "Statistical Data": 10, Recommendation 53; *National Defense Authorization Act* for Fiscal Year 2017, (Pub. L. No. 114-328) s140a requires the establishment within four years of uniform standards and criteria for collecting military justice data across all of the military services.

36. Davis "Workplace and Gender Relations Survey" 2016: ix; Winkle et al., "Survivor Experience": vii.

37. Winkle et al., "Survivor Experience": 32.

38. Devon M. Alvarez, "Death by Hazing: Should there be a Federal Law Against Fraternity and Sorority Hazing?" *Journal of Multidisciplinary Research* 7 no. 2 (2015): 43; Kirsten M. Keller et al, *Hazing in the U.S. Armed Forces: Recommendations for Hazing Prevention Policy and Practice* (RAND Corporation, 2015).

39. Morral et al., "Sexual Assault and Sexual Harrasment": 90 Elizabeth R. OuYang, "Can Military Courts Deliver Justice to a Subordinate Hazed by Superiors?" *Asian American Policy Review* 23 (2012): 81; See e.g., Kirk Semple, "Army Officer Reaches Deal in the Suicide of a Private," *New York Times*, December 18, 2012: A24.

40. Rough and Armor, "Sexual Assault": 210–11.

41. Morral et al., "Sexual Assault and Sexual Harrasment" Vol 2: 92.

42. Holly Hemphill et al., "Defence Advisory Committee on Women in the Services Report" *DACOWITS*, May 17, 2013: ii.

43. Banner, "Institutional Sexual Assault": 136–37 "UCMJ has the capacity to penalize a much broader range of infractions than civilian criminal codes . . . However . . . the UCMJ currently is underutilized in this regard"; Robert Reed et al., "Sex Crimes and the UCMJ" in *Report for the Joint Service Committee on Military Justice*, Department of Defense, 2005: 2.

44. Morral et al., "Sexual Assault and Sexual Harrasment" Vol 2: 77–84.

45. Ibid., xxiii, 81 "Even among part-time reservists, most who experienced a sexual assault in the past year indicated that the incident involved military personnel or settings (85 percent)."

46. Anne-Claire Blok, "Sexual Violence in the U.S. Military" (Human Rights Council, April–May 2015): 4–5.

47. Jefferson P. Marquis et al., "Improving Oversight and Coordination of Department of Defense Programs That Address Problematic Behaviors among Military Personnel" (RAND Corporation, 2017) https://www.rand.org/pubs/research_reports/RR1352.html 20; See Jennifer S. Knies, "Two Steps Forward, One Step Back: Why the New UCMJ's Rape Law Missed the Mark" *The Army Lawyer* August (2007): 1.

48. Marquis et al., "Improving Oversight": 36; Brenda S. Farrell et al., "Sexual Violence. Actions Needed to Improve DOD's Efforts to Address the Continuum of Unwanted Sexual Behaviors" (US Government Accountability Office, 2017) https://www.gao.gov/assets/690/689086.pdf: 12.

49. SAPRO, "Department of Defense Annual Report on Sexual Assault in the Military" (Department of Defense, 2018) http://sapr.mil/public/docs/reports/FY17_Annual/DoD_FY17_Annual_Report_on_Sexual_Assault_in_the_Military.pdf: 3.

50. Ibid., 3.

51. David Usborne, "Soldiers, Sexual Abuse—and the Serial Killer: The US Military's Secret Sexual Assaults" *The Independent*, June 28, 2013 http://www.independent.co.uk/news/world/americas/soldiers-sexual-abuse-and-the-serial-killer-the-us-military-s-secret-sexual-assaults-8679271.html.

52. Carol E. Tracy et al., "Rape and Sexual Assault in the Legal System" *Women's Law Project and AEquitas* June 5–7, 2013 http://jpp.whs.mil/Public/docs/04-Meetings/sub-20150507/03_Rape_SexAsslt_LegalSystem_WLP_AEQuitas_20120605.pdf: 7; See Usborne "Soldiers, Sexual Abuse"; Tom Philbin and Michael Philbin, *The Killer Book of Serial Killers* (Sourcebooks, Inc., 2009) Ch 21; Kirsten E. Gillibrand et al., "The Relationships between Military Sexual Assault, Post-Traumatic Stress Disorder and Suicide, and on Department of Defense and Department of Veterans Affairs Medical Treatment and Management of Victims of Sexual Trauma," *One Hundred Thirteenth Congress Second Session*, February 26, 2014 http://www.fdsys.gov/: 5 "According to the American Psychiatric Association, 90 percent of all rapists and serial rapists will commit an average of 3 to 600 rapes in a lifetime. This is not just a problem within the military. It becomes a societal and national security risk to us all."

53. Marin R Castro, "Sexual Assault in the Military" (United States Commission on Civil Rights, 2013) http://www.usccr.gov/pubs/09242013_Statutory_Enforcement_Report_Sexual_Assault_in_the_Military.pdf.

54. David Lisak and Paul M. Miller, "Repeat Rape and Multiple Offending among Undetected Rapists" *Violence and Victims* 17 no. 1 (2002): 73.

55. Ibid., 78.

56. Ibid., 78; See further, Lisa M. Schenck, "Informing the Debate about Sexual Assault in the Military Services: Is the Department of Defense Its Own Worst Enemy?" *Ohio State Journal of Criminal Law* 11 (2014): 579.

57. Jessica Wright et al., "Annual Report on Sexual Harassment and Violence at the Military Service Academies Academic Program Year 2013–2014" (Sexual Assault Prevention and Response Office, February 2015): The definition of unwanted sexual contact used in the Service Academy Gender Relations Survey is behaviorally based and not intended to designate specific UCMJ offenses; Mary Padilla and Kristin Williams, "Workplace and Gender Relations Survey of Reserve Component Members: Tabulations of Responses" (Human Resources Strategic Assessment Program, April 2013).

58. Wright, "Annual Report": 7–8; Rough and Armor, "Sexual Assault": 215.

59. Wright, "Annual Report": 8.

60. Ibid., 8.

61. Rough and Armor, "Sexual Assault": 214.

62. Wright, "Annual Report": 8.

63. Rough and Armor, "Sexual Assault": 211.

64. Clara Bingham, "Code of Dishonor" *Vanity Fair*, December 2003 http://www.vanityfair.com/news/2003/12/airforce200312: "A recent Defense Department inspector general's draft survey revealed that 80 percent of all sexual assaults at the academy go unreported, meaning that the true 10-year casualty list could be as high as 700. The same survey indicated that 7.4 percent of last year's female student body at the academy were victims of rape or attempted rape, and 18.8 percent were victims of sexual assault. (By way of comparison, a 2000 Department of Justice study reported that nationwide 1.7 percent of female college students claimed to have been raped.)"

65. Michael J. Davidson, "Court-Martialing Cadets" *Capital University Law Review* 36 (2008): 635–73.

66. Lohman, "Silence of the Lambs": 231, citing Naomi Woolf, "Rape in the Military a Culture of Coverup" *The Guardian*, June 15, 2012 https://readersupportednews.org/opinion2/273-40/11931-rape-in-the-military-a-culture-of-coverup.

67. Ellen P. Embrey et al., "Task Force Report on Care for Victims of Sexual Assault" (Department of Defense, April 2004) http://www.sapr.mil/public/docs/research/Task-Force-Report-for-Care-of-Victims-of-SA-2004.pdf: viii, 56–59. The task force specifically rejected the ability to directly compare sexual assault rates between military and civilian populations. They referred to various reports including FBI Uniform Crime Reporting (UCR) rates of sexual assault and the military services' own reported statistics, derived from reports to law enforcement. These reports are comparable because they are both collected by law enforcement agencies and define sexual assault similarly.

68. This definition of rape became effective from January 1, 2013.

69. Criminal Justice Information Services Division Preliminary Semi-Annual Uniform Crime Report, January–June, 2016 https://ucr.fbi.gov/crime-in-the-u.s/2016/preliminary-semiannual-uniform-crime-report-januaryjune-2016/tables/table-3 the violent crime figures for 2013–2016 include the offense of murder, rape (revised definition), rape (legacy definition), robbery, and aggravated assault; See also, "Reporting Rape in 2013 Summary Reporting System (SRS) User Manual and Technical Specification" (U. S. Department of Justice. Federal Bureau of Investiga-

tion, 2014) https://ucr.fbi.gov/crime-in-the-u.s/2016/preliminary-semiannual-uniform-crime-report-januaryjune-2016/tables/table-3.

70. Hunter Peebles, Amanda Grifka, Lisa Davis, "Military Workplace Climate" Ch 9 in Winkle et al., "Workplace and Gender Relations": 232; "2012 Workplace and Gender Relations Survey of Active Duty Members: Survey Note and Briefing," Defense Technical Information Center, 2013; "Department of Defense Annual Report on Sexual Assault in the Military: Fiscal Year 2012," US Department of Defense, 2012, Vol 1: 7–8; Bastick, "Integrating a Gender Perspective": 37.

71. Winkle et al., "Workplace and Gender Relations": 234.

72. Ibid., 251.

73. Davis et al., "Workplace and Gender Relations": 364.

74. See *National Defense Authorization Act,* Fiscal Year 1989, (Pub. L. No. 100-456) 10 U.S.C. § 1034 (*Military Whistleblower Protection Act* 1988); *National Defense Authorization Act* Fiscal Year 2014 (Pub. L. No 113–66); (*Military Whistleblower Protection Enhancement Act* of 2013 (Pub. L. No. 113-66).

75. Brenda S. Farrell, "Whistleblower Protection DoD Needs to Enhance Oversight of Military Whistleblower Reprisal Investigations" (United States Government Accountability Office, May 2015); See also Department of Defense Inspector General Memorandum, Government Accountability Office (GAO) Report on Whistleblower Protection: Actions Needed to Improve DoD's Military Whistleblower Reprisal Program (Feb. 24, 2012).

76. Rachel A. Woldoff and Karen G. Weiss, "'Stop Snitchin': Exploring Definitions of the Snitch and Implications for Urban Black Communities" *Journal of Criminal Justice & Popular Culture* 17 (2009): 184, 185 cited in Banner, "Institutional Sexual Assault": 138. "Army's urge a 'duty to speak,' they are fighting against a significant and deeply held perception that they are acting as a 'snitch,' a 'traitor who reveals group secrets or cooperates with a group's enemies . . . the ultimate backstabber.' The more exclusive the social group, the more likely the label will apply."

77. Shauna, Stahlman, et al., "Self-Reported STIs and Sexual Risk Behaviors in the U.S. Military: How Gender Influences Risk" *Sexually Transmitted Diseases* 41, no. 6 (2014): 359–64.

78. National Intimate Partner and Sexual Violence Survey, 2010 summary report cited in Rough and Armor, "Sexual Assault": 213.

79. Stahlman et al., "Self-Reported STIs."

80. Lisa M. Schenck, "'Just the facts, ma'am: How military appellate courts rely on Factual Sufficiency Review to Overturn Sexual Assault Cases When Victims Are "Incapacitated"' *Southwestern Law Review* 45 (2016): 523: "The Department of Defense (DoD) generates elaborate annual reports exceeding 1,000 pages discussing sexual assaults and efforts to reduce their occurrence. The prevalence of the role that alcohol consumption plays in sexual assaults is not specifically summarized for the DoD as a whole in any one report."

81. Ibid., 541–42 ". . . the FY 2014 RAND Corporation survey [found] that '25 percent of men and 41 percent of women had been drinking at the time of the assault.'"

82. Brenda S. Farrell, "Whistleblower Protection. DoD Has Improved Oversight for Reprisal Investigations but Can Take Additional Actions to Standardize Process

and Reporting" (US Government Accountability Office, September 7, 2016); But *cf* J. Michael Dahm, "Innocent until Investigated" *Proceedings Magazine* 142 no. 4 (2016) https://www.usni.org/magazines/proceedings/2016-04/innocent-until-investigated.

83. Farrell, "Whistleblower Protection."

84. Carson, "The Historical Roots": 10–11.

85. Holtzman et al., "Statistical Data": 15.

86. Holtzman et al., "Statistical Data": citing "DoD Response to JPP Request for Information" 164A, April 5, 2017, http://jpp.whs.mil/Public/ docs/03_TopicAreas/07-CM_Trends_Analysis/20170407/20170407_JPP_RFI_164_165_DoD.pdf: 15.

87. See, e.g., Jean Zimmerman, *Tailspin: Women at War in the Wake of Tailhook* (Doubleday, 1995).

88. See, e.g., J. Richard Chema, "Arresting 'Tailhook': The Prosecution of Sexual Harassment in the Military" *Military Law Review* 140 (Spring) (1993): 1.

89. Zimmerman, *Tailspin*: 6.

90. Leslie J. Coletti, "In Search of a New Culture: The Sexual Violence against U.S. Military Women by Their Fellow Soldiers, 1978–Present" *Dietrich College of Humanities and Social Sciences Thesis* (2010) http://repository.cmu.edu/cgi/view content.cgi?article=1049&context=hsshonors: 143; Kingsley R. Browne, "Military Sex Scandals from Tailhook to the Present: The Cure Can Be Worse Than the Disease" *Duke Journal Of Gender Law & Policy* 14 (2007): 749.

91. Coletti, "In Search of a New Culture": 163.

92. Melissa Healy, "Pentagon Blasts Tailhook Probe, Two Admirals Resign" *Los Angeles Times,* September 25, 1992: 2.

93. See e.g., Robert L Beck, *Inside The Tailhook Scandal: A Naval Aviator's Story* (Fulton Books Inc, 2016); Zimmerman, *Tailspin.*

94. *Coughlin v. Hilton Hotels Corp*., 879 F. Supp. 1047 (D. Nev. 1995). Hilton Hotels Corporation appealed and the appeals court upheld both the decision and the award in 1997.

95. Browne, "Military Sex Scandals."

96. Ibid., 760.

97. Behan, "Don't Tug on Superman's Cape": 110. "Soldiers may seek removal of letters of reprimand filed in their Military Personnel Records Jacket or their Official Military Personnel File by appealing to designated appeal authorities."

98. Browne, "Military Sex Scandals": 762. "The Senate allowed Kelso to retire with his four stars in 1994. The vote was 54 to 43."

99. Ibid., 753.

100. Eric Schmitt, "Judge Dismisses Tailhook Cases, Saying Admiral Tainted Inquiry" *New York Times,* February 9, 1994 http://www.nytimes.com/1994/02/09/us/judge-dismisses-tailhook-cases-saying-admiral-tainted-inquiry.html.

101. Coletti, "In Search of a New Culture": 137; Schmitt, "Judge Dismisses Tailhook Cases."

102. Schmitt, "Judge Dismisses Tailhook Cases."

103. Browne, "Military Sex Scandals": 756–57.

104. Ibid.

105. Coletti, "In Search of a New Culture": 136, 139.

106. See e.g., Browne, "Military Sex Scandals"; Beck, *Inside The Tailhook Scandal.*

107. Pauline Collins, *Civil-Military "Legal" Relations: Where to from Here? The Civilian Courts and the Military in the United Kingdom, United States and Australia.* (Leiden: Brill Nijhoff, 2018); Diane H. Mazur, "Rehnquist's Vietnam: Constitutional Separatism and the Stealth Advance of Martial Law" *Indiana Law Journal* 77 (2002): 701.

108. Collins, *Civil-Military "Legal" Relations.*

109. Stephen Gageler, "Deference" *Australian Journal of Administrative Law* 22 (2015): 151, 152.

110. Coletti, "In Search of a New Culture"; See also, Mic Hunter, *Honor Betrayed: Sexual Abuse in America's Military* (Barricade Books, 2007).

111. Coletti, "In Search of a New Culture": 132.

112. 518 U.S. 515 (1996).

113. Coletti, "In Search of a New Culture"; Elizabeth L. Hillman, "Front and Center: Sexual Violence in U.S. Military Law" *Politics and Society* 37 no. 1 (2009): 101; Kilborn, "Sex Abuse Cases"; Robert D. Shadley, *The Game: Unraveling a Military Sex Scandal* (Beaver's Pond Press, 2013).

114. UCMJ art 134.

115. UCMJ art 125.

116. Neil A. Lewis, "Ex-Sergeant Pleads Guilty to Having Sex with Trainees" *New York Times*, April 8, 1997 http://www.nytimes.com/1997/04/08/us/ex-sergeant-pleads-guilty-to-having-sex-with-trainees.html: he was sentenced to one year but served four months in prison.

117. Coletti, "In Search of a New Culture": 105; *United States v. Simpson,* 58 M.J. 368 (C.A.A.F. 2003). *United States v. Simpson*, 55 M.J. 674 (Army Ct. Crim. Appeals. 2001).

118. Dana Michael Hollywood, "Creating a True Army of One: Four Proposals to Combat Sexual Harassment in Today's Army" *Harvard Journal of Law & Gender* 30 (2007): 151, 159.

119. Hillman, "Front and Center":107; Martha Chamallas, "The New Gender Panic: Reflections on Sex Scandals and the Military" *Minnesota Law Review* 83 (1998): 305, 311.

120. Richard S. Siegfried et al., "The Secretary of the Army's Senior Review Panel Report on Sexual Harassment" (U.S. Dept. of Defense, July 1997) http://www.dtic.mil/dtfs/doc_research/p18_13.pdf; See Hollywood, "Creating a True Army of One": 160.

121. Siegfried, et al., "The Secretary of the Army's": 2; see further T. S. Nelson, *For Love of Country: Confronting Rape and Sexual Harassment in the U.S. Military* (Routledge, 2002): 90–91.

122. Hollywood, "Creating a True Army of One": 161–62.

123. Zoë Carpenter, "20 Years Ago, an Army Veteran Reported a Sexual Assault. She's Still Waiting for Justice" *The Nation*, February 24, 2014 https://www.thenation.com/article/nearly-two-decades-after-speaking-veteran-waits-sexual-assault-reform/.

124. Jane Gross, "Sergeant Major Gets One-Step Demotion but No Time in Jail" *New York Times*, March 17, 1998 http://www.nytimes.com/1998/03/17/us/sergeant-major-gets-one-step-demotion-but-no-time-in-jail.html.

125. Hollywood, "Creating a True Army of One": 162–63; Chamallas, "The New Gender Panic": 305, 310–12.

126. *McKinney v. White,* 291 F.3d 851, 852 (D.C. Cir. 2002) McKinney was unsuccessful.

127. See *National Defense Authorisation Act* for the Fiscal Year 2015 (Pub. L.114–92).

128. See, *Stubbs v. United States*, 744 F.2d 58, 59 (8th Cir. 1984); Hollywood, "Creating a True Army of One"; Schenck, Informing the Debate": 588; Kim Strosnider, "FBI Investigates Charges That Female Cadets at the Citadel Were Hazed" *Chronicle of Higher Education* 43(18) (1997) A51; Kilborn, "Sex Abuse Cases."

129. Hollywood, "Creating a True Army of One": 160.

130. Nancy Kassebaum-Baker et al., "Federal Advisory Committee on Gender-Integrated Training and Related Issues" (U.S. Dept. of Defense, December 16, 1997) http://www.defenselink.mil/pubs/git/report.html.

131. Hollywood, "Creating a True Army of One": 166; Chamallas, "The New Gender Panic."

132. Phillip O'Connor, "New Sex Scandals at Fort Leonard Wood" *St. Louis Post-Dispatch*, November 23, 2008.

133. Coletti, "In Search of a New Culture": 107.

134. Chamallas, "The New Gender Panic": 336–37.

135. Lohman, "Silence of the Lambs": 151, 262.

136. *United States v. Delmar G. Simpson*, US Army Court of Criminal Appeals 55 M.J. 674 2001; *United States v. Delmar G. Simpson*, Appellant No. 02-0001 Crim. App. No. 9700775 July 1, 2003.

137. Lewis, "Ex-Sergeant Pleads Guilty."

138. Ellen Goodman, "'Great And Sustained Discipline' Required" *The Spokesman-Review*, May 2, 1997 http://www.spokesman.com/stories/1997/may/02/great-and-sustained-discipline-required/; Michael I. Spak and Jonathan P. Tomes, "Sexual Harassment in the Military: Time for a Change of Forum" *Cleveland State Law Review* 47 (1999): 335.

139. Richard J. Newman, "Upheaval at the Academy" *Air Force Magazine* (January 2004): 56, 57; Hillman, "Front and Center"; Colleen Dalton, "The Sexual Assault Crisis in the United States Air Force Academy" *Cardozo Women's Law Journal* 1 (2005): 177.

140. Janine P. Felsman, "'To Support and Defend' against Sexual Misconduct: Calling on Future Military Leaders to Bridge the Cultural Divide" *Ohio State Journal of Criminal Law* 11 no. 1 (2014): 353.

141. Kilborn, "Sex Abuse Cases."

142. T. K. Fowler et al., "Panel to Review Sexual Misconduct Allegations at the U.S. Air Force Academy" (Senate Armed Services Committee, House Armed Services Committee, Secretary of Defense, September 22, 2003) https://www.scribd.com/document/106779977/Report-of-the-Panel-to-Review-Sexual-Misconduct-Allegations-at-the-USAF-Academy.

143. Ibid., 14–34.

144. Mary L. Walker, "The Report of the Working Group Concerning Deterrence of and Response to Incidents of Sexual Assault at the U.S. Air Force Academy" June 17, 2003.

145. Kilborn, "Sex Abuse Cases": 57.
146. Fowler et al., "Panel to Review Sexual Misconduct": 75–81.
147. Ibid., 4–6, 35–36.
148. Ibid., 1–2, 37–40.
149. Ibid., 101–5.
150. See e.g. David W. Graney, *Rogue Institution: Vigilante Injustice, Lawlessness, and Disorder at the Air Force Academy* (Wheatmark Inc, 2010): 270–72.
151. Fowler et al., "Panel to Review Sexual Misconduct": 61.
152. UCMJ art 2(a) (2).
153. Davidson, "Court-Martialing Cadets."
154. Robert E. Murdough, "Barracks, Dormitories, and Capitol Hill: Finding Justice in the Divergent Politics of Military and College Sexual Assault" *Military Law Review* 223 no. 2 (2015): 233, 242.
155. Elizabeth Byrne, "ADFA cadet found not guilty of raping woman after night out in Canberra" *ABC News*, July 5, 2017 http://www.abc.net.au/news/2017-07-05/adfa-cadet-found-not-guilty-of-rape/8680872.
156. Gerald L. Hoewing et al., "The Report of the Defense Task Force of Sexual Harassment and Violence at the Military Service Academies" (Department of Defense, June 2005).
157. Ibid., Executive Summary: 3.
158. Ibid., 45.
159. Embrey et al., "Task Force Report on Care for Victims"; See also, Michael L. Dominguez, Roger A. Brady, and John Speigel, "Report Concerning the Assessment of USAF Sexual Assault Prevention and Response" (Department of Air Force, August 2004)
160. *National Defense Authorization Act* for Fiscal Year 2005 (Pub. L. 108-375).
161. *National Defense Authorization Act* for Fiscal Year 2005 (Pub. L. 108-375) s 571.
162. Reed et al., "Sex Crimes": 1.
163. *National Defense Authorization Act* for Fiscal Year 2006 (Pub. L. 109-163).
164. *National Defense Authorization Act* for Fiscal Year 2012 (Pub. L. 112-81).
165. 69 M.J. 338, 345 (C.A.A.F. 2011).
166. James Risen, "Attacked at 19 by an Air Force Trainer, and Speaking Out" *New York Times*, February 26, 2013 http://www.nytimes.com/2013/02/27/us/former-air-force-recruit-speaks-out-about-rape-by-her-sergeant-at-lackland.html.
167. Margaret Woodward, "Developing America's Airmen: A Review of Air Force Enlisted Training" in *Commander Directed Investigation Report* (U.S Air Force, November 2, 2012): xiv–xxiii.
168. Woodward "Developing America's Airmen": 6.
169. Risen, "Attacked at 19."
170. "A Complete List of the 35 Basic Military Training Instructors Court-Martialed in the Lackland Air Force Base Sex Scandal," 2016 https://militaryjusticeforall.com/.../a-complete-list-of-the-35-basic-military-training-ins....
171. Woodward "Developing America's Airmen": Appendix G.

172. Jackie Speier, "Rep Speier Demands Protection for Military's Most Vulnerable; Introduces Legislation to Shield Trainees from Sexual Assault by Instructors" *Press Release*, January 28, 2013 https://speier.house.gov/media-center/press-releases/rep-speier-demands-protection-militarys-most-vulnerable-introduces; Jackie Speier, "House Armed Services Committee Hearing" January 23, 2013: "All sexual advances by a training instructor toward a trainee are indefensible because consent is impossible in this power dynamic. Trainees are taught from day one that nothing an MTI says ends with a question mark—recruits must obey every order given and every task demanded."

173. Wilson Brissett, "Air Force Academy Questioned for Response to Sexual Assault" *Airforce Magazine*, December 14, 2017 http://www.airforcemag.com/Features/Pages/2017/December%202017/Air-Force-Academy-Questioned-for-Response-to-Sexual-Assault.aspx; Danielle Rogowski, "Quis Custodiet Ipsos Custodies? The Current State of Sexual Assault Reform within the U.S. Military and the Need for the Use of a Formal Decision Making Process in Further Reform" *Seattle University Law Review* 38 (2015): 1139.

174. Jackie Speier, Letter to Secretary of Defense General Hagel, Commandant of the Marine Corp, General Amos and Principal Deputy Director Halbrooks, May 8, 2013.

175. Thomas James Brennan, "Hundreds of Marines Investigated for Sharing Photos of Naked Colleagues" *The War Horse*, March 4, 2017 https://www.revealnews.org/blog/hundreds-of-marines-investigated-for-sharing-photos-of-naked-colleagues/.

176. "Military Academy Sexual Harassment Report Survivors of Sexual Assault and Harassment in Military Academies" (House Armed Services Subcommittee on Military Subcommittee on Military Personnel, May 2, 2017) https://www.c-span.org/video/?427730-1/victims-testify-sexual-assaults-military-academies; see also Ian Duncan, "Midshipmen and Cadets Testify before Congressional Panel about Sexual Assault and Retaliation" *The Baltimore Sun*, May 2, 2017 http://www.baltimoresun.com/news/maryland/politics/bs-md-naval-academy-sexual-assault-hearing-20170502-story.html.

177. Senate Armed Services Committee (SD-G50) Marines United Social Media Nude Photos Investigation, Gen Robert Neller, C-Span, March 14, 2017 https://www.c-span.org/video/?425339-1/senators-press-marine-corps-commander-accountability-nude-photo-controversy: 00:35:47.

178. Senate Armed Services Committee (SD-G50) Senator Kirsten Gillibrand, 00:42:30.

179. Ibid., 00:42:50.

180. Stephanie Gardiner, "'Jedi Council' Sex Ring Leader Hastings Fredrickson Sentenced to 15 months," *The Sydney Morning Herald*, February 9, 2015 https://www.smh.com.au/national/nsw/jedi-council-sex-ring-leader-hastings-fredrickson-sentenced-to-15-months-20150209-139wqo.html.

181. James S. Laporta and Rory Laverty, "Marines Keep Sharing Women's Nude Photos in Secret Groups after Getting Busted" *The Daily Beast Company LLC*, March 10, 2017 http://www.thedailybeast.com/marines-keep-sharing-womens-nude-photos-in-secret-groups-after-getting-busted.

182. Paul J. Larkin Jr, "Revenge Porn, State Law, and Free Speech" *Loyola of Los Angeles Law Review* 48 (2014): 57; Sarah Bloom, "No Vengeance for 'Revenge Porn' Victims: Unraveling Why This Latest Female-Centric, Intimate-Partner Offense Is Still Legal, and Why We Should Criminalize It" *Fordham Urban Law Journal* 42 no. 1 (2016): 234; Christina Cauterucci, "The Military's Nude-Photo Sharing Scandal Is Worse Than We Thought" *slate.com*, March 15, 2017 http://www.slate.com/blogs/xx_factor/2017/03/15/the_military_s_nude_photo_sharing_scandal_is_getting_worse.html.

183. Brennan, "Hundreds of Marines."

184. Banner, "Institutional Sexual Assault": 138.

185. Cauterucci, "The Military's Nude-Photo."; Brennan, "Hundreds of Marines": "The group has a code of conduct pinned to the top of its page: no discussing Marines United; no threats, harm or harassment; and no racist and illegal posts. These acts violate not only the group's stated code of conduct, but also Facebook's terms of use. The initial link on the page to the image collection read: 'Here you go, you thirsty fucks . . . this is just the tip of the iceberg. There is more coming.'"

186. Brennan, "Hundreds of Marines."; Dan Lamothe, "For the First Time, the Marine Corps Plans to Have a Female Infantry Officer among Its Ranks," *Washinghton Post*, September 21, 2017 https://www.washingtonpost.com/news/checkpoint/wp/2017/09/21/for-the-first-time-the-marine-corps-expects-to-have-a-female-infantry-officer-among-its-ranks/?utm_term=.58e7aef0bba7.

187. Bloom, "No Vengeance"; Paul J. Larkin, "Revenge Porn."

188. Zachary Cohen, "Navy, Marines Prohibit Sharing Nude Photos without Consent," *CNN*, April 19, 2017 http://edition.cnn.com/2017/04/19/politics/navy-marines-nude-photo-scandal-regulations-change/index.html; Andrea González-Ramírez, "The Navy & The Marines Have Made Revenge Porn Illegal—Here's Why," *Refinery29*, April 20, 2017 http://www.refinery29.com/2017/04/150816/navy-marines-revenge-porn-scandal-explained.

189. Duncan, "Midshipmen and Cadets."

190. "More Nude Photos of Female Military Personnel Shared Online, 1 Year after Marines United Scandal" *RT News*, March 10, 2018.

191. Farrell et al., "Sexual Violence."

192. Ibid., 13.

193. *National Defense Authorization Act* for Fiscal Year 2018 (Pub. L. No. 115-91) s 917a.

194. "Nude Photo Scandal Grows to 21 Felony Cases as Military Scours Web for Evidence" *CBS News*, May 5, 2017 www.cbsnews.com/.../nude-photo-scandal-grows-felony-cases-military-scours-web-ev...: "It's the kind of investigation that could go on forever. A simple word search of 'uniformed military nude' got nearly 80 million hits."

195. Sig Christenson, "Changes Driven by Lackland Scandal Not Complete" *San Antonio Express News*, September 9, 2014 http://www.mysanantonio.com/news/local/military/article/GAO-Changes-after-Lackland-scandal-not-finished-5744288.php.

196. Schenck, "Informing the Debate": 588.

197. Elizabeth Becker, "Army Demotes Retired NATO Commander Who Admitted Affairs with Wives of Subordinates" *New York Times*, September 3, 1999 http://www.nytimes.com/1999/09/03/us/army-demotes-retired-nato-commander-who-admitted-affairs-with-wives-subordinates.html.

198. Becker, "In 1952, Maj. Gen. Robert Grow, the military attache in Moscow, was tried on charges of dereliction of duty and was suspended from command for six months."

199. Bradley Graham, "Army Busts a General to Colonel" *The Washington Post*, November 17, 1999 https://www.washingtonpost.com/archive/politics/1999/11/17/army-busts-a-general-to-colonel/3d48564f-6b1f-46c6-9e5b-c8b9cb4ab5a5/?noredirect=on&utm_term=.5b6881c6cb04.

200. Lolita C. Baldor, and Jeffrey A. Sinclair, "U.S. Army General, Charged with Forcible Sodomy, Adultery," *Huffington Post*, November 26, 2012 http://www.huffingtonpost.com/2012/09/26/jeffrey-sinclairarrested_n_1916919.html.

201. Heidi L. Brady, "Justice Is No Longer Blind: How the Effort to Eradicate Sexual Assault in the Military Unbalanced the Military Justice System" *University of Illinois Law Review* (2016): 193, 211–214.

202. Gregg Zoroya, "General Avoids Jail Time in Case Involving Affair with Subordinate" *USA Today,* March 20, 2014 http://www.usatoday.com/story/news/nation/2014/03/20/sinclair-general-affairsubordinate-army-sexual-assault/6557033/.

203. Brady, "Justice is no Longer Blind": 214; Lohman, "Silence of the Lambs"; Craig Whitlock, "Sordid Details Spill Out in Rare Court-Martial of a General," *The Washington Post*, August 14, 2013 https://www.washingtonpost.com/world/national-security/sordid-details-spill-out-in-rare-court-martial-of-a-general/2013/08/14/f6c89c68-008d-11e3-a661-06a2955a5531_story.html?tid=a_inl&utm_term=.45fad70961d0: "another Army Brig. Gen. Roger B. Duff, pleaded guilty in June 2012 after facing a court-martial and retired."

204. *United States v. Howell* No. 201200264, 2014 CCA LEXIS 321, unpublished op. (N.M.Ct.Crim.App. 22 May 2014); *United States v. Averell*, 201300471 (N.M.C.C.A. 2014); Rustico, "Overcoming Overcorrection."

205. Brady, "Justice Is No Longer Blind": 227.

206. Rustico, "Overcoming Overcorrection": 2053.

207. Craig Whitlock, "Disgraced Army General, Jeffrey A. Sinclair, Receives Fine, No Jail Time," *The Washington Post*, March 20, 2014 https://www.washingtonpost.com/world/national-security/disgraced-army-general-jeffrey-a-sinclair-receives-fine-no-jail-time/2014/03/20/c555b650-b039-11e3-95e8-39bef8e9a48b_story.html?utm_term=.85e429089966; Alan Blinder, "General in Sex Case to Retire with a 2-Rank Demotion Jeffrey Sinclair to Receive Benefits, but at Lower Level," *New York Times*, June 21, 2014, A15; See Zoroya, "General Avoids Jail"; Brady, "Justice Is No Longer Blind": 229: "Two VPA provisions are particularly relevant. Section 3(c)(1) requires written performance appraisals of all Service members that must "include an assessment of the extent to which each such members supports the sexual assault prevention and response program of the Armed Force concerned." Additionally, Section 3(c) (2) requires that commanding officers' performance appraisals

include an evaluation of whether or not they have "established a command climate in which . . . allegations of sexual assault are properly managed and fairly evaluated." These provisions incentivize unlawful command influence because evaluations are used to identify those Service members who are best qualified for promotion. Service members who are passed over twice for promotion are forced to either retire or leave the military." (footnotes omitted)

208. Brady, "Justice Is No Longer Blind": 241.

209. Rustico, "Overcoming Overcorrection": 2054.

210. "Military Sexual Assault Amendment Defeated in Defense Bill Markup" Part 2 Clip of Fiscal Year 2018 Defense Authorization Markup, 2017 https://www.c-span.org/video/?c4675219/military-sexual-assault-amendment-defeated-defense-bill-markup; Michael Biesecker, "Army General Fined, Reprimanded in Sex Case" *Daily News*, March 20, 2014 http://www.military.com/daily-news/2014/03/20/army-general-fined-reprimanded-in-sex-case.html.

211. Whitlock, "Disgraced Army General"; Blinder, "General in Sex Case"; Thom Shanker, "West Point Sergeant Pleads Guilty to Videotaping Female," *The Washington Post*, March 7, 2014: A18.

212. Michael S. Schmidt and Matt Apuzzo, "David Petraeus Is Sentenced to Probation in Leak Investigation," *New York Times*, April 23, 2015: A16.

213. Craig Whitlock and Adam Goldman, "Pentagon Will Not Discipline Petraeus in Sex-and-Secrets Scandal," *The Washington Post*, January 30, 2016 https://www.stripes.com/news/us/pentagon-will-not-discipline-petraeus-in-sex-and-secrets-scandal-1.391456.

214. Tom Vanden Brook, "Disgraced Army General Fired after 'Inappropriate' Relationship with Young Woman on Staff" *USA Today*, June 23, 2017 https://www.usatoday.com/story/news/politics/2017/06/23/disgraced-army-general-fired-after-inappropriate-relationship/422902001/: "Maj. Gen. James Baldwin was the last division commander to be relieved after an investigation found him negligent in at attack that left 33 dead and 83 wounded at Fire Support Base Mary Ann in Vietnam on March 28, 1971."

215. Tom Vanden Brook, "Army Demotes 'Swinging General' after Investigation into Affairs, Lifestyle" *USA Today*, December 16, 2016 https://www.usatoday.com/story/news/politics/2016/12/16/army-demotes-swinging-general-david-haight/95493058/.

216. See Lolita C. Baldor, "Two-Star General Demoted after Affair" *The Associated Press*, December 16, 2016 http://www.armytimes.com/news/your-army/2016/12/16/two-star-general-demoted-after-affair/.

217. Whitlock, "Disgraced Army General"; Brady, Justice Is No Longer Blind": "In June 2014, Lt. Col. Morse was reprimanded for 'molesting a female officer at a sexual assault prevention conference,' while Lt. Col. Krusinski was reprimanded 'for drunkenly fondling a woman in a bar against her will.' Neither faced any punishment beyond a reprimand."

218. *Morse v. Biehl and Agar*, Brief in support of petition for extraordinary writ in the nature of a writ of prohibition, US Army Court of Criminal Appeals. http://www.caaflog.com/wp-content/uploads/LTC-Morse-v.LTC-Biehl-and-COL-Agarl-brief.pdf.

219. Robert Draper, “The Military’s Rough Justice on Sexual Assault” *New York Times*, November 26, 2014 https://www.nytimes.com/2014/11/30/magazine/the-militarys-rough-justice-on-sexual-assault.html.

220. Nancy Montgomery, “Emails Show General Warned against Reversing Wilkerson Verdict” *Stars and Stripes*, August 29, 2013 https://www.stripes.com/news/emails-show-general-warned-against-reversing-wilkerson-verdict-1.238114.

221. UCMJ Article 60; Rogowski, “Quis Custodiet Ipsos”: 1156–57.

222. Draper, The Military’s Rough Justice.”

223. Ibid.: “Christensen says he received his annual performance review and found that he was downgraded for the first time. His superiors informed him that he would soon be assigned to be a judge on the appellate court. The appellate court was widely understood to be the Air Force’s dumping ground for JAG misfits.” [33].

224. Broussard, “Restoring Balance”: 10; Whitlock, “Sordid Details.”

225. Broussard, “Restoring Balance.”

226. See Draper, “The Military’s Rough Justice”; Taylor, “Senate Rejects Bill.”

227. Embrey, “Task Force Report on Care for Victims.”

228. Bruce Fleming, “Mishandling Sexual Assault, and Other Military Problems” *Society* 52 no. 6 (2015): 521, 523. “Other recent cases of visible Navy malfeasance in the fleet, at far less than the four-star level, include topless (and bottomless) pool parties put on by a Navy Captain in Bahrain, numerous skippers relieved for improper sexual relations with subordinates or drunkenness, the commanding officer of Fort Jackson, the Army’s largest training base, was suspended in May 2013 because allegations of sexual misconduct.” http:// www.military.com/daily-news/2013/05/22/fort-jackson-coaccused-of-adultery-suspended.html?ESRC=eb.nl.

229. Whitlock, “Sordid Details”; Draper, “The Military’s Rough Justice.”

230. Jackie Speier, “Military Rape Speech 26” https://www.youtube.com/watch?v=SJhNpjA1ZrE.

231. Mark F. Light, “The Navy’s Moral Compass. Commanding Officers and Personal Misconduct” *Naval War College Review* 65 no. 3 (2012): 136.

232. Matthew Burris, “Thinking Slow about Sexual Assault in the Military” *Buffalo Journal of Gender, Law & Social Policy* 23 (2014–2015): 21.

233. David A. Schlueter, “The Military Justice Conundrum: Justice or Discipline?” *Military Law Review* 215 (2013): 4.

234. Fleming, “Mishandling Sexual Assault”: 525.

235. Lewis Carroll, *Alice’s Adventures in Wonderland: Through the Looking Glass and What Alice Found There* (Philadelphia: H. Altemus, 1895).

Chapter Three

Survivors, Perpetrators, and the Institutional Responses

SURVIVORS AND PERPETRATORS

By now you will have a clear picture, having read the cases in the previous chapter, of the extent of the problem. You may have also deduced that band-aid measures do not address the problem. This leaves civilian control of the military and the military institution weakened and in moral decline. The matters described raise questions around why it should be this way and what can be done about it. First it is useful to remember some of the consequences and then to look at the nature of the responses by the institutions, not only the military but the courts along with the legislature and the executive.

Consequences include whether other potential survivors will be encouraged to report, and whether perpetrators are encouraged or discouraged by the message they are sent. Whether a discipline process can ever be achieved in a separate society that seeks exceptionality, but is still very publicly accountable and in the public spotlight, is an essential question. What do discipline failures do to the institution and its reputation, and to those who may have thought of joining? Often not taken into account is the cost to the military of losing high-level decorated and acclaimed senior military personnel with many years of experience, both survivors and perpetrators, who mostly retire as a result of these matters. In addition, there is the cost to the taxpaying public of training such persons, only to have their service lost. Where is the equality of a system of rule of law in which members of a coterie can choose to resign, or get administrative punishments that avoid jail terms for criminal offences, when in the civilian criminal system perpetrators have no such option? Citizens can ask how that is reasonable. Further, if the perpetrator is allowed to retire and they happen to be a serial offender released without genuine punishment, or even being placed on a sex offender's register, how does that show any regard for the citizenry the military is supposed to protect? Finally, is there a genuine understanding of the wrong done? It is often said of perpetrators that they are amazing soldiers who would give their life for their country and they are often highly decorated, but if they do not understand the importance of their actions then how can the coterie culture ever change?

General Sinclair's lawyer said in referring to his retirement he is a ". . . highly decorated war hero who made great sacrifices for his country, and it's right that he be permitted to retire honorably."[1] Being a great warrior may make one feel untouchable, particularly when not subjected to the same law as everyone else in a democracy. Sinclair, allegedly having admitted to making derogatory comments about women demonstrates this by his response when staff challenged him he said: "I'm a general, I'll say whatever the [expletive] I want."[2] This signifies feeling above the law in his protected separate coterie. What these leaders miss is that when morality and ethical codes are breached, it is a short step to greater dishonesty. If this lack of respect can be shown to internal team members then how can citizens rely on their military leaders to uphold the Geneva Conventions and the laws of war when dealing with the enemy or civilians in a conflict zone? Clearly, there can be no such certainty. Sexual and other abuses of power therefore go to the heart of discipline and fundamentally undermine the very laws of war that have made war still an acceptable method of resolving conflicts.

Examples of this ethical absence were plentiful in the recent conflicts in both Iraq and Afghanistan. A brave soldier, Justin Watt, brought the rape of a young girl and her murder, together with her entire family's murders, in the Mumudiyah killings to light. His own father cautioned him against speaking out and he suffered death threats rather than praise for his trouble. The stories of sexual abuse of prisoners at Abu Ghraib, and of those removing body parts from deceased combatants in Afghanistan, happened in an atmosphere of perceived privilege. Being cloaked by a cone of protection enabled a feeling of impunity to develop. Only those with a genuine moral compass and extreme bravery have been able to stand up against this.[3]

Survivors regularly report that the initial assault is one thing but the subsequent handling by the institution, if the matter is reported, is often significantly more damaging, "It's a terrible feeling when someone does this to you and gets away with it, and then you report it and the system punishes you. It's almost worse than the actual act, that the system failed you."[4] Involuntarily discharge is the outcome from reporting in up to 90 percent of the cases.[5] Too many survivors suffer depression, Post Traumatic Stress Disorder (PTSD), or suicidal ideation when they feel there is no further recourse to address their suffering.[6] Lieutenant Helmer found herself investigated and leaving the military when she complained of sexual assault. The alleged perpetrator on the other hand was removed from his command but suffered no other punishment or charges and remained in his job.[7]

The few perpetrators that are punished have also seen unhappy outcomes, such as Sergeant Walker, who continued to claim he never raped anyone and all sexual encounters were consensual. Walker died by suicide having allegedly never accepted that he had received a fair and just trial.[8] The rates of death by suicide in the military profession can tell their own story and this is addressed further in the Australian context.[9] However, not only is there the tragic loss of young lives but the lasting impact on the family and the community, a factor which can never be fully understood as regards long-term consequences.[10] Despite this, an acceptance or normalization seems to have descended, and even civilian courts seem unable to understand that ". . . a right to be free from sexual assault lies in a lack of understanding of the harm resulting from such events."[11]

Retired Air Force Technical Sergeant Jennifer Norris, giving evidence before the House Armed Services Committee in 2013, noted that perpetrators often went unpunished, and they received full benefits when they eventually were honorably discharged.[12] It is claimed that sexual assault perpetrators and rapists ". . . have an estimated 86.5 percent chance of keeping [their] crime a secret and a 92 percent chance of avoiding a court-martial."[13] Twenty years after her assaults and rape, Brenda Hoster spoke of her experience at the hands of her superior, Sergeant Major Gene McKinney, in 1996. Hoster reported that superiors told her to sort out her concerns with McKinney herself.[14] She felt that nothing had changed, with Congress just churning the debate repeatedly. For Hoster, additional frustration left her wondering why she went through the torment by speaking out at all.

It takes a few brave souls telling their stories openly to portray directly the nature and depth of the issues compounded by the initial wrong act. The following testimony delivered to a congressional hearing indicates the degree of the problems:

> At a point during the investigation, I was forced to provide proof by confronting my rapist to try to get a confession. I was asked to make repeated recorded phone calls and then go to his home while wearing a body wire. I asked him to tell me what happened. I got a full confession. My perpetrator was arrested and charged with several counts, including sexual assault and sodomy. The trial lasted a week. Even with overwhelming evidence, the court [martial] found him guilty of lesser charges. The court decided he would receive a bad conduct discharge, no jail time, and they took his 23 years of service as kudos. He was ordered to NCIS headquarters for fingerprinting, where they determined he had gnawed the skin from his fingertips on both hands so he could not be fingerprinted. He refused to

> register on the sex offenders database by simply saying, ''No, I don't have to.'' Nothing was done, and to this day, I don't know where my perpetrator is. Not knowing his location leaves me looking over my shoulder for the rest of my life. I was not afforded the same rights as rape victims in the civilian world. Where are my choices?[15]

This epitomizes the very reason that the military have to be brought under the one mainstream civilian criminal system. The coterie otherwise becomes an organization infiltrated by perpetrators, holding their own criminal tendencies with impunity. The Australian Royal Commission cited research findings supporting reluctance to report and institutional stasis where hierarchical power differences make motivation to change difficult. These well-established practices can foster abuse in such institutions.[16]

The climb up the hierarchy of the military attracts a competitive need to prove one's strength, often perceived through masculine ideals. This means doing better and more of everything, including sexual conquests, drinking more, and having one or more adulterous affairs, in the misguided belief it might mean you are also a better killer on the battlefield.[17]

While legislation has adjusted the law, for example by preventing the convening officer from overturning panel verdicts, criminalizing revenge against complainants, removing the statute of limitations on sex crimes, and making dishonorable discharge mandatory for those convicted of a sex crime,[18] the reporting of sexual assault remains within the chain of command. Encouragement to report is therefore still minimal. As Hoster argues, years after her experience how could one have confidence that speaking out makes any difference. Yet most survivors claim a key motivation in speaking out is so that no one else ever has to go through what they have experienced.[19] Unfortunately, Hoster's experience is more the norm than the exception, as most do not report. Of those who do report, a significant percentage appear encouraged to drop the complaint. In the Aberdeen scandal they had not been taken seriously or worse, incurred the ire of their supervisor, and no further action resulted. Twenty-seven percent at that time said the perpetrator was counselled or transferred to a new location, and one in five woman believed their work performance review suffered due to their complaints.[20] SAPRO in its 2018 report stated: "the reports received last year in FY16 represented only about a third of the estimated 14,900 Service members who indicated experiencing a sexual assault during the same time period. Consequently, reporting rates are a poor estimate for how often sexual assault occurs."[21]

The US Brooker Naval Health Research Center has recorded Marines with PTSD as "11 times more likely to receive a misconduct discharge" than a marine who had not deployed and was not diagnosed with PTSD.[22] The result is a fundamental difference in access to health care and compensation for disabilities for the individual who is honorably discharged, as opposed to one receiving a dishonorable misconduct discharge.[23] The Australian Joint Standing Committee on Foreign Affairs, Defence and Trade's (Joint Committee) Report 2013 on the *Care of ADF Personnel Wounded and Injured on Operations* noted significant differences in treatment and access to support for those discharged with a condition recognized by the Department of Veteran's Affairs, and those who develop a condition post discharge.[24]

Overall, it is impossible to even begin to consider the costs and consequences not only of abuse but of the double impact when the institutional response also creates harm. Many say this doubling up of the breach of trust has as much impact as the initial assault. On the other side the perpetrators, if treated lightly, continue to offend and never have the opportunity to reflect on, and reform, their behavior. If charged and convicted, they go through a system that differs from the experience of citizens in the primary society. Sometimes they are ejected into the primary society without thought for the protections that society needs. The question stands–what has the military institution done to address these issues?

INSTITUTIONAL ACTIONS AND RESPONSE

The institutional response now seems to follow a fairly well-developed pattern. It starts with internal inquiries, often with unsatisfactory conclusions, or a denial of any systemic problems, instead blaming it on a few bad apples who are not worthy of being in the military. If more than the initial complainant come forward, then usually a higher level or even independent government or external inquiry may occur. Recommendations are made, some of which are accepted and then implemented through many changes to many layers of rules, directives, and policy advisories, often over many years. These then have to be checked via an external oversight mechanism such as Congress, the Senate or legislature to see that changes are being observed.[25] Usually sometime during this change phase, another scandal breaks with another complainant or complainants coming forward and the costly, lengthy cycle is commenced all over again. In Australia, there may be a Senate inquiry. In the US, the Senate Armed Services Committee and the House Committee on Armed Services may report on the issue if it is in their remit. These are committees often replete with ex-military, who are now congressional representatives and senators. Some senators actively advocated against changes to the Don't Ask Don't Tell policy and transgender changes.[26] Using veterans and retired military figures to people reviews, task forces, and panels means that a narrowed, often antiquated, worldview is the only lens provided for the problem. The perspective remains internal to the coterie. Instead, it requires fresh eyes and new approaches, often ones that only civilians can bring. Lurie has argued that the introduction of the UCMJ in 1950, overturning a long outdated system, occurred principally because the UCMJ drafting committee was comprised mostly of civilians. This "was recognition that the military had been unable to impose on itself the type of military justice reforms sought by the external legal order."[27]

One of the key arguments supporting internal military inquiries is that they enable lessons to be learned quickly so that the problem can be prevented and the organization can be highly efficient. This argument is entirely broken by the observance of practice in which lessons never seem to be learned, nothing happens quickly, and problems continue, as identified in the many examples described in this work. The enormous amount of taxpayers' money spent on the many inquiries seems to be passed over. Each of the yearly survey reports costs a substantial amount. Just one example is the 2014 RAND Report, which was estimated to cost the DoD approximately $920,000, made up of $755,000 in expenses and $165,000 in DoD labor.[28]

The DoD was slow to respond in an encompassing manner to the early complaints. However, there have been actions taken, seemingly enough to dissipate criticism in most instances. It took the Iraq conflict in 2004, before then Secretary of Defense, Donald Rumsfeld, established SAPRO.[29] However, this body has had a role limited to accounting through surveys and reporting, along with developing support programs for survivors of abuse, and delivery of training for members on desirable behavior, with the aim of keeping leaders to a high standard of conduct and therefore leadership. Like many of the changes made with the best intensions, they have brought their own issues. Concerns have arisen about the close connections between those members, mostly officers, involved in training or who attended training in the area of sexual assault, and their involvement as court-martial panel members.[30] A secret coterie disciplining its own raises concerns around unlawful command interference, panel bias, and an inability for members to receive impartial due process when dealing with criminal behaviors.[31]

Change appears to be largely reactionary. The most significant three changes to the UCMJ have arisen out of complaints by military personnel. The first change came after the Vietnam War experience and was driven by a desire to reduce command influence in the discipline process back then. As a result, the *Military Justice Act* 1968 was passed, enabling the JAG to allocate military lawyers to general courts-martial.[32] Until 1969 "law officers," presided over courts-martial but were under the convening authority's command.

The second change saw the passing of the *Military Justice Act* 1983, which enabled appeals to the Supreme Court by *certiorari*, with leave from the United States CAAF.[33] The act did not bring courts-martial into alignment with an article III court status,[34] but did change the processes for selection of counsel and judges. No significant change has resulted from these amendments, given the small number of matters that get to the Supreme Court and their scarce success when they do, which is no doubt due to the Supreme Court's deference to CAAF as a specialist military body. It is important to note that the military operates a very different system of review, with the primary level of review conducted by the Courts of Criminal Appeals (CCA) for each separate service area.[35] Established in response to outcries about the discipline system after WWII, these bodies received extraordinary powers of review in an effort to even out any perceptions of "rough justice" or lack of due process available in the civilian system, and to ensure some consistency in terms of punishments.[36] Other than overturning a verdict or increasing a sentence, the CCA may weigh evidence, ascertain credibility of witnesses (without the benefit of seeing and hearing their evidence), determine issues of fact and law in approving, or not, findings of guilt by the court-martial process, and assessing the appropriateness of the sentence.[37] However, it would seem that the evidence has not supported the rationale for their establishment in regards to sentencing. A five-year study of around 4,000 CCA determinations across the services, by Weber,[38] reports that UCMJ article 66 (c)

> was most frequently used to reassess a sentence when a legal error affected a finding of guilt (203 of the approximate 4000 cases), with remedies for excessive post-trial delay being granted less frequently (57/4000), and with disapproval of portions of a sentence deemed inappropriately severe occurring very infrequently (23/4000). In only two cases were sentences reassessed after being compared to closely related offenses (uniformity justification).[39]

The lack of uniformity in sentencing risks offending the equality principle in the rule of law and ultimately the civilian and military members' support for the discipline system. The costs involved in sustaining this level of review would be obviated by simply bringing the military under the one civilian justice system. Military accused are given a choice as to who will determine their sentence. This can range from a hearing and a sentence by a member panel, or judge alone, or a guilty plea before a judge and sentencing by panel members, or a plea and sentence heard by a judge alone.[40] There are no mandatory minimum sentences[41] and mixing criminal sentencing and workplace discipline leaves the military a wider array of discretion in "punishments" such as rank reduction and discharge. Since 2017, provision is made for government appeals against a sentence on the vague basis that it violates the law or is "plainly unreasonable."[42] This option is not available in Australia.[43] Congress chose this path, rather than the suggestion by the Military Justice Review Group regarding the adoption of sentencing guidelines.[44] It does not reflect equality with the civilian population as the range is far broader, allowing a choice of options for discipline and potentially ones that are likely to give the most lenient sentence. Another difference from the civilian system is the military practice of joining all charges in one court-martial hearing and providing one unitary sentence.[45]

A third adjustment, due to complaints by survivors of sexual and other abuse in the military, resulted in the most encompassing investigation of the UCMJ in over 30 years.[46] The Military Justice Review Group, established in 2013 by then Chair of the Joint Chiefs of Staff, General Martin Dempsey, ultimately led to the *Military Justice Act* 2016.[47] The tranche of changes were aimed at encouraging the reporting of sexual offences, addressing victim support, discouraging retaliation, and dealing with offenders by dismissal or dishonorable discharge at a minimum.[48] Adjustments also included to the pre-trial procedures to ensure, where possible, that proceedings be conducted by an impartial Judge Advocate.[49] The changes saw the military discipline system becoming an ever-closer replication of the civilian system. This begs the question of why there should be two systems operating side by side at huge expense to the taxpayer, especially if one is not working to produce the outcomes that are claimed as justification for its existence.

Other changes have included reform of the definition of rape in the UCMJ in 2006[50] in an attempt to reflect changes in society and to respond to the various scandals. The new article 120 covered 14 different sex-related offences, from indecent exposure to forcible rape. Up until then, the military courts-martial and appeal courts had to try to breathe some updated meaning into article 120.[51] Recognition of increasing sexual autonomy saw the military appellate court give its seal of approval to an affirmative consent standard.[52] The court preferred accepting that rape was a sexual assault lacking consent, preferably affirmative consent, and that force only be considered when addressing the level of seriousness attached to the offence, rather than having to find evidence of force to establish the commission of the offence.[53] Unfortunately, the 2006 amendments in article 120 (t)(16) caused their own issues, with a shift in the burden of proof to the accused on the issue of consent, and then back to the government to prove beyond reasonable doubt that the defense did not operate. The aim was to shift the focus to the accused and away from the victim. This change placed an unconstitutional burden on the accused and led to calls, as early as 2009, by the Task Force on Sexual Assault in the Military to go back to the drawing board for a rewrite. The task force had a further 83 recommendations for improvement in 2009, including addressing the lack of review and evaluation of SAPRO work.

In June 2012, the *National Defense Authorization Act* again authorized amendments to article 120. The essential changes simplified the requirements, made the offences gender neutral, separated child sexual offences into two new articles (120(b) and 120(c)), and addressed the constitutional issues on burden of proof. Unfortunately, the changes bought their own further issues. Retrospective issues meant there were now three versions of article 120 (pre 2007, post 2007, and post 2012) applicable depending on the time of the alleged offence. The lack of a statute of limitations on sex crimes makes the law complicated for those applying and enforcing it. Consent is now merely a possible defense in relation to any of the elements regarding force.[54]

This unfortunately showed a lack of understanding and engagement with the civilian expertise concerning the crime of rape. As Knies discusses, the issue is not about violence or force. Sexual offending is about the loss of personal sexual autonomy and bodily integrity, and this can arise without clear violence but through abuse of power, rank, and position, as a form of constructive force, particularly in such a rigid hierarchical closed institution.[55] MacKinnon argues persuasively that the approach to rape from a focus on consent is misplaced. Instead, it should be about equality in personal interactions, given the element of power and control attached to such crimes:

> Intrinsic to consent is the actor and the acted-upon, with no guarantee of any kind of equality between them, whether of circumstance or condition or interaction, or typically even any interest in inquiring into whether such equality is present or meaningful, at least in the major definition of the most serious crime. Put another way, the concept is inherently an unequal one, simultaneously silently presupposing that the parties to it are equals whether they are or not.[56]

Female politicians, such as Senators Gillibrand, Spier, Tsongas, McCaskill, and Boxer, have instigated many attempted changes.[57] This has been an epic battle, resisted by the Pentagon and the Joint Chiefs of Staff. Overall, their efforts have included attempts to remove prosecution authority from the military to an independent body.[58] This has been strenuously resisted and remains unachieved to date. Gillibrand noted that her proposed *Military Justice Improvement Act* was only ever a small "step in the right direction" in trying to bolster faith in a broken system.[59] It was not without division on the side of those seeking change, with Gillibrand's proposal not receiving the support of McCaskill and others. McCaskill's alternative proposal saw better results with the passing of the *National Defense Authorization Act* for Fiscal Year 2014.[60] McCaskill believed the reforms she was able to get through the Senate with a 97-0 vote of overwhelming support would achieve a ". . . laundry list of things that are going to protect victims, that are going to bring perpetrators to justice, that are going to hold commanders accountable."[61] That laundry list aimed to move the protection from the accused towards the survivor by limiting the role of convening authorities and providing greater protections for survivors of sexual assaults. It included changes, such as those responding to the Franklin incident, by limiting the article 60 ability of commanders to overturn a court-martial outcome, and changing the article 32 pre-trial hearing to align it more with a civilian grand jury preliminary hearing rather than its prior investigative role. The latter was a response to the extreme questioning that occurred in a navy football article 32 hearing in 2013.[62]

The Department of Defense Judicial Proceedings Panel has produced a series of reports around sexual assault since its inception in 2014.[63] In its final report, and in handing over the baton to its successor the Defense Advisory Committee on Investigation, Prosecution, and Defense of Sexual Assault in the Armed Forces (DAC-IPAD), it explicitly reemphasized certain recommendations. These included:

> . . . continuing to analyze adult-victim sexual assault court-martial data on an annual basis . . . and . . . consider analyzing the following patterns that the JPP discovered in its analysis of fiscal year 2015 court-martial data:
>
> a. Cases involving military victims tend to have fewer punitive outcomes than cases involving civilian victims; and
> b. The conviction and acquittal rates for sexual assault offenses vary significantly among the military Services; and
> . . . continue the review of the new Article 32 preliminary hearing process.[64]

The Defense Advisory Committee on Women in the Services (DACOWITS) in 2013 had made a recommendation for removal of the chain of command from prosecution to defense legal experts.[65] As addressed in chapter 1, argument 3, taking away the commanders' ultimate say over those they command, is considered a threat to the military hierarchical power and is claimed to dissipate order and discipline. While the Pentagon did make a slight adjustment, by requiring decisions to charge perpetrators in relation to sexual offences be made by more senior commanders, the sustaining of the chain of command remained. US Defense Secretary Leon Panetta released a memo restricting authority in such cases to prevent those lower in rank than colonel or Navy Captain from referring matters to prosecution.[66]

Argument 3 was regularly made in objection to Senator Gillibrand's proposal to remove sexual assault offences from the chain of command, namely that changing the reporting process would undermine commanders' authority and therefore their ability to achieve discipline in the ranks. This argument is blind to the obvious reality that the commander's ability to keep discipline has already been devastated by the sexual harassment and abuse scandals. Deciding to court-martial a unit member, or not, is likely to make other members take sides and at least one side will resent the commander's decision and undermine control. That commanders alternatively referring criminal offending to the civilian authorities for prosecution can maintain obedience is never addressed when relying on argument 3.

Relying on commanders to instill discipline, when they may themselves be abusing power or behaving badly, has many downsides. Commanders have the power over those under them in order to put the functional imperative of the organization, fighting wars, always at the forefront. This has been taken to mean being able to ignore someone's criminal conduct if their skills, or just their mere presence, is believed to be required to maintain the fighting capacity of the unit. Such consideration ignores the destruction to the vital ingredient "trust" when members of a unit abuse and assault each other, when the pressures within the group work to induce harassment and bullying of someone who is seen to complain, to be different, or to be other. Ignoring criminal conduct could not be more damaging to the functional fighting capacity of a unit and yet commanders can be tempted to use their power to suppress these matters in order to avoid the spotlight. Having commanders make such decisions over those under them is problematic from many viewpoints, not least because they are also subject to others overseeing their work reviews and promotion. After all, if assaults are occurring under their command perhaps their leadership is questionable, and certainly, they risk tarnishing their own record. Losing large pensions and retirement entitlements remains a threat to their decision-making and conduct.

Commanders as judges of whether conduct warrants punishment, and the degree of punishment, really just present a costly facade of justice. It would be simpler to acknowledge it for what it is and let the commander mete out direct punishment. Currently, an overwhelming majority of criminal matters are dealt with through administrative punishments under cover of privacy laws, a small few get to a court-martial, and an even smaller number result in a finding of guilt and genuine punishment.[67]

Regrettably, the almost continual litany of incidents fails to instill confidence; rather, an organization lacking transparency and punishing its own, or not, as the case may be, leaves a broken system. Far from discipline, control and behavior better than the civilian standards, which the justifications have relied upon for the existence of a separate system, the opposite seems to occur. The message from the cases is that senior people, who carry the responsibility for upholding the law within the separate coterie, may be offenders themselves. This system stands outside the mainstream, creates its own internal rules, and then decides whether it follows them. There seems to be some general disjunction between the real significance of sexually motivated, or abuse of power, offending and that of other offences, such as those perceived to relate directly to war fighting. However, the reality is that these offences go to the heart of war fighting, as they demonstrate loss of discipline, moral weakness, and lack of candor. The justification for adultery remaining an offence in the US military can feasibly be found in this reasoning. If one wants another sexual partner, then doing it legitimately and getting a divorce first is the moral and legal approach. It is about honesty, morality, not bending rules, not opening oneself to blackmail, espionage, or other threats, nor providing poor or non-existent leadership.[68] If this occurs within one's own special coterie and team, it is likely that much worse has the potential to occur in conflict when dealing with enemy combatants and other civilian populations. What assurance exists that what the military does in the citizen's name is honorable and upholds the Geneva Conventions?

While bad human behavior concerning sexual offending can never be eradicated entirely, what can be achieved is a change in the institutional response and in the broader society's methods of dealing with it. In these cases, lessons really can be learned and implemented to avoid mistakes being repeated. The civilian tolerance of the abandonment of the separate military coterie by the US Supreme Court comes at a cost that eventually demands an answer.

THE US COURTS INFLUENCE

The US Supreme Court appears to have abandoned military personnel because of judgments by then Chief Justice Rehnquist, an ex-military person that enabled the military to become a true coterie. Operating as a separate society, the civil courts largely refuse to touch military matters because of the uniqueness of discipline within the military allegedly creating a special situation that advises against judicial intrusion.[69] The wrong turn taken by Rehnquist CJ has derailed the civil-military relationship, and failure to redress this dislocates the military enterprise and jeopardizes the democratic civilian system of control.[70]

It is argued that when one joins the armed forces, one is dedicating one's life to a cause beyond considerations of the personal. The life of a soldier in combat bears no resemblance to that of a civilian. This notion appears to have been taken to the extreme in the US courts' adoption and application of the *Feres* doctrine followed by US legislation protecting certain organizations' employees from suit.[71] The doctrine is underpinned by the courts' reliance on the importance of protecting military command and discipline. In *Feres v. United States,*[72] the Supreme Court held that members of the military could not sue the United States for negligent torts arising out of, or incident to, their military service on the basis that, irrespective of whether the suit alleges negligence or an intentional tort, it would be disruptive of military discipline. The court in *Everett v. United States*, when applying *Feres*, specifically emphasized the "need to protect military discipline" as arising from the "peculiar and special relationship" between the soldier and her superiors.[73] This reverence by courts for the "special" needs of the military has been utilized by the courts to remove democratic demands for the control of the military by civilian authority.

Many after *Feres* have asked why military personnel should be treated differently; they are still a citizen of the state but with added obligations. They are still subject to the civilian justice system and should be able to access it in appropriate situations. That they have an added responsibility does not preclude the military organization from dealing with individuals after they have been in the civilian courts. This is not through re-trial or refusal to allow any civil damage claims, but in the standard fashion that, if you get a criminal conviction or civil judgment for a tortious wrong, you can be removed from practicing, be disciplined, or not be promoted. If you are injured through a co-worker's negligence you can expect better, including being able to exercise your rights through the civilian tort law. Situations of war fighting can be demarcated, and there are no grounds to establish courts are incapable of distinguishing the demarcation line.

Just as the UCMJ has had to have an upgrade since 1950, so should the *Feres* decision from the same year. The *Federal Tort Claims Act* 1946, (FTCA) provides citizens with a moral code of reasonable expectations about their conduct where it causes damage to another. To define sexual assault as service-related is an appalling statement that admits failure. It actually normalizes the behavior as something the civilian courts, through overly deferent attitudes, are prepared to turn a blind eye. Trust by the courts in the legislator and, in turn, the military institution to look after itself based on loyalty to the institution obviates the duty of the court to uphold law and ensure individual rights are protected. Uncannily, the consequence is, as Banner notes in *Day v. Massachusetts National Guard*,[74] that claims arising from hazing are likely to be precluded by *Feres* purely because such practices "are no strangers to military life."[75]

Courts are established to provide justice for citizens and determine disputes, so citizens do not turn to self-help such as the rapist naming and shaming websites. They are an integral part of the structure of democratic government, and to deny a segment of the tax paying public their due because of special military entitlement claims is to deny the impact the court's attitude has on the functional capacity of the military. It is quite contrary to the deferential claim that courts cannot interfere in military matters because they have no knowledge of such things. Courts in other parts of the world are able to step in and find a more balanced approach. This contrasts with decisions in comparative countries, for instance the UK, where courts have a greater readiness to reach into the domain of the political and hold the executive accountable, particularly where individual rights are an issue.[76]

The view of the military as a separate coterie is found not only in *Feres v. United States*[77] but in other decisions by the Supreme Court in which CJ Rehnquist played a significant role. *Rostker v. Goldberger;*[78] *Chappell v. Wallace;*[79] *United States v. Stanley,*[80] and *Goldman v. Weinberger,*[81] are just some of a series of decisions in which the Supreme Court has withdrawn, even when constitutional rights and protections are raised. In *Chappell,* a *Bivens*-style claim was made, but failed. *Bivens v. Six Unknown Named Agents*[82] was a case concerning Federal Narcotics agents entering Biven's home without legal search and seizure warrants. This was held to be in breach of Biven's Fourth Amendment rights, enabling a claim for damages by Bivens. *Chappell* concerned a claim against navy officers for discriminatory actions but it failed on the basis that a damages claim could not be bought against a superior officer. Chief Justice Burger relied on Arguments 1, 2, and 3 outlined in chapter 1 as the usual justifications in stating:

> [t]he special status of the military has required, the Constitution has contemplated, Congress has created, and this Court has long recognized two systems of justice, to some extent parallel: one for civilians and one for military personnel. The special nature of military life—the need for unhesitating and decisive action by military officers and equally disciplined responses by enlisted personnel—would be undermined by a judicially created remedy exposing officers to personal liability at the hands of those they are charged to command.[83]

Stanley is a high-water mark of the court's neglect of the military society. In this case, the court enabled the military to administer LSD non-consensually as part of an experiment for which Stanley was a human guinea pig.[84] Claiming that review of a decision by the military to use personnel in this way would call into question "military discipline and decision-making [and would] require judicial inquiry into, and hence intrusion upon, military matters"[85] is nothing but abandonment of the court's duty. The use of the phrase "incident to service" as a test leaves open nearly every activity, including crime that involves sexual elements and experiments on humans. One can be forgiven perhaps in wondering what has happened to the United States, a nation that took such care in addressing the WWII military experiments on citizens by another nation.[86]

Rehnquist's CJ influence in this area has extended to enabling the development of other coteries such as university colleges, where sexual assaults have also become problematic in these insulated establishments. Rehnquist J in *Board of Curators of the University of Missouri v. Horowitz* set up a precedent, enabling others to follow, when stating, "[c]ourts are particularly ill-equipped to evaluate academic performance."[87] This standard excuse, that the courts have no competence to make decisions on academic matters and that universities can be trusted to do this better, enables decision making by such institutions beyond the Article III courts. Notwithstanding the *Disclosure of Campus Security Policy and Crime Statistics Act (Clery Act)*[88] mandating the reporting by colleges and universities of crimes occurring on campus to the US government, university hierarchies ensure complex systems protect the institution's reputation in a *la bella figura* manner that leaves survivors often without proper outcomes.[89]

Courts leave the executive and legislature without guidance or a judicial check, instead relying on these arms, and ultimately the people through the political process, to provide the only constraint. The rule of law is applicable to all with the executive being no exception. If the courts adopt a deferential approach in questions of national or military interest, or university education, they create exceptional coteries. It risks fragmenting the primary society's dominant legal system.

In *Kori Cioca and others and Courtney Hurd v. Rumsfeld and Gates,*[90] court action was taken by survivors of sexual assaults arguing a *Bivens* claim, seeking damages against the highest civilian authorities, such as former Secretary of Defense Robert Gates and Donald Rumsfeld. Although the court in this case admitted the allegations were "egregious,"[91] it felt it was excluded from making a decision. Despite *Bivens*[92] citing a cornerstone constitutional case of *Marbury v. Madison*[93] that "[t]he very essence of civil liberty certainly consists in the right of every individual to claim the protection of the laws, whenever he receives an injury,"[94] *Bivens* set the standard. If anything, subsequent case law has been more severely limiting. Only twice in 40 years has the Supreme Court allowed a new application of the remedy[95] and never in a matter involving the military.[96] This flies in the face of civilian control of the military, in which the judiciary is one of the three arms of the system that aids in maintaining that control by supporting the other two arms, rather than abrogating its role.

The argument the courts rely on for abstention requires interpreting the constitutional wording to mean that it "delegates authority over military affairs to Congress and to the President as Commander in Chief . . . [and] contemplates no comparable role for the judiciary."[97] This relies on the separation of powers erroneously because it only talks of these branches acting within power when making laws for the Congress and rules for the president. It does not mean there is no role for the court to observe its function of adjudicating on the limits of the law and rule making. The Constitution does not contemplate the judiciary vacating its duty to adjudicate and to provide remedies in matters in which Congress is given the power to make laws, for instance in Article 1 section 8 about matters such as borrowing money, weights and measures, or postal services, so why the exception for the military?

The position prevails despite the statement by the Supreme Court that "[t]here is no 'military exception' to the Constitution."[98] The court must acknowledge its duty, as arbiter interpreting the Constitution that it chooses the degree of deference it will apply in any particular case. The Fifth Circuit noted there are limits to deference, providing an example such that "[it] could not stay its hand if, for example, it [were] shown that only blacks were assigned to combat positions while whites were given safe jobs in the sanctuary of rear echelons."[99] It is hard to predict a logic in this, as such an example would still require questioning of commander's decisions. Yet this is the main basis that the courts have avoided finding liability by the military and its leaders for failure to implement work practices to protect or prevent retaliation and further suffering by members who have been victims of assault and sexual abuses. The staunch claim that to do so would be a judicial intrusion too far into the military domain, because it requires questioning management decisions regarding matters of control, supervision, and discipline of military members, fails to address the role of the court. As the third organ of government, participating in assisting the other two arms, the legislature and executive, and working in a fully functioning democratic structure of governance, the court has a duty to ensure rights are upheld and all citizens receive an equality of treatment under a rule of law and under the Constitution.

Congress, the president, and military commanders are under the Constitution, not outside of it, and the court is the determiner of whether that is happening.[100] The courts have boxed themselves into a narrow and circular argument that the military is untouchable because the military domain is beyond the court's reach and expertise. Both sides use the separation of powers in support of their position. The courts rely on *Stanley*[101] to justify a separation of powers based on the power claimed to be given by the Constitution to the political arm, such as Congress, for passing legislation on "Army, Navy, and militia."[102] However, such a view does not address the reality that the Supreme Court is the body to have taken such an interpretation and that over time, if good justification exists, the court is not bound by its past and can interpret the Constitution in a manner that allows it to be a living, breathing document. That is, the claim by the survivors who argue the court's role is to support the political arms of governance and "[i]f the judiciary refuses to adjudicate any claims alleging that the military ignored Congressional mandates, the military enjoys the very type of power not subject to checks and balances that the drafters of the Constitution feared."[103]

In *Klay, et al., v. Panetta*[104] the court found support for its position of extreme deference given the amount of congressional involvement in legislating on the issues surrounding sexual abuse in the military. This approach is blind to the role of the court in assisting correct enforcement of the legislation through its interpretation and application. Congress does not apply and enforce the law, which is the role of the courts. *Klay* saw twelve navy and marine members seeking redress for breach of constitutional rights, not from their attackers but from military leadership, for their failures such as enabling offenders through providing "moral waivers" to facilitate persons with prior criminal convictions into the military coterie, and permitting interference by commanders into investigations into sexual assaults. The rights they allege were breached included "Fifth Amendment rights to bodily integrity, due process, and equal protection; a First Amendment right to speak about their assaults without retaliation; and a Seventh Amendment right to have juries try their assailants."[105]

The survivors in *Klay* argued that leaders had not observed the law by avoiding carrying out legislative demands such as creating a centralized database for reporting sexual assaults.[106] Circulatory arises in the form of the Supreme Court asking Congress to legislate to direct the courts to intervene, rather than the Supreme Court fulfilling its already clear and existing duty to interpret the law and the Constitution in a way that recognizes legality. This means not allowing an institution such as the military to have free reign in how it treats its members, who also happen to be primary citizens under the US Constitution. Why would it be inappropriate to consider whether congressional intention is upheld by adjudicating on matters such as whether a non-judicial punishment is more appropriate than discipline for commission of what, under the general law, would be a criminal offence? If the Supreme Court feels it cannot do this, purely because it is the military, then it is time the criminal law was honored by being enforced through the civilian criminal system.

It was odd that the Court of Appeals in *Klay* found it an improper judicial inquiry to determine whether a matter fell within the civilian rather than the military domain, given that historically, courts and articles of war have supported the dominance of the civilian courts given the civil-military control principle.[107] A system that permits the highest court to let pass "brutal and criminal assaults, compounded by a degrading and humiliating institutional response,"[108] as described by the District Court, due to the matter arising "out of or . . . in the course of activity incident to [military] service,"[109] is a failed system. This behavior opens a slippery slope for the militarization of the civilian domain, as other institutions attempt to make similar arguments for exceptional treatment. Beyond the scope of this work is a widening literature on police behavior where police feel above the law and the courts have restricted the ability for citizens to bring actions for damages in tort.[110]

Lawyers have sought a number of ways to try to get the courts to be brave enough to revise their position. In *Saum v. Widnall*,[111] an attempt was made to argue for equitable relief through a declaratory judgment that constitutional rights were contravened.[112] Unfortunately, pursuing restitution was considered a step too far.[113] No doubt, creative lawyers will continue to try to seek justice for survivors in anticipation that the statement in *Chappell* held some meaning: "[it] has never held, nor do we now hold, that military personnel are barred from all redress in civilian courts for constitutional wrongs suffered in the course of military service."[114]

In the meantime, we see the confusion that abounds in the case law after the Rehnquist Supreme Court's judgments that wound back the foundations of the civil-military relationship, and the understanding that civil courts are to be used, if open and operating, at all times in preference to courts-martial. In *Cioca v. Rumsfeld*,[115] the two most senior civilian figures supervising military matters, Gates and Rumsfeld, were sued by 28 plaintiffs on the basis that they held ultimate responsibility for control of the military, and they had failed to ensure the culture of abuse and retaliation had been addressed.[116] The case was dismissed on appeal. The court found that rape is "incidental to" or essentially an occupational hazard of military service.[117] The court claimed the "incident to service test" was one it could apply readily as it needs less inquiry.[118]

It certainly attracts minimal inquiry as almost all conduct can be considered incident to service. The court claimed that a test, requiring some genuine investigation, may lead to interference with military decision-making or discipline and this, by its very nature, would give rise to the outrageous possibility of the court reaching an erroneous decision. This spurious argument could apply to anything that Congress has power to legislate on. It surely does not mean the purpose and role of the court is not to also participate as intended by the people in the constitutional pact. The court approved a claim that *Bivens* suits never apply in military matters, even when the Constitution is violated, because the inquiry itself would disrupt the military.[119] Applying the "incident to service" test ". . . it is clear that the allegations raised . . . are either incident to, or arise out of, their service in the military."[120] *Cioca* failed because it was said the claim against the military leaders for failure to manage the sexual abuse would lead to further damage by intruding into the military management, which is a matter for Congress as the legislator and not for the courts:

> Rather, our decision reflects the judicial deference to Congress and the Executive Branch in matters of military oversight required by the Constitution and our fidelity to the Supreme Court's consistent refusal to create new implied causes of action in this context.[121]

The claims made in *Cioca* were unsuccessful but they clearly delineated the areas of major concern, including:

> The opportunity for command to choose to charge offenders with adultery rather than rape or other sexual offending;
> Having military, not civilian authorities, investigate and prosecute sex crimes;
> Allowing convicted sex offenders an honorable discharge with full retirement benefits;
> Failure to stop command retaliation against those reporting; and
> Failure to address domestic violence offending more seriously.[122]

Not to be deterred, further action that relies on injunctive relief to prevent military discipline procedures that violate constitutional rights of due process, a fair trial and freedom of speech are likely. Civil liability for failure to prevent harm, due to intentional, negligent, or reckless conduct, operates to ensure institutions observe acceptable standards of conduct. This exists independently of the criminal law and is designed to ensure survivors are compensated for wrongs done in a restorative manner, and injunctive relief, available in tort law, can address institutional failures. Such actions often rely on class lawsuits. However, a general constraint on such suits is that they further limit the rights of individuals to seek redress, particularly when they are in a closed system such as the military coterie.[123] Bringing administrative law actions to test whether a decision maker has fulfilled their lawful obligations or not should not be above the law for someone in a publicly funded role, particularly if outside of combat action.

Taking a look at just a few of the decisions of the CAAF shows the divergent paths developing when the highest military appeals court feels it is not bound by the precedent of the highest civilian court. In the process, the civil control of the military becomes a redundant principle. CAAF has noted it is dealing with a growing number of child pornography cases.[124] In the civilian realm, these are prosecuted under the *Child Pornography Prevention Act* of 1996 (CPPA). This act was interpreted by the US Supreme Court to require that the providence inquiry establish that the images of children were real and not "virtual" or computer-generated images.[125] CAAF was able to avoid this requirement and confirm convictions in child pornography cases, using misconduct prejudicial to good order and discipline or service discrediting, rather than the CPPA.[126]

The centralization of power in a system in which Congress and the executive are given to believe they have ultimate freedom presents a significant threat to individuals, giving the executive a dominance not dissimilar to ancient royalty. All actions, including those of the president as the executive and the commander in chief of the military, wearing two hats, must operate within the constraints of the Constitution. Unconstrained freedom to act, because it concerns the military interest, needs to be amenable to be judged under the law in a democracy. This is done via the highest court, the US Supreme Court, as the guardian of the Constitution. The court denies its role when it adopts notions of the separations of power that ignore the changed conditions in which the institutions of government operate. This includes the two-party political system, and in the US, with "democracy" exercised precariously when voting is non-compulsory, and occurs only every two years for midterm congressional members and four years for president and congressional membership.

The arbitrary consequences of the Supreme Court's approach to the military find expression in the tragic case of the "Mahmudiyah Killings," involving the gruesome murder of the family of 14-year-old Abeer Qassim al-Janabi, and then her rape and murder on March 12, 2006.[127] The ensuing case, *United States v. Green*[128] indicates the offences were committed in a combat zone by US military personnel, including an immediate supervisor of Green's. An Iraqi war veteran, Green was nevertheless a civilian at the time the truth emerged, as he was discharged in May 2006. Therefore, he was prosecuted as a civilian, being one of the first to be indicted and convicted under the *MEJA*.[129] Green's four co-offenders, still attached to the military, went through the military discipline system. The one criminal episode in this case highlights the inconsistency of the different processes, rights, and punishments when the military continues to be treated as a separate society. Green received the more harsh punishment of a life sentence from a civilian court.[130] His military conspirators received punishment that was far more lenient because the Convening Authority capped the three offenders' sentences, making them eligible for parole, for two of them after 10 years, and for the other after 20 years.[131] Having the two systems provides accused with the ability to contest jurisdiction, as did Green, in order to try to receive the most favorable outcome. Not unsurprisingly he claimed he should have been subject to military discipline, as there was nothing to distinguish him from the other offenders in the one episode of offending.

Suggesting the equal protection required by the rule of law, he interestingly argued they should all have been addressed in the military system rather than in the civil.[132] Unfortunately for Green, the equal protection argument stands stronger when argued in the reverse, as it should cover all US citizens, not enable a special coterie to receive different, and in this case lighter, treatment. It is curious indeed that the military claims to maintain a separate system in order to enforce stricter obedience and control, yet the civilian system delivered the harsher punishment. Assertions of impunity for military personnel find support when soldiers receive treatment that is more lenient. It also explains why some soldiers are unlikely to want to abandon the discipline system even though it has uncertain constitutional protections.

The court's role, particularly as regards the human rights and freedoms and protections of the individual, is to ensure the elected arms of government do not have unlimited power to capriciously control the lives of their citizens, which includes military personnel. The constitutional reading adopted by the Supreme Court encourages the other two arms of government to feel free to make any law for "military necessity," irrespective of rights and freedoms. Despite seeming reluctance by some judges to *Feres* ("when a court is forced to apply the *Feres* doctrine, it frequently does so with a degree of regret"),[133] an opportunity to rectify the situation was passed over in *Ortiz v. United States.*[134] This case was settled without court resolution yet again avoiding the *Feres* unfairness. *Ortiz* involved a military agent's medical negligence resulting in damages to the child of a military member during the birthing process.[135] While compensation may be available, avoiding a court's public ruling on the matter leaves malpractice in military hospitals to endure, while being subsidized by the primary society carrying the burden of the cost of those injured by the negligent conduct.

Human rights are something the US can proudly claim to be early supporters of, with the Bill of Rights Amendment to the Constitution in 1791 and the Eleanor Roosevelt–led Universal Declaration of Human Rights (UDHR) 1948. It was not until after the atrocities of WWII that human rights became a focus at the international level. The development of instruments in the international legal order sees countries undertaking to limit their sovereignty to the extent necessary to protect the rights of all individuals, including minorities. The relationship between the individual and the state moves away from the political to the legal, where the political will of the majority has to operate in harmony and respect the rights of the individual under a rule of law that operates in the domestic constitutional and international domain.[136] However, despite the early adoption of human rights, resistance has been strong in recent years with the executive in the US going to extraordinary lengths to avoid the application of the *Rome Statute* and the International Criminal Courts (ICC) operation in relation to its citizens, in particular its military.[137]

The general isolationism of US courts, in particular the Supreme Court, is ubiquitous. Michael Ignatieff has stated, "American judges are exceptionally resistant to using foreign human rights precedents to guide them in their domestic opinions [perhaps] anchored in a broad popular sentiment that the land of Jefferson and Lincoln has nothing to learn about rights from any other country."[138] Fidell also has noted that while impressive changes are happening in other countries, in the US military, "[i]t is an unfortunate but undeniable fact that historically, American military justice jurisprudence has shown little interest in foreign military justice developments. The bar and the bench can share responsibility for arguments not made, or, if made, disregarded."[139]

In Australia, the situation is different in relation to civil tortious claims. *Groves v. The Commonwealth*[140] settled an action in negligence against the Commonwealth, demonstrating it is possible for a military member under the common law to recover damages caused by the negligence of another member while on duty in peacetime.[141] This has found recent support in *FJ v. Commonwealth of Australia*[142] when the Victorian Court of Appeal confirmed the *Military Rehabilitation and Compensation Act* 2004 (MRCA) s 388 does not bar civil damages arising out of pregnancy and childbirth.[143] However, in the criminal domain the Australian High Court adopts the deferent position of the US Supreme Court.

The court's deference to the military needs greater constitutional contextualization than relying purely on reference to historical tradition and practice, given the evolutionary changes that have occurred since the historical cases relied on were decided. The general refusal by the Supreme Court to acknowledge and uphold the rights of the individual when they are employed by the military, and the resistance by the US to the application of international human rights instruments to its soldiers, mean that many are suspicious of the degree to which its military operates under, and within, the rule of law.[144]

RESISTANCE TO CHANGE

Command responsibility no longer functions in the way intended and no other area than sexual assaults has demonstrated this more clearly.[145] Many have noted the military institution's tactics for avoiding change and deflecting external criticism.[146] Major changes to military discipline were demanded after the civilian experience of being involved in the military during WWII. Roan described the situation in the US as follows:

> Many were concerned with the almost summary disposition of cases, the lack of rights afforded to an accused, and the perceived unlawful command control over the system. The system appeared arbitrary, with too few protections for the soldier and too much power for the commander. Rear Admiral Robert J. White described the ground swell of criticism against military justice: "The emotions

suppressed during the long, tense period of global warfare were released by peace, and erupted into a tornado-like explosion of violent feelings, abusive criticism of the military and aggressive pressures on Congress for fundamental reforms in the court-martial system."[147]

Survivors continue the common refrain over half a century later. Sullivan notes that the "Department of Defense controls the internal process of suggesting changes to military law, public participation in matters of military justice is rare. . . ."[148] The problem is that the band-aid piecemeal approach fails to address the fundamentals of the culture and the issues. The navy porn photo scandal surfaced, despite previous bids to address sexual harassment, because these fundamentals had not changed and so this particular form of exploitation was not closed off. Military personnel will continue to find ways to express their belief in a heterosexual male cultural entitlement and it will persist as long as it remains outside the mainstream civilian criminal and workplace discipline system.

An internal investigation as a standard response enables the military coterie to close its doors to further external gaze and provides a time lapse in which to gather resources for a response that fits its needs and removes some of the passion from the story. This was the experience when Brennan broke the story of the photo scandal in the *War Horse*. Despite his attempts to elicit comment from the Secretary of Defense and the Commandant of the Marines, both avoided comment due to the ongoing investigation.[149] The battlefront has become internal as the military tries to track down social media sites in what appears to be a failing attempt to curtail this activity. A year after the photo scandal arose, around 55 punitive actions were taken, but members seem to remain impervious to the lesson of acceptable behavior.[150] Resorting to the dark Web and other sites, the disrespect for their colleagues shows a broken system of trust and discipline that makes the justification for strong discipline, separate from the civilian criminal law, unsustainable.

Senators Speier and Gillibrand have been strong and constant voices in calling out the failure of the military to prevent abuses that it has known about but has failed to respond to in concerted ways. Senator Speier's expression of justifiable outrage reached a crescendo when one of the chief sexual assault investigation officers appointed was himself charged with sexual assault in the McKinney scenario.[151] McKinney, accused of sexual harassment after appointment to lead the commission, tasked to deal with it, and receiving only a demotion and reprimand for obstruction of justice, underlines the problem of eradicating this activity within a closed coterie.[152] Senator Speier identified the military leadership as big at beating its chest and saying all the right words, and Congress as culpable while the sexual assault numbers had increased by 30 percent, with 26,000 rapes and sexual assaults in the military and one-third of women serving in military reporting sexual harassment in 2013. All the money, training, and prevention attempts appear not to have stemmed the assaults. Senator Speier exhorted it is "time to roll up our sleeves and do something real . . . and to stop nibbling around the edges."[153] The ongoing claims of retaliation raise the question for survivors as to why they would report when they are not likely to get any justice but indeed, more persecution. The senator's suggested solution was to take reporting of sexual assault away from the chain of command but still keep it within the military by setting up an independent body staffed with experts in dealing with these crimes, much like Australia's Inspector General of the Australian Defence Force (IGADF).[154] Speier declared that military "justice" is "seen as a sham when zero tolerance evaporates and becomes zero accountability, making the military just look incompetent."[155]

Senator Gillibrand and McCaskill's legislation eventually saw some changes but the system of separate military discipline was largely left intact.[156] While the reforms in 2014 were extensive, such as providing for victims' advocates where they are a member, it left civilian survivors unaddressed and resulted in further amendments and adjustments subsequently.[157] Attempts to overcome retaliation by moving such claims higher up to the Inspector General have not eliminated the possibility of ostracism.[158] Removal of the five-year limitation on sexual offending was a positive move; however, as noted, the changes to article 32 hearings and other changes brought further complications.[159]

Spilman raises some of the issues, claiming that "[u]ltimately, Congress did not give military crime victims any new rights in the revised article 60(d)."[160] Of the 15 recommendations made by the Human Rights Watch Report in 2015, none suggested abandoning the current system, instead only adding extra band-aid measures.[161] The solution needs to go further than mere cosmetic fiddles.[162] Unfortunately, Senator Speier and others refer to the military system as a justice system. What they fail to grasp is that it is not a justice system but a workplace discipline system that has absorbed the ordinary criminal law and, under the cloak of privacy and operational command, excludes the operation of the civilian criminal justice system. The civilian criminal system is a state punishment of criminal law infringement in a public manner where justice can be seen to be carried out.

As Speier rightly asks: what is the point of requiring reporting if at the same time "'. . . we will keep it under the rug' by restricting or redacting the reports"?[163] To support the assertion, Speier referred to the court-martial of Wilkerson for sexual assault. Lieutenant Major General Craig Franklin, in reinstating Wilkerson to active duty, claimed he simply felt Wilkerson's character, as a good "family man," was of greater import than polygraph evidence of guilt, relied upon by the court-martial panel. Christensen, an experienced military prosecutor involved in prosecuting the Wilkerson matter, has described witnessing a "commander testify at sentencing that a non-commissioned officer who had just been convicted of sexually molesting his daughter, a 13-year-old with a developmental disability, was nonetheless of great value to the unit and should therefore be retained."[164] The good soldier defense was addressed somewhat by McCaskill's legislative amendment, but it does not really address the effect of this on a commander, nor on the panel service members when they make decisions as to what will happen.[165] When sentencing it is not just the past but also the future usefulness of a member that may be relevant, particularly if it is believed they can be rehabilitated. As Spak and McCart have written:

> The theory is simple: good soldiers do not commit crimes. Because service members receive periodic performance evaluations and often commendations and decorations for duty performance, adducing evidence of good military character is seldom difficult.[166]

Given most matters are not reported, or if they are the commanding officer decides if and how they will be dealt with, many matters, if they do get to this stage, only result in administrative punishment. The overturning of a guilty verdict in a court-martial when something actually reaches that stage means the "code is broken . . . and the military is damaging itself."[167] The Judicial Proceedings Panel analysis of 738 sexual assault cases resolved for the year 2015 found that

> the overall conviction rate for any offense did not vary significantly among the military Services. Notably, cases involving a military victim had a lower conviction rate than cases involving a civilian victim, and cases in which the victim was the spouse or intimate partner of the accused had a lower conviction rate than all other cases. Finally, penetrative offense cases were two and a half times more likely than contact offense cases to be dismissed before trial.[168]

Rustic argues that the statistics show that between 2011 and 2014 the conviction rate for sexual abuse offences rose to 127 percent from 55 percent of final dispositions.[169] While this is expected with the upturn in attention to these matters, he argues it may show an over-concern to be seen to be addressing the matter, at the cost of achieving real cultural change and appropriate reform of the discipline system.[170] This shifts the pendulum back to the alleged perpetrators' fair trial rights, as the swings and roundabouts continue.

The Judicial Proceedings Panel reported the difficulties when trying to compile statistics due to "lack of sufficient information."[171] Somewhat unbelievably, "the data required to meet the JPP's congressional tasks were not available or collected by any entity within the DoD, including the annual DoD SAPRO report. The JPP independently collected the needed information directly from case files maintained by the military Services,"[172] in an attempt to meet its tasks. Their recommendations for changes in the SAPRO data collection, as already noted, were resisted.[173]

Another reason for bringing the military discipline within one unified criminal justice system is to reduce the divergences in the law applicable to military and civilians under the separate systems, which only results in undermining both. An example of the difference is in funding for military defense counsel, who may not operate under independent budgets like a civilian defense counsel. In the US, there is a claimed imbalance in training, support, and funding for defense counsel as opposed to trial counsel.[174] The Pentagon's review after the repeal of the Don't Ask Don't Tell policy accepted that it would not damage military effectiveness as those opposed had claimed, although well over 50 percent of marines were against removal of the policy.[175] Military members and civilians can rightly feel the different treatment as an injustice, as they individually may argue that one system or the other is more or less in their favor. This undermines a central pillar of democracy that the rule of law ensures, namely that there is one equal law for all.

CONCLUSION

Substantive change is not forthcoming in the piecemeal approach dominated and controlled by military or ex-military figures. Rather, a radical overhaul that requires strong civilian input into the implementation of change that a majority of military personnel and the primary society can accept is needed to reclaim an otherwise militarized space. Change is unlikely to occur unless prompted by strong individual leadership. Whether this is presidential, legislative, or judicial, or, as is usually the case, coming from those most affected, the military survivors, where their treatment results in a public demand for change. Potential for this arises each time another scandal is reported.

Consideration of how this institution can be trusted to be in charge of defending a nation if it cannot address its internal offending remains. One can feel like a lone wolf howling on an empty mountainside, perhaps with some other strays joining the pack occasionally. Unfortunately, the state of civil-military relations in the US, and history itself, demonstrates that the chance of controlling the coterie and separating the internal discipline system to function as a normal workplace discipline code, where criminal conduct is dealt with in the civilian criminal system, is remote in the extreme. It will take much more than horrific abuse claims or miscarriages of justice, which have all occurred. It will take a massive groundswell of ordinary military members to bring a change of heart. This is unlikely to happen when many in power positions benefit from the system's protections. What is left? Courageous civilian leadership with insight and awareness and a Supreme Court, Congress, and Senate that back it up. This would be an extreme event if it were to occur.

The military machine rumbles on in a most powerful way. Veterans gain political power and ensure enough opposition to change to make it an unstoppable force, and one not within the bounds of the notion of the civil-military control paradigm. In the 114th Congress there were just over 100 veterans[176] and significant numbers, around 14 percent on average, of veteran state legislators with post-2001 veterans making up around 20 percent.[177] Just under half the members sitting on the Armed Services Committee are veterans. While this makes sense, as their experience is relevant to the matters in hand, it also raises the issue of confirmation bias in decision making in the military societies' interests. However, where there is a will there is a way and if there is a genuine desire to stop the abuse then a movement to address it in the way proposed here could be genuinely accepted and encouraged.[178]

The reality remains that a separate coterie provides minimal deterrents to perpetrators as they infiltrate a hierarchical system that enforces a very patchy discipline. This discipline, in large part, seems to rely on fear, uncertainty, and the personalized, and therefore arbitrary, exercise of individual power based on hierarchy in a secret coterie protected from external eyes. Survivors have little recourse to see punishment of the perpetrators, or to claim damages from the institution and superiors who have been negligent in their oversight. This is not how it is in the civilian system where claims for redress are open to survivors. Damages claims against negligent employers for harassment and other assaults in the workplace are a regular aspect of civilian justice and work as a legitimate and powerful deterrent of activity deemed unacceptable by civilian society.[179]

NOTES

1. Alan Blinder, "General in Sex Case to Retire with a 2-Rank Demotion Jeffrey Sinclair to Receive Benefits, but at Lower Level" *New York Times*, June 21, 2014: A15.

2. Craig Whitlock, "Disgraced Army General, Jeffrey A. Sinclair, Receives Fine, No Jail Time" *The Washington Post*, March 20, 2014 https://www.washingtonpost.com/world/national-security/disgraced-army-general-jeffrey-a-sinclair-receives-fine

-no-jail-time/2014/03/20/c555b650-b039-11e3-95e8-39bef8e9a48b_story.html?utm_term=.85e429089966.

3. Francine Banner, "Institutional Sexual Assault and the Rights/Trust Dilemma" *Cardozo Public Law, Policy and Ethics Journal* 13 (2014): 97, 138–39; Terry L. Price, "Explaining Ethical Failures of Leadership" *Leadership & Organization Development Journal* 21(4) (2000): 177.

4. Clara Bingham, "Code of Dishonor" *Vanity Fair,* December 2003 http://www.vanityfair.com/news/2003/12/airforce200312.

5. Sara Darehshori, "Booted. Lack of Recourse for Wrongfully Discharged US Military Rape Survivors" May 19, 2016 https://www.hrw.org/report/2016/05/19/booted/lack-recourse-wrongfully-discharged-us-military-rape-survivors; See further, *National Defense Authorization Act* for Fiscal Year 2013 (Pub. L. No. 112-239).

6. Kirsten E. Gillibrand et al., "The Relationships between Military Sexual Assault, Post-Traumatic Stress Disorder and Suicide, and on Department of Defense and Department of Veterans Affairs Medical Treatment and Management of Victims of Sexual Trauma" *One Hundred Thirteenth Congress Second Session,* February 26, 2014 http://www.fdsys.gov/; Thomas W. Britt et al., "Morale as a Moderator of the Combat Exposure-PTSD Symptom Relationship" *Journal of Traumatic Stress* 26 (2103): 94.

7. Hannah Brenner, Kathleen Darcy, and Sheryl Kubiak, "Sexual Violence as an Occupational Hazard and Condition of Confinement in the Closed Institutional Systems of the Military and Detention" *Pepperdine Law Review* 44 (2017): 881, 927; James Risen, "Attacked at 19 by an Air Force Trainer, and Speaking Out" *New York Times*, February 27, 2013 http://www.nytimes.com/2013/02/27/us/former-air-force-recruit-speaks-out-about-rape-by-her-sergeant-at-lackland.html 52.

8. Sig Christenson, "Ex-Lackland Instructor Dead in Apparent Suicide" *mySAnantonio.com*, September 2, 2014 https://www.mysanantonio.com/news/local/military/article/Ex-Lackland-instructor-dead-in-apparent-suicide-5728749.php.

9. Alex Gallacher et al., "The Constant Battle: Suicide by Veterans" (Foreign Affairs, Defence and Trade References Committee, August 2017) https://www.aph.gov.au/Parliamentary_Business/Committees/Senate/Foreign_Affairs_Defence_and_Trade/VeteranSuicide/Report.

10. See e.g., Julie Cerel, John R. Jordan, and Paul R. Duberstein, "The Impact of Suicide on the Family" *The Journal of Crisis Intervention and Suicide Prevention* 29 no. 1 (2008): 38.

11. Banner "Institutional Sexual Assault": 161–62.

12. Magalie Laguerre-Wilkinson and Phil Hirschkorn, "Pentagon Battling Military Rape 'Epidemic'" *CBS News*, January 28, 2013 http://www.cbsnews.com/news/pentagon-battling-military-rape-epidemic/.

13. Brenner, et al., "Sexual Violence": 927.

14. Zoë Carpenter, "20 Years Ago, an Army Veteran Reported a Sexual Assault. She's Still Waiting for Justice" *The Nation*, February 24, 2014 https://www.thenation.com/article/nearly-two-decades-after-speaking-veteran-waits-sexual-assault-reform/.

15. Gillibrand et al., "The Relationships between Military Sexual Assault": 62.

16. Peter McClellan, Robert Fitzgerald, and Helen Milroy, "Royal Commission into Institutional Responses to Child Sexual Abuse" December 15, 2017 https://www.childabuseroyalcommission.gov.au/final-report: 169.

17. See Zimmerman, *Tailspin*: 55 cited in Leslie J. Coletti, "In Search of a New Culture: The Sexual Violence against U.S. Military Women by Their Fellow Soldiers, 1978–Present." *Dietrich College of Humanities and Social Sciences Thesis* (2010): 1–62. http://repository.cmu.edu/cgi/viewcontent.cgi?article=1049&context=hsshonors: 33 ". . . fighter pilots at the top, cause those below to feel the need to prove themselves even more. They did this by partying harder, drinking more, and sleeping with more women."

18. See *National Defense Authorization Act* for Fiscal Year 2017 (Pub. L. No. 114-328) *National Defense Authorization Act* for the Fiscal Year 2014 (Pub. L. No.113-66).

19. Carpenter, "20 Years Ago."

20. Peter T. Kilborn, "Sex Abuse Cases Sting Pentagon, but the Problem Has Deep Roots" *New Yourk Times*, February 10, 1997 http://www.nytimes.com/1997/02/10/us/sex-abuse-cases-sting-pentagon-but-the-problem-has-deep-roots.html.

21. SAPRO, "Department of Defense Annual Report on Sexual Assault in the Military" (Department of Defense, 2018) http://sapr.mil/public/docs/reports/FY17_Annual/DoD_FY17_Annual_Report_on_Sexual_Assault_in_the_Military.pdf: 13.

22. John W. Brooker, "Improving Uniform Code of Military Justice Reform" *Military Law Review* 222 (2014): 1, 102.

23. Ibid., 103.

24. Australian Joint Standing Committee on Foreign Affairs, Defence and Trade's (Joint Committee) Report, 2013 on the *Care of ADF Personnel Wounded and Injured on Operations*: 96–97.

25. Bingham, "Code of Dishonor": ". . . by September, 61 academy women had told Colorado senator Wayne Allard's office they had been raped or assaulted, four top academy administrators had been replaced, dozens of rules and regulations had been changed, and the Pentagon had launched three investigations, which in turn were being closely scrutinized by Congress."

26. Banner, "Institutional Sexual Assault": 115.

27. Jonathan Lurie, *Military Justice in America. The U.S. Court of Appeals for the Armed Forces, 1775–1980* (University Press of Kansas, 1998): 97.

28. Jessica Wright et al., "Annual Report on Sexual Harassment and Violence at the Military Service Academies Academic Program Year 2013–2014'" (Sexual Assault Prevention and Response Office, February 2015): 1.

29. Stella Cernak, "Sexual Assault and Rape in the Military: The Invisible Victims of International Gender Crimes at the Front Lines" *Michigan Journal of Gender & Law* 22 (2015): 207, 228.

30. Greg Rustico, "Overcoming Overcorrection: Towards Holistic Military Sexual Assault Reform" *Virginia Law Review* 102 (2016): 2027, 2056 ". . . and civilian defense attorneys have pointed out that the same service members who are digesting countless hours of sexual assault awareness and response training on a regular basis are also serving as court-martial members in sexual assault cases. In fact, since

the vast majority of court-martial members are officers, many of these court-martial members have not only attended SAPR courses but also taught SAPR courses to their subordinates."

31. Rustico, "Overcoming Overcorrection"; Latisha Irwin, "Justice in Enlisted Administrative Separations" *Military Law Review* 225 (2017): 35.

32. UCMJ art 26(a) and 26 (c), requiring the use of military judges; Pub. L. No 90-632, 82 Stat. 1335 (1968).

33. UCMJ art 67a (a), (1988 & Supp. V 1993); Pub. L. No. 98-209, 97 Stat. 1393 (1983).

34. *Weiss v. US* (1994) 510 US 163, 179 (Rehnquist CJ); UCMJ art 60—convening authorities given wide discretion to modify sentences and findings.

35. Elizabeth Holtzman et al., "Statistical Data Regarding Military Adjudication of Sexual Assault Offenses for Fiscal Year 2015" (Judicial Proceedings Panel, Septemeber 15, 2017): 19–20, 45–46.

36. Dru Brennerbecka, "Assessing Guidelines and Disparity in Military Sentencing: Vive la Difference!" *Federal Sentencing Reporter* 27(2) (2014): 109–10; Steven M. Immel, "Development, Adoption, and Implementation of Military Sentencing Guidelines" *Miltary Law Review* 165 (2000): 159.

37. UCMJ art 66 (c).

38. Jeremy Stone Weber, "Sentence Appropriateness Relief in the Courts of Criminal Appeals" *Air Force Law Review* 66 (2010): 79.

39. Ibid., 100, 126.

40. Megan N. Schmid, "This Court-Martial Hereby (Arbitrarily) Sentences You: Problems with Court Member Sentencing in the Military and Proposed Solutions" *Air Force Law Review* 67 (2011): 245, 250; Bradford D. Bigler, "Rebalancing Military Sentencing: An Argument to Restore Utilitarian Principles within the Courtroom *Military Law Review*" 225 (2017): 1: "The fiscal year (FY) 2017 *National Defense Authorization Act* (NDAA) 2017 § 5182 includes a provision for all sentencing to be conducted by military judge alone, unless elected otherwise by an accused who has been tried before members."

41. Manual for Courts-Martial, United States app. A12 (2012).

42. *National Defense Authorization Act* for Fiscal Year 2017 (Pub. L. No. 114-328) § 5301.

43. JA Woodward, "Director of Military Prosecutions Annual Report for the Period 1 January to 31 December 2016" Department of Defence, Commonwealth of Australia, 2017 [126].

44. See Military Justice Review Group, A Bill, Department of Defense, 2016 http://www.dod.gov/dodgc/images/military-justice2016.pdf; Bigler "Rebalancing Military Sentencing": 6: "In addition to the appeal provisions included in the FY2017 NDAA, the Military Justice Review Group proposed an amendment to Article 56 that would have allowed for government appeal where the sentence reflected an improper application of a sentencing factor."; Andrew S Effron et al., "Report of the Military Justice Review Group. Part I UCMJ Recommendations" (December 22, 2015).

45. Brennerbecka, "Assessing Guidelines": 110: "Unlike federal courts where two or more charges may only be joined in one trial if they are related, customary military

practice has been to join all known charges, even if 'distinct, separate, and completely unrelated,' in a single trial. As the 'quid pro quo' for this expansive joinder practice, a military court-martial enters a gross or unitary sentence for all offenses of which the accused is convicted."

46. Effron et al., "Report of the Military."

47. *Military Justice Act* 2016 enacted in *National Defense Authorization Act* for Fiscal Year 2017 (Pub. L. No. 114-328); See further Effron et al., "Report of the Military."

48. *Military Justice Act* 2016 amending the UCMJ for example arts 6a, 32, 43, 46, 56, and 60.

49. *Military Justice Act* 2016 amending the UCMJ art 32(b).

50. *National Defense Authorization Act* for Fiscal Year 2006 (Pub. L. 109-163), UCMJ new art 120 taken from option 5 of the JSC report; Carson and Carson, "The Historical Roots."

51. Jack Nevin and Joshua R. Lorenz, "Neither a Model of Clarity nor a Model Statute: An Analysis of the History, Challenges, and Suggested Changes to the New Article 120" *Air Force Law Review* 67 (2011): 296.

52. Quil Lawrence, "When Civilians Accuse Troops of Rape, Military Courts Often Decide" *npr Newscast,* April 3, 2015 http://www.npr.org/2015/04/03/397267336/when-civilians-accuse-troops-of-rape-military-courts-often-decide; Stella Cernak, "Sexual Assault."

53. Danielle Rogowski, "Quis Custodiet Ipsos Custodies? The Current State of Sexual Assault Reform within the U.S. Military and the Need for the Use of a Formal Decision Making Process in Further Reform" *Seattle University Law Review* 38 (2015): 1139.

54. Ibid., 1163.

55. Jennifer S. Knies, "Two Steps Forward, One Step Back: Why the New UCMJ's Rape Law Missed the Mark" *The Army Lawyer (*August 2007): 1.

56. Catharine A. MacKinnon, "Rape Redefined" *Harvard Law & Policy Review* 10 (2016): 431.

57. See Robert Draper, "The Military's Rough Justice on Sexual Assault" *New York Times*, November 26, 2014 https://www.nytimes.com/2014/11/30/magazine/the-militarys-rough-justice-on-sexual-assault.html: "Military Justice Improvement Act . . . came within five votes of passage in the Senate in March"; Lisa Mascaro, "Senate Rejects Stronger Military Sexual Assault Bill" *Los Angeles Times,* March 6, 2014 http://articles.latimes.com/2014/mar/06/nation/la-na-military-sexual-assault-20140307.

58. "Military Sexual Assault Amendment Defeated in Defense Bill Markup" (2017) Part 2 *Clip of Fiscal Year 2018 Defense Authorization Markup* https://www.c-span.org/video/?c4675219/military-sexual-assault-amendment-defeated-defense-bill-markup: "The *Military Justice Improvement Act* (MJIA) attempted to remove the decision to prosecute criminal sexual assaults from the survivor's chain of command to independent military failed in 2014, 2015 and 2017." See also Kay Steiger, "This Lawsuit Could Change How the Military Handles Sexual Assault" *Think Progress.org*, April 2, 2015 https://thinkprogress.org/this-lawsuit-could-change-how-the-military-handles-sexual-assault-b6d70f7e200c/.

59. Draper, "The Military's Rough Justice": "Senator Gillibrand . . . acknowledged that removing prosecutorial authority from the chain of command 'isn't a silver bullet. . . . It's just a step in the right direction. It's the kind of tool you need to help people have faith in the system.'"

60. Holtzman et al., "Statistical Data": 41.

61. Darren Samuelsohn, "McCaskill's Sexual Assault Bill Passes" *Politico Pro*, October 3, 2014 http://www.politico.com/story/2014/03/claire-mccaskill-military-sexual-assault-bill-104499.

62. Annys Shin, "Judge Finds Midshipman Not Guilty in Naval Academy Sex Assault Case," *The Washington Post*, March 20, 2014 https://www.washingtonpost.com/local/judge-to-rule-in-naval-academy-sexual-assault-case-after-hearing-closing-arguments/2014/03/20/d9211394-b040-11e3-b8b3-44b1d1cd4c1f_story.html?utm_term=.812c59957df4; See also Marc Edward Rosenthal, "Where Is the Justice? The Sexual Assault Crisis Plaguing the Military and a Lack of Meaningful Justice" *University of Miami National Security & Armed Conflict Law Review* 41 (2013): 295.

63. See, Judicial Proceedings Panel http://jpp.whs.mil/.

64. Holtzman et al., "Statistical Data": 31–32.

65. Holly Hemphill et al., "Defence Advisory Committee on Women in the Services Report" May 17, 2013.

66. Zachary D Spilman, "Not Helping: How Congressional Tinkering Harms Victims during the Post-Trial Phase of a Court-Martial" *Columbia Law Review* 114 (2014): 70; Lorelei Laird, "Military Lawyers Confront Changes as Sexual Assault Becomes Big News" *ABA Journal*, September 1, 2013 http://www.abajournal.com/magazine/article/military_lawyers_confront_changes_as_sexual_assault_becomes_big_news/.

67. Mark E. Bojan, "Bad Paper: Reforming the Army Reprimand Process" *Military Law Review* 224 (2016): 1150; Brennerbecka, "Assessing Guidelines": 112:"Unitary sentencing affects the fundamental data upon which any statistical analysis of military sentencing depends. Additionally, the complexity of the multiple components of a military criminal sentence also makes sentence comparison with any statistical accuracy impossible."

68. See Dean C. Ludwig and Clinton O. Longenecker, "The Bathsheba Syndrome: The Ethical Failure of Successful Leaders" *Journal of Business Ethics* (1993): 265.

69. See *United States v. Stanley*, 483 U.S. 669 (1987).

70. See Pauline Collins, *Civil-Military "Legal" Relations: Where to from Here? The Civilian Courts and the Military in the United Kingdom, United States and Australia* (Leiden: Brill Nijhoff, 2018).

71. In 1965 the Department of Veterans Affairs, 79 Stat. 1156, 38 U. S. C. §4116 (1970 ed.), now codified at 38 U. S. C. §7316 (2006 ed.) and the *Medical Malpractice Immunity Act*, 90 Stat. 1985, 10 U. S. C. §1089, 1976 commonly known as the Gonzalez Act, conferred immunity on military medical personnel. Subsequently this legislation was followed by legislation covering medical practitioners more broadly in the *Federal Employees Liability Reform and Tort Compensation Act* (Liability Reform Act), 102 Stat. 4563, the Westfall Act; See *Levin v. U.S.*, 568 U.S. 2013; 11–1351 (2013); See further, Michael Rust, "Expansion of the Feres Doctrine" *Emory*

Law Journal 32 (1983): 237; David Saul Schwartz, "Making Intramilitary Tort Law More Civil: A Proposed Reform of the Feres Doctrine" *The Yale Law Journal* 95 no. 5 (1986): 992, 998; Ann-Marie Woods, "A More Searching Judicial Inquiry: The Justiciability of Intra-Military Sexual Assault Claims" *Boston College Law Review* 55 (2014): 1329.

72. 340 U.S. 135 (1950).

73. 492 F.Supp. 318, 325–26 (S.D. Ohio 1980).

74. 167 F.3d. 678, 685 (1st Cir. 1999).

75. Banner, "Institutional Sexual Assault": 135. See also *Lanus v. United States*, No. 12-862, S. Ct. (June 27, 2013) (order denying cert.).

76. See "Military Law—Justiciability—Eastern District of Virginia Dismisses Suit against Government for Military Sexual Assaults—Baldwin v. Department of Defense No. I:15-cv-oo424 (E.D. Va. Oct. 14, 2016)" *Harvard Law Review* 130 (2017): 2243; *R (Smith) v. Secretary of State for Defence and Another* 2009] EWCA Civ 441 (18 May 2009); *R (Smith) v. Secretary of State for Defence* [2010] UKSC 29; In Australia *Mabo v Queensland [No 2]* (1992) 175 CLR 1 and *A v. Hayden* (1984) 156 CLR 532.

77. 340 US 135 (1950); See, further, Barry Kellman, "Judicial Abdication of Military Tort Accountability: But Who Is to Guard the Guards Themselves?" *Duke Law Journal* (1989): 1597.

78. 453 US 57 (1981).

79. 462 US 296 (1983).

80. 483 US 669 (1987).

81. 475 US 503 (1986).

82. 403 US 388 (1971).

83. 462 US 296, 303–04 (1983) (Burger CJ) (internal citation omitted).

84. See Stephanie A Levin, "The Deference That Is Due: Rethinking the Jurisprudence of Judicial Deference to the Military" *Villanova Law Review* 35 (1990): 1009.

85. *Stanley*, 483 U.S. 682 (1987).

86. See e.g., Mary L. Dudziak, "Law, Power, and 'Rumors of War': Robert Jackson Confronts Law and Security after Nuremberg" *University of Southern California Legal Studies Working Paper Series* (2012) Paper 88.

87. *Board of Curators of the University of Missouri v. Horowitz* 435 U.S. 78, 90–92 (1978).

88. *US Code Title 20 Education* § 1092.

89. Banner, "Institutional Sexual Assault": 146.

90. 720 F.3d 505 (4th Cir, 2013). See also *Lebron v. Rumsfeld*, 670 F.3d 540 (4th Cir. 2012).

91. *Kori Cioca and others and Courtney Hurd v. Rumsfeld and Gates* 720 F.3d 505,508 (4th Cir, 2013).

92. 403 U.S. 388 (1971); 456 F.2d 1339 (2nd Cir. 1972).

93. 5 US (1 Cranch) 137, 163 (1803).

94. 403 US 388, 389 (1971).

95. *Davis v. Passman,* 442 U.S. 228 (1979), a congressional staffer could sue a congressman for alleged violations of the Due Process Clause of the Fifth Amendment; *Carlson v. Green*, 446 U.S. 14 (1980), a suit against federal prison officials

for an alleged violation of the Cruel and Unusual Punishments Clause of the Eighth Amendment.

96. *Stanley*, 483 U.S. 669, 682 (1987); *Chappell*, 462 US 296, 304–305 (1983).

97. *Orloff v. Willoughby*, 345 U.S. 83, 93 (1953) "Judges are not given the task of running the Army."

98. *Saum v. Widnall*, 912 F. Supp. 1384, 1392 (D. Colo. Jan 29, 1996) (Kane CJ) citing *Steffan v. Aspin* "[t]here is no 'military exception' to the Constitution." (8 F.3d 57 [D.C. Cir. 1993], 62 (Mikva CJ) (noting that when the Supreme Court has deferred to military judgment, it has been careful to do so only within the confines of ordinary constitutional analysis (citing *Rostker v. Goldberg,* 453 U.S. 57, 67, 101 S. Ct. 2646, 2653, 69 L. Ed. 2d 478 (1981)), *rev'd on other grounds en banc sub nom. Steffan v. Perry,* 41 F.3d 677 (D.C.Cir.1994).

99. *Minds v. Seaman*, 453 F.2d 197, 199 (5th Cir. 1971).

100. See e.g., Colleen Dalton, "The Sexual Assault Crisis in the United States Air Force Academy" *Cardozo Women's Law Journal* 1 (2005): 177.

101. *Stanley,* 483 U.S. 669, 682, (1987).

102. *US Constitution* Article 1; section 8, clauses 15 and 16.

103. *Klay, et al., v. Panetta* 758 F.3d 369 (2014). See also Edward Sherman, "Legal Inadequacies and Doctrinal Restraints in Controlling the Military" *Indiana Law Journal* 49 (1974): 539.

104. *Klay, et al., v. Panetta* 758 F.3d 369 (2014); *Klay v. Panetta,* 924 F.Supp.2d 8 (D.D.C.2013).

105. *Klay, et al., v. Panetta* 758 F.3d 369, 372 (2014); See *Klay v. Panetta,* 924 F.Supp.2d 8 (D.D.C.2013), 223–240.

106. *Klay, et al., v. Panetta* 758 F.3d 369, 372 (2014).

107. 758 F.3d 369, 375 (2014)—"Plaintiffs' suit invites a civilian court to adjudicate . . . whether . . . military (rather than civilian) authorities investigate and prosecute sexual assaults. This is precisely the kind of 'judicial inquiry into, and hence intrusion upon, military matters' that the Supreme Court disavowed in *Stanley.* 483 U.S. at 682, 107 (1987) S.Ct. 3054."

108. 758 F.3d 369, 372 (2014); *Klay v. Panetta,* 924 F.Supp.2d 8 (D.D.C.2013).

109. 758 F.3d 369, 372 (2014).

110. Craig B. Futterman, H. Melissa Mather, and Melanie Miles, "The Use of Statistical Evidence to Address Police Supervisory and Disciplinary Practices: The Chicago Police Department's Broken System" 1(2) *DePaul J. for Soc. Just.* (2008): 251.

111. 912 F. Supp. 1384 (D. Colo. 1996).

112. 912 F. Supp. 1384, 1394 (D. Colo. 1996).

113. 912 F. Supp. 1384, 1394–95 (D. Colo. 1996) "Where, as here, plaintiff seeks no prospective relief, the Declaratory Judgment Act is an inappropriate vehicle for asserting constitutional claims. . . . Based on the foregoing, Saum's constitutional claims are reviewable under the *Lindenau-Mindes* test only to the extent the equitable relief sought is in a form other than a monetary award."

114. 462 U.S. 296, 304 (1983).

115. *Cioca* 720 F.3d 505 (4th Cir. 2013); See also *Klay v. Panetta,* 758 F.3d 369 (D.C. Cir. 2014).

116. Jesse Ellison, "Judge Dismisses 'Epidemic' of Rape in Military Case" *The Daily Beast*, December 13, 2011 http://www.thedailybeast.com/judge-dismisses-epidemic-of-rape-in-military-case.

117. *Cioca* 720 F.3d 505, 512 (4th Cir. 2013).

118. 720 F.3d 505, 512 (4th Cir. 2013).

119. 720 F.3d 505, 512 (4th Cir. 2013) 621–22 "The law is now settled that Bivens suits are never permitted for constitutional violations arising from military service, no matter how severe the injury or how egregious the rights infringement."; Brenner, et al., "Sexual Violence."

120. *Cioca* 720 F.3d 505, 513 (4th Cir. 2013).

121. 720 F.3d 505, 518 (4th Cir. 2013); See also Elizabeth L. Reidy, "Gonzalez v. United States Air Force: Should Courts Consider Rape to Be Incident to Military Service?" *American University Journal of Gender, Social Policy and Law* 13 (2005): 635–68.

122. *Cioca* 720 F.3d 505, 513–514 (4th Cir. 2013).

123. Brenner, et al., "Sexual violence": 929–30.

124. H. F. "Sparky" Gierke, "The Use of Article III Case Law in Military Jurisprudence" *Army Lawyer* August (2005): 25, 32, 37.

125. *Ashcroft v. Free Speech Coalition* 535 U.S. 234 (2002).

126. *United States v. Mason* 60 M.J. 15 (2004); *United States v. Irvin*, 60 M.J. 23 (2004) discussed in Gierke, "The Use of Article III": 37.

127. See Jim Frederick, *Black Hearts: One Platoon's Descent into Madness in Iraq's Triangle of Death* (Harmony Books, 2010); *Redacted* (directed by Brian De Palma, Film Farm the HDNet Films, 2007) 1:30:00, fictional film influenced by Mahmudiyah.

128. *United States v. Green* US Court of Appeals Sixth Circuit Nos. 09-6108/6123.

129. 18 USC Sec 3261(b).

130. Brett Barrouquere, "Steven Green Spared Death Penalty for Iraqi Rape, Murders," *Huffington Post*, May 21, 2009 http://www.huffingtonpost.com/world/the-news/2009/05/21/.

131. Norbert Basil MacLean, "Separate and Unequal Military Justice" *Los Angeles Times*, September 10, 2008 http://www.latimes.com/opinion/la-oew-maclean10-2008sep10-story.html: All three received a dishonorable discharge and are housed in the Disciplinary Barracks at Fort Leavenworth, Kansas.

132. *Green* 654 F.3d 637, 649 (6th Cir. 2011), (Martin J) Court of Appeal found his discharge meant that at the relevant time, namely the laying of the charge, he was in a different position from his co-conspirators.

133. *Ortiz v. U.S. ex rel. Evans Army Cmty. Hosp.*, 786 F.3d 817, 822–23 (10th Cir. 2015); See *United States v. Stanley*, 483 U.S. 669 (1987) (Brennan, J., dissenting 704-06; O'Connor J, dissenting 709-10).

134. Brenner and Kubiak, "Sexual Violence as an Occupational Hazard": 950.

135. Patricia Kime, "Tragedy and Injustice: The Heartbreaking Truth about Military Medical Malpractice" (2016) *Military Times*, July 10, 2016 https://www.militarytimes.com/pay-benefits/military-benefits/health-care/2016/07/10/tragedy-and-injustice-the-heartbreaking-truth-about-military-medical-malpractice/.

136. See Samuel Brenner, 'I Am a Bit Sickened': Examining Archetypes Of Congressional War Crimes Oversight after My Lai and Abu Ghraib" *Military Law Review* 204 (2010): 1.

137. Butch Bracknell, "The U.S. and the International Criminal Court: An Unfinished Debate," *Los Angeles Times*, May 26, 2011; Contrast this with the UK ratification of the *Rome Statute* on October 4, 2001, and the domestic implementation in the *International Criminal Court Act* 2001 UK; Australia ratified the *Convention* on July 1, 2002, and implemented it domestically in the *International Criminal Court Act* 2002 (Cth).

138. Michael Ignatieff (ed), *American Exceptionalism and Human Rights* (Princeton University Press, 2005): 277.

139. Eugene Fidell, "A World-Wide Perspective on Change in Military Justice" *The Air Force Law Review* 48 (2000): 195, 197.

140. (1982) 150 CLR 113; 40 ALR 193.

141. [2007] HCA 29 (19 June 2007), (Gummow, Hayne and Crennan JJ), [38].

142. [2017] VSCA 84 The Commonwealth lodged an application to the High Court seeking special leave from the decision of the Court of Appeal on the basis that FJ's pregnancy and childbirth was a compensable injury under the MRCA, and therefore an action for common law damages does not lie against the Commonwealth as it is barred by section 388 of the MRCA. The High Court refused leave to appeal.

143. *White v. Director of Military Prosecutions* [2007] HCA 29 [38] (June 19, 2007) "the civil law of obligations does not cease to run merely because the obligations in question bind or confer rights upon a defence member."

144. See e.g., Thomas Wayde Pittman and Matthew Heaphy, "Does the United States Really Prosecute Its Service Members for War Crimes? Implications for Complementarity before the International Criminal Court" *Leiden Journal of International Law* 21 (2008): 165.

145. Lindsay Hoyle, "Command Responsibility—a Legal Obligation to Deter Sexual Violence in the Military" *Boston College International & Comparative Law Review* 37 (2014): 353; David A. Schlueter, "American Military Justice: Responding to the Siren Songs for Reform" *Air Force Law Review* 73 (2015): 193; Jessica A. Turchik and Susan M.Wilson, "Sexual Assault in the U.S. Military: A Review of the Literature and Recommendations for the Future" *Aggression and Violent Behavior* 15 no. 4 (2010): 267; Lindsy Nicole Alleman, "Who Is in Charge, and Who Should Be? The Disciplinary Role of the Commander in Military Justice Systems" *Duke Journal of Comparative & International Law* 16 (2006): 169; Shelbi Nicole Keehn, "Striking a Balance between Victim and Commanding Officer: Why Current Military Sexual Assault Reform Goes Too Far" *Columbia Journal of Law and Social Problems* 48 (2015): 461.

146. See e.g., Diane H. Mazur, "Rehnquist's Vietnam: Constitutional Separatism and the Stealth Advance of Martial Law" *Indiana Law Journal* 77 (2002): 701; Jacoba Brasch, *More Martial than Court: From Exceptionalism to Fair Trial Convergence in Australian Courts-martial* (PhD Thesis, University of New South Wales, 2011); Steven B. Lichtman, "The Justices and the Generals: A Critical Examination of the U.S. Supreme Court's Tradition of Deference to the Military, 1918–2004" *Maryland Law Review* 65 (2006): 907.

147. James B Roan and Cynthia Buxton, "The American Military Justice System in the New Millennium" *Air Force Law Review* 52 (2002): 185, 188.

148. Dwight H. Sullivan, "Country Reports" (Paper presented at the Continuity and Change in Militay Justice, London, December 12, 1998): 7–8.

149. Thomas James Brennan, "Hundreds of Marines Investigated for Sharing Photos of Naked Colleagues" *The War Horse,* March 4, 2017 https://www.revealnews.org/blog/hundreds-of-marines-investigated-for-sharing-photos-of-naked-colleagues/.

150. "More Nude Photos of Female Military Personnel Shared Online, 1 Year after Marines United Scandal" *RT News*, March 10, 2018; Jared Keller, "At Least 30 Marines Face Courts-Martial in 'Marines United' Investigation" *Task & Purpose*, May 1, 2017 https://taskandpurpose.com/marines-nude-photo-scandal-court-martial/.

151. See further, Hollywood, "Creating a True Army of One."

152. Coletti, "In Search of a New Culture": 41.

153. Jackie Speier, "Military Rape Speech 26" https://www.youtube.com/watch?v=5Zgzn-qVKLM&feature=youtu.be.

154. Jackie Speier, "Reps Speier, Braley and Meehan Introduce Bipartisan Bill to Prevent Military Commanders from Overturning Convictions" *Press Release*, March 12, 2013 https://speier.house.gov/media-center/press-releases/reps-speier-braley-and-meehan-introduce-bipartisan-bill-prevent-military Congressman Braley, said, "Sexual assault in the military is a persistent problem that hasn't gone away and the military has resisted making the changes necessary to eliminate it from the ranks. Victims of these terrible crimes deserve the same protection they would receive if they were civilians. There should be no sheltering of violent criminals just because they happen to be subject to military rules and regulations."

155. Speier, "Military Rape Speech 26."

156. Rustico, "Overcoming Overcorrection": 2029.

157. *National Defense Authorization Act* for Fiscal Year 2014, Pub. L. 113-66.

158. Rosenthal, "Where Is the Justice?": 340.

159. Spilman, "Not Helping"; Suzanne Simms, "Revision of Article 60 and the Military Convening Authority's Clemency Power: An Alternative to the Enacted Legislation" *National Security Law Journal* 2 no.2 (2014): 301.

160. Spilman, "Not Helping": 79.

161. Darehshori, "Booted."

162. See e.g., Hollywood, "Creating a True Army of One"; Michael I. Spak and Jonathan P. Tomes, "Sexual Harassment in the Military: Time for a Change of Forum" *Cleveland State Law Review* 47 (1999): 335.

163. Speier "Military Rape Speech 26."

164. Draper, "The Military's Rough Justice."

165. Brennerbecka, "Assessing Guidelines": 109.

166. Spak, "Sexual Harassment": 94 (Footnotes omitted)

167. Speier, "Military Rape Speech 26."

168. Holtzman et al., "Statistical Data": 39.

169. Rustico, "Overcoming Overcorrection": 2030–31.

170. Ibid.: 2031 "Well-intentioned policies can backfire when they fail to address deep, structural problems. Furthermore, any progress made towards ameliorating

sexual assault in the military will prove fleeting if the investigation, prosecution, and trial processes remain entirely within the discretion of commanders who are not well-positioned to manage this complex legal issue."

171. Holtzman et al., "Statistical Data": 4, 6.

172. Ibid., 6.

173. Ibid., 10.

174. Heidi L. Brady, "Justice Is No Longer Blind: How the Effort to Eradicate Sexual Assault in the Military Unbalanced the Military Justice System" *University of Illinois Law Review* (2016): 193, 230.

175. Jeh Charles Johnson and Carter F. Ham, "Report of the Comprehensive Review of the Issues Associated with a Repeal of 'Don't Ask, Don't Tell'" (Department of Defense, November 30, 2010): 4.

176. "Military Veterans in the Next Congress" *Los Angeles Times*, November 5, 2014 http://spreadsheets.latimes.com/military-veterans-in-the-next-congress/.

177. Rebecca Burgess, "Veterans in the 115th Congress" *AEIdeas*, November 18, 2016 http://www.aei.org/publication/veterans-in-the-115th-congress/.

178. Sig Christenson, "Changes Driven by Lackland Scandal Not Complete" *San Antonio Express News*, September 9, 2014 http://www.mysanantonio.com/news/local/military/article/GAO-Changes-after-Lackland-scandal-not-finished-5744288.php: "'Protect Our Defenders' founder Nancy Parrish predicted the military would continue to fight a losing battle against sexual assault in the ranks until an independent office oversees those cases."

179. Laguerre-Wilkinson and Hirschkarn, "Pentagon Battling."

Chapter Four

The Australian Military Experience—Discipline and Morality

BACKGROUND

Australia has experienced a sustained series of reviews and inquiries into the treatment of women in the defense, suicide of soldiers, and allegations of abuse, including sexual abuse.[1] These have all indicated a very long history of such behavior. The 2016 Defence Abuse Response Taskforce Final Report (DART)[2] spanned seven decades of all possible types of abuse, including individuals, groups, adult, children, women, and men, within the three arms of defense. Costing around $140 million, it presented a culture that has failed to learn from past mistakes. Risk factors identified included the operation of the chain of command, discouragement and lack of reporting, deficiency of consequences, and an environment fueled by drug and alcohol consumption. The then Minister for Defence, in 2013, observed that around 80 percent of those experiencing abuse did not report the abuse.[3] DART was instigated by an earlier review undertaken in 2011 and conducted by an independent Australian law firm, DLA Piper.[4] This review had been prompted by yet another event described as the "Australian Defence Force Academy Skype Sex Scandal," revealed due to the female survivor going to the media.[5] In addition, the Royal Commission into Institutional Responses to Child Sexual Abuse[6] heard submissions related to the Australian Defence Force, with some survivors giving public testimony for the first time regarding abuse they had experienced in some cases over sixty years earlier.

Not unlike the US, Australian military personnel's poor treatment for survivors takes the form of dishonorable discharge, career loss, and poor reintegration, or inappropriate counselling and support. The Director of Military Prosecutions (DMP) has reported a "general dissatisfaction by the Services at the current state of the military justice system."[7] The story is one of a military culture unable to address the problem of abuse and risking a lack of public respect. This chapter considers the findings of the DART taskforce, along with other related review recommendations, and some of the cases that have been reported. It concludes with observations suggesting a way to address this growing challenge for the military in a society that increasingly demands observance of individual human rights. Certainly, the *Defence Force Discipline Act*, 1982 (DFDA) outlines an understanding that an individual's rights are a paramount concern, but with a rider that such rights exist only insofar as they can operate alongside the demands of the act:

> s 3 (18) The provisions of this Act in so far as they protect the individual are in addition to, and not in derogation of, any rights and freedoms of the individual, whether under the law of the Commonwealth or of a State or Territory, and this Act is not intended to exclude or limit the operation of any law of the Commonwealth or of a State or Territory providing for those rights and freedoms in so far as it is capable of operating concurrently with this Act.

Dissatisfaction by those subjected to the military discipline process has been clearly expressed as a system that:

- is excessively tied up in process, too slow, and too hard to use;
- is too soft in terms of the punishments that can be imposed;
- fails to contribute to instilling a sense of personal accountability;
- fails to support proper discipline and the authority of rank;
- provides little disincentive to bad behavior with inadequate penalties and powers of punishment; and
- lacks transparency in that there should be public disclosure of disciplinary consequences.

An IGADF Military Justice Audit Survey of the navy found these feelings to be widespread and the following claims were reiterated:

- 30 percent believed that the complexity of the DFDA discourages people from laying charges;
- 46 percent believed that processes involved in investigating offences took too long;
- 44 percent believed that processes involved in trying offences took too long;
- 29 percent believed that adverse administrative action processes took too long; and
- 8 percent did not believe that the military justice system provided sufficient feedback to victims and complainants.[8]

That the DFDA prescribes no specific sexual offences, relying only on the subsumed civilian law under the DFDA s 61, may be a very good reason to consider its inadequacy in dealing with the full range of behaviors that should attract discipline in the form of criminal punishment. Due to Defense receiving continual and ongoing allegations of sexual abuse, the then Secretary of the Department of Defence established a plethora of inquiries and reviews, on April 11, 2011, to respond to the allegations and to determine an appropriate way to address the complaints and the more general issues raised. These reviews included the following, alongside the two (DLA Piper and DART) already mentioned:

- an inquiry, under Defence regulations, to be conducted by Mr. Andrew Kirkham QC, into the management of the "Skype incident of March 2011" (Kirkham inquiry);
- a review of the treatment of women at ADFA and the treatment of women in the ADF, and pathways for women into ADF leadership;
- a review into employment pathways for women in the Department of Defence;
- a review of the use of alcohol in the ADF;
- a review of social media and Defense;
- a review of personal conduct of ADF personnel; and
- a review of management of incidents and complaints in Defense.[9]

The Inspector General of the Australian Defence Force (IGADF), in the Review of the Management of Incidents and Complaints in Defence including Civil and Military Jurisdiction,[10] considered the interface between military discipline and civilian criminal justice reporting, which is characterized by a multiplicity of overlapping policy, and the need for a single complaint-handling agency.[11] In this regard, the Inspector General welcomed the Complaint Management, Tracking and Reporting System (COMTRACK) initiative, but noted a need to adequately resource the body.[12] The Defence Force Ombudsman, in submissions to the IGADF, noted that there was a lack of clarity for command in the operation of the civilian-military interface for certain complaints and he further raised the appropriateness of an administrative or discipline response. The Ombudsman also noted the absence of an appropriate hotline, not only for military persons but also for civilians wishing to report an incident involving a military member. Particularly concerning were perceptions of a conflict of interest and lack of impartiality by the IGADF.[13] The Ombudsman dismissed these perhaps too easily as a perception of bias. However, the perception is relevant, whether the bias is actual or not is another matter entirely. The IGADF also noted the overlay of complaints bodies.

Within the military, these include the Inspector General Defence own investigations; the Defence Whistleblower scheme with accompanying hotline;[14] the Australian Defence Force Investigative Service (ADFIS), which deals with disciplinary investigations; the Fairness and Resolution Branch, which aims to assist in resolving matters at the lowest level; and the Office of the IGADF, which oversees, by inquiry, the operation of the military discipline system.

The civilian system has its own bodies in the administrative complaints area. These include the Commonwealth Ombudsman, who also acts as Defence Ombudsman, and various State and Territory Ombudsmen; and specialist tribunals such as the Administrative Appeals Tribunal, Veterans Review Board, the Human Rights Commission Tribunal, the Australian Commission for Law Enforcement Integrity, the Inspector General of Security and Intelligence, the Office of the Australian Information Commissioner, and the Social Security Tribunal.[15] The Administrative Appeals Tribunal also reviews decisions where any Commonwealth legislation provides for such review.[16] Most concerning, in a second report by the IGADF, was the over-duplication of audit and risk, raising the complexity and cost in the military above the experience of civilian organizations. Such activity obfuscates, rather than increases, efficiency and effectiveness, the latter being one of the justifications by the military for maintaining independence in this area:

> The audit function of Audit and Fraud Control Division accounts for 45 staff with a personnel budget of less than $6 million and an operating budget of under $2 million, out of a total of at least 400 FTE audit and/or assurance positions across Defence costing more than $47 million per year. The total cost is much higher than would be expected when compared to other organizations of similar size. It reflects overlap and duplication.[17]

The ADF, like the US military, has a number of discipline options. Australia has both its administrative system and discipline system addressing criminal offending on three levels: courts-martial, Defence Force Magistrates, and summary authorities. Defence Force Magistrates are senior legal military officers, often reservists, providing an alternative to a court-martial and acting as a restricted form of court-martial. Summary Authorities are also appointed through the chain of command and operate across three levels, Subordinate Summary Authority (SSA), Commanding Officer (CO), and Superior Summary Authority, to provide limited lesser punishments. Discipline Officers,[18] who deal with DFDA minor breaches of service offences by non-commissioned rank and officer cadets, where there is no factual dispute and the member admits the misconduct, provide the lowest level of control. All levels are subject to some form of review. The model is primarily adversarial with even minor offences requiring proof beyond reasonable doubt, despite these matters being akin to workplace discipline, with the continuum between these and criminal offending not delineated.[19] This attracts a disincentive for use of discipline at the higher end of criminal offending.[20] The lowest level of control has proved popular, as it is seen as quick and efficient. There has been an increasing use of this informal process instead of the other discipline options. Fairness is somewhat questionable, as submission to this style of discipline requires acceptance of the offending, thus perhaps placing pressure on members to admit guilt they would otherwise deny. If an accused does not admit to offending, the matter has to go to a service-level tribunal.[21] The US likewise has a summary discipline system described as Non-judicial Punishment.[22] It avoids the consequences and the humiliation associated with a court-martial but has other impacts of significance for military members.

The outcome of the very extensive *Rethinking Systems of Inquiry, Investigation, Review and Audit in Defence* amounted to the then Chief of the Defence Force, General D.J. Hurley, acknowledging the need to address the recommendations in the report, but concluding that most of the outcomes could be achieved by implementing action within the existing structure in order to minimize disruption. This involved some guidance and policy reform and an attempt to make the IGADF more independent.[23]

Broderick concluded in her final report, after having been involved in extensive reviews of the military as the Sex Discrimination Commissioner in the Australian Human Rights Commission that while many changes in policy and reform of culture had been undertaken, ongoing oversight and vigilance would be required.[24] Australian military survivors expressed a lack of faith in the military ever being able to handle sexual and general abuse and discrimination complaints properly.[25] The Director of Military Prosecutions reported in 2016 on an

> . . . increase in the number of prosecutions for low-level sexual misconduct perpetrated by males on subordinate female members of the Defence Force. Such offences alleged sexual misconduct by male senior NCOs or officers . . . threatening failure if there was a refusal to engage in a sexual relationship . . . [with] Many of the incidents . . . committed in training establishments. It is apparent . . . that other incidents go unreported because the complainant does not believe that he or she will be believed and many just want to move on with their careers. . . .[26]

Perhaps the most significant aspect of the DLA Piper Review was that it resulted in the law firm receiving over 1,112 communications between April and October 2011 complaining of abusive treatment.[27] The overwhelming numbers led to the Minister for Defence establishing the DART process, which commenced in November 2012. Apologies came from the Minister of Defence to survivors of abuse and from the Chief of Defence Force to the public.[28] DART was initially meant to assist survivors of physical and sexual abuse, or workplace harassment and bullying that occurred prior to a cut-off date of April 11, 2011, and in particular the HMAS Leeuwin and Australian Defence Force Academy (ADFA) 24 matters. The latter related to survivor stories in 24 matters arising from ADFA. However, due to subsequent allegations and issues, DART had two extensions to the terms of reference. The first, in June 2015, and the second on November 11, 2015. DART's work concluded in 2016 with its final and twelfth report.[29] Over the life of DART, it received 2,439 complaints of which 1,751 reached a standard of plausibility considered to be within the terms of reference. This standard was used as it was less concerned with legal standards such as "beyond reasonable doubt," because the focus was on survivors, many of whom now suffered drug and alcohol abuse and mental health problems as an outcome of the abuse. The plausibility test looked to the reasonableness of the allegations on the available information, taking into account that the oldest complaint related to an incident occurring over sixty years prior.

The DART process was designed to redress past wrongs in the sense of hearing and respecting survivors, and enabling some of them to come forward and tell their story for the first time. A counselling and a reconciliation model, along with capped reparation payments were adopted. The reparation payments were not compensatory but rather an acknowledgment of wrongs that should not have occurred. The payments did not rely on confidentiality or exclude future legal action. They ranged from $5,000 to $50,000, and 1,723 payments totaling $66.63 million were made.[30] Approximately just over a third of the survivors took up the offer of counselling, which utilized a trauma-informed practice. Those undertaking counselling represented 68 percent males and 32 percent females. Overall, survivors were 73 percent males and 27 percent females.[31]

The restorative engagement approach of DART was possibly the most advanced used to date in dealing with trauma survivors. It involved training facilitators in a respectful survivor conferencing process handling high emotional content. For those participating in the mostly face-to-face conferencing, 352 senior Defence officers and 619 survivors, the experience was reported as delivering a surprising and often profoundly positive impact.[32] DART found the main concerns of the survivors were twofold: 1) to finally have acknowledgment from the institution, and where possible the abuser, that they had been wronged; and 2) to ensure others would never have to go through what they had experienced.[33]

Significant findings by DART included that many of the survivors were children (27 percent) when the abuse occurred, during their initial recruitment and training. Abuse was often perpetrated by more senior recruits or staff in positions of hierarchical authority, and "difference" ranging from age, religion, appearance, or illness tended to attract the abuse. The effects were often long lasting and the culture of defense was prohibitive of reporting.[34]

DART made eight recommendations. These focused around training those handling the survivors, and awareness raising to ensure proper management in dealing with, and advising, survivors.[35] Also important was acknowledging that it could take years before a survivor can talk about or even begin to consider reporting abuse.

DART recommendations 1, 2, and 7 contained some of the most telling concerns for the purposes of this work. First, there was a desire to ensure that those within Defence who are involved in the investigations, such as the officers employed by the IGADF and ADFIS, now under the overarching umbrella of the Joint Service Police Group,[36] observe and have training in civilian policing best practice—particularly when dealing with sexual assault and abuse.[37] Secondly, and most importantly, those civilian criminal offences involving acts of abuse, unless they are minor offences or offences occurring out of jurisdiction, ought to be investigated and prosecuted through the civilian justice system.[38] This recommendation reinforces the civil-military principle of civilian precedence over the military. However, it is a principle that has been gradually eroded as Defence has contained more and more of its activity within its institutional walls. Thirdly, a need to have some outside superintendence was identified to ensure changes in policy, training and other reforms actually occur. This role was recommended for the Defence Force Ombudsman who independently reports to Parliament. It is clear from DART that trust was broken for many Defence members and the institution.

The many reviews did result in the prosecution of two individuals involved in the ADF Skype incident. This prosecution took place through the normal civilian criminal justice system rather than the military court-martial system, because cadets are not a "defence member" as defined by the DFDA, in the same way that reservists, while not on duty, are not subject to discipline under the DFDA. This can create its own dilemmas for jurisdiction and claims for the need to compel obedience and greater discipline. The Jedi Council incident involved activities by reservists. *Chief of the Defence Force v. Gaynor* also concerned behavior of a reservist that arguably bought the military into disrepute, yet as a reservist, Gaynor could not be charged with disobeying a lawful command.[39]

In regards to investigation and civilian justice versus military discipline, it was apparent that ADFIS had investigated civilian criminal offences assimilated under s 61(3) *Defence Force Discipline Act* 1982, and in some cases, instead of handing over to the civilian police, apparently kept the matters in-house by dealing with them as administrative or service offences such as prejudicial conduct.[40] It also was claimed that ADFIS discouraged survivors from reporting to the civilian authorities. It is interesting that the culture at the ADF Academy, as part of which the 24 allegations by women of abuse arose, saw all woman survivors disinclined to report to the civilian authorities.[41]

Through the detailed scrutiny of 67 matters, DART noted that the following reasons existed to justify using the civilian justice system, instead of the military discipline system, when prosecuting offenders:

1. no criminal record results from a conviction in the military system;
2. relevant offenders are not placed on the sex offender register;
3. there is no exposure to civilian sanctions such as probation, parole, and good behavior bonds;
4. there is no access to drug treatment options and other offender programs;
5. there is no opportunity for survivor impact statements as part of the sentencing process;
6. the survivor's eligibility for compensation under survivors of crime schemes is affected;
7. prosecutions under the *Defence Force Discipline Act* are subject to a statutory limit of five years, which would not apply to a criminal prosecution based on the same alleged offence; and
8. police may not have access to a convicted member's conviction record because the conviction is not recorded in police intelligence databases.[42]

The Australian High Court decisions limit the jurisdiction of military punishment under the DFDA to "service connected" matters, which maintain discipline for the particular needs of the military. This more restrictive approach is exemplified by the US case of *O'Callahan,*[43] now overturned in the US by *Solorio,*[44] in which then Chief Justice Rehnquist adopted the status test, relying simply on whether a person was a military member. However, the Australian High Court service test adopted in *Re Tyler; Ex parte Foley*[45] has effectively evolved to permit almost any military matter being dealt with by the military. The argument is reduced to any behavior affecting military morale and reputation being a matter for military discipline. This relates to the status of those whose behavior is under scrutiny and thus encompasses far more than the original service test envisaged:

> In the military context, the commission of crimes by defence members, even when off duty and extraneous to their service, can reflect on their fitness, and on the reputation of the ADF as a whole. Parliament may thus decide, as it has, that any crime committed by a defence member may be prosecuted as a service offence.[46]

Proponents of the service test, Justices Brennan and Toohey in *Re Tracey; Ex parte Ryan,*[47] acknowledged at the time that the subjective assessment of the service connection could lead to questions of "impression and degree."[48] In *White v. Director of Military Prosecutions,*[49] the High Court, by a six to one majority, permitted ordinary criminal offences committed by military personnel under civilian law, even while off duty, to be heard by service tribunals, or as defense disciplinary matters, instead of by the civilian courts. Ultimately, the Defence Force Discipline Appeal Tribunal, a non-court, asserted a preference for the status test in Australia:

> as recognized in *Solorio,* the "service status" test has the advantage of providing a much clearer and cleaner test than that of "service connection." The DFDA . . . legislation is framed in terms of the "service status" test . . . no decision of the High Court rejects the "service status" test, and it has never been held that, insofar as the DFDA embraces the "service status" test, it is beyond power. Accordingly, even if the "service connection" test were not satisfied, in the absence of any decision of the High Court precluding its acceptance, we would find jurisdiction on the basis of the "service status" test.[50]

A memorandum of understanding exists between the Director of Military Prosecutions (DMP) and the Director of Public Prosecutions (DPP), which requires consultation and consent before an assimilated serious criminal offence such as murder or sexual assault can be pursued in the military jurisdiction particularly when committed within Australia.[51] However, although the consent requirement exists, a warrant for arrest, charging, and holding in custody can all occur prior to obtaining any consent.[52] This rather shrouded process has lost sight of the reason for its existence, which is to respect civil-military control and ensure most matters are dealt with in the civilian justice system unless there are extremely good grounds to deal with it in the internal military discipline system. Opportunity for uncertainty exists when certain sexual offences, such as indecent assault, do not require DPP approval before being pursued in the military domain. The memorandum speaks of service offences, yet the current state of the case law in Australia remains unclear on determination of what this means.

The then government and ADF rejected the extensive 2005 *Senate Inquiry into the Effectiveness of Australia's Military Justice System* recommendation that all criminal offences, irrespective of location, be referred to the civilian authorities.[53] It was claimed the Senate inquiry members acknowledged the importance for the chain of command to have control over discipline.[54] Certain sexual offences under the *Crimes Act* 1990 Part IIIA are to be referred to the DPP for consideration of jurisdiction to prosecute.[55] None of these factors provide justification to reject the recommendation made by the Senate.

Ironically, the need to maintain high morale and discipline, cited as one justification for a separate discipline system, seems to be defeated by the internal system in which so much sexual and physical abuse and harassment is sustained. It is informative to consider standard claims made for maintaining the status quo. These include arguments 1, 2, and 3 outlined in chapter 1, such as "adversely affecting command and morale" and the "military necessity to maintain a strong fighting force." These were put forward in 1992 as justification for dismissing anyone in the Australian military who was homosexual. Three other justifications for removing homosexuals were proposed: national security, due to the stigma attached; health issues such as AIDS; and that children in defense need protection from such behavior.[56] This was in the early 1990s, and while these claims could certainly be dismantled as arguments that look somewhat silly now, cultural change occurs slowly. Not until Anzac Day 2017 could wreaths be laid acknowledging the contributions to service across the generations of lesbian, gay, bisexual, transgender, intersex, and queer (LGBTIQ) service members.[57] The 1986 ADF instruction on homosexual behavior in the defense force, reaffirmed in June 1992 but overturned in November of the same year by then Prime Minister Paul Keating, had an annexure B that outlined unacceptable sexual behavior by defense members.[58] Paragraph 4 is telling in attitude, and one that still seems to support resistance today:

> This obligation defines the limits of the ADF concern regarding the sexual behavior of members. Sexual behavior which is inconsistent with this obligation is termed unacceptable sexual behavior and will normally warrant disciplinary and/or administrative action, where such behavior:
>
> a) is prejudicial or is likely to be prejudicial to group cohesion;
> b) is prejudicial or is likely to be prejudicial to command relationships;
> c) is prejudicial or is likely to be prejudicial to the attainment of military objectives through reducing the operational effectiveness, health or safety of the individual or the group;
> d) takes advantage of, or threatens the person or personal integrity of subordinate of underage persons;
> e) brings or has the potential to bring discredit on the ADF; or
> f) is unlawful under either civil or military law.[59]

These claims are now clearly redundant, adding to the many reasons that justify no longer maintaining the military discipline system as a separate system. Evidence from the DART investigation shows that of the 1,723 reparation payments made, 97 percent contained a component to acknowledge a failing by the institution in managing the complaint. Initiation practices including bastardisation, a term encompassing harassment and bullying, often continued without a response from the institution. Physical injuries and errant and unusual behavior seemingly go unobserved by those in charge despite a hierarchical command environment.

As part of the drive to cultural change, defense have implemented various directives and policies. These have included instructions supporting respect for equity and diversity and have encouraged commanders to model this change by taking action that eliminates unacceptable behavior.[60] Some evidence of the changing culture saw ADF members permitted for the first time in 2013 to march in their uniform in the famous Sydney LGBTI Mardi Gras,[61] and the acceptance of women in combat as the Gillard government moved to allow in 2011.[62] Public commentary, particularly in social media, was also included in the instructions for change and extended to reserve military personnel.[63]

Bernard Gaynor, a reservist who joined the military in 1997, served as an officer in the active army from 2002–2011, and became a major in 2013 while part of the reserve forces, tested the strength of this commitment. In 2013, he made comments reflecting his views of the LGBTI community and members of the Islamic religion on his personal blog website, Facebook, and Twitter account.[64] Refusing to desist and take down his comments when requested by the Chief of Army, Gaynor's commission was eventually terminated. The matter went to the federal court on a constitutional challenge.[65] Gaynor was claiming that the directive restricted his implied public freedom of political speech. The single judge accepted Gaynor's argument, stating:

> It may be the case that members of a full time regular service are rarely (if ever) free to publicly express opinions against the policies of the ADF or the decisions of their superiors but the same cannot always be said about members of Reserves. Such persons are often not on duty. They are private citizens, in substance, when not on duty and not in uniform. Military discipline under the Defence Discipline Act (sic) does not apply to them. In my view, their freedom of political communication cannot be burdened at those times.[66]

This position was overturned on appeal to the full court in 2017.[67] There, the court found that the single court judge had erred in their application of the implied freedom of speech test. Unlike the First Amendment to the US Constitution, the Australian Constitution has no such explicitly included rights. The High Court has resolved to imply a limited freedom of speech into the Australian Constitution. However, it does not provide individual personal rights of free expression, instead focusing more generally on the legislative power to pass legislation that acts in a restrictive manner on the ability for public political communication to occur freely.[68] The impugned Defence regulation 85 in *Gaynor* was considered to apply to the suitability of officers, and supporting diversity in opinions and outlook, yet requiring ". . . respect and tolerance, without which diversity cannot flourish."[69] Thus, it was directed at the appropriateness of an officer's behavior in a leadership position and was not focused on limiting free communication or the subject matter of any communication. In *Gaynor*, the court noted ". . . the lack of tolerance and respect for fellow officers and other ADF members about whom he was speaking [was] aptly described as extreme, including his refusal to accept and abide by orders and directions given to him."[70] The appellate court observed that Gaynor's behavior was incompatible with that expected of a leader, even a reservist, demonstrating an incapacity ". . . to operate within the hierarchal structures of the ADF in ways that advance the cohesiveness of the armed forces."[71]

The attention to prioritizing group cohesion, military command objectives, and reputation over breaches of the law shows an ongoing focus of the military institution. This is identified by the military attitude when the media is involved in reporting internal incidents. Foster has found a general hostility towards the media from within defense. He claims the perception is of a media that is antagonistic and works to damage the reputation of the military, ". . . because the one thing the ADF feared more than an adverse outcome on the battlefield was bad press and the damage that this might do to its reputation."[72] Hostility towards the media is an entrenched feature of the ADF's coterie culture and is a central feature of the military's vision of its relations with civil society, according to Foster and others.[73] This fear of loss of reputation and antagonism to the media is common within coteries, confirming the *la bella figura* syndrome.[74] A major cultural repositioning has to occur to acknowledge individual well-being, which remains unaddressed and at odds with the prioritized military ethos. In attempts to simultaneously contain and redress the situation, defense has set up yet another internal body—the Sexual Misconduct Prevention and Response Office (SeMPRO), which is designed to improve education, revise policies, and publish statistics. Much like its US cousin, the Sexual Assault Prevention and Response Office (SAPRO), it has a limited remit and reports internally to the Chief of Defence.[75] Lack of substantive redress impacts on survivors, perpetrators, and extended others as is witnessed in the following case vignettes.

CASE VIGNETTES, FROM THE INQUIRIES

Abuse can take many forms. Sexual and physical abuse often are the most abhorrent. However, DART noted the high prevalence of both sexual and workplace harassment and bullying.[76] This type of behavior is perhaps more insidious and harder to uncover, but the consequences are potentially equally destructive. Also noted by DART was the reality that perceptions of the impact of the abuse are distinctly individual, and there is no correlation between the objective type of the abuse and the subjective impact on the individual.[77] What is common is the repression by a culture that condemns "dobbing."[78] A survivor, particularly one going to the media or to a body outside the coterie's control, also euphemistically referred to as "beyond the wire," presents a peril to the hierarchical system of authority and fraternal code of honor, perhaps more aptly named a code of (dis)honor. Despite this repression, a few brave persons are still prepared to speak out. Then independent senator, Jackie Lambie, an ex-service member herself, successfully advocated for three investigations in relation to the matters now described.

The Constant Battle: Suicide by Veterans

A former Special Air Service (SAS) member came forward publicly to give evidence before a Senate inquiry into suicide among veterans.[79] He spoke of his family's suffering and being "blacklisted" by the military institution. His complaint lay on two fronts. First, he claimed he was the survivor of sexual abuse during interrogation training in 2006[80] and second, his brother, also a service member, had been the survivor of harassment that he believed had adversely affected him.[81] The brother had received psychological help following the death of a friend. Later he felt sidelined when given a job looking after exhibits in a regiment museum instead of returning to his position in the SAS where, as a highly trained soldier, he had participated in multiple tours of duty.[82]

Dr Scally's submission to the Foreign Affairs, Defence and Trade References Committee, "The Constant Battle: Suicide by Veterans," expresses his experience in the military as a regimental medical doctor serving for 21 years:

> I wish to elucidate that not all harm occurs overseas; indeed, I have seen significant trauma and morbidity occur in the barracks and field training environment (including training deaths, injury and suicides). I have witnessed gross mistreatment verging on torture and have been compelled to be complicit to it. I have witnessed the persecution of soldiers by sub-unit commanders who were previously the subject of a parliamentary enquiry into . . . psychopathic bullying, yet were nonetheless deemed fit to take command, and further ruin young lives. I have been threatened with imprisonment for not changing my medical opinion to suit the wants of command.[83]

The Department of Veterans Affairs has received recommendations for improvement as a result of "The Constant Battle" Senate inquiry. The *Veterans Entitlement Act* 1920 (Cth) and the *Safety, Rehabilitation and Compensation*

Act 1988 (Cth) are just some of the legislative instruments operating in this domain.[84] One simple recommendation addresses the issue of the complex web of legislation and administrative burdens veterans have to try and navigate in order to access support when in a vulnerable state.[85] For the military, making claims for special treatment as an institution capable of being ready to fight and manage a war, and therefore operating on efficiency, responsiveness, and flexibility, the allegation of bureaucratic regulatory overload seems too common.

Due to the claims made and Senator Lambie's push, the Senate referred two more inquiries to the Foreign Affairs, Defence and Trade References Committee: one looked at the circumstances related to the SAS officer's claim of sexual abuse during Resistance to Interrogation training, and another into the matter of the Jedi Council described below.[86] The three inquiries came on top of the many inquires undertaken internally in Defence as well as independently by other bodies.[87] What they signify is the ongoing cost to the taxpayer of maintaining a broken system, one that seems never capable of being truly fixed no matter how many inquires may be undertaken or how much fiddling around the edges occurs.

The Resistance to Interrogation training inquiry noted that after 2006 this training was rebadged as "Conduct after Capture." One participant raised the degree of usefulness of the training, stating "[t]he crux is that it is actually a misnomer to call it 'training,' because no instruction was given, there was no feedback, there was no evaluation and there was no coaching."[88] Similar issues arose as with the Survival, Evasion, Resistence, and Escape (SERE) program in the US, including the use of this training for other potential purposes, such as training the trainer in certain interrogator tactics; questionable levels of consent; potential for a breach of the UN *Convention Against Torture and Other Cruel, Inhuman or Degrading Treatment or Punishment,* and the conflicted position for psychologists and medical personnel involved in the training. The committee recommended that information on the participants be retained by the military and be accessible to the Department of Veterans Affairs, and that an independent arm's-length third party be permitted to review the participants for potential psychological harm after the hardest, level C, training for Conduct after Capture had occurred.[89]

A member of defense tasked with assisting members with mental health issues made claims in 2013 of having experienced abuse. As an army psychologist for 16 years, holding some responsibility for the welfare and mental health of deployed military and having served in many campaigns, including in Bougainville, East Timor, the Solomon Islands, Iraq, and the Middle East, Morgan said his claim was mishandled with non-compliance in reporting deadlines, including by the most senior ranks of defense.[90] The member overcame fear of personal consequences to express frustration at what he perceived as little change in the way survivors of abuse were treated, notwithstanding the extensive number of inquiries and reports:

> I can categorically say that no matter all of the cultural reviews, the establishment of the abuse tribunal and the DLA Piper report, nothing has changed about the way Defence reacts to abuse . . . My personal experience tells me that the Army's abuse management strategies that I've seen—delay, deter and deceive—are still in force now . . . They say one thing in public and do another thing in private.[91]

The inquiry into suicides found that high levels of complexity in the legislative regime provided to assist veterans needed to be addressed. Also noted were contributing factors to suicide such as sexual abuse, bullying, and harassment.[92] The government has responded to the committees, report into military member's suicide with agreement to the majority of the twenty-four recommendations and an expenditure of $31 million to support their new initiatives. This includes establishing a national de-identified veterans' suicide register to enable a closer understanding of the problem. The government softened on an early budgetary reluctance and extended non-liability health care to free and immediate health care for anyone who has served one day with the military—removing the prior requirement of three years' service.[93] Improving the transition to civilian life has been given attention by providing an annual physical and mental health checkup and a white card to discharging military personnel, to enable access to mental health treatment when they feel it is needed.[94]

The Jedi Council

Another incident reflecting the issues is known as the "Jedi Council" saga. It provides an insight into the many aspects of abuse. Overarching in this was the inability of the separate defence institution to deal with the event in a manner that satisfied anyone. Named, inaccurately, as a perversion of the fictional "Jedi Council," which was portrayed in the *Star Wars* movie as the Jedi Order, a spiritual, philosophical, and paramilitary organization combining religion and warrior attributes in a meritocratic hierarchal secretive organization aimed to fight evil and bring about good, the real so-called Jedi Council of the ADF brought about harm, not good. However, it did have the attributes of a separate secretive coterie, subject to its own rules. The group filmed or photographed women, often without their knowledge, during sexual activity and the resulting digital media files were sent by email to a substantial number of defense personnel, possibly 172, not all necessarily group members.

The emails were often headed "Dear Jedi Council" and conveyed descriptions around the activity depicted.

One serving member who received these emails was a lieutenant colonel but, as it turned out, he never opened the uninvited emails but deleted them instead. Nevertheless, then Chief of Army, Lt. General David Morrison, allegedly gave enough information for the public to be able to identify the person, along with two others who were stood down, before the outcome of an investigation had substantiated any wrongdoing. The ADF denied providing anyone's name to the media in the subsequent inquiry.[95] Famous for his speech that went around the world and exhorted the military to overcome such sex scandals, and later named Australian of the year, David Morrison's actions nevertheless drew comment.[96] Despite the lieutenant colonel's claim that he and his family's lives were destroyed, he stated that he required no more than a public apology.[97]

Senator Jackie Lambie had gained access to a New South Wales police report into the Jedi Council matter that had allegedly suggested investigation irregularities by ADFIS.[98] In the Foreign Affairs, Defence and Trade References Committee Inquiry into "Matters Raised by NSW Police, Strike Force CIVET," the exchange of offensive emails by the Jedi Council, and an independent police investigation by NSW police detectives carried out in July 2012, were the subject of scrutiny. Allegations of other inappropriate conduct by ADFIS staff and investigations by the IGADF suggested a potential culture that not only may not uphold appropriate standards expected from an investigative body but also may propagate disrespect.[99] At the conclusion of the Jedi investigation, nine members had their service terminated while another seven managed to avoid this outcome, even though six of the seven received a censure. The inquiry noted that the remaining 176 defence members and employees identified as involved in Operation JARRAH were assessed individually by their chain of command. Generally, an administrative sanction applied.[100]

Most concerning was that the Foreign Affairs, Defence and Trade References Committee reported that they were unable to fully report due to difficulties in obtaining evidence. A jurisdictional objection was made by the NSW police commissioner suggesting a federal government body could not intrude on state police operations and "[a]ny purported scrutiny of NSW Police's actions which are available if the POA Report is produced should not be undertaken by the Commonwealth Parliament, including a Senate Committee, but by the NSW Parliament."[101] The committee responded in relation to the refusal by NSW police to provide their report, suggesting that it was an unusual response given the committee had never requested the report.[102] The committee noted that the IGADF had carried out a second inquiry, which found "serious shortcomings with ADFIS investigative practices and procedures" requiring measures to improve the Australian Defence Forces' "understanding and investigation of cybercrime and ICT misuse."[103] Perhaps surprising for an organization dedicated to the cutting-edge defense of Australia's security, Senator Lambie commented that

> [w]hile the Committee rightfully does not rely upon the draft CIVET report due to the inability to establish its status, the draft report did raise very serious concerns about the proper workings of federal agencies that have thus far evaded proper Parliamentary scrutiny.[104]

ADF Skype Matter

Prior to the two particular cases described, the sex scandal "Skype incident," leading to the DLA Piper and the DART process, had occurred. A young female cadet, unbeknownst to her, had been live videoed while having consensual sex at the Australian Defence Force Academy.[105] Subsequently the survivor, now known as "Kate," was allegedly hazed through disciplinary proceedings against her by the management of ADFA in relation to other matters. This was acknowledged by the then Minister for Defence as "inappropriate, insensitive, wrong [and] almost certainly faulty in the law."[106]

Despite the many inquiries instigated by the 2011 Minister of Defence's response to the Skype sex scandal, an investigative journalist reporting in 2014 found that there was a lack of awareness among cadets of the inquiry process, and even if they were aware, a lack of faith and trust in a system that had already failed them so badly.[107] The Kirkham Inquiry, set up to look at the specific ADF Skype incident, concluded there had been no wrongdoing in pursuing disciplinary action against the cadet.[108] The perpetrators were charged and found guilty by a jury within the civilian system, for indecency and using a carriage service for the offence. Both perpetrators managed to elude imprisonment, due to their age and previous good character, and they received twelve-month good behavior bonds.[109] Kate responded by stating: "[a]s Defence culture stands at the moment, I think we still have a really long way to go before I would feel confident in being able to say, 'Yes, it's a good career choice for females.'"[110]

By coming forward, Kate empowered many others to feel able to make aligned claims. In 2013, her bravery was recorded by being awarded *Daily Life's* woman of the year,[111] but this could never redress the personal cost in losing her career, being discharged on medical grounds, and left to follow a different career. Kate indicated she would continue to fight "for as long as it takes" to keep the issue alive for the public.[112] The stamina needed for this is colossal. As Thornton has noted, very few woman can sustain a prolonged action.[113] Nevertheless, some woman hold out, while also trying to sustain a career despite the negative workplace. The reality is that systemic harassment is insidious in nature as it fashions a male dominance in a male domain of generalized power. Broderick's extensive 2012 review on women serving in the Defence Force[114] advocated increasing the targets for gender employment and punishing managers who failed to address abuse and sexual harassment. However, implementation is a slow process.

Case 40—Royal Commission into Institutional Response into Child Sexual Abuse

The Royal Commission into the Institutional Response to Child Sexual Abuse focused on abuse reported in relation to the military bases Leeuwin, Western Australia, and Balcombe, Victoria. This was due to the similar nature and extent of abuse reported to have occurred over a similar period of time, yet coming from different services situated on opposite sides of the country.[115] The evidence portrayed a climate of widespread abuse, involving unequal power by older males over younger males, in an informal hierarchy engaged in ritual hazing practices that were accepted as part of a rite of passage into the coterie.[116]

HMAS Leeuwin was a navy base located onshore in Western Australia. It operated between 1960 and 1984 as a training institution for junior recruits. Around 13,000 boys aged between 15 and 16 years passed through the base in their entry into the navy. The training was conducted over 12 months. For the first six months, the boys were ranked "Junior Recruit Second Class" after which they progressed to "Junior Recruit First Class." Once they had successfully completed the training they went on to further officer training or were allocated to a navy ship. The intake of recruits was staggered over three monthly intervals, supporting an unofficial hierarchy system, which so easily lent itself to abuse. The colloquial names given to each staggered recruitment intake tells a story. The newest recruits were titled the "new grubs," the next group the "grubs," the next the "shits," and the most senior the "top shits."[117] Their welfare needs, including discipline, was overseen by two Divisional Officers, each responsible for two separate divisions of around 100 recruits, and they were assisted by a Petty Officer and a Chief Petty Officer, who were ranked as senior sailors.[118]

Concerning is that abuse at Leeuwin had seen two previous inquiries, one in 1971, conducted by Navy Judge Advocate General Rapke, and referred to as the Rapke Report. This related to a publicized bashing of a junior recruit. The mother of the 15-year-old survivor had reported the matter in the media.[119] Rapke's report exonerated the officers as largely upstanding and diligent service personnel. He consigned the matter to an over-enthusiastic group bashing that had been inflicted on the survivor by four or five recruits due to his stepping outside his "unofficial" level of hierarchy in applying his own bullying. Rapke's report, not released due to the age of the alleged survivors and privacy concerns of those involved, received some coverage in the media. It would appear that the survivor and perpetrators had all received similar discipline. Rapke seemed most concerned with the media coverage and was keen to emphasize the isolated nature of such incidents as being due to some "bad apples." Rapke did not consider the abuse was systemic or institutionalized. It was reported that he felt ". . . confident that if [the survivor] or any other of the lads involved continues with his naval career, he will find happiness and satisfaction in that career and perhaps even benefit from the miserable experiences he has been subjected too."[120] This is the language of "a rite of passage" that survivors indicated they were encouraged to believe and accept.

More enlightened than Rapke, in 2014, DART's investigation of accounts of abuse by 238 former junior recruits acknowledged that the level of abuse was more serious and widespread, including sexual abuse, and was perpetrated by not only junior recruits but also participating staff members.[121] Given Rapke's response, it is perhaps no surprise that more than 40 years later it was still a culture in which complaining about abuse is discouraged. An aberrant *la bella figura* attitude was sustained by the lack of appropriate management where survivors did attempt to report abuse, with no actions taken and in some cases an active dissuading from making the complaint. DART found that this arose because of the stigma attached, leading to shame at having been abused, along with fear of discharge, or threats of further abuse for "dobbing" by reporting, and a general lack of trust in reporting to other staff members.[122] That the unofficial system of hierarchical bullying and abuse continued was due in part to the institutional "blind-eye" to such *la brutta figura* matters.

While 36 survivors of child sexual abuse at Leeuwin contacted the Royal Commission, the commission heard evidence from only five of these survivors. These five, two being abused by staff and three by fellow recruits, indicate a pattern of abuse occurring within their first six months at the Leeuwin base when they were aged 15–16 years. One of the survivors had given evidence to Rapke in 1971. He testified that prior to this, he had been warned that if he indicated it was anything other than "boys being boys" he would suffer repercussions. This survivor endured a "boys being boys" culture, in which regular acts of anal and oral sex were performed on and by him that involved both junior recruits and staff, while he was 16 years of age. His attempt to report to a chaplain met with threats that any reporting could endanger him further. After running away, which for him seemed his only option, he alleged that when he was caught, further sexual abuse occurred when in the custody of the naval police. At his court-martial the Divisional Officer, whom he had told about his abuse, described him as a troublemaker resulting in his "unsuitable discharge."[123]

The Balcombe Barracks, an Australian army base on the Mornington Peninsula, Victoria, which operated from 1948 to 1982, provided 7,500 trade apprenticeships educating female and male recruits from secondary schools for four years in technical and clerical trades. Again, the recruits were divided into companies with each comprised of three platoons commanded by a sergeant, a company sergeant major, and a clerk and storeman. Senior apprentices were given the unofficial rank of hut corporal with apprentices expected to report any incidents to them before reporting to divisional staff. This entrenched an unofficial hierarchical power structure ripe for abuse of the junior "sprogs."[124]

A Manual of Personnel Administration was the only procedural document, which has now mysteriously disappeared, that dealt with all complaints no matter the age or whether sexual abuse was alleged.[125] Twelve survivors contacted the Royal Commission regarding their abuse while children at the Balcombe Barracks, and evidence was heard from five of these survivors. This compares to the 68 complaints (30 involving children) provided to DART about physical or sexual abuse at Balcombe. A number of the survivors alleged that on numerous occasions anal penetration occurred where a broom handle was used, and these survivors still, in 2014, were denied any compensation due to their inability to produce contemporaneous evidence.

The Royal Commission found the complaints were to be made to Divisional Officers with no special procedures for child sexual abuse complaints. However, for an organization that prides itself on efficiency, the procedures were complicated by their overlay in a number of different source documents.[126] The now lost "log-books" provided the only records of complaints. Only one of the five survivors giving evidence made a written complaint at the time of the incident, which ultimately resulted in no action being taken.[127]

Bastardisation was a general all-encompassing term used to cover incidents of bullying, harassment, and abusive initiation practices. Four navy staff, including the chaplain at the time, gave evidence to the Royal Commission. Many years later, in 2016, even after the closing of the base, they still tended towards a denial of the abuse or the extent of it. Retired Rear Admiral Peter Sinclair was given charge of Leeuwin after the Rapke report to improve the situation. Yet, Sinclair, who served from 1948 to 1989, and was to be governor of New South Wales from 1990 to 1996, told the Royal Commission that, despite working to ensure the abuse did not continue, he was appalled to hear of it now, and simply could not understand how it could occur.[128] This was notwithstanding his evidence of experiencing ". . . a terribly uncomfortable and not very exciting"[129] initiation himself and awareness of inappropriate sexual initiation activities such as "nuggeting"—the covering in boot polish of another's testicles. Such a rite of initiation was considered acceptable, but not widespread.[130] The entire approach to allowing initiation practices such as these or initiation of any sort is in need of a cultural change that seems yet to be comprehended by coterie institutions. The apparent shock and surprise by senior military figures tends to be a repeated refrain. Vice Admiral Ray Griggs, commenting on the DART evidence and findings, expressed that the evidence ". . . absolutely sickened me,"[131] acknowledging a failure in the duty of care by the military establishment.

The Royal Commission also inquired in detail into the complaints emanating from Australian Defence Force Cadets because these were not addressed in any other inquiries; and Defence continues to recruit children from the age of 13.[132] Cadets can remain to the age of twenty and from age eighteen they can transition into "Adult Cadet Staff Members," eligible to apply to become instructors of cadets. From age nineteen, they can become officers overseeing cadets.[133] The ADF Cadets collectively cover the three services. Cadets are not members of the ADF, and the ADF service chiefs are responsible for the cadets.[134]

A common problem arising in this environment is inappropriate relationships between instructors and cadets. Although attempts to prevent these have been made since 2004, it would appear that the issue remains unresolved. As an institution, the defense force, which prides itself on efficiency, seemed to have little clear understanding of the legal requirements regarding the age of consent and, more importantly, the obligations of those in positions of authority. While a federal system means the criminal law varies across states, applying differing ages of consent, it became clear during the Royal Commission that inaccurate or incomplete information in relation to these laws was present in the cadet and instructor training materials.[135] This is despite the issuing of various policy manuals, including those that forbid relationships of a close personal nature between staff and cadets, training around the age of consent, and reporting obligations and duties to the civilian authorities.[136] For a military, it is a major concern that the trainers, nor the cadets, understand their obligations as part of the duties they are expected to ultimately fulfill in the forces.

The Royal Commission heard evidence from seven witnesses concerning five cases of alleged child sexual abuse, out of the 25 survivors that contacted the commission. From 2001, Defence had kept records of incidents of allegations of child sexual abuse, which indicates 154 recorded allegations up to the time of the Royal Commission's inquiry in 2016. Almost one third, 51 allegations, involved adult instructor assaults on a cadet, 10 involved ADF staff, and the remainder saw other cadets as perpetrators.[137]

Key concerns for the Royal Commission were how the management of complaints or allegations of child sexual abuse internally affected the capacity to protect children, and how internal investigations influenced criminal investigations. The lack of satisfactory processes became highlighted by the tragic case of one cadet. Due to a relationship with a 30-year-old instructor when she was only 15 years old, she was told she had a choice of resigning or being dishonorably discharged. She ended up taking her own life by suicide. The pain for her family was made all the greater when it became clear that a decision to reinstate the cadet had been made before her death, but she had not been advised in a timely manner.[138] The perpetrator was relocated, eventually leaving the military.

The Royal Commission found some common factors that surrounded abuse episodes, including that those to whom abuse was to be reported were sometimes the abusers; if reported, further abuse or loss of job prospects was a possibility;[139] a desire to get just desserts by waiting for suitable rank to enable the survivor to become the abuser; a blurring between abuse and punishment; and fear of being accused of being homosexual, leading to discharge.[140]

Other common traits found were that most abuse tends to occur during out-of-hours activity or under cover of night. Vice Admiral Griggs indicated in his evidence that the internal procedures at Leeuwin should have provided high levels of supervision. He indicated that duty staff were present in the recruits' accommodation blocks at all times, except during short absences for meals, alongside a system of roving patrols. However, the survivors giving evidence indicated that this was not the case and the recruits' accommodation blocks were not patrolled, with most abuse occurring at night.[141]

Hierarchical entrenchment of power played a significant role. The staggered recruiting and separation into two divisions set up a hierarchical competitive system that was heightened through the selection of Divisional Officers from leading junior recruits, who were empowered to report their peers and to give direct orders to junior recruits where it was thought to lead to good order and discipline. An attempt to address this had occurred after the Grey Review,[142] through the removal of the hierarchical cadet structure and its replacement with a mentoring approach. Residential Support Officers (RSO) were created in 2012 to operate as mentors/supervisors in order to assist with supervision in the residential location and overcome isolation of first-year cadets during their transition.[143]

As a footnote to these proceedings Major Griggs, who had a prominent role in giving evidence to the Royal Commission, became embroiled in his own controversy, having a relationship with a lower-ranked member of the military.[144] Adultery is not an offence in the Australian military and a different approach to married members having affairs is taken to that of the US. Largely seen as a private matter, unless fraud or issues of rank and line management are involved, the military generally does not interfere. Still, such behavior by senior leaders can have repercussions on discipline at a moral level.

THE INSTITUTIONAL RESPONSE

The government response to the DLA Piper Report included a continuation of much of the Pathway to Change Reforms that had commenced in 2012 as part of an Evolving Defence Culture.[145] The strategy had arisen out of seven reviews into Defense culture and other reform proposals. At least fourteen major reviews occurred between 1995 and 2011 alone and the reviews continue.[146] Reforms occurred at ADFA after 2011 with the goal to provide a safer, more inclusive workplace. Culture was a key concern, with the *Review into the Treatment of Women at ADFA* recommending attention to:

- ADFA's role and purpose
- Equity and diversity
- ADFA's structure and staffing
- Midshipmen and cadets as young people and future leaders
- Accommodation and supervision
- Minimizing risk, managing incidents, and ensuring the safety of the workplace
- Advice and referral
- Data.[147]

To get a sense of the inquiry landscape, some of what follows provides an overall portrait, beyond matters already discussed. In 2011 and 2012 Elizabeth Broderick, Sex Discrimination Commissioner, reported on her review into the treatment of women in the ADF.[148] The review indicated considerable discrepancies in the recording of the number of assaults between the Values, Behaviour and Resolution Branch (VBR) of the Defence Department, the Service Police Central Records Office of ADFIS, and the IGADF 2011 report. The commissioner considered this to be

> concerning, as it means that trends cannot be followed, offenders and repeat offenders cannot be tracked and areas in which sexual abuse are occurring cannot be identified with accuracy. It also means that targeted preventative strategies

> cannot be properly put in place. Of considerable concern is that the failure to capture incidents of sexual abuse accurately can place ADF members at risk of harm from undetected or untracked offenders.[149]

This echoes the similar state of statistics reporting in the US, by which useful statistics, providing meaningful evidence that enable exact comparisons, are difficult to obtain. Civilian prosecution authorities do not keep records that distinguish a matter as one involving the military—either as related to offenders or survivors. This all indicates a general preponderance of either non-concern or lack of transparency. The government accepted the Broderick recommendation to establish the Sexual Misconduct Prevention and Response Office (SeMPRO) to coordinate and improve survivor support and timely responses, as well as assembling information on rates and types of abuse and related misconduct.[150] Although it took some time to implement, SeMPRO also has an education and policy function. A further outcome from both the Broderick's Report and the DLA Piper Review was the assurance of confidentiality for any reporting of harassment or abusive conduct, and the possibility of a dignified and expedited exit without financial or other penalty from the military.[151]

In the 2016–2017 reporting cycle, SeMPRO indicated it had received 265 formal reports of sexual misconduct, indicating little change from the 2013–2014 numbers and generally only fluctuating up or down by around 5 percent over the last four years.[152] Unfortunately, however, SeMPRO was the subject of a number of concerns. SeMPRO, not unlike its US counterpart SAPRO, only deals with sexual abuse. Other matters, such as sexual harassment, physical abuse, and discrimination are addressed by the VBR in ADFIS.[153] Not until after the Royal Commission into Institutional Responses into Child Sexual Abuse did SeMPRO consider the policies and practices of the ADF cadets, and only in October 2016 were support services offered to cadets, their families, officers, and instructors in a 12-month trial.[154] Furthermore, these policies and practices would appear to lack insight into male tendencies not to report sex offences, when considering SeMPRO's claims that sexual offences are gendered crimes because formal reports are by females in "eight out of every ten victims."[155] This raises concerns for around 80 percent of males in defense, many of whom may not be reporting. The DART Review referred to a hotline provided as having a deficit focus as part of a personal service, which diminishes the building of trust. Other issues included exceptions to the restriction of disclosures that needed more explanation to survivors, and there was room for still further improvement in the communication with survivors, particularly with regard to their options for support and forensic evidence gathering and the provision of face-to-face support.[156]

DART suggested the following six features were causal to the abuse in ADFA:

- issues of gender and culture within the male-dominated environment at ADFA, including the cadet hierarchical structure that was in place until the late 1990s;
- concerns about the suitability and experience of some staff members in supervising young people in a mixed gender environment;
- inadequate levels of supervision and security in the ADFA accommodation;
- excessive use of alcohol by cadets;
- issues with reporting of abuse, including inadequate policies and procedures regarding the management of reports of abuse and a culture, which discouraged abuse; and
- a failure of leadership to prevent, stop, and respond to abuse.[157]

In response to the nine Recommendations by the Foreign Affairs, Defence Report and Defence and Trade References Committee Process to Support Victims of Abuse in Defence, the government noted most but only agreed with one recommendation, namely that Volume 2 of the DLA Report should be released without being redacted or conveyed in summary form. The government rejected the recommendation to continue the superintendence activities of DART beyond June 2015.[158]

The Senate Foreign Affairs, Defence and Trade Committee Report on the DLA Piper Report encouraged Defense to have senior members participate in the restorative engagement established by the DART program, with an independent review to see if a similar continuing program should exist and an independent review of the completion of the Pathway to Change to understand its effectiveness.[159] The Eggleston Senate report recommended that research using anonymized data received by DART would be fruitful, and that the Inspector General's recommendation for support officers be implemented.[160]

The renewed batch of inquiries saw Defense become busy with a number of programs. However, the long list of inquiries can obscure just what is happening. Probably one of the most significant was a major inquiry in 2005 by the Senate into the *Effectiveness of Australia's Military Justice System*.[161] This inquiry was broad-ranging, covering both the discipline and the administrative inquiry system. It resulted in a substantive change with the introduction of the new Australian Military Court (AMC). Sadly, due to the then Howard government's response of only partially adopting the Senate's recommendations, after advice from Defense, which claimed a need for operational effectiveness by maintaining control over the discipline of soldiers, the AMC ultimately failed. Ironically, defensive in protecting Ch III courts, the High Court in *Lane v. Morrison*[162] found the military court unconstitutional, returning the military to its separate historic courts-martial system.[163] Since this outcome, the military justice system has reverted to the prior courts-martial system with interim legislation and the situation remaining in place nearly a decade later. This was notwithstanding the ongoing inquiry environment plainly showing a lack of ability in the institution to achieve the desired level of control and good moral behavior.

Prior to the High Court's decision, earlier in 2009, a further independent report reviewing the new court structure had reported favorably that all but six of the thirty recommendations in the Senate Report, which had been accepted by the government, had been implemented. In a type of numbers game, the report also contentedly noted that of some 382 recommendations in reviews conducted in the ten years 2000–2009, only 28 remained to be implemented.[164]

There is no denying that Defence took some steps to address systemic issues identified in the DLA Piper Report. A key response was the adoption of a strategy for cultural change through implementing the *Pathway to Change—Evolving Defence Culture*.[165] This strategy encompassed Defence's cultural ambitions to be realized through a five-year plan. It required gathering much of the reviews advice in order to focus on key areas, namely leadership inclusivity and accountability; values and behavior education; reform of ADFA and other training establishments; improved management of ADF personnel career pathways; and improved complaints management processes. The Royal Commission heard from Vice Admiral Griggs that these key changes were mostly completed with the focus now moving to their normalization.[166] Senior Defence members also engaged in a review and an audit into the inquiry system itself, including the military discipline system,[167] but it was criticized by DART for its restricted consultation.[168]

The IGADF made 1,336 recommendations and suggestions towards improving military discipline arrangements and procedures in the period 2014–2015, and 900 in 2015–2016.[169] By December 2016, it was said that actions and recommendations were complete and Defence was now shifting to stabilizing and evaluating the changes. Part of the process has involved collaboration with the Human Rights Commission visiting bases and reviewing data as an external oversight mechanism to ensure cultural reform is real.[170] Complaints of unacceptable behavior showed a decrease, amounting to around 1 percent of ADF, or 668 incidents, being formally recorded by 2016–2017. This number has to be considered against a backdrop in which only 10–20 percent of matters are addressed as serious enough to warrant a formal discipline or administrative response, the majority being resolved at the earliest and lowest possible stage, often using alternative dispute resolution methods.[171]

The closed nature of coteries leads to the risk of groupthink and failure to hear the critical voice. Thus, the very thing such societies fear most—reputational damage—becomes inevitable. Being open to outside input, involving the civilian side of the civil-military equation, can only improve performance. The Orme Report, *Beyond Compliance–Professionalism, Trust, Capability in the Australian Profession of Arms*, provided a classic example back in 2011.[172] While many apt and well-made points were clear in the report, it suffered from a common fatal flaw in such matters. It was comprised mostly of current or retired military members and looked to other militaries to solve its problems, when often these militaries come from a similar background suffering similar problems, which they have also failed to grapple with over time. This internalized and unconscious bias operates within a closed bubble that requires bursting. The bursting was encouraged by DART, with the committee exhorting a continued engagement with external bodies such as the Australian Human Rights Commission.[173] The challenge is for the highest civilian courts, such as the High Court, to also heed this call and change its default approach.[174]

The Orme Report acknowledged that a different culture was needed and that incremental change was not enough, while it also rightly recognized the forest of red tape, with policies and procedures becoming a contributing source of problems.[175] While showing some insight into the problem of a warrior culture that engages in insider and outsider behavior, and in which sexual conquest is equated with combat prowess, the review then took a backward turn, falling into reliance on two of the aspects that arguably contribute to this. Citing Huntington the review drew on hierarchy and the distinctive "Profession of Arms" as the answer.[176] It also looked to the US and UK, taking a workplace health and safety approach adopted in the UK to the crash of a military aircraft known as the "Nimrod" disaster.[177] The unlikely nature of such a model, which demands open communication in a flattened structure with the key component of critical thinking and the critical voice being accommodated, was misunderstood when trying to apply it to a closed strictly hierarchical culture. The core belief in adopting an operationally focused culture is questioned. The literature contests that other fundamental structural changes are needed before a culture can change, and by focusing on the human elements over the organizational values, more genuine results are likely.[178] The review never addressed the DFDA's adoption of the criminal laws but comment was made that "the DFDA provides a very similar balance of obligations and protections to those that apply to the civilian criminal law," while noting that the issue of a self-administered discipline system was onerous.[179] This statement, and the acceptance that "an effective system regulating personal conduct must be transparent, demonstrate that people are held to account, and be timely,"[180] along with acknowledging "human infallibility," misses the central problem. The problem is that the coterie administers a criminal punishment system ruled by discretionary human decisions, which makes it separate and different from the criminal system of the primary society, in which the law is imposed through observing a rule of law rather than a rule by men.

Perhaps unsurprisingly, despite the flurry of activity to implement the various recent reviews, new allegations continue to arise. These have included the Jedi Council sex scandal in June 2013 and, in the same month, a further scandal involving hazing of recruits that included sex acts.[181] This is not unexpected in the sense that no system will eradicate abuse, because humans will always be humans. What it does indicate, however, is the expenditure of huge sums of public funding in these reviews, and seemingly "busy" reforms have seen the problem continue apparently unabated. The reality is that abusive behavior is fostered in a culture that remains resistant to the outside, that seeks to distinguish itself as "elite" and maintains its own internal discipline beyond that of the civilian society it is ultimately part of and accountable to. The question left unanswered is whether the sexual abuse and other harassment activities would be any worse if the military was subject to the same system of criminal punishment and discipline as the civil society, or more importantly perhaps, whether they would be less, and whether discipline in the military would be damaged or in fact improve?

Notwithstanding the declared approach of "zero tolerance"[182] and increased reporting, perhaps due to survivors feeling greater confidence in the updated processes and the ethical and cultural change programs, the reality remains that perpetrators are removed and released into civilian society. Thus civilian society becomes the place for military failures, without accountability to the public for the inadequate response to these individuals' conduct. That institutional change requires outsiders to ensure cultural adjustment and relevancy, in alignment with the primary society, becomes a constant need when secret coteries strongly protect their separateness.[183]

CONCLUSION

Despite the perpetual inquiries and reports, along with various changes, the DLA Piper report sadly indicated that "the military has not been able to provide evidence that all—or even many—of the alleged perpetrators identified during previous inquiries were called to account."[184] The secret coterie is left with a lack of confidence from both members and the public, achieving the very opposite of the desired reputational outcome, through its reluctance to address *la brutta figura.* Regardless of the well-intentioned statements, such as those by Defence Force Chief David Hurley, that everything would be done to stamp out abuse, the DLA Piper investigators claimed a lack of open cooperation. The law firm cited difficulties in obtaining information from the ADF and receiving an insurmountable stack of material after the requested deadlines had passed, resulting in this material remaining un-investigated.[185]

Notwithstanding the ever-closer alignments with those of the civilian systems it remains that, the executive arm, through an internal disciplinary process, provides military discipline. This was a key problem for Kirby J in *White v Director of Military Prosecutions.* The judge in dissent considered that the Australian Constitution did not allow for citizens, who are also military personnel, to be tried without a jury, as called for under s80 of the Constitution and in line with the requirements of Ch III courts.[186] No attempt was made by the majority to balance the military demands against the equally, or arguably more important, historical demands of democracies, as regards the rule of law and separation of powers. The majority did not consider the historical importance of the need for civilian control of the military. This position by the courts does not give support to a legislature struggling to address the growing military coterie and its demands.

What is wrong here is the piecemeal, but complicated and expensive, inquiry process. Inquiries tend to focus on one aspect such as one arm of the military, or a certain rank level or type of military personnel, for example women, rather than addressing the whole system. Those inquires that have been broader, and have included significant change recommendations, have often resulted in the military influencing the government response to accord with the military's desires.

None of these activities is surprising when some common sense is applied. Research has been available for many years to empirically establish the nature of power and group behavior, particularly in institutions of hierarchical power. What is concerning is how the separate society manages to keep these matters concealed while prioritizing reputation over all else. Such attitudes and environment, providing a secret protective network, evidently lead to cover-ups and this fortifies abuse. For instance, in the appointment of DART chairperson and former West Australian Supreme Court Judge Len Roberts-Smith, it may have seemed that his position as a military reservist of major general rank was useful, but it may also have been perceived as possibly clouding belief in a fully independent review. Robert Cornall eventually took over from Roberts-Smith as chairperson, but not before Roberts-Smith indicated that a stand-alone royal commission into the HMAS Leeuwin cases was unwarranted.[187] The ADF has managed to evade a Royal Commission into its operations despite such calls having been voiced since its inception in 1951. Originally given 12 months to do its work, the DART final report was submitted in November 25, 2014, taking 24 months longer than intended.

Defence's response to the reviews seems to lag in timing and appears as if little steps are taken rather than a more sweeping approach being embraced. Buried in reviews, the small incremental steps lack a general possibility of substantive cultural and structural change. DART noted the hierarchical and environment risk factors and the long-held anti-dobbing culture that needed to be taken into account, while Defence merely reports statistics or survey results in an effort to be seen to be monitoring the issues.[188] The old adage of "prevention being better than a cure" is apt here. Submissions made to the Broderick Review suggested that academy training for cadets was a costly exercise at around $300,000 per cadet, and that a more appropriate way to provide undergraduate education for cadets was required: "ADFA will be eternally vulnerable to the risks of misbehavior by its students."[189] Vital reforms would require a dedicated urgency that appeared to be lacking when it came to revising the processes for managing responses to sexual assaults. These included requirements for administrative or disciplinary action to be taken, which were not released for a further three years after the DLA Piper review in the form of the revised Defence Instructions (General).[190]

Clearly, the justification that incorporates the whole of the civil criminal law into the military system is in need of revision. Civilian society still demands order to function and uses coercion, such as criminal punishment and workplace discipline, to maintain this.[191] A specialized legitimate constitutional civil court (Art III US; Ch III Australia) could still satisfy the military demands in this regard.[192] There is no reason the criminal law cannot have specific offences applying to a class of persons that satisfy a particular category, which would not be a breach of the rule of law. The law is only applicable to that segment of society that fulfills the essential elements of the crime; for instance, criminal offences by company directors and other professionals falling in specific categories are provided for within criminal codes.[193] A soldier in a modern democracy maintains their joint civilian status while providing professional soldiering. They no longer only need drills in military methods and tactics but they need an understanding of political science, history, international relations, sociology, psychology, and human organizational management systems. The next chapter highlights the importance of this broader knowledge by looking at how other militaries and institutions have addressed matters such as leadership and values.

NOTES

1. Clint Arizmendi, "A Culture of Reviews" *Australian Defence Force Journal* 192 (2013): 81; Elizabeth Broderick, "Advice to the Minister for Defence the Hon. Kevin Andrews" (Australian Human Rights Commission, June 24, 2015): 37–47.

2. Robert Cornall, "Defence Abuse Response Taskforce" Final Report "DART" (Commonwealth of Australia, March 2016) https://www.defenceabusetaskforce.gov.au/reports/Documents/dart-final-report.pdf.

3. Stephen Smith MP, "Paper Presented on the Defence Abuse Response Taskforce" *Press Release*, June 20, 2013 http://www.minister.defence.gov.au/2013/06/20/minister-for-defence-stephen-smith-paper-presented-on-the-defence-abuse-response-taskforce/.

4. Alan Eggleston, "Report of the DLA Piper Review and the Government's Response" (Foreign Affairs, Defence and Trade References Committee, June 2013).

5. Daisy Dumas, "Woman of the Year Is ADFA Skype Sex Scandal Cadet" *Sydney Morning Herald*, December 16, 2013 http://www.smh.com.au/national/woman-of-the-year-is-adfa-skype-sex-scandal-cadet-20131215-2zfcz.html.

6. Peter McClellan, Robert Fitzgerald, and Helen Milroy, "Royal Commission into Institutional Responses to Child Sexual Abuse," December 15, 2017 https://www.childabuseroyalcommission.gov.au/final-report.

7. JA Woodward, "Director of Military Prosecutions Report for the Period 1 January to 31 December 2016" (Department of Defence, April 18, 2017): 4, [9].

8. Minister for Defence, the Hon Stephen Smith MP, "Sex Discrimination Commissioner to Lead Review of the Australian Defence Force Academy and the Australian Defence Force" *Media Release*, April 11, 2011: C. W. Orme, "Report of the ADF Personal Conduct Review. Beyond Compliance–Professionalism, Trust, Capability in the Australian Profession of Arms" (Department of Defence, 2011): 52.

9. See Broderick "Advice to the Minister": 6, 37–47, providing a good overview of the inquiries and reports up to the end of 2014.

10. Geoff Earley, "Review of the Management of Incidents and Complaints in Defence Including Civil and Military Jurisdiction" (Department of Defence, September 6, 2011) http://www.defence.gov.au/Publications/Reviews/SystemsInquiry/.

11. Ibid., Recommendation 33, 43.

12. Ibid., Recommendation 36, 45.

13. Commonwealth and Defence Force Ombudsman, "Management of Disciplinary Complaints. Submission by the Commonwealth and Defence Force Ombudsman" in *IGADF Review* (2011) Enclosure 1 in Earley, "Review of the Management."

14. See DI(G) PERS 45-5 *Defence Whistleblower Scheme*.

15. See Earley, "Review of the Management": Annex B to Enclosure 4.

16. *Administrative Appeals Tribunal Act* (Cth) 1975 and the *Administrative Appeals Tribunal Regulation* (Cth) 2015.

17. Earley, "Review of the Management": Audit Phase Second Report February 25, 2014: 1.

18. Laurence Street and Air Marshal Les Fischer, "Report of the Independent Review on the Health of the Reformed Military Justice System" (January 23 2009): [48], 13; ". . . the ADF's major [military justice system] success story is the widespread employment and popular support for the [Discipline Officer] Scheme."; Mark Cunliffe, Geoffrey Brown, and Gerard Fogarty, "Re-Thinking Systems of Inquiry, Investigation, Review and Audit in Defence, Annex G: Specialist Roles and Processes" (2014): 6.1.9, 31: "Since 2001, the use of the Discipline Officer Scheme in the ADF has more than doubled from 2,333 infringements in 2001 to 5,285 in 2011."

19. Michael Inman, "Defence Criminal Investigations Hamstrung by Discipline Laws: Prosecutor" *The Sydney Morning Herald*, January 6, 2018 https://www smh.com.au/national/defence-criminal-investigations-hamstrung-by-discipline -laws-prosecutor-20180105-h0dyiq.html: "The military's top prosecutor used her annual report to argue the Australian Defence Force should consider abandoning the current military discipline system—based on the largely adversarial civil criminal justice model."

20. See Rodger Gyles, "HMAS Success Commission of Inquiry Allegations of Unacceptable Behaviour and the Management Thereof" (Department of Defence, December 2011): Part III Report: [2.12]: "That makes the investigation of even a minor matter a difficult task."

21. Cunliffe et al., "Re-Thinking Systems of Inquiry": 6.1.8. Summary discipline system; 6.3.3: 30, 32. "The modern US and UK systems also permit an accused member to elect to be tried by Court-martial if they do not wish to be dealt with by a summary authority."

22. UCMJ art 15.

23. Cunliffe et al., "Re-Thinking Systems of Inquiry" Summary of decision following consideration of Report on Stage B http://www.defence.gov.au/Publications/Reviews/SystemsInquiry/docs/Summary_of_agreed_reforms.pdf.

24. Broderick, "Advice to the Minister."

25. 22 "A number of victims, including some who were still serving, [said] they were not confident in the ability of the military to properly and transparently manage any future complaints."

26. Woodward, "Director of Military Prosecutions Report": 4–5, [13]-[14].

27. Gary Rumble, Melanie McKean, and Dennis Pearce, "Report of the Review of Allegations of Sexual and Other Abuse in Defence. Facing the Problems of the Past" DLA Piper Review (October 2011) Volume 1.

28. Rumble et al., "DLA Piper Review": xxxix; Simon Cullen, "Smith Delivers Apology for Defence Force Abuse" November 26, 2012 http://www.abc.net.au/news/2012-11-26/taskforce-to-consider-royal-commission-into-adf-abuse/4391934.

29. Cornall, "DART."

30. Ibid., 1, 15.

31. Ibid., 21.

32. Ibid., 19–20.

33. Ibid., 64

34. Ibid., 50.

35. Ibid., 6.

36. Dave Devlin, "Joint Service Police Group Launched" June 17, 2017 http://news.navy.gov.au/en/Jun2017/Events/3794/Joint-Service-Police-Group-launched.htm#.WnKXv2iCzIU; Gary L Jones, "Collaborative Policing: A Facilitated Approach to AFP/RACMP Inter-Agency Co-Operation" (2017) https://www.army.gov.au/our-future/blog/strategy/collaborative-policing-a-facilitated-approach-to-afpracmp-inter-agency-co; T. Dawe and D. Connery, "Army-Police Interoperability: Collective Contributions to Future Land Power" *Australian Army Land Power Forum* 2017 https://www.army.gov.au/our-future/blog/amphibious-joint-interagency/army-police-interoperability-collective-contributions.

37. Cornall, "DART": 41–43. See further, *Inspector-General of the Australian Defence Force Regulation* 2016 Pt 3, Division 1 s 6 (1) (a) "the following persons are eligible to be appointed as an inquiry officer, inquiry assistant or Assistant IGADF: (a) a member of the Defence Force, of any rank."

38. Cornall, "DART": 43–44.

39. *Chief of the Defence Force v. Gaynor* [2017] FCAFC [151].

40. Cornall,"DART": 42.

41. Ibid., 37–39.

42. Ibid., 43.

43. *O'Callahan v. Parker* 395 US 258 (1969).

44. *Solorio v. United States* 107 S. Ct 2924 (1987).

45. (1994) 181 CLR 18.

46. *Williams v. Chief of Army* [2016] ADFDAT 3 [49] (Tracey and Hiley JJ).

47. *Re Tracey* (1989) 166 CLR 518.

48. Ibid., 570.

49. *White v. Director of Military Prosecutions* [2007] HCA 29.

50. *Williams v. Chief of Army* [2016] ADFDAT 3 [50]-[51] (Tracey and Hiley JJ).

51. DFDA s 63 (1); See Lyn McDade, "Director of Military Prosecutions Annual Report for the Period 12 June 2006 to 31 December 2007" Department of Defence, Commonwealth of Australia, 2008: 1–59: Annex B "Memorandum of Understanding between the Australian Directors of Public Prosecution and the Director of Military Prosecution," May 22, 2007; Jurisdictional considerations and issues have been considered in Rumble et al., "DLA Piper Review": 38; Defence and Trade References Committee, The Senate Foreign Affairs, "The Effectiveness of Australia's Military Justice System" (June 2005).

52. DFDA s 63 (2).

53. Senate Foreign Affairs, "The Effectiveness of Australia's Military Justice System": Recommendation 1; Department of Defence, Government Response to the Senate Foreign Affairs, Defence and Trade References Committee "Report on the Effectiveness of Australia's Military Justice System" (October 2005).

54. Government Response "Report on The Effectiveness of Australia's Military Justice System": 13–14 ". . . [t]he maintenance of effective discipline is indivisible from the function of command in ensuring the day-to-day preparedness of the ADF for war and the conduct of operations" and "[r]ecourse to the ordinary criminal courts to deal with matters that substantially affect service discipline would be, as a general rule, inadequate to serve the particular disciplinary needs of the Defence Force."

55. DFDA s 63 (1)(a)(ia).

56. Gary Brown, "Homosexuality and the Australian Defence Force: The Issues" (Department of Parliamentary Library, 1992).

57. See further, Shirleene Robinson, "Witch-Hunts and Surveillance: The Hidden Lives of Queer People in the Military" *The Conversation*, April 25, 2017 https://theconversation.com/witch-hunts-and-surveillance-the-hidden-lives-of-queer-people-in-the-military-76156; Dylan Welch, "Fighting the Enemy Within" *The Sydney Morning Herald*, April 16, 2011 http://www.smh.com.au/federal-politics/political-opinion/fighting-the-enemy-within-20110415-1dhu1.html.

58. Brown, "Homosexuality": 15.

59. Ibid.: Annexure B unacceptable sexual behavior by defence members. [4].

60. See e.g., Defence Instruction (General) October 2001: 18 (1).

61. Robinson, "Witch-hunts"; But *cf* Miranda Devine, "Mardi Gras: Why Were Aussie Soldiers Allowed to March?" *The Queensland Times*, March 6, 2017 https://www.qt.com.au/news/mardi-gras-why-were-aussie-soliders-allowed-march/3151185/.

62. Robert Burton-Bradley, "ADA Says Women Not Suited for Land Combat Because of Rape Risk" *News Ltd*, April 13, 2011 https://www.news.com.au/national/victims-demand-defence-forces-abuse-inquiry/news-story/68ef2a3438534fdb16bfab9a48caf88b?sv=20ee52be2c7757c1f375cbf9bbc53d71.

63. *Defence Act* 1903 (Cth) s 9A (2); DI(G) ADMIN 08- 2 "Use of Social Media by Defence Personnel," January 16, 2013: [19] ". . . Defence personnel must not post material that is offensive towards any group or person based on any personal traits, attributes, beliefs or practices that exploit, objectify or are derogatory of gender, ethnicity or religion. Such behavior involving social media may amount to conduct that could constitute an offence against provisions of the DFDA, the *Public Service Act* 1999 or amount to a breach of the APS Code of Conduct." This policy extended to army reserve members not on duty.

64. *Gaynor v. Chief of the Defence Force (No 3)* [2015] FCA 1370, [117]-[118].

65. [2015] FCA 1370 [186]; *Chief of the Defence Force v. Gaynor* [2017] FCAFC 41

66. [2015] FCA 1370 [280]–[287].

67. [2017] FCAFC 41 [112]. *Defence Legislation Amendment (First Principles) Act* 2015 (Cth). On 1 October 2016, the *Defence (Personnel) Regulations* were repealed and replaced by the *Defence Regulations 2016* (Cth).

68. *Chief of the Defence Force v. Gaynor* [2017] FCAFC 41 [47]-[65]. See further, *Cunliffe v. The Commonwealth*, 182 CLR 272, 326 (Brennan J) "The implication is negative in nature: it invalidates laws and consequently creates an area of immunity from legal control, particularly from legislative control."

69. *Chief of the Defence Force v. Gaynor* [2017] FCAFC 41 [108].

70. Ibid., [109]–[110].

71. Ibid., [106].

72. Kevin Foster, "Looking for Failure? Why the ADF Hates the Australian Media" *The Conversation*, August 13, 2013 https://theconversation.com/looking-for

-failure-why-the-adf-hates-the-australian-media-16800 [15]; Kevin Foster, *Don't Mention the War: The Australian Defence Force, the Media and the Afghan Conflict* (Monash University Publishing, 2013).

73. Jonathan Turley, "The Military Pocket Republic" *Northwestern University Law Review* 97 (2002): 1, 76.

74. McClellan, "Royal Commission."

75. Cornall, "DART": 47.

76. Ibid., 28–30.

77. Ibid., 6, 59.

78. Thornton, "Sexual Harrasment"; See further, *Williams v. Robinsons* 2000 EOC 93-112 HREOC.

79. Alex Gallacher et al., "The Constant Battle: Suicide by Veterans" (Foreign Affairs, Defence and Trade References Committee, August 2017) https://www.aph.gov.au/Parliamentary_Business/Committees/Senate/Foreign_Affairs_Defence_and_Trade/VeteranSuicide/Report: reporting 118 suicides since 2000.

80. Eoin Blackwell, "Former SAS Trooper Evan Donaldson Declines $1 Million Settlement Offer from Defence" *The Huffington Post*, June 16, 2016 http://www.huffingtonpost.com.au/2016/06/16/former-sas-trooper-evan-donaldson-declines-1-million-settlement/; Alex Gallacher et al., "Operation of the Australian Defence Force's Resistance to Interrogation Training" (Foreign Affairs, Defence and Trade References Committee, 27 March 2017).

81. Michael Koziol, "Former SAS Trooper Breaks Down Telling Senate Inquiry of Brother's Attempted Suicide" *The Sydney Morning Herald*, November 18, 2016 http://www.theherald.com.au/story/4303048/former-sas-trooper-breaks-down-telling-senate-inquiry-of-brothers-attempted-suicide/?cs=4219.

82. Ibid.; Blackwell, "Former SAS Trooper Evan."

83. Gallacher et al., "The Constant Battle": Submission 59, 3.

84. See as amended by *Safety, Rehabilitation and Compensation Legislation Amendment (Defence Force) Act* 2017.

85. Gallacher, et al., "The Constant Battle": Suicide XXV, Chapter 3, 42–43, Chapter 4, 53–58.

86. Alex Gallacher et al, "Matters Raised by NSW Police Strike Force Civet" (Foreign Affairs, Defence and Trade References Committee, 2017); "Operation of the Australian Defence Force's (ADF) Resistance to Interrogation (RTI) Training, November 10, 2016, Senate referred the matter to the Foreign Affairs, Defence and Trade References Committee for inquiry and report by 20 March 2017 http://www.aph.gov.au/Parliamentary_Business/Committees/Senate/Foreign_Affairs_Defence_and_Trade/ADFRTI.

87. Senate Foreign Affairs, Defence and Trade Committee report, *Mental Health of Australian Defence Force Members and Veterans*, September 2016.

88. Gallacher et al., "Matters Raised by NSW": 13 [2.42].

89. Ibid., 15–17.

90. Hayden Cooper, "Officer Breaks Ranks to Condemn ADF's 'Neglect' of Abuse Victims" *ABC 7:30 Report*, March 8, 2013 http://www.abc.net.au/news/2013-03-07/army-officer-says-adf-fails-abuse-victims/4558834.

91. Hayden Cooper, "Officer Breaks Ranks"; "Clarification–Chief of the Defence Force interview on ABC's 7:30 program–7 March 2013" March 8, 2013 https://news.defence.gov.au/media/on-the-record/clarification-chief-defence-force-interview-abcs-7:30-program-7-march-2013. See further Eggleston, "Report of the DLA Piper Review": 51 (Submission 22).

92. Gallacher et al., "The Constant Battle": 22, [3.34].

93. Australian government, "Response to the Foreign Affairs, Defence and Trade Committee Report The Constant Battle: Suicide by Veterans" (Australian government, October 2017): 3.

94. Ibid., 3–4.

95. Gallacher et al., "Matters Raised by NSW Police": 2.16, 8 "Defence at no time in its public announcements regarding the investigation and resolution of this matter named any individuals involved, whether as an alleged participant, witness or survivor . . . Defence's internal inquiries and investigation did not identify any Defence member or individual who may have disclosed this information to the media."

96. Miranda Devine, "It's Not Too Late to Say Sorry, David Morrison. Many Are Still Waiting to Hear a Few Simple Words" *The Daily Telegraph*, October 22, 2016 https://www.dailytelegraph.com.au/rendezview/its-not-too-late-to-say-sorry-david-morrison-many-are-still-waiting-to-hear-a-few-simple-words/news-story/fa861060b1187f75598c0dbcff4288e9.

97. Andrew Greene and Dylan Welch, "Police Say Defence Failed to Cooperate with Jedi Council Sex Scandal Investigation" *ABC News*, November 23, 2016 http://www.abc.net.au/news/2016-11-23/police-say-defence-failed-to-cooperate-with-investigation/8051974.

98. Gallacher et al., "Matters Raised by NSW"; Gallacher et al., "The Constant Battle."

99. Patrick Lion, "ADF Investigation Service Sent 'Insulting and Humiliating' Emails" *News Corp Australia Network*, June 21, 2013 http://www.news.com.au/national/adf-investigation-service-sent-8216insulting-and-humiliating8217-emails/news-story/c28fdce4d40bb66dc3a3d1287a5c34bf; Ian McPhedran, "Senior Australian Defence Force Investigator Risked Execution When She Carried Heroin from Afghanistan to Dubai," *The Courier Mail*, May 29, 2012 http://www.couriermail.com.au/news/national/senior-australian-defence-force-investigator-risked-execution-when-she-carried-heroin-from-afghanistan-to-dubai/news-story/f0660e4a3f100e8ccb82c252eb8d40f7?sv=52c55107288d9e56cb068dea0e794d87.

100. Gallacher et al., "Matters Raised by NSW": 6 [2.7]-[2.8].

101. Ibid., Appendix 2 Item 3.

102. Ibid., 9 [3.3].

103. Ibid., 10 [3.7].

104. Ibid., 13 [1.2]

105. Ian McPhedran, "Defence Sex Scandal: Cadet Secretly Filmed Liaison with Colleague" *Adelaide Advertiser*, April 6, 2011, 17.

106. Minister for Defence, the Hon Stephen Smith MP, "Interview with David Speers SKY News PM Agenda" *Transcript*, April 6, 2011 cited in Eggleston, "Report of the DLA Piper Review": 6.

107. Michael Brissenden and Alex McDonald, "Former Deputy Commandant Warned Australian Defence Force Academy Not the Best Way to Train Next Generation of Officers" *ABC Four Corners*, June 10, 2014 http://www.abc.net.au/news/2014-06-09/former-deputy-commandant-issued-warning-on-adfa/5510658.

108. Minister for Defence, the Hon Stephen Smith MP, "Outcomes of the Kirkham Inquiry" *Media Release*, March 7, 2011.

109. Christopher Knaus and Michael Inman, "ADFA Skype Scandal Cadets Sentenced, Avoid Jail" *The Canberra Times*, October 23, 2013 http://www.canberratimes.com.au/act-news/adfa-skype-scandal-cadets-sentenced-avoid-jail-20131023-2w0hz.html: "The Minister stated that the [Kirkham] inquiry had found that neither the ADFA Commandant, nor the Deputy Commandant, had made an error of judgement in their decision to commence and conclude disciplinary proceedings against the female cadet. Nonetheless, the Minister remained of the view that this was an error of judgement. The Minister indicated that the inquiry report would not be publicly released."

110. Dumas, "Woman of the Year": [13].

111. Ibid.

112. Ibid.

113. Thornton, "Sexual Harrasment": 440.

114. Australian Human Rights Commission, *Review into the Treatment of Women in the Australian Defence Force Academy*, Phase 1 Report, October 2011: 99–100 recommending a hotline and establishing a database; Australian Human Rights Commission, *Review into the Treatment of Women in the Australian Defence Force*, Phase 2 Report, August 2012: 36–37 establishing a dedicated Sexual Misconduct Prevention and Response Office (SeMPRO) and the ability for complainants to make confidential approaches to SeMPRO.

115. McClellan, "Royal Commission" Case Study 40, August 2016: 7 [26] "Royal Commission has been contacted by 111 people about incidents of child sexual abuse within the ADF. Of those 111: 50 contacts were about child sexual abuse at either Leeuwin or Balcombe, and 26 were about child sexual abuse within the ADF Cadets. Also 30 people about allegations of child sexual abuse that occurred at other ADF establishments."

116. McClellan, "Royal Commission": 377.

117. Ibid., Case Study 40: 7 [34].

118. Ibid., 7 [35].

119. Judge Rapke's "Report on Recruit's Charges: Connolly Admitted Bullying," *Navy News*, 1971; McClellan, "Royal Commission" Case Study 40, August 2016: [37].

120. Rapke's "Report on Recruit's": 6; See "DPP Quits over Promotion 'Misjudgment'" *ABC News*, May 15, 2011 http://www.abc.net.au/news/2011-05-15/dpp-quits-over-promotion-misjudgment/2694324. Raptke was dismissed from office as Victoria DPP at age 60 in 2011 due to tensions around appointment of a female prosecutor to a high-level position.

121. McClellan, "Royal Commission" Case Study 40: 7 [38].

122. Cornall, "DART": 31.

123. McClellan, "Royal Commission" Case Study 40, Opening Submissions: [68].

124. Ibid., [95].

125. Ibid., [99].

126. Ibid., Overview: [43]—The procedures could be found in—"the Queen's Regulations and Admiralty Instructions, as varied by the *Regulations and Instructions for the Royal Australian Navy ABR 5016* (RAN Regulations and Instructions), General Navy Orders, and the *HMAS Leeuwin Ship's Standing Orders* (Leeuwin Ship's Standing Orders)."

127. Ibid., Opening Submissions: [49]; see also [74] "Mr Frazer made a claim for compensation to DVA in 2001. The claim was initially rejected due to a lack of corroborating evidence. Following an appeal to the Administrative Appeals Tribunal, Mr Frazer's claim was accepted when he was able to locate a witness to his abuse."

128. Ibid., Case Study 40, Report: 40: 45.

129. Joanna Woodburn and Philippa McDonald, "Child Abuse Royal Commission: Former Navy Officer Says Abuse 'Surprised and Horrified' Him" *ABC News*, June 22, 2016 http://www.abc.net.au/news/2016-06-22/child-abuse-royal-commission-navy-base-rite-of-initiation/7533556.

130. McClellan, "Royal Commission" Case Study 40, Report: 46.

131. Michael Brissenden, "HMAS Leeuwin: Navy Chief Says Defence Turned a Blind Eye to 'Sickening' Abuse against Young Sailors" *ABC News*, June 18, 2014 http://www.abc.net.au/news/2014-06-18/navy-chief-says-defence-turned-blind-eye-to-hmas-leeuwin-abuse/5533766.

132. McClellan, "Royal Commission" Case Study 40, Opening Submissions: [30], Report: [74].

133. Ibid., Opening Submissions: [134].

134. *Cadet Forces Regulation 2013* (Cth).

135. Currently, the legal age when an individual is able to validly consent to sex is: 17 years in Tasmania and South Australia; 16 years in the Australian Capital Territory, New South Wales, the Northern Territory, Victoria, Western Australia, and Queensland. In Queensland, the age of consent for anal sex is 18 years of age. Notwithstanding the age of consent, legislation in the Australian Capital Territory, the Northern Territory, New South Wales, Victoria, Western Australia, and South Australia makes it an offence for a person in a supervisory role to have sexual intercourse or intimacy with a person under their special care who is aged 16 or 17 years.

136. McClellan, "Royal Commission" Case Study 40, Opening Submissions: [152]-[164]: "Pursuant to the Child Protection Policies, AAFC members have mandatory reporting obligations that require any adult supervisor who becomes aware of any suspected or known child sexual abuse to report the matter immediately to local authorities (civilian police and child protection agencies) and report up the chain of command"; [166]: "There will be evidence that Defence is currently consolidating its policies concerning minors in the ADF and ADF Cadets and that a central policy document known as the Youth Policy Manual (YOUTHPOLMAN) will be produced"; The YOUTHPOLMAN from August 2017 prohibits any sexual interaction between Defence and Cadet Adults (including cadets over the age of 18) and Cadets and Other Minors under the age of 18 in any Defence context, 1.2, 1.23.

137. Ibid., [138].

138. Ibid., [171]-[177].

139. Ibid., [193]: "CJF feels she was bullied and refused a promotion as a result of speaking out against the way the investigation was conducted and also for involving the Director General of the AAFC in the investigation."

140. Ibid., [54]: "child sexual abuse were viewed through the general prism of "unnatural" or homosexual acts at the time. The institutional response to such acts was laid down in a variety of Navy Orders that made 'buggery,' 'indecent assault' and an 'act of gross indecency with a male person' offences punishable by discharge from the Navy"; [62]: "survivors will say that they made, or attempted to make, reports about incidents of abuse to staff and that they were not believed, or told that the abuse was 'a rite of passage' into the Navy, or that no action was taken. One survivor will give evidence that he reported abuse to a staff member and was subsequently threatened with dishonorable discharge"; Girard Dorney, "Australia Investigates Horrific Abuse of Over 200 Teenage Boys at Navy Base" *Vice News*, July 21, 2014 https://news.vice.com/article/australia-investigates-horrific-abuse-of-over-200-teenage-boys-at-navy-base.

141. McClellan, "Royal Commission" Case Study 40, Opening Submissions: [51].

142. Bronwyn Grey, "Review into Harassment and Sexual Offences at the Australian Defence Force Academy" (Australian Defence Force, 1998).

143. Broderick, "Advice to the Minister": 50–51.

144. David Wroe and Deborah Snow, "An Officer, If Not Quite a Gentleman" *The Sydney Morning Herald*, December 1, 2012 https://www.smh.com.au/national/an-officer-if-not-quite-a-gentleman-20121130-2am0m.html; Rory Callinan, "ADF Knew of Officer's Affair with Ray Griggs, but Husband Didn't" *The Australian,* March 21, 2018 https://www.theaustralian.com.au/national-affairs/defence/adf-knew-of-officers-affair-with-ray-griggs-but-husband-didnt/news-story/376f21c59c684488e18c59d74315e3fb. See also *King v. Chief of Army* [2012] ADFDAT 4.

145. Eggleston, "Report of the DLA Piper Review."

146. Report to the Senate on the Elimination of Sexual Harassment in the ADF, 1995; Women in the ADF: two studies, 1996 (Burton Report); Kathryn Quinn, "Sexual Harassment in the Australian Defence Force" (Commonwealth of Australia, 1996) http://www.defence.gov.au/fr/reports/shinadf.pdf; Brigadier Hon A. R. Abadee, "A Study into Judicial System under the DFDA" (1997); Bronwyn Grey, "Review into Harassment"; Defence Ombudsman's Own Motion Investigation—Own motion investigation into how the Australian Defence Force responds to allegations of serious incidents and offences. Review of Practices and Procedures, 1998; Military Justice Procedures in the ADF, Joint Standing Committee on Foreign Affairs, Defence and Trade, 1999; Report of an Inquiry into Military Justice in the ADF, 2001 (Burchett Report); Senate Foreign Affairs "The effectiveness of Australia's military justice system": Defence Ombudsman's Own Motion Investigation—Management of Unacceptable Behaviour Complaints in the ADF, 2007; Rumble et al., "DLA Piper Review"; Street and Fischer, "Report of the Independent Review"; Gyles, "HMAS Success."

147. Broderick, "Advice to the Minister": 49, 182: Appendix A provides a detailed description of the reforms.

148. Elizabeth Broderick, "Report on the Review into the Treatment of Women at the Australian Defence Force Academy" (Australian Human Rights Commission, 2011) https://defencereview.humanrights.gov.au/reports; Elizabeth Broderick, "Report on the Review into the Treatment of Women at the Australian Defence Force, Phase Two of the Review into the Treatment of Women in the Australian Defence Force" (Australian Human Rights Commission, August 22, 2012) http://defence review.humanrights.gov.au/reports.

149. Broderick, "Phase Two of the Review": 254

150. Ibid., Recommendation 18 & 19, 36–37.

151. Ibid., 254, 270–271; Eggleston, "Report of the DLA Piper Review": 20 [2.52].

152. Department of Defence, "Sexual Misconduct Prevention and Response Office Supplementary Report 2016–17, A Supplement to the Defence Annual Report 2016–17" (SEMPRO, 2016–2017) http://www.defence.gov.au/annualreports/16-17/Downloads/SeMPRO-Report-1617.pdf:4.

153. Broderick, "Advice to the Minister": 67.

154. Department of Defence, "Sexual Misconduct Prevention": 11.

155. Ibid., 10.

156. Alex Gallacher, "Processes to Support Victims of Abuse in Defence" (Senate, Foreign Affairs, Defence and Trade References Committee, October 2014: [6.18]-[6.19].

157. Broderick, "Advice to the Minister": 49.

158. Australian Government, "Processes to Support Victims of Abuse in Defence" *Response to the Foreign Affairs, Defence and Trade References Committee Report* (May 2015).

159. Gallacher, "Processes to Support Victims of Abuse": 40–41; Department of Defence, The Defence Committee, "Pathway to Change: Evolving Defence Culture a Strategy for Cultural Change and Reinforcement" (Department of Defence, 2012) www.defence.gov.au/pathwaytochange/; Australian Human Rights Commission, "Pathway to Change: Collaboration for Cultural Reform in Defence, Women at ADFA: Measures to Promote Gender Equality and Assessment of Their Adequacy" (Department of Defence. Australian Human Rights Commission, March 26, 2014) https://defencereview.humanrights.gov.au/publications/report-review-treatment-women-australian-defence-force-academy/3-women-adfa-measures.

160. Eggleston, "Report of the DLA Piper Review": Recommendation 5, xi; Recommendation 7 xii.

161. Senate Foreign Affairs, "The Effectiveness of Australia's Military Justice System."

162. *Lane v. Morrison* [2009] 239 CLR 230.

163. [2009] 239 CLR 230; Andrew D Mitchell, "Too Close for Comfort: Lane v. Morrison and Its Effect on Australian Military Justice" *Public Law Review* 21 no. 1 (2010): 9; Alison Duxbury, "The Curious Case of the Australian Military Court" *Oxford University Commonwealth Law Journal* (2010): 155.

164. Street and Fischer, "Report of the Independent Review": [87], [88], [89] .

165. The Defence Committee, "Pathway to Change."

166. McClellan, "Royal Commission": [37].

167. See Cunliffe et al., "Re-Thinking Systems of Inquiry."

168. Len Roberts-Smith, "Sixth Interim Report to the Attorney-General and the Minister for Defence" (June 2014): 23–24.

169. Australian Defence Force, "Annual Report" (Department of Defence, 2014–2015) http://www.defence.gov.au/annualreports/14-15/part-three/chapter-9.asp: Ch 9; Australian Defence Force, "Annual Report" (Department of Defence, 2015–2016) http://www.defence.gov.au/AnnualReports/15-16/Chapters/chapter-5.asp#ReportOfIGADF Ch 6.

170. Australian Defence Force, "Annual Report" (Department of Defence, 2014–2015) Ch 7.

171. Ibid., 107.

172. Orme, "Report of the ADF."

173. Gallacher, "Processes to Support Victims of Abuse": [6.16].

174. Pauline Collins, *Civil-Military "Legal" Relations: Where to from Here? The Civilian Courts and the Military in the United Kingdom, United States and Australia.* (Leiden: Brill Nijhoff, 2018).

175. Orme, "Report of the ADF": [21], [43].

176. Ibid., [42], [112].

177. Ibid., [102]-[104].

178. See e.g., Jay W. Lorsch and Emily McTague, "Culture Is Not the Culprit" *Harvard Business Review* (2016): 96.

179. Orme, "Report of the ADF": Annex C, 52.

180. Ibid., [95].

181. Alys Francis, "ADF Recruits Performed Sex Acts in Hazing, Sources Say" *9News National*, June 22, 2013 http://news.ninemsn.com.au/national/2013/06/22/12/11/adf-recruits-performed-sex-acts-in-hazing-sources.

182. Gallacher, "Processes to Support Victims": 48, [4.6].

183. Banner, "Institutional Sexual Assault": 165–166; See, Jacoba Brasch, *More Martial than Court: From Exceptionalism to Fair Trial Convergence in Australian Courts-Martial* (PhD Thesis, University of New South Wales, 2011).

184. Eggleston, "Report of the DLA Piper Review": 13.

185. Simon Cullen, "Sexual Predators May Have Targeted Military: Report" *ABC News*, July 10, 2012 http://www.abc.net.au/news/2012-07-10/government-releases-report-into-adf-sex-abuse/4121056 ". . . the report's authors have criticized the way Defence has dealt with the latest inquiry, saying obtaining information from the ADF was 'particularly problematic.' They say the review team received a vast quantity of material—'over a metre-high stack'—in the days and weeks after the internal deadline for documents. The report says the material was too voluminous and too late for it all to be considered"; Roberts-Smith, "Sixth Interim Report": 23.

186. [2007] HCA 29 held that the "defence power s51 (vi) is sufficient to enable Parliament to provide for disciplinary powers to be exercised judicially by officers of the armed forces. The power exercised, while judicial in nature, is not the judicial power of the Commonwealth pursuant to Ch III, but is supported solely by section 51(vi) to maintain or enforce discipline"; But *cf* Alexander Street, "Submission No 2 of

Alexander Street SC" *AMC (Transition Provisions and Consequential Amendments) Bill 2012*, July 11, 2012 http://www.aph.gov.au/DocumentStore.ashx?id=3846db08-d509-42cd-8c36-e3eb12fb9157: 3–9.

187. Len Roberts-Smith, "Seventh Interim Report to the Attorney-General and the Minister for Defence" (Defence Abuse Response Taskforce, September 2014): 12; Cornall, "DART": paras [5], [36]-[40].

188. Gallacher, "Processes to Support Victims": [6.20].

189. Brissenden and McDonald, "Former Deputy Commandant."

190. Gallacher, "Processes to Support Victims": [6.17].

191. See e.g., *Australian Federal Police Act 1979* (Cth) (AFP Act) and the *Australian Federal Police Categories of Conduct Determination 2006* (Cth) establish the disciplinary regime relevant to AFP appointees, category 3 conduct, the investigator may recommend any one or more of the following: termination; remedial action; training and development action; or any other action that the commissioner can take in relation to the AFP appointee. See *Public Service Act* 1999 (Cth) s15 Breaches of the Code of Conduct (1) An Agency Head may impose the following sanctions on an APS employee in the Agency who is found (under procedures established under subsection (3)) to have breached the Code of Conduct:

(a) termination of employment;
(b) reduction in classification;
(c) re-assignment of duties;
(d) reduction in salary;
(e) deductions from salary, by way of fine;
(f) a reprimand.

192. *White* [2007] HCA 29 [134] (Kirby J) "There is absolutely no reason why the functions assigned under the Act to service tribunals could not be performed by a Ch III court."

193. See e.g., *Criminal Code Act* 1995 (Cth) Part 2.5 Corporate Criminal responsibility; Part 5.5 Prescribed terrorist organization.

Chapter Five

Lessons from Others

EXPERIENCES IN OTHER MILITARIES

Post-communist states saw total transformation in their militaries after the fall of the Soviet Union in 1989. While the experience was individualized to each state's circumstances, it was a remarkably quick and significant transformation. The case of the Czech Republic provides a demonstration of how change in the military society is possible. The new Czech Republic sees the separation of powers and institutional structures along similar lines to Western democracies such as the US and Australia. A president can appoint top military officers and is the supreme commander of defense.[1] However, somewhat like Australia, this power is limited through parliamentary authority and any presidential decisions are based on agreement with the prime minister and the minister of defense. The legislative power is the same with regards to controlling the budgetary purse strings, but is stronger than in Australia or the US as the legislature decides whether the military goes to war, rather than the executive.[2] Of especial interest is the abandonment of military discipline with its own specialized courts in 1993. The Czech military, numbering around 80,000 prior to 1989, has reduced to around 22,000 persons who are now subject to the mainstream criminal justice system.[3] It would appear that the sky has not fallen in. Quite the contrary, the Czech Republic can report having a military that went from "control through scandals" reported in the media in the early to mid-1990s[4] (not unlike the US and Australia), to a newly reframed and functioning military within a civil-military controlled democratic state. This is not to say there were no road bumps initially, as a country with citizens suspicious of its military was now placing civilians in charge.[5]

Certainly, the transformation was dramatic following the "Velvet Revolution," so-called because with the demise of the USSR the change was largely bloodless, beginning with a mass demonstration in 1989. Free elections were first held in 1990 and the result saw the division of the former Czechoslovak Socialist Republic into two states in 1993, the Czech Republic and Slovak Republic. Soldiers were able to choose which new state they would serve and many went with the Czech Republic.[6] Moving from a totalitarian Communist Party–controlled state to a modern democratic market economy saw a number of purges of the membership of the military and a dramatic downsizing. On January 1, 2005, conscription was replaced with a system of volunteer professional soldiers. Initial changes were swift with a complete refresh of commanding officers of the general staff by 1993, and a reduction in generals from 240 in 1989 to 20 by 1996.[7] Now the military is an all-volunteer professional force of around 22,000 with a small reserve force of approximately 1,000 and around 8,000 civilian employees in the Ministry of Defence.[8]

These events, plus the new détente, saw citizens questioning the need for a military at all, leaving military morale low. Czech citizens largely disengaged from their military, perhaps more so than other Western democracies, because of the dramatic change from a state of military pervasiveness through all of society during the Cold War to the post-Cold War feeling of freedom.[9] The military purpose had gone, from defense of the nation as part of the front-line Eastern Bloc countries ready to prevent Western European invasion, to finding security through joining with NATO in March 1999 and moving to a peacekeeping focus.[10] In order to do this, certain reforms were inevitable. Becoming part of NATO stimulated the further goal of joining the European Union in 2004. For small states, being under the protection of an internationalized security force has advantages. The aim of advancing peace and stability and fulfilling peacekeeping duties, crisis management, and other public benefits in non-traditional military domains became more relevant.[11] Participation in NATO brought with it requirements to fulfill certain standards and norms. The Czech Republic's National Defense Concept 2005 and the White Paper on Defence 2011 contained much of the reform proposals.[12] Woman now represent around 14 percent of the military workforce. Since 2003, ministerial orders from the Minister of Defence have ensured a code of ethics and moral oath by soldiers for professional service.[13] As with all change, the period of transition saw many soldiers leave. However, it appears that after the adjustment, with the abolition of the military courts-martial and integration within the civilian justice system, there is little evidence of a breakdown in internal discipline or inability to perform functionally.

Evidence of harassment and hazing practices during the communist era affected the image of the Czech military as it has with many others.[14] The replacement of the longer-term military personnel by a new generation of soldiers[15] brought with it one body, the Personnel Agency, which carries responsibility for maintaining statistical data and personnel records, preventing unacceptable social behavior, upholding crime prevention, health, well-being, and education, and ensuring the care for veterans and retired soldiers.[16] This is in recognition that the quality of the soldiers' experience is vital to the overall defense performance and stability. In 2004, a specific University of Defence was established in Brno. Its aim is to provide high-level qualifications for senior officers based on lifelong education principles. Civilians and foreign students also attend the university in an integrated manner.

The Czech military now has an internal system of workplace discipline like any other organization, which does not replace the operation of normal criminal law. It would appear the Czech Republic has fully embraced the new democratic military[17] and consolidated established democracies such as the US and Australia could learn much from this. There is no subsuming of the criminal law within defense as occurs in Australia and the US. Rather the Czech Republic Criminal Code sets aside certain offences particular to the military, such as Crimes against Military Conscription Section XI; Military Crimes Section XII; Crimes against Humanity and Peace, and War Crimes Section XIII.[18] The Criminal Code specifically applies to a military person as per the following:

> s. 114 para 1 (1)—If the Criminal Code requires a special attribute, capacity or position of an offender for commission of a criminal offence, the offender or accomplice of this criminal offence may be only a person who has the required attribute, capacity or position. An offender or an accomplice of a military criminal offence according to Chapter Twelve of the Special Part of this Code may be only a soldier.[19]

The military police was established in January 1991 and falls directly under the minister of defence.[20] The Criminal Procedure Code confers civilian police powers on the military police. Military police may investigate crimes by military personnel, including in foreign jurisdictions.[21] These are referred to the civilian prosecutor who has conduct of all such matters, if necessary after a soldier is repatriated from the foreign jurisdiction. Military police are integrated with civilian police in their training. The Criminal Code article 52 contains the full panoply of sentencing options, including military options such as demotion in rank. Minor offences can still be dealt with as a workplace discipline matter.[22] Generally, the crime rate in the Czech Republic armed forces is stable.[23] The majority of offending appears to relate to traffic and drug offences with some dishonesty offences. In 2015, only 36 matters were referred to the Public Prosecutor and seventeen were dealt with through workplace discipline. Perhaps most interesting is the Crime and Prevention Programme engaging in preventive training and intervention, which found, when checking 2,181 military persons, that only 23 registered positive for alcohol and 5 for psychotropic drugs.[24]

NATO countries that still have some form of military courts include the UK, Luxembourg, Poland, Switzerland, and Turkey, but many have replaced these with the civilian justice system (Czech Republic, Denmark, Finland, France, Germany, Italy, Netherlands, Norway, Spain, Sweden), or at least are progressing in that direction.[25] Countries outside the US and Australia have led the way by adopting legislation, or even constitutions, that limit their military discipline, particularly where serious violation of human rights have occurred.[26] Both France and Germany have abolished the use of military courts during peacetime, including trial of military offences and of breaches of ordinary criminal offences committed by military persons.[27] This is the exclusive province of civil judges. Military courts only operate when military personnel are serving in time of war in foreign states, although this is also subject to the civil courts' review.[28] This compares with the trial by military courts-martial of civil criminal matters with no distinction between peacetime and war, and now potentially applying to civilians in the US, being supported by the highest civil domestic courts in the US and Australia.

In the Americas, Costa Rica stands out as a country that can provide a distinct alternative, having abolished its national military permanently under the Costa Rican Constitution.[29] It is of note that the country has not suffered any invasion or collapse, as is often suggested will happen if a country is to disband its military. However, reliance on other countries able to come to Costa Rica's aid remains, should defense ever be required.[30] The legal model of permanent neutrality adopted by Switzerland in the nineteenth century provides another model of the way in which states can show restraint in engaging the need for a large military.[31] The Argentinean government in 2009 abolished its separate military discipline system, bringing all matters within the civilian court system during peacetime. Again, it has not led to any dire consequences.[32]

In Canada, the system remains similar to Australia and the US, with a separate military punishment incorporating the civilian criminal law. However, the case of *R. v. Généreux*, in 1992[33] saw the Canadian Supreme Court find the dual purpose of military punishment and criminal law standards applying to military members, meaning that the military system was subject to the requirements of the Constitution including the Canadian Charter of Rights and Freedoms s11(d). This required the appointment of judges within the military system to conform to the charter. After *Généreux* the Judge Advocate General's appointment of judges on an ad hoc basis was not considered independent, as their own career could be affected by the perceived "quality" of their opinions.[34]

Closer to Australia, the creation of a new army for Timor Leste raised interesting issues peculiar to that country. Due to an already established civilian justice system and the conditions of low wages and pre-existing fighting forces, a very pared-back system of military discipline was developed. This shows how using the existing civilian system can be sufficient, with a few specific offences used for short-term punishment (maximum 28 days confinement) by commanders to maintain local discipline. It was acknowledged that there would be no out-of-jurisdiction operations by the military and they would always be close "to towns and therefore to District Courts . . . the soldiers being subject to civil law for civil offences"[35] was agreeable. The importance of "the military system [being] compatible with the civil system, the latter clearly having primacy" was recognized.[36] Timore Leste adopted the local inquisitorial system to use for commanders untrained legally, in order to discover any facts on which to base punishment for breach of discipline.

It has been noted by Mr. Louis Joinet in his report to the UN Sub-Commission on the Promotion and Protection of Human Rights[37] that the trial of military personnel accused of serious human rights violations is still undertaken by military tribunals in many states. However, the situation is changing around the world with more military offending being placed under the civil justice system. The High Court of South Africa has declared that establishing military courts in that country is incompatible with its Constitution.[38] The move to limit military control of discipline is occurring as

> [m]ore and more constitutions and fundamental laws strictly limit the military jurisdictions [Colombia (art. 213), Greece (art. 96.4), Guatemala (art. 209), Haiti (arts. 42 and 267.3), Honduras (art. 90), Italy (art. 103), Mexico (art. 13), Nicaragua (art. 93), Paraguay (art. 174) and Venezuela (art. 49)] or even abolish them in peacetime (Austria, Denmark, France, Germany, Norway and Sweden).[39]

The continued demand of the military and executives in the US and Australia that, due to historically claimed needs for expediency and command control of discipline, the military must remain separate and outside the constraints of the civil system of justice, and in a sense beyond the rule of law, is hard to justify. Decaux proposes that the alternative is simple:

> Either military justice conforms to the principles of the proper administration of justice and becomes a form of justice like any other, or it constitutes "exceptional justice," a separate system without checks or balances, which opens the door to all kinds of abuse and is "justice" in name only.[40]

Members see, as a duty, the resistance by the military to anything that is perceived to touch on maintaining a tight and efficient fighting force. However, this can incur significant reputational cost that in its own way can damage the ability to maintain a functional fighting force, through its effects on morale and on recruitment and retention of military personnel. Looking to other areas, we can see parallels where similar institutions have experienced the damaging effects of their operations. The sexual abuse allegations in the Catholic Church have shown that "[t]he consequence of departing from its own pastoral morality produced profound moral and reputational damage to the institution.[41] It is instructive to consider such institutions.

EXPERIENCES IN OTHER SEPARATED COTERIES

Other areas in which total institutions operate within a specified domain, such as prisons, colleges, immigration detention, and religious organizations, have many of the attributes of secret coteries and thus attract attention and criticism when dealing with sexual assault matters. However, research has generally been specific to each of these types of institutions on an individual basis. Commonality among such institutions includes hierarchically ranked leaders with power over large cohorts of often young mixed genders, survivors and perpetrators living in close quarters or known to each other, and the usage of drugs or alcohol.[42] In turning to these institutions, the military may learn some relevant lessons. Media coverage and legal constitutional requirements have resulted in changes in the operation of some coteries. Justifications for internal control also vary. However, in an interesting twist, one sees the influence of the military on the thinking of these institutions, as they push for means to distinguish their position from the primary society in order to receive a specialized approach to offending and discipline. This militarization of the civilian domain creates a fragmented society in which the law operates differently for the citizen and the coterie members.

Tertiary Education Institutions

The gradual erosion of the common civil criminal law is taking place by a process of stealth. Bozarth states in relation to US colleges:

> The Department of Education exerts large amounts of influence on the state university system through 20 U.S.C. § 1681(a), commonly known as Title IX: "No person in the United States shall, on the basis of sex, be excluded from participation in, be denied the benefits of, or be subjected to discrimination under any

> education program or activity receiving Federal financial assistance." Arguing that sexual assault creates a hostile and threatening environment for the alleged victims, thus giving them unequal treatment, the Department of Education used Title IX as the justification to promulgate guiding documents addressing sexual assault adjudication.[43]

The US Department of Education made changes in 2011 giving universities remit to investigate and resolve allegations of sexual assault reaching beyond just students on campus to non-students and off-campus students. The extension was supported by Congress to allow for swift results through minimum due process. Such processes enable further erosion of the law as memorandums of understanding between the civilian law enforcement agency and the colleges result in establishing a "privatized" jurisdiction that supports the coterie.[44] The slippery slope leads to the colleges' approach, not unlike the military, as non-specialist student service administrators seek to protect the institutional reputation, in the interest of *la bella figura*, in undertaking any investigations.[45] This diminishing of the criminal justice system results in confusion. An obligation that it is reported immediately to the civilian police should be common to all alleged criminal behavior, so that a skilled investigation, protecting the interest of both parties, not just the institution's, enables correct evidence gathering, due process throughout, a common standard of proof, punishment processes, and appropriate counselling services. Colleges should remain focused on their core duties, such as the provision of education and ensuring a safe campus with appropriate security, well-lit buildings, and the elimination of fraternities.

The situation in Australian university private residential colleges and allegations of deadly hazing practices have received attention through two reports and media coverage. Elizabeth Broderick, then Human Rights Commissioner, who, between 2011 and 2015, conducted numerous reviews into women in the ADF, also produced the Cultural Renewal at the University of Sydney Residential Colleges Report.[46] This was criticized for its methodology by a separate report, "The Red Zone," produced by the End Rape on Campus Australia Group,[47] which suggested using focus groups rather than individual survey or interview data in a situation where individuals are vulnerable to pressure produced a sanitized report.[48] It is apparent that, like the militarized hierarchical system that supports young people being placed in leadership positions of power, exercised over junior-ranked "freshers," abuse of the power, unless closely supervised, is nearly always inevitable. This, together with *la bella figura*, has ingrained a bunkering attitude in the university coterie that produces perceptions of elitism deserving of special power. A similar attitude is suggested as a factor underlying Crompvoet's Report into the Australian SAS, which is described as:

> an organization rift [sic] by internal tensions and rivalry (especially between SASR and commando units), a pattern of elitist/condescending behaviors towards support personnel, perceptions of senior leadership failure and cover-ups—real or imagined, and misdemeanours or more serious offences in the field, as well as a culture of drug and alcohol abuse.[49]

Much like the US universities, a creeping belief in the ability not to report crime, but to investigate internally to protect the institution, is observed.[50] Both universities and the military appeal to parents by suggesting they can offer an elite experience for their children in institutions that have respect and authoritative pride as safe institutions. As Banner aptly describes, ". . . university and the military each assume a 'state like' role in members' lives."[51] The lessons of situations where coteries investigate and discipline their own cohorts go unheeded.

Churches

Churches provide salient lessons. They have seen reviews take place over a considerable period concerning abuse of children in Ireland,[52] the US,[53] Canada,[54] Belgium,[55] the Netherlands,[56] England and Wales,[57] Scotland,[58] and Australia.[59] The Catholic Church is just one religious institution that has closed ranks and has gone to extreme lengths to coverup and protect its brand reputation. At the former Catholic Church institution in Tuam, County Galway, they literally just buried their guilt, at least from 1925 to 1961. The Commission of Investigation into Mother and Baby Homes found around 800 remains of babies and children up to three years old. Nuns ran the institution.[60] The impetus for the closed ranks appears to relate to cannon law, in particular the Code of Cannon Law and the attitude demanded by *la bella figura*. While the Catholic Church operates under the civilian justice system, it still has a semblance of internal law that singles it out as a special coterie under the leadership of the Vatican, with the Pope at the helm.

Having voiced condemnation of sexual abuse, the actions of the church have been less transparent in support for survivors, with the senior church elite having knowledge of the issue for decades.[61] The Australian Royal Commission into Institutional Response to Child Sexual Abuse noted that 2,500 survivor stories involved the Catholic Church. This represented 61.8 percent of all religious institutional sexual abuse claims and 36.2 percent of all survivors.[62]

Lessons from the Royal Commission, although specific to children, are relevant to all who find themselves members of coterie-like institutions. When the public become aware through media reporting, governments are forced to respond. However, the unfortunate and repeated experience is that little changes. As the Royal Commission noted, ". . . inquiries rarely led to reform. Instead, authorities attempted to manage 'damage control' by closing down institutions and limiting investigations."[63] Knowing why this is the case is fundamental to bringing permanent change, rather than repeating the inquiry syndrome. Common observations about the institutions were found and are set out here, with emphasis given to those aspects particularly likely to exist in the military:

- *some institutions are more likely than others to enable adult perpetrators*, and children with harmful sexual behaviors, to sexually abuse . . . and to *make it more difficult for the abuse to be detected and addressed*;
- the level of risk within a particular institutional context is influenced by the *types of activities and services provided, the physical environment, the characteristics of the [members] in the institution, and, to an extent, organizational management;*
- *some institutions, such as closed institutions, carry more risk of . . . sexual abuse than others* and these institutions need to be alert to their heightened risk;[64]
- abuse is *more likely in institutional contexts where the community has an unquestioning respect for the authority of an institution;*
- *Cultural, operational and environmental factors* within institutions can all affect the likelihood of . . . sexual abuse and the prospect that abuse will be identified, reported, and responded to appropriately;
- institutional cultural factors include *leadership and organizational culture*, which shape assumptions, values, beliefs, and norms. This influences, among other things, how individuals behave when interacting . . . *what is understood to be appropriate and inappropriate behavior*, and how . . . well-being and safety is prioritized. They can include risk factors such as the failure to listen to . . . or *prioritizing the reputation of an institution over the safety and well-being* of [members];
- *operational factors include governance, internal structure, day-to-day practices*, the approach to the implementation of safety policies and the recruitment, *screening and training of employees*. They can include *risk factors such as institutional hierarchies that inhibit identification of abuse and allowing perpetrators to remain in positions where abuse can continue.*[65]

Any institution that falls within these parameters may be prone to lowered moral behavior and therefore has an obligation to respond in a way that will minimize the risk of abuse. Many of the findings provide some of the most recent information on sexual assault within institutions, enabling greater understanding, and although specific to children, the cadets in the military are firstly of a young age and secondly, much of this is relevant across ages. The commission found that males represent the majority of survivors of sexual abuse in institutions, including in the military, as well as in other areas such as sports clubs, schools, youth detention, religious activities, and out-of-home care, where reporting incidents may be less likely and males are themselves less likely to report abuse.[66] Females on the other hand were found to often enter into destructive sexual activity in institutions, which "fostered a culture of authority, command, and control rather than focusing on the care and wellbeing of residents."[67] With regards to the perpetrators, common characteristics, also important in the military context, included:

- outward charm, but aggressive and controlling behavior when in private;[68]
- position of authority within the institution using their role, power and the trust attributed to them to take advantage of opportunities;[69] and
- older boys used the power they held in an institution to sexually abuse others in charge of disciplining the younger boys: "we were given military rank and positions and it was normally the boys directly above you in rank that dished out the punishments and abuse."[70]

Perpetrators can be linked to the type of institution in which they operate. This includes the ability to access victims, find excuses for their behavior, and thus avoid punishment.[71] The Royal Commission identified four definitional types of perpetrators: "fixated, persistent" perpetrators; "opportunistic" perpetrators; "situational" perpetrators; and "professional" perpetrators.[72] Fixated persistent perpetrators will gravitate to an occupation that facilitates an environment in which they can actively manipulate. Opportunistic perpetrators tend to exploit opportunities given by their role and power within an institution.[73] Situational perpetrators may engage in abuse to release their life stress from factors such as social isolation, self-esteem, and an absence of positive adult models in their lives. Such perpetrators tend to be in positions of trust and will have fewer victims, but they will abuse their victim for longer.[74] Professional perpetrators use their workplace and employment to camouflage their activity and they may show traits of any of the preceding typologies. However, they are often better educated, have less antisocial behaviors, more impulse control, and show an ability to adapt based on how others perceive them in their context.[75] Institutions that operate an internal criminal punishment system can facilitate abuse by attracting the typical perpetrators described. This is particularly so in hierarchical power institutions in which authority provided by rank, respect based on institutional reputation, and poor criminal enforcement enable degrees of tolerance and values such as *la bella figura* to reign.[76]

The military practice of prohibiting contact between cadets and their family is an additional factor in isolating survivors from support networks. This also applies to detention facilities. Some researchers suggest a notion of whole-of-institution grooming.[77] Exploitation of the institutional procedures and practices, such as commanders referring matters that may be criminal in behavior for lesser administrative processes, or reducing charges to ensure they fit in a lesser category, are just some possible ways for manipulation of an institutional setting. Using rank and position, or establishing impressive reputations such as the "good soldier" are mechanisms by which professional perpetrators can proceed to groom a whole institution.[78] From this, a belief that a survivor cannot successfully prevent further abuse, together with little external superintendence, a culture of impunity can rapidly arise.

Institutions in which dependence on others is important foster confirmation bias.[79] Members often seek to protect the institution above their own or other members' concerns.[80] Primary society's respect for the institution enables the avoidance of scrutiny and any disclosure of *la brutta figura*.[81] The secret coterie of the military is enabled by concealing and avoiding unfavorable activity so their reputation is protected.[82] Unfortunately, such an approach can lead to significant damage when matters leak through the cracks.

The Royal Commission found that such institutions seemed to avoid reporting criminal conduct to the civilian police and engaging with the primary justice system.[83] Further deflecting investigation by calling it "anti the institution" prevents an invasive gaze.[84] Much like the warrior myth in the military, the internal belief system and doctrines inhibit the ability to respond to the abuse. In the church, this includes belief in forgiveness of sins, such as those of the perpetrators.[85] This culture, when operating in a total institution in which discipline is internalized, can nurture an environment ripe for manipulation, reducing detection and elimination of abusive behavior. Culture is established by the leaders and cements the disposition of an institution: ". . . culture of an institution is created primarily by those in leadership positions, through the way in which they model behavior and communicate assumptions, values and beliefs."[86]

The turn of the twentieth century saw certain activities, such as adultery, debauchery, sodomy, bestiality, and the sexual abuse of children, promulgated in the first Code of Canon Law, 1917, as canonical crimes, referred to as "delicts" to be tried by canonical courts. A further major development occurred in 1922 when Pope Pius XI pronounced a top-secret instruction delivering a cloak of secrecy over all child sexual abuse (also homosexual, bestial, and confessional soliciting) matters. This document, known as *Crimen Sollicitationis*, brought all such matters under the jurisdiction of the Holy Office, thereby attaching the "secret of the Holy Office" to any information gained during canonical inquiries and trials of these cases.[87]

The secret of the Holy Office imposed a permanent cloak of silence over anyone involved, including the bishops, survivors, and witnesses, by threatening automatic excommunication. This document was to undergo changes that expanded its coverage. In 1962, Pope John XXIII extended it to priests in religious orders. In 1974, the "secret of the Holy Office" was renamed as the "pontifical secret" or *Secreta Continere* by Pope Paul VI, and extended to include "delicts against faith and morals," as well as child sexual abuse by clergy, religious brothers and sisters, and laypersons.[88] Cloaking not only inquiries and trials, but also the allegations, in the strictest of secrecy, the *Secreta Continere* continues in force.[89] That the secret is itself kept secret is apparent from the evidence provided by Bishop Robinson in the Royal Commission hearing in Australia:

> How can that be, that the Pope can issue a decree which is relevant to your work, in both 1922 and again in 1962, and you not know about it? [Answer] . . . the only answer I could give you is secrecy. The Vatican can sometimes be so secret that, quite literally, quoting the gospels, the left hand does not know what the right hand is doing, and that they can be so secret that even . . . I did not know about the existence of this document until about 2000.[90]

Pope John Paul II introduced further extensions in 1983, with a revised Code of Canon Law reaffirming adoption of a pastoral and therapeutic approach to clergy who are sex perpetrators, and rendering removal of such perpetrators by local bishops more difficult. A limitation of time in bringing actions was reduced to five years from the date of the abuse, instead of the seven years in the 1917 Code. Such a reduction for crimes in which survivors can take many years before they can even come to tell someone is capricious and offensive. As the Royal Commission noted, "[l]imitation periods and immunities are arbitrary barriers to prosecutions, particularly given the lengthy periods of delay associated with the reporting of child sexual abuse. They can only work injustice against survivors."[91]

In 2002, Pope John Paul II issued a *motu proprio*, or a personal decree. The decree increased the limitation period to 10 years from the survivor's eighteenth birthday but it confirmed the pontifical secret. Further, it also directed that if a local ordinary conducted a preliminary investigation that suggested an allegation of sexual abuse of children under 18 years of age was true, it must be referred to the Congregation of the Doctrine of the Faith, which would give individual ad hoc instructions on how the case would progress.[92] Again, in 2010, Pope Benedict XVI provided further revision to the *motu proprio*, extending the limitation to 20 years after a survivor turned 18 and enabling dismissal or deposition from the priesthood of a priest according to the gravity of the offence.[93] Prior to this, dismissal was only available in "more serious cases," where there was no possibility of the perpetrator reforming. Tapsell has indicated that a Spanish Canon lawyer, Aurelio Yanguas SJ, in 1946 declared that the purpose of the secrecy was to protect the church's reputation by diverting the matters before they reached the civil authorities' notice.[94] All subsequent Popes maintained this secrecy, which had overturned prior decrees that perpetrators were to be reported to civil authorities.[95]

The documents portray the deeper underlying ecclesial culture of the secret coterie, in which entitlement based on a long history, much like that of the military, incurs a certain deference from state institutions, including the civilian police. This practice enables secret coteries a space to develop their own "so-called" process for discipline. In such societies, morality is the first to fail. If society as a whole cannot be privy to the behavior of these protected groups, then decline in their internal moral standards will be inevitable, and ultimately this damages not only the coterie but also the society that permits its existence.

These coteries also portray a cultural inheritance, in particular the Italian belief in *la bella figura*, the demand to manifest a good appearance for the world. This belief is unshakable as part of codes of honor that reach back to Roman times. It is instilled in the group–whether clans, families, institutions, or even states, and the members of such coteries ignore it at their peril. This ubiquitous thinking has enabled the churches for many centuries to practice forgiveness of wrongs and hide *la brutta figura* from the public, as such wrongs are an unpardonable failure. Like a two-sided coin, beauty and the beast, failures are seen as *la brutta figura*, the ugly side, and to make these public means losing face and public reputation.

The operation of secret coteries outside the mainstream civilian justice system enables a perceived conflict between their internal institutional workings, such as the military discipline law or the canon law, and the civil law common to all. This was a theme observed in the Australian Royal Commission in regards to the Catholic Church. A document called "A Guide to Understanding Basic Congregation of the Doctrine of the Faith Procedures concerning Sexual Abuse Allegations" was created by the Congregation of the Doctrine of the Faith in 2010.[96] This document required local ordinaries to comply with civil law requirements for the reporting of child sexual abuse, when a state had such laws. Only the US was permitted this exception in 2010. However, taking a black letter law approach, if the civil laws were not clear, or in any way did not require mandatory reporting, then the secrecy prevailed. This attitude was described in the Royal Commission as an example of internal institutional doctrine that can restrict the workability of any policy.[97]

The interpretation enabled the church to take a restrictive approach to avoid reporting when it was not explicitly required by the civil law. Questions of genuine morality or obligations to the democratic system within which the coterie operates were not relevant for this determination. This, along with the pontifical secrecy have operated to protect the Catholic Church from disclosing abuse that has been going on for a long time. The Royal Commission indicated that in Australia alone, from 1980 to 2015, there were a documented 4,444 incidents of sexual abuse of children.[98]

If the aim of the canon law was to protect the reputation of the church and its priests, it has only had the opposite effect. The internal process known as *Towards Healing* claims to seek a just and compassionate healing response to survivors, while also considering the perpetrator. The church claims that around 2,215 survivors accessed the process from 1996 to 2013.[99] A survivor making a complaint to the church can go through a process that includes having a contact person appointed to record the nature of the complaint. This presents problems for the gathering of forensic evidence via police interviews, which should always happen first. Although the process indicates that survivors should be encouraged to report to the police, this duty appears not to be always observed. However, it needs to occur so that evidence is not contaminated by others interviewing or taking down details of the survivors' stories under less than forensic conditions. Police are specially trained in taking forensic statements that do not contaminate the evidence, which offers the best chance of successful prosecution within the legal system. As the Royal Commission in Australia has shown, not only do institutions have policies that demonstrate a failure to understand the importance and duty to prioritize reporting in the civilian legal system, but they have, in fact, processes that engage in internal investigations by people with little or no specialized knowledge or training. Even when they do have policies in place there is often a failure to observe the self-created policy.[100]

This is sufficient to raise alarm, but it is worse when the stories indicate that the *Towards Healing* process itself was often not understood or followed, with imprecision in the roles for lawyers and insurers, misunderstanding of conflicts of interest, perceptions of bias, confidentiality, transparency, and power imbalance.[101] If the authority does not agree with the complaint, a meeting is held between the authority and the survivor, who is required to recall the abuse again with the intention of some negotiated outcome and possible "discipline" of the perpetrator.[102] This is all outside the civil and criminal justice system and it presents major challenges to that system.[103] The institutional closing of ranks stultifies any possibility to overcome *la brutta figura* and to address the issues fully. As Bishop Greg Thompson from Newcastle, resigning the day before he gave evidence at the Royal Commission, indicated, the risk to those who speak out includes threats and ostracism from powerful cliques within the coterie.[104]

While the possibility of introducing criminal offences for errant institutions was considered by the Royal Commission, it concluded that despite some institutions having a "criminogenic" culture, either contributing to or even causing criminal behavior, this was not a recommendation it was prepared to make.[105] However, an offence applicable to individuals within an organization for failure to protect those in their care or for whom they may hold a duty of care, to protect them from a substantial risk of abuse by an adult associated with the institution, was recommended. The recommendation extended to creating a criminal offence for owners, managers, staff members, and volunteers (excluding foster and kinship careers) who failed to report sexual abuse of children within an institutional context. This operates in circumstances where they know, suspect, or should have suspected (on the basis that a reasonable person in their circumstances would have suspected, and it was criminally negligent for the person not to suspect), that an adult associated with the institution was sexually abusing or had sexually abused a child.[106] Religious confessionals have been contentious in this domain because of the call for religious freedom to follow the obligations of one's belief system. However, as the Royal Commission pointed out and resolved in recommendation 32:

> The criminal offence of failure to report should apply in relation to knowledge gained or suspicions that are, or should have been, formed, in whole or in part, on the basis of information disclosed in or in connection with a religious confession.
>
> The legislation should exclude any existing excuse, protection or privilege in relation to religious confessions to the extent necessary to achieve this objective.[107]

It has been suggested that an alternative for the confessional dilemma would be to follow the approach adopted by canon law concerning those who falsely defame a priest, namely to require the perpetrator to hand themselves to the police before they seek absolution in a confessional.[108] This would deny the perpetrator a means of receiving confidential absolution, which the Royal Commission considered enabled some perpetrators to commit further offences.[109] It would also avoid challenges of religious freedom and the spectacle of priests preferring to go to jail over breaking the confessional seal.[110]

A resistant and slow response supports the Royal Commission's comments regarding criminogenic organizations providing a safe space for criminal conduct. Lack of reform to canon law, to ensure observance of the civilian legal systems within which the churches sit, arises from the higher echelons of the secret coterie. It would appear that, despite some bishops from Ireland, Australia, the US, and England seeking, at least since 1996, a mandatory reporting to the civilian authorities in the canon law, irrespective of what civil laws require, they have been unsuccessful. The Pope has rejected the requests each time.[111] Bishop Geoffrey Robinson confirmed at the Royal Commission "[h]owever great the faults of the Australian bishops have been over the last thirty years, it still remains true that the major obstacle to a better response from the Church has been the Vatican."[112]

Much as we see the military hierarchy protecting its patch and its senior members, the church has protected its senior figures from *la brutta figura.* That it was not only the Catholic Church is clear from the wide-ranging religious institutions investigated by the Royal Commission. For instance, all but 1 of the 23 Anglican dioceses in Australia together received 1,115 complaints of child sexual abuse, involving 569 named and a further 133 unnamed perpetrators between 1980 and 2015.[113] The Royal Commission revealed a diffused and decentralized power structure in which each diocese largely self-managed the abuse allegations in an unfettered manner.

Conflicts of interest that arise around friendships, where alleged clergy have offended, have been afforded a lot of protection at various levels, either at a committee level or in the local parish. People refuse to accept that their loved priest has been an offender. The results, which only include survivors who were able to lodge a complaint, are likely to underreport the true scale of child sexual abuse within the church.[114] The case study of an Anglican-run home for abandoned children revealed levels of abuse that parallel the types of abuse found in the Abu Ghraib scandal involving the US military internment in Iraq in 2004:

> If children soiled their sheets, the sheets would be wrapped around the child's head with the urine and excrement still on them. Witnesses . . . described punishment involving standing in awkward positions for long periods and being beaten if they moved . . . being forced to stand naked for hours with . . . arms outstretched and a bible in each hand. Staff and older girls took shifts to watch him, and he was hit if he bent his elbows or dropped his arms below his shoulders.[115]

Operating separately from the primary civilian justice system does not prevent secret coteries calling in the aid of the law when it suits its purposes. Relying on legal arguments and civilian lawyers, coteries use the law, rather than their professed values such as high discipline and order, or concern and care for members, in order to avoid responsibility. In the case of the churches considered by the Royal Commission, this included obfuscation through uncertainty as to the legal body responsible, and using the statute of limitations and defenses such as tortious non-vicarious liability.[116] Much of the handling of allegations made by survivors involved mismanagement and failure to follow even their own policy, such as reporting to a Professional Standards Director, or police.[117] Survivors experienced coverups, such as confidential agreements attached to monetary payments and *la brutta figura* keeping everything hidden, thereby creating a re-traumatization.[118]

Having secret coteries operate their own criminal investigations outside the civilian justice system has clearly led to failures and different treatment. The process for the Anglican Church included a bishop making a decision whether to charge an offence under the Offences Canon of 1962. This included possibly setting up a board of inquiry and, if the perpetrator denied the allegations, a diocesan tribunal conducted a "trial" applying rules of evidence—not clearly elicited as to whose rules of evidence—resulting in a recommendation that a bishop may choose to follow or not.[119] This sounds very familiar as it brings to mind the power of a commanding officer in disciplining military personnel.[120]

Notwithstanding these internal processes and policies, a reverend of the church, ordained in 1963, was charged and convicted by the civilian system of sexual assault of a 16 year old in 1968 and placed on a two-year good behavior bond. In seeming disregard of the civilian law, the reverend was transferred to work as a music teacher and to provide pastoral care to children under the supervision of an archdeacon in charge of the North Coast Children's Home.[121] This enabled further offending for which the reverend was eventually convicted and imprisoned. Despite awareness by his bishop over a period of ten years, no disciplinary action was taken against the reverend by anyone utilizing the church's internal processes. The communication between the church and the civilian police was in this case demonstrably less than desirable.[122] Those in charge knew of a summary of allegations that disclosed serious criminal behavior but failed to inform the police. When given a chance to explain this failure to the Royal Commission, the comment was "no idea."[123]

La bella figura is such an ingrained way of thinking that people are unaware of its influence on their actions. The interaction of the canon law and civil law has presented a major dilemma where none should exist. It is *de rigueur* that civilian law prevails. As Bishop Robinson noted before the Royal Commission, "the laws and procedures of the church must not prevent a bishop from obeying the reasonable laws of the State."[124] However, Bishop Robinson quoted from a document prepared by the Congregation of the Doctrine of the Faith, showing the resistance an elite coterie can present: "[t]he Church cannot let itself be influenced by public opinion, at times deliberately stirred up, in order to adapt itself to the mentality and way of acting of the secular world."[125]

The police need to get the best evidence. This means investigating a matter while it is fresh, including interviewing and taking statements from witnesses in a forensic manner, before such evidence becomes corrupted through a survivor being required to repeat their claims many times. Having survivors interviewed by, often untrained, people within the internal institutional system, and with perhaps different desired ends, does not aid a criminal prosecution. The standard practice in the civilian system where a crime may have occurred is for an allegation to be investigated by the police. The person is often stood down from their duties while the investigation occurs or they are arrested once enough evidence is gained and released on bail or held in custody while they await trial. Any internal workplace disciplinary actions follow after the outcome of the criminal trial is known, as the burden of proof is less.

The Royal Commission noted a general feeling among survivors of disappointment in the way institutions have dealt with them.[126] An inappropriate dealing has many consequences. These include enabling perpetrators to continue their crimes, destabilizing society and its criminal justice institutions by enabling impunity, impeding justice, and hiding the extent of the problem. The cost to society of survivors' trauma cannot be calculated as one can never know what capacity the survivor might have had to contribute to society had they not been abused. This is countered by the effects of drug and alcohol abuse, suicide, and other outcomes, which tend to become intergenerational.[127] The Royal Commission heard evidence of what an ideal response, at a minimum, should look like. Importantly, such a response would give priority to the safety and welfare of the survivor, something that is notable in its absence from the churches' internal response processes. These also are bereft of the importance of providing support services for not only the survivors, but also others, such as parents and staff touched by the offending, and the review and superintendence of the process to ensure it is clear and observed.

Most important in all of this is the institution's need to avoid acting as a secret coterie outside the civilian system and instead to report to, and cooperate with, the civilian police, prosecution, and justice system.[128] The public justice system always has room for improvement and much work in that area continues, but it represents society's agreement about what behavior is unacceptable at a criminal level, and how to punish this behavior, to honor victims of crime, to deter would-be perpetrators, and to rehabilitate existing offenders. There are public, or state, criteria involving the entire citizenry, much of which goes beyond, but also includes, the victim's interests. The latter particularly includes protection from the perpetrator, and through the punishment, a public acknowledgment of the wrong done to the survivor and the suffering they have incurred. This provides an added educational awareness to the entire community that has been shown to be vital in overcoming the historical numbness that result in a refusal to accept that "good" institutions (often secret coteries) can have people doing bad things. Part of the belief is that members are above the ordinary, and a special aura then attaches to them. These are all relevant to the healing of a survivor of abuse.

The criminal justice system has also been molded over centuries, and continues to be molded, to accommodate protections for an accused perpetrator at the same time as the one that may have suffered at their hands. This signifies a democracy at work in which all are equal under a rule of law and not a rule by men or individual secretive institutions. The Australian Royal Commission firmly supported maintaining a civilian criminal response. The reasons included punishment of the perpetrator in recognition of the wrong done, not only to the survivor but to the entire community, as part of an understanding that such crime is not just a private matter between the perpetrator and victim; to educate and raise awareness of such offences in order to encourage reporting and convictions; and to act as a deterrent for potential perpetrators, for example by increasing the risk of detection:

> . . . seeking a criminal justice response to institutional child sexual abuse is an important way of increasing institutions,' governments' and the community's knowledge and awareness not only that such abuse happens but also of the circumstances in which it happens.[129]

Maintaining a strong criminal system supports the proper functioning of a democracy and is an important aspect for survivors and perpetrators for the many reasons outlined. This does not mean the criminal justice system is an unchanging stagnate one, as many advancements to aid survivors, while maintaining integrity in the system and fairness to perpetrators, are balanced in the process. These include taking video evidence of interviews with young survivors, use of victim compensation schemes, and even possibly a criminal restorative approach utilizing victim offender mediation.[130] The Royal Commission considered and rejected the idea of using formal restorative justice approaches, preferring instead to support the criminal law response.[131] However, this did not exclude consideration of restorative practices within the civil law arena as covered in the *Redress and Civil Litigation Report* (2015).[132]

The biggest lesson is that by operating as a secret coterie and excluding the proper workings of the state's legal jurisdiction, an enclave is created in which violent offenders and pedophiles can flourish. The aim to protect reputation and to deter the prying eyes of the state, because they are a society in which morals are to be of the highest Christian order, resoundingly comes unstuck. The risk of losing parishioners, now experienced as the coverup ultimately failed, as most coverups inevitably do, could have been avoided. This experience has salient parallels directly with the military coterie.

It is not the military or churches alone that have perpetrators of sexual abuse. The Royal Commission received allegations relating to more than 1,000 institutions that included, along with the churches of all denominations and the military, educational, sporting, healthcare, juvenile detention facilities, theatre and music groups, and generally any organization in which children congregate away from parental supervision, such as child care, foster care, and respite care.[133] This would appear to be self-evident if one acknowledges that a criminal perpetrator will seek the source of their prey, then such institutions will inevitably be a hotspot for those with pedophiliac tendencies. The institutions range from public to private, including both for- and not-for-profit companies and religious organizations and charities. All fit under the umbrella of the one civilian and criminal justice system. However, the worst offending ubiquitously occurred in institutions that were allowed to develop their own means of handling potential crimes on an in-house basis. The most supported in this is the military, which is given a hands-off deference based on the Supreme Court's jurisprudence and an interpretation of the US Constitution that has in turn influenced the Australian High Court's approach to the military.

Next are the churches, which, through a long history, have been accorded some degree of independence through their own declared systems of canon law. The remainder operate under incorporated constitutions written by the group, or in some cases statutory instruments. The culture of blind obedience and fear works in both the military and the church, and it operates to protect the coterie through loyalty to small enclaves, connected through a rank and hierarchical system in which *la bella figura* infuses the cultural blindness:

> The church is not good at handling faults within itself. It tends to ignore them, to cover them up, to do anything, but not look at them . . . it leads to a morality of doing things because you are afraid rather than doing things because they are right; not making up your own mind; you obey the law of someone above you and you don't really think for yourself.[134]

Some have identified the institutional failure across the board as driven by a divide between rights and trust. Banner describes the individual, and perhaps groups, as having a rights-centric approach and the institution as holding a legitimacy based on trust. The latter is dependent on reputation that enables both member and civic belief in large institutions.[135] A balance generally ensures that individuals feel that rights are maintained and their trust is well placed. However, when the two are unbalanced, the institution becomes troubled. Banner observes "[u]nwanted sexual contact happens . . . in these locations with greater frequency than they do . . . in society as a whole."[136] Institutions such as the church, military, universities, and detention centers provide closed hierarchical structures, accommodating the use of internal processes that deny civilian rights and avoid the primary civilian governance. Unfortunately, these institutions are most frequently dealing with young adults or even children and in locations in which alcohol and drugs may be prevalent.

The Point of Connection

One may wonder how the issue of sexual abuse in churches is relevant to abuse in the military. Apart from the fact that both are major institutions within democracies, there are some fundamental and shared historical origins that may explain the conduct of these secret coteries, as related to their special laws and feelings of elite separatism from the mainstream civilian society. Foley explains how this works:

> At the heart of the protective stance was a culture of "clericalism" which takes as its premise that priests who are "ontologically changed, or marked out by God through ordination as special people whose very nature has been changed [as a consequence of their ordination] . . . deserve to be treated differently." The canon law provisions are designed to protect this privilege so that all investigations of clergy sexual assaults are to be carried out in a way which allows priests to be "treated more leniently than every other citizen."[137]

To understand this, one has to return to the beginnings of the church in Europe, and particularly the Catholic Church in Rome, and to the beginnings of military codes for control of conduct as part of the Roman and European approaches. To explore the cultural connection and location with its Roman ties, it is necessary to digress a little to absorb some accepted cultural attributes that are particular to the Italian psyche. An understanding of the nature of *la bella figura*, the male hierarchical culture, the associated difficulty for civic governance, and a preference for small communities making coteries responsible to their own[138] can all aid in understanding the psyche behind the response of the churches and the military. Historically, it arises from common cultural origins.

The Italian connection, and more particularly the Roman military influence, can be identified in codes for military discipline, with many codes based on a detailed borrowing from others, carrying them through antiquity to the present day.[139] Sixteenth-century military literature was frequently written in the Italian language.[140] The English military, during the age of Elizabeth, had served in European wars and observed Italian command during the wars between Charles V and Francis I.[141] English military codes, such as the code of the Earl of Leicester, and Richard II, 1385, provide early examples in which the articles of war commence with religious stipulations.[142] Gustavus Adolphus' Articles of War in 1621, some 236 years after Richard II's Articles, were created for the citizen-soldiers in Adolphus' conscript Swedish military and the articles set out the duties of soldiers as well as the consequence for breaching those duties. Interestingly, a commander's responsibility to soldiers was not mentioned, but the first 16 articles covered religion in a Protestant vein. Religion had a pervasive presence intermixing with military groups. Adolphus encouraged chaplains to operate within the military cohort.[143] As Hagan observes,

> . . . resemblance among codes permits the reasonable inference to be drawn that each followed the other in more than just time. Gustavus Adolphus's code was not the beginning of modern articles of war. It was but one of a succession of such codes, each relying heavily on those that had been used before. They all, of course, bear a marked resemblance to Roman martial laws.[144]

Documents such as the early fourth-century Roman work *De Re Militari*, by Vegetius, and printed in 1473; a penal code called *Carolina* and promulgated by Charles V, Holy Roman Emperor from 1519 to 1556; and the codes of the Elizabethan military, all have a common lineage.[145] As Sherrill states in relation to the US:

> The job of drafting the original military code for this country in 1776 was so distasteful that most members of the Continental Congress committee assigned the task shirked it, and the job was left to John Adams. Adams had such a strange notion of what the new nation stood for that he copied the handiest tyrannical code available. . . . It was Adams' timourous notion that "nothing short of the Roman and British discipline could possibly save us. . . . There was extant, I observed, one system of Articles of War which had carried two empires to the head of mankind, the Roman and the British. . . ."[146]

The military, like the churches, is comprised of smaller groups within the overall structure. The early English military contained a group of between 100 to 200 men led by a captain. The captain's reputation was often not a good one. Hagan describes that

> . . . captains were colorful and sometimes courageous; more often, they were simply corrupt. . . . Their crimes ranged from petty thievery to mass murder. Immorality, cowardice, absenteeism, disgraceful neglect of men and provisions, disregard for even a modicum of military discipline, ignorance of training procedures and tactics—these were but some of their faults, so that the name of captain became odious to soldier and citizen alike.[147]

Sutcliffe indicates that the Romans had incurred similar problems:

> . . . the principall caise of the neglect of military discipline proceedeth from fraude, negligence, and insufficiency of Officers. He therefore that desireth to bring things into order, must begin with reformation of Officers, who both first brought in, and since have continued many disorders, in the proceedings and practice of armes.[148]

Similarly, bishops and cardinals headed dioceses with priests in charge of congregations within a diocese. These small tight-knit groups of men established a system of internal loyalties to their particular group, held together by the hierarchical structure demanding obedience and respect to their code. Like the captains, the church leaders had a variable reputation.[149]

Leadership of the small groups to this day remains a key factor in how the group behaves towards all those within and without the group. The transition from the Dark Ages through to the Middle Ages involved moves to achieve improved moral behavior. Rules covering matters such as an officer and gentleman and fraternization were supported by the feudal caste system in which hierarchical loyalty, faith, and breach of faith were enforced through severe discipline.[150]

One can rightly ask what has changed from these early beginnings in a system that has remained stable and often unchanging over a long period, being reliant on a philosophy that supports a secret coterie. The feudal system from which the notion of coteries arises relied on an unbreakable understanding and enforcement of the social mores of the time.[151] This history provides an understanding out of which the current system grew, and within which, despite good actions by good people, strands of *la bella figura* persist.

The Roman military law was able to maintain an influence through the Dark Ages to the Renaissance, aided by a classical revival.[152] This classical revival started out of Italy in the thirteenth century when the *condottieri,* studying the art of war, arguably modernized its development in Europe. Works from the Renaissance period such as *The Art of War* by the Italian Machiavelli[153] drew on Roman military practice and had a profound influence on military thinking around many aspects, including leadership and discipline.[154] Machiavelli drew heavily on Roman law in his work and consulted with the Italian *condottieri*.[155] He devoted considerable thought to the role of command and the importance of leadership. Machiavelli was not alone in his influence.

Pierino Belli, an Italian Catholic who served as a high-level advisor to the Holy Roman Emperor, Charles V, and King Philip II of Spain, and who was nominated counsellor to the Duke of Savoy in 1561 and in 1563, was as an early thinker with considerable influence on the laws of war. In particular, he addressed the conduct of military personnel's behavior and their punishment.[156] His principle beliefs were based in natural law and he aimed to alleviate some of the brutality of war, particularly for civilians.[157] Belli drew on both Roman law and Canon law when deriving his principles, for instance on the right of self-defense.[158] Importantly, these principles maintained, at the time, the obligation for soldiers to be subject to ordinary civilian law.

He relied for example on the Roman law rule that a soldier who invades a home at night can be treated as all home invaders and were given no special rights.[159] Alberico Gentili, who lived from 1552–1608, was another Italian lawyer, influential through his chair of civil law at Oxford, in introducing Italian and Roman thinking into England.[160] This group of Italians, among others, have, from the fifteenth century onward, influenced the laws of war, including codes for military conduct. After the English Reformation Italian Protestants found a refuge in England, their small number could transmit Italian cultural patrimony, thus bringing influences into English military thinking.[161] The court-martial ironically is a continental clone that has remained attached to English military discipline, while European countries have moved to abandoning a courts-martial system in favor of working closely with their civilian justice systems.

At the same time, canon law had travelled, bringing the influence of Roman codes via the bishops engaged in offices of state:

> The church lives by Roman law (*ecclesia vivit lege Romana*) was the saying, for the law of the Roman Catholic Church entwined itself with Roman law in order to incorporate ancient Rome's principles of justice, and in order to share in the esteem in which ancient Rome was universally held.[162]

Hence, the story that underlines military discipline has a strong connection to the Roman law, and Italian cultural and legal principles often filtered through canon law. The English system, from which military discipline in both Australia and the US arose, drew heavily on these influences. Ultimately, the military developed a separate code of discipline in parallel to the common law, but this had not always been the case. The statute of Edward I in 1279 gave the sovereign the ability to command and discipline all military forces through the exercise of the royal prerogative. This exclusive control extended specifically to disobedience, desertion, and cowardice. In the eighteenth century, Blackstone claimed that military discipline was not connected to any settled legal principles but was rather more "an indulgence than a permission of law," and consisted of a series of arbitrary decisions.[163] These ad hoc decisions arose as part of the historical development of militaries and their control. It has been claimed variously that discipline was delivered through the Chivalry Court of the Lord High Constable and Earl Marshal,[164] or constables and marshals who were military officers.[165] During Elizabeth I's reign, she nominated a Judge Martial (or Marshal) to accompany the Earl of Leister's army in 1587–1588.[166] Meron claims that Richard II established the first comprehensive articles of war in 1385 at Durham, and that Henry V, in 1419, added capital offences to better enforce military discipline and protect foreign non-combatants. Severe punishments provided for the death penalty, mutilation, flogging, and forfeiture of possessions.[167] As Squibb confirms:

> [u]ntil the passing of the Mutiny Act legalised the maintenance of a standing army the legal basis of military discipline was of a purely temporary nature, resting upon whatever Ordinances or Articles of War happened for the time being to be in force. In times of peace . . . there was no military law.[168]

So it appears that during the seventeenth century, instead of a fixed code, articles of war were provided for by military commanders operating under royal commission,[169] but in peacetime the military law could never operate while "the king's courts [were] open for all persons to receive justice according to the laws of the land."[170] Civil offences committed by military persons proceeded through the ordinary civil courts in the early medieval times.[171]

It was not until a century after The Hundred Years' War (1337–1453)[172] that the concerns arising from disbanded military men acting as mercenaries prompted the monarchs of Europe to establish national armies. These developments required payment by the sovereign of the members in return for their loyalty, and they were housed in garrison locations controlled by strict Spartan-like codes of military discipline.[173] These coterie establishments led to the direct development of the idea of the elite soldier class, with their internal structures, administration, and rules. The development of the coterie was a gradual one but was clearly connected with the idea of a separate society. The derivation from the Roman Empire, when the soldier was subjected to the rule of his commander, through to the establishing in the 1600s of permanent standing militaries controlled by a central authority, usually a sovereign monarch in a hierarchical command structure, is clear.[174]

Oliver Cromwell, who in 1642 was a parliamentarian, not a monarch, led the New Model Army (1645)[175] as the first real standing army in England. Again, the environment of its founding was enveloped in religious discipline and fervor, uniting the army in its cause. Cromwell sought to curb the king's power by ensuring Parliament could defend the citizens' just rights. Cromwell's military claimed that it represented the people, who needed protection from the monarch who was not acting in their best interests. This gave rise to concerns about the civil-military relationship. Finer has subsequently identified the risk by noting that when "[t]he military draw this distinction between the nation and the government in power, they begin to invent their own private notion of the national interest. . . ."[176]

The *Petition of Right* 1627[177] established that only the civilian courts, common law and equity, were to apply to soldiers and citizens in the UK during peacetime. The subsequent *Mutiny Act* 1689[178] was established to deal with the specific incidents involving the desertion of soldiers from William of Orange, and it was only meant to be a temporary measure for six months. Instead, it became more permanent in setting out the particular grounds for discipline in the armed forces. This legislation attempted to locate the military within the constitutional structure, under the control of the monarch. It provided Parliament with a controlling check by requiring regular consent, at certain intervals, for the military to continue. The courts contributed to this containment of military power by hearing cases. The annual consent was repeated in the preamble of the *Mutiny Act* up until 1878, and thereafter every five years, and it remains relevant today.[179] This progeny of military discipline has a link to how sexual and other internal abusive behaviors have been enabled.

AN ELITE CULTURE OF SECRECY

Sexual abuse has arisen in secret coteries, such as churches, and where power and the law is in the hands of mostly men in a hierarchical and tightly controlled separate manner. The dogma, teachings, laws, and customs have derived from classical Roman and Italian influences in which the cultural tendency to present a best picture, *la bella figura,* means that anything that may damage that impression is hidden away. The pedigree of the belief systems of these two institutions comes from a single stream as their source. This means that even the apex of power, such as the Pope in the case of the Catholic Church, or the commander in chief of the military, will find breaking with that traditional source an extraordinarily difficult thing to do, even if in reality their position makes it easy to direct a change. Pope John Paul II could have directed a very different outcome, but for almost twenty years after the first public stirrings around the degree of abuse erupted, silence and concealment was the response. To have done otherwise would entail implying that those who have gone before were wrong, and in a system where loyalty to the members is essential, this becomes a perceived impossibility. Bishop Robinson stated that "before ordination as a bishop, every candidate is required to take an oath of loyalty to the pope—not God, not the church, but the pope. Every bishop is meant to be 'a pope's man,' and bishops take this oath seriously."[180] That the church coterie has evolved to become stronger and more protected over time, much like the military since the *Petition of Right* in the UK, is clear:

> The Acts of the Apostles show that Peter, the first pope, was not above criticism and had to answer to the church for his actions (11:1–18). Today, on the contrary, the pope is held to be above criticism, is not answerable to the church and

> must be protected and defended in every way possible. This culture of obsessive secrecy has been a powerful factor in the mishandling of abuse.[181]

Much like the continuing difficulty in obtaining clear and useful data, the operation of secrecy in the churches is aided by the inability to obtain accurate statistics and lack of clear and transparent reporting to civilian authorities:

> We could never get full figures because . . . in a religious order the superior would handle a case, or mishandle it, whichever, but he would leave no written records, so that when he went out of office and his successor came, quite literally, the successor did not know what happened. . . .[182]

This historical contextual outline indicates how the separate society has been sustained. Yet the first part of the chapter has indicated that the modernization of many countries' militaries has reinforced the distinction between the civil and military domains, and has reasserted the dominance of the civilian through eliminating courts-martial and military control of criminal behavior. This has not led to the dire consequences used as arguments justifying sustaining the current courts-martial system and the combination of criminal and workplace discipline as they exist in the US and Australia, but instead has seemingly worked efficiently and given soldiers equality of treatment. Unfortunately, the next chapter shows how sustaining coteries influences the operation of a democracy from within the system of government in the US and Australia, resulting in a form of militarization of the primary society.

NOTES

1. Military Strategy of the Czech Republic (Prague: Ministry of Defence, April 2012).
2. Czech Republic Defence is governed by the *Constitutional Act* No. 1/1993, the Constitution of the Czech Republic; *Constitutional Act No.* 110/1998; *Security of the Czech Republic*—Act No. 219/1999; *Armed Forces of the Czech Republic*—Act No. 221/1999; *Professional Soldiers*—Act No. 220/1999; *Course of Conscription or Alternate Service and Military Exercises and Some Legal Relations of Reserve Soldiers*—Act No. 222/1999; *Arrangements for Defence of the Czech Republic*—Act No. 585/2004; *Conscription and its Ensuring (the Conscription Act)*—Act No. 124/1992; *Military Police*—Act No. 153/1994; *Intelligence Services of the Czech Republic*—Act No. 289/2005; Tomas Zipfel, "The Politics and Finance of Civil-Military Reform in the Czech Republic" *Journal of Communist Studies and Transition Politics* 17 no. 1 (2001): 96, 108.
3. See Act No. 141/1961 Coll. *Criminal Procedure Code*. The civil courts deal with all criminal offences committed by military personnel.

4. Zipfel, "The Politics and Finance": 109.

5. Larry L Watts, "Reforming Civil-Military Relations in Post-Communist States: Civil Control vs. Democratic Control" *Journal of Political and Military Sociology* 30 no. 1 (2002): 51.

6. Zipfel, The Politics and Finance": 3, 101; Zdenek Kríž, "Army and Politics in the Czech Republic Twenty Years after the Velvet Revolution" *Armed Forces & Society* 36 no. 4 (2010): 627.

7. Zipfel, "The Politics and Finance": 3, 100.

8. Military Strategy of the Czech Republic (Prague: Ministry of Defence, April 2012) no. 32: "National defence is a civic duty and a moral obligation at the same time. The legal duty of citizens to defend their homeland has not ceased despite the transformation of the Armed Forces of the Czech Republic into an all-volunteer force."

9. Roman Blasek, "Perception of Security Risks by the Population of the Czech Republic" *The Journal of Slavic Military Studies* 11 no. 3 (1998): 89, 90–91 "Czech citizens showed the lowest fear of global conflict (12 percent) of 50 countries in a 1995 Gallup poll. The same poll saw 31 percent of US citizens believed global conflict would occur in the next 10 years."

10. Military Strategy of the Czech Republic (Prague: Ministry of Defence, April 2012) no. 26: "The Armed Forces are capable of participating in peace enforcement, peace support or peacekeeping operations and post-conflict stabilisation and reconstruction missions. In addition, the personnel of the Armed Forces of the Czech Republic may also perform tasks as part of humanitarian missions, rescue and evacuation efforts and take part in additional civilian operations and observer missions led by international organizations."; Daniel N. Nelson, "Civil Armies, Civil Societies and NATO's Enlargement" *Armed Forces & Society* 25 (1998): 137.

11. Zipfel, "The Politics and Finance": 3; Štefan Sarvaš, "The NATO Enlargement Debate in the Media and Civil-Military Relations in the Czech Republic and Slovakia" *European Security* 9 no. 1 (2000): 113.

12. The Ministry of Defence of the Czech Republic, "White Paper on Defence" (Department of Communicationand Promotion, 2011); "The Long Term Perspective for Defence 2030" (Ministry of Defence of the Czech Republic, 2015) http://www.army.cz/images/id_8001_9000/8503/THE_LONG_TERM_PERSPECTIVE_FOR_DEFENCE_2030.pdf.

13. Czech Armed Forces National Report for CWINF Year 2003 Annex E to IMSTAM(WIN)005-04 https://www.nato.int/ims/2003/win/national_reports/czech.pdf.

14. Jirí Hodný and Radim ŠTastný, "Bullying in the Army of the Czech Republic" *The Journal of Slavic Military Studies* 10 no. 1 (1997): 128; David M. Glantz, "Military Training and Education Challenges in Poland, the Czech Republic, and Hungary" *The Journal of Slavic Military Studies* 11 no. 3 (1998): 18.

15. Glantz, "Military Training": 10.

16. Ministry of Defence & Armed Forces of the Czech Republic, Personnel Agency http://www.army.cz/en/armed-forces/organisational-structure/general-staff/personnel-agency-87195/.

17. Kříž, "Army and Politics"; Rostislav Mazurek and Vladimír Karaffa, "Doctrine of the Armed Forces of the Czech Republic" (Ministry of Defence, Joint Forces Command, University of Defence and Training and Doctrine Directorate, 2004) http://www.army.cz/assets/en/ministry-of-defence/strategy-and-doctrine/acr_doctrine 2004.pdf.

18. Criminal Code No. 40/2009 Coll. Chapter XII–Military Criminal Offences (Sections 375–399).

19. Criminal Code No. 40/2009 Coll. 114 para. 4 clarifies when one is considered a soldier.

20. Act No. 124/1992 Coll., as amended.

21. Marek Frystak, "Pre-Trial Proceedings in the Czech Republic" *Jurisprudence* 3 no. 121 (2010): 251, 261.

22. Criminal Code No. 40/2009 Coll. Chapter VII, XII, provides for specific sentence options on military crimes. The most serious offences receive sanction where there is danger to society, lesser workplace breaches are handled by officers exercising disciplinary powers; see also Act No. 221/1999 Coll., on Career Soldiers.

23. "Report on Internal Security and Public Order in the Czech Republic in 2015" (Ministry of the Interior of the Czech Republic, Security Policy and Crime Prevention Department Analyses and Strategies Unit, 2016) www.mvcr.cz/soubor/report-on-internal-security-2015.aspx: 6–7.

24. Ibid., 7: "A total of 43 officers of the Armed Forces of the CR were sentenced in 2015. Sentences were most frequently issued for causing danger under the influence of drugs (12 officers), blackmail (4 officers) and theft (4 officers)."

25. Bastick, "Integrating a Gender Perspective": 31–36; Julio Ríos-Figueroa, *Constitutional Courts as Mediators: Armed Conflict, Civil-Military Relations, and the Rule of Law in Latin America* (Cambridge University Press, 2016): 49–50.

26. Louis Joinet, "Issue of the Administration of Justice through Military Tribunals" (E/CN.4/Sub.2/2002/4, UN Sub-Commission on the Promotion and Protection of Human Rights 54th session, July 9, 2002); See, Constitutions of *Bolivia* (art. 34), *Haiti* (art. 42.3), and *Venezuela* (art. 29); See also legislation in *Colombia (Military Penal Code and the Act on Genocide, Enforced Disappearance, Torture and Illicit Displacement of Populations*), in Guatemala (Decree No. 41 of 1996) and Nicaragua.

27. Edward F. Sherman, "Military Justice without Military Control" *The Yale Law Journal* 82 no. 7 (1973): 1398.

28. Joinet "Issue of the Administration": [16], [27].

29. Costa Rican Constitution November 8, 1949, Article 12.

30. David P. Barash, "Costa Rica's Peace Dividend: How Abolishing the Military Paid Off" *Los Angeles Times*, December 15, 2013 http://articles.latimes.com/2013/dec/15/opinion/la-oe-barash-costa-rica-demilitarization-20131208.

31. Congress of Vienna and the Treaty of Paris of 1815 recognizes Switzerland's neutral status. See Edgar Bonjour, *Swiss Neutrality: Its History and Meaning* (London: George Allen & Unwin Ltd., 1946) and J. F. L. Ross, *Neutrality and International Sanctions* (New York: Praeger, 1989).

32. Leonardo Filippini and Karina Tchrian, "Argentina's New Military Justice System—a Review of Law 26394" *Derecho Penal y Criminología* 91 (2010): 103;

See e.g., J McClelland, "Starting from Scratch: The Military Discipline System of the East Timor Defence Force" *Journal of Conflict and Security Law* 7 (2002): 253.

33. 1 S.C.R. 259, 286 (Can.).

34. Victor Hansen, "The Impact of Military Justice Reforms on the Law of Armed Conflict: How to Avoid Unintended Consequences" *Michigan State International Law Review* 21 (2013): 229, 236.

35. McClelland, "Starting from Scratch": 258.

36. Ibid., 257–58: "As the force would not be deploying overseas the need to have a system of military discipline . . . did not arise. Civil matters could be dealt with in the civil system, thereby imbuing an element of reassurance of FDTL accountability. Accordingly, the scope of jurisdiction vis a vis offences could be limited to military breaches of discipline."

37. Joinet, "Issue of the Administration": 4.

38. Ibid., [23]; [17] "On the 29 March 2001, the High Court of South Africa declared that the act establishing military courts was incompatible with the new Constitution citing Andries Diphapang Potsane/Minister of Defence: 'There has been a radical break with the past. . . . The military is not immunized from the democratic change. Maintaining discipline in the defence force does not justify the infringement of the rights of soldiers, by enforcing such military discipline through an unconstitutional prosecuting structure (14.6).'"

39. Ibid., [16].

40. Emmanuel Decaux, Draft Principles Governing the Administration of Justice through Military Tribunals (Decaux Principles), UN Commission on Human Rights 62nd Sess., U.N. Doc. E/CN.4/2006/58 (13 January 2006): [11]; See also Leandro Despouy, Civil and Political Rights, Including the Question of Independence of the Judiciary, Administration of Justice, Report of the Special Rapporteur on the Independence of Judges and Lawyers, UN Commission on Human Rights, 62nd Session UN Doc E/CN.4/2006/52 (13 January 2006); Gabriel Knaul, Report of the Special Rapporteur on the Independence of Judges and Lawyers, UN Commission on Human Rights 68th Session UN Doc A/68/285 (7 August 2013): [15], [20]—"Several countries have abolished the operation of military tribunals in peace time altogether and transferred the responsibility for adjudicating alleged wrongdoings by military personnel to the ordinary courts and/or disciplinary bodies."

41. Tony Foley, "Institutional Responses to Child Sexual Abuse: How a Moral Conversation with Its Lawyers Might Contribute to Cultural Change in a Faith-Based Institution" *Legal Ethics* 18 no. 2 (2015): 164, 177.

42. Banner, "Institutional Sexual Assault": 129.

43. Graci Bozarth, "Strange Bedfellows: The Military, the University, and Sexual Assault" *University of Missouri-Kansas City Law Review* 84 (2016): 1003, 1022 (footnotes omitted).

44. Ibid., 1024–25.

45. Ibid., 1028; Banner, "Institutional Sexual Assault"; Hannah Brenner, Kathleen Darcy, and Sheryl Kubiak, "Sexual Violence as an Occupational Hazard and Condition of Confinement in the Closed Institutional Systems of the Military and Detention" *Pepperdine Law Review* 44 (2017): 881; Kathy Bagot, "Administrative

Accountability in Prisons" *Australian Journal of Administrative Law* 9 (2002): 143; Matthew Groves, "The Purpose and Scope of Prison Discipline" *Criminal Law Journal* 26 (2002): 10.

46. Elizabeth Broderick, "Cultural Renewal at the University of Sydney Residential Colleges" (November 29, 2017).

47. Nina Funnell and Anna Hush, "The Red Zone Report. An Investigation into Sexual Violence and Hazing in Australian University Residential Colleges" (EROC Australia, February 28, 2018).

48. Allison Langdon, "D Is for Disgrace Episode 1–3" *60 Minutes*, March 4, 2018 https://www.9now.com.au/60-minutes/2018/episode-3.

49. Nick McKenzie, Chris Masters, and David Wroe, "Secretive and Elite SAS Soldiers Grilled about Alleged War Crimes," *Canberra Times*, June 8, 2018 https://www.canberratimes.com.au/politics/federal/secretive-and-elite-sas-soldiers-grilled-about-alleged-war-crimes-20180608-p4zkau.html.

50. Langdon, "D is for Disgrace": Langdon asked "since when were crimes not reported for police investigation"; Foley, "Institutional Responses."

51. Banner, "Institutional Sexual Assault": 130.

52. Sean Ryan et al., "The Commission to Inquire into Child Abuse" (Government of Ireland, May 20, 2009) http://www.childabusecommission.ie/index.html; Yvonne Murphy, Ita Mangan, and Hugh O'Neill, "Commission of Investigation. Report into the Catholic Archdiocese of Dublin" (July 2009); Anthony Hart, David Lane, and Geraldine Doherty, "Historical Institutional Abuse in Northern Ireland between 1922 and 1995" (January 20, 2017) https://www.hiainquiry.org/; See generally, McClellan, "Royal Commission": Final Report Volume 16, Religious Institutions Book 1: 178–207 for a discussion of the many inquiries in different states.

53. Karen Terry and Jennifer Tallon, "The Nature and Scope of Sexual Abuse of Minors by Catholic Priests and Deacons in the United States 1950–2002" (The United States Conference of Catholic Bishops, February 2004); Karen J. Terry et al., "The Causes and Context of Sexual Abuse of Minors by Catholic Priests in the United States, 1950–2010" (United States Conference of Catholic Bishops, May 2011).

54. Roderick A. Macdonald et al., "Restoring Dignity: Responding to Child Abuse in Canadian Institutions" (Law Commission of Canada, March 2010) http://www.lcc.gc.ca.

55. Stephen Castle, "Pervasive Abuse Found in Belgian Church" *New York Times*, September 11, 2010: 8A.

56. Timothy P. Schilling, "Sex Abuse in the Dutch Church. A New Report Scandalizes an Already Diminished Flock" *Commonweal Magazine*, January 11, 2012 https://www.commonwealmagazine.org/sex-abuse-dutch-church.

57. Alexis Jay et al., "The Independent Inquiry into Child Sexual Abuse" (March 12, 2015) https://www.iicsa.org.uk/.

58. Anne Smith, "The Scottish Child Abuse Inquiry" (Scottish Government, 2015) www.childabuseinquiry.scot.

59. McClellan, "Royal Commission" Final Report: 256–259—See the many inquires since 2000 listed.

60. Rozina Sabur, "Mass Grave of Up to 800 Children Found Underground at a Former Home for Unmarried Mothers and Their Babies in Ireland" *The Telegraph* March 3, 2017 https://www.telegraph.co.uk/news/2017/03/03/mass-grave-800-children-found-underground-former-home-unmarried/; See also Peter Tyrrell and Diarmuid Whelan, *Founded on Fear* (Transworld Ireland, 2006).

61. Rachel Browne, "Church Laws Deliberately Misused to Cover Up Sex Claims: Royal Commission" *Sydney Morning Herald*, February 9, 2017 http://www.smh.com.au/nsw/church-laws-deliberately-misused-to-cover-up-sex-claims-royal-commission-20170208-gu8tm0.html "Canon lawyer and whistleblower priest Father Thomas Doyle told the hearing Australian Catholic church authorities have been aware of allegations of clerical child sexual abuse for decades. Canon law has been used as an excuse in some instances by ecclesiastical authorities for not proceeding and taking direct action against reports of child sexual abuse."

62. McClellan, "Royal Commission" Final Report Vol 2 Nature and Cause: 12.

63. Ibid.: 243; Lisa Millar, "Ireland Has Lessons for Australia Eight Years after Its Own Child Abuse Commission of Inquiry" *ABC News*, December 14, 2017 http://www.abc.net.au/news/2017-12-14/what-can-australia-learn-from-irelands-own-commission-of-inquiry/9250596.

64. McClellan, "Royal Commission" Final Report Vol 2 Nature and Cause: 5.3, 158 "'Closed' institutions typically have full control over the children in their care. In these institutions, children are subject to strict rules and procedures, are entirely dependent on the institution, and are isolated from the outside world. There is often little external oversight or support. They are generally higher risk environments for children."

65. Ibid., 16, 73—This accords with research from other studies that "cite withdrawal of complaints by victims as a key factor in the early attrition of sexual assault cases."

66. Ibid., 97 "Victims, particularly males, may be less likely to disclose sexual abuse by a woman because they feel that they would not be believed or taken seriously."

67. Ibid., 104.

68. Ibid., 94.

69. Ibid., 95.

70. Ibid., 103.

71. Ibid., 124.

72. Ibid., 17, 127.

73. Ibid., 23, 31, 128.

74. Ibid., 34–36, 37, 129.

75. Ibid., 130–31.

76. Ibid., 169, 179.

77. Ibid., 43 "entire communities can be affected by grooming. . . . Research indicates that perpetrators may target and groom entire organizations, as well as the children and individuals who work within them."

78. See M. Proeve, C. Malvaso, and P. DelFabbro, *Evidence and Frameworks for Understanding Perpetrators of Institutional Child Sexual Abuse,* report prepared for

the Royal Commission into Institutional Responses to Child Sexual Abuse, Sydney, 2016, 31: "'Institutional grooming' is a mechanism that enables perpetrators to take advantage of features of an institutional environment in order to circumnavigate any barriers and to use organizational frailties in order to pursue their interests with minimal detection."

79. McClellan, "Royal Commission" Final Report Vol 2 Nature and Cause: 170.

80. Ibid., 162 "Research has identified instances where staff have responded to disclosures of child sexual abuse by protecting the organization's reputation over responding to victims."

81. Ibid., 192 "A family's trust and loyalty to the institution could also create opportunities for perpetrators to groom the child and the family."

82. Ibid., 162 "We examined many instances where an institution's leadership tried to prevent abuse allegations being made public to protect the institution's reputations."

83. Ibid., 163 ". . . institutions that rely on internal processes or 'closed systems' to deal with breaches of conduct . . . may fail to report abuse to the police or other external authorities."

84. Ibid., 163 "The research suggests . . . in some instances instead of referring allegations to the police for investigation, the Catholic Church has carried out its own investigations and made decisions about the guilt and punishment of alleged perpetrators."

85. Ibid., 173.

86. Ibid., 159.

87. For a detailed discussion of canon law, see McClellan, "Royal Commission" Transcript produced by DTI 24/08/2015 (156) 16005; McClellan, "Royal Commission": Case Study 16, The Melbourne Response; See also Kieran Tapsell, "On Abuse: Francis Yet to Make Critical Clerical Changes" *National Catholic Reporter*, July 28, 2017 https://www.ncronline.org/news/accountability/abuse-francis-yet-make-critical-clerical-changes.

88. See *Sacramentorum Sanctitatis Tutela* of Pope St. John Paul II applies Article 1(4) of the 1974 Instruction of Pope Paul VI, *Secreta Continere*, Substantive Norms Part 1 concerning the most serious crimes http://www.ncrnews.org/documents/norms_de_gravioribus_delictis.pdf.

89. McClellan, "Royal Commission": Transcript produced by DTI 24/08/2015 (156) 16005.

90. Ibid., Transcript produced by DTI 24/08/2015 (156) 16054.

91. McClellan, "Royal Commission": Criminal Justice Report, Executive Summary Pts 1 and II Criminal Limitation periods: 46.

92. McClellan, "Royal Commission": Case Study 16, The Melbourne Response: 127.

93. Ibid.

94. Kieran Tapsell, "Child Sexual Abuse and the City of Man: A Response to Philip Almond" *ABC Religion and Ethics* Opinion, October 23, 2017 http://www.abc.net.au/religion/articles/2017/10/23/4754231.htm.

95. See further, Desmond Cahill and Peter Wilkinson, "Child Sexual Abuse in the Catholic Church: An Interpretive Review of the Literature and Public Inquiry

Reports" (August 2017) *Centre for Global Research, School of Global, Urban and Social Studies* https://www.rmit.edu.au/content/dam/rmit/documents/news/church-abuse/child-sex-abuse-and-the-catholic-church.pdf.

96. McClellan, "Royal Commission" Final Report Vol 2 Nature and Cause: 173.

97. Ibid., "Research has suggested that religious doctrine can limit the effectiveness of policy changes to prevent abuse. In some instances, this is because of religious principles that direct an institution to use internal systems for dealing with misconduct without recourse to civil authorities."

98. McClellan, "Royal Commission" Case Study 50 Catholic Church Authorities: 7 [26].

99. McClellan, "Royal Commission" Interim Report Volume 1, 2014: 170.

100. McClellan, "Royal Commission" Final Criminal Justice Report, Recommendation 32: "Any person associated with an institution who knows or suspects that a child is being or has been sexually abused in an institutional context should report the abuse to police."

101. McClellan, "Royal Commission" Interim Report Volume 1, 2014: 172.

102. McClellan, "Royal Commission": Report of Case Study No. 8 Mr. John Ellis's experience of the Towards Healing process and civil litigation.

103. McClellan, "Royal Commission": Transcript produced by DTI 24/08/2015 (156) 16055 ". . . we had already made the decision to have Towards Healing and to follow that, and . . . the Australian bishops were well aware that they were outside church law and that their document had no standing in church law."

104. Christopher Knaus, "Royal Commission Reveals Scale of Child Sexual Abuse in Anglican Church" *The Guardian*, March 17, 2017 https://www.theguardian.com/australia-news/2017/mar/17/royal-commission-reveals-scale-of-child-sexual-abuse-in-anglican-church: "Newcastle bishop, Greg Thompson, resigned . . . after trying for years to force reforms within the church. He told the royal commission on Friday that the church's response was still being hampered by factionalism 'You have relationships . . . where people are aligned to groups, to factions. So within a diocese, let alone across the country, there are factions and allegiances which cut across a common response, particularly when there are beliefs and attitudes that have not come to terms with history.'"

105. McClellan, "Royal Commission" Criminal Justice Report, Executive Summary Pts 1 and II: 57 "Institutions themselves may be 'criminogenic,' in that they are likely to cause or produce criminal behavior, or they may contribute to offending indirectly. The criminal law may also be more appropriate than civil law for punishing and deterring wrongdoing because conviction carries with it serious consequences and social stigma."

106. Ibid., Recommendation 36.

107. Ibid., Recommendation 32: "Any person associated with an institution who knows or suspects that a child is being or has been sexually abused in an institutional context should report the abuse to police. . . ."

108. Kieran Tapsell, "Sex Abuse and the Seal of the Confessional" *National Catholic Reporter*, August 18, 2017 https://www.ncronline.org/news/opinion/sex-abuse-and-seal-confessional.

109. McClellan, "Royal Commission" Criminal Justice Report: 53–54.

110. Tapsell, "Sex Abuse."

111. Kieran Tapsell, "On Abuse: Francis Yet to Make Critical Clerical Changes" *National Catholic Reporter*, July 28, 2017 https://www.ncronline.org/news/accountability/abuse-francis-yet-make-critical-clerical-changes; John Allen, *All the Pope's Men: The Inside Story of How the Vatican Really Thinks* (New York: Doubleday, 2004).

112. Tapsell, "Child Sexual Abuse."

113. McClellan, "Royal Commission" Case study 3, North Coast Children's Home: The alleged abuse took place at the hands of 285 laypeople and 247 ordained clergy. The Royal Commission referred 84 alleged perpetrators to police.

114. Knaus, "Royal Commission Reveals."

115. McClellan, "Royal Commission" Case study 3, North Coast Children's Home: 12.

116. Ibid., 21, 23–24; See McClellan, "Royal Commission" Report of Case Study No. 8 Mr. John Ellis's experience of the Towards Healing process and civil litigation.

117. McClellan, "Royal Commission" Case study 3, North Coast Children's Home: 40–45.

118. Ibid., 37.

119. Ibid., 53–55: Findings 21–23.

120. Ibid., 51 noting parallels in processes with military discipline.

121. Ibid., 52.

122. Ibid., 45, 57.

123. Ibid., 58.

124. McClellan, "Royal Commission" Transcript produced by DTI 24/08/2015 (156) 16048.

125. Ibid., 16062; Transcript produced by DTI 24/08/2015 (156) 16007 "The conflict between canon law and civil law was a theme of the Australian report"; See also Geoffrey Robinson, "For Christ's Sake: Confronting the Culture of Abuse within the Catholic Church" *ABC*, November 13, 2012 http://www.abc.net.au/religion/articles/2012/11/13/3632146.htm; Geoffrey Robinson, "Confronting Power and Sex in the Catholic Church: Reclaiming the Spirit of Jesus" *Sophia* 47 no. 2 (2008): 231.

126. McClellan, "Royal Commission" Criminal Justice Report": 166.

127. Ibid., 25–26, 112, 115. The impact of child sexual abuse may be lifelong, and the impact on their families and the broader community may continue into subsequent generations.

128. Ibid., 168.

129. Ibid., 14, 193.

130. Ibid., 14: Recommendation 1, 3.

131. Ibid., 13.

132. Ibid., 13,189 ". . . we are not satisfied that formal restorative justice approaches should be included as part of the criminal justice response to institutional child sexual abuse, at least in relation to adult offenders . . . victims . . . of institutional . . . sexual abuse should have access to justice through both criminal justice responses and redress and civil litigation."

133. Ibid., 100 "(the Forgotten Australians report) found that, between the 1920s and 1970s, more than 500,000 children were placed in care."

134. McClellan, "Royal Commission": Transcript produced by DTI 24/08/2015 (156) 16082.

135. Banner, "Institutional Sexual Assault": 102; See further, Thierry Devos et al., "Conflicts among Human Values and Trust in Institutions" *British Journal of Social Psychology* 41(2002): 481–94.

136. Banner, "Institutional Sexual Assault": 128.

137. Foley, Institutional Responses": 174 (footnotes omitted).

138. Christopher W Behan, "Don't Tug on Superman's Cape: In Defense of Convening Authority Selection and Appointment of Court-Martial Panel Members" *Military Law Review* 176 (2003): 190; Robinson, "Confronting Power."

139. William R. Hagan, "Overlooked Textbooks Jettison Some Durable Military Law Legends" *Military Law Review* 113 (1986): 163, 184; Norman G. Cooper, "Gustavus Adolphus and Military Justice" *Military Law Review* 92 (1981): 129.

140. Hagan, "Overlooked": 184.

141. Ibid.

142. Ibid., 190 "the code of Richard II . . . begins with a stern call for religious order."

143. Ibid., 187–88 "Gustav Adolf. . . was not the first . . . to begin his military code with articles that protected and forced the exercise of religion."

144. Ibid., 198.

145. Ibid., 178.

146. Robert Sherrill, *Military Justice Is to Justice as Military Music Is to Music* (Harper & Row, 1969): 68–69.

147. Hagan, "Overlooked": 191.

148. M. Sutcliffe, *The Practice, Proceedings, and Lawes of Armes* (London 1593) 336 cited in Hagan, "Overlooked": 191.

149. See e.g., Cahill, and Wilkinson, "Child Sexual Abuse."

150. Kevin W. Carter, "Fraternization" *Military Law Review* 113 (1986): 61, 64.

151. Ibid., 64: "Every class within the feudal caste system had its own customary notions and habits regarding social relationships. Violation of these socially accepted rules of conduct was considered a breach of faith. Breach of faith was the most repugnant crime in a feudal society founded upon loyalty to one's superiors and it was severely and promptly punished by general infamy and dishonor."

152. Hagan, "Overlooked": 201.

153. Niccolò Machiavelli, *The Art of War 1517–1520* (Neal Wood trans, Bobbs-Merrill, 1521); John Sloan, "Machiavelli on War" http://www.xenophon-mil.org/milhist/renaissance/machessy.htm "Machiavelli drew on two sources for his theories on the military history and practice of contemporary Europe, especially Italy; and the military history and practice of ancient world, especially the Roman Republic."

154. See e.g., Hale, *War and Society in Renaissance Europe, 1450–1620* (Leicester University Press, in association with Fontana Paperbacks, 1985).

155. Sloan, "Machiavelli on War": "The Italian condotierri had long since established schools of warfare in which they sought to study and develop both strategy and

tactics. . . . As an avid student of the art, Machiavelli no doubt questioned every leader he met and engaged in constant discussion of military affairs . . . in . . . *The Art of War* . . . he uses the distinguished condoterri, Fabrizio Colonna, as his mouthpiece. . . ."

156. David B. Kopel, Paul Gallant, and Joanne D. Eisen, "The Human Right of Self-Defense" *Brigham Young University Journal of Public Law* 22 (2007): 43, 69–70.

157. Ibid., 69.

158. Ibid., 70: "Belli's citations for the principle were to a Roman law rule about personal defense, and to a Canon law (Catholic Church law) rule about warfare."

159. Ibid., 70: "Belli argued that soldiers should, in most cases, be subject to the ordinary law applicable to everyone else."

160. Ibid., 72; see also Benedict Kingsbury and Benjamin Straumann, *The Roman Foundations of the Law of Nations: Alberico Gentili and the Justice of Empire* (Oxford University Press, 2010).

161. Michael Wyatt, *The Italian Encounter with Tudor England: A Cultural Politics of Translation* (Cambridge University Press, 2012).

162. Kopel et al., "The Human Right": 120.

163. Samuel Warren, *Blackstone's Commentaries Systematically Abridged and Adapted to the Existing State of the Law and Constitution* (W Maxwell, Bell Yard, Lincoln's Inn., 1855) quoting Sir Matthew Hale, 324; Antony Buckingham, *A Brief History of Australian Military Law* Australian MP History Website www.home.iprimus.com.au/buckomp: [6].

164. Stephen Payne Adye, *A Treatise on Courts-Martial, to Which is Added an Essay on Military Punishments and Rewards* (J Murray, 3 ed, 1786): 1–2 "The Court of Chivalry or Marshal's court, the judges of which were the lord high constable and earl marshal, is the fountain of martial law in England . . . they become part of the aula regis established by William the Conqueror, under the direction of chief justiciar, and composed of the great officers of ftate, each of whom had his particular jurisdiction, the constable and marshal presiding in matters of honor and arms, and determining according to the law military and the law of nations and when Edward I. new-modelled the whole frame of our judicial polity, and broke and subdivided the aula regis, into distinct courts, they were appointed to preside over the Court of Chivalry. . . ." See further, Frederick Bernays Wiener, *Civilians under Military Justice. The British Practice Since 1689 Especially in North America* (The University of Chicago Press, 1967); But *cf*, G. D. Squibb, *The High Court of Chivalry: A Study of the Civil Law in England* (Oxford University Press, 1959) in which Squibb disputes the role of the High Court of Chivalry in military matters: 3–4.

165. Squibb, *High Court of Chivalry:* 4–5.

166. David Grummitt, "The Court, War and Noble Power in England, c. 1475–1558," in Steven Gunn and Antheun Janse (eds), *The Court as a Stage: England and the Low Countries in the Later Middle Ages* (Boydell Press, 2006): 145 "The appointment of a special officer to conduct courts-martial during war campaigns can be traced back to the reign of Elizabeth I when a Judge Martial (or Marshal) accompanied the Earl of Leicester's army to the Low Countries in 1587–1588. . . . However, recent research suggests that the Judge Martial was independently responsible for military discipline; See further, Operational Selection Policy OSP46, Records relating to Military Law and Courts-Martial, National Archives http://www.nationalarchives

.giv.uk/documents/osp46.pd.pdf: 5; The Court of Chivalry was inactive for several centuries when the case of *Manchester Corporation v. Manchester Palace of Varieties Ltd* [1955] 1 All ER387, put the continued existence of the High Court of Chivalry beyond question; See also, Squib, *High Court of Chivalry:* 8–9.

167. T. Meron, *Henry's Wars and Shakespeare's Laws*: *Perspectives on the Law of War in the Later Middle Ages* (Clarendon Press, 1993): 91–93.

168. Squibb, *High Court of Chivalry:* 12.

169. J. F. Pipon and J. K. Collier, *Manual of Military Law* (William H Allen, 3rd Revised ed, 1860):14 "each war, each expedition, had its own edict."

170. Warren, "Blackstones Commentaries": 413.

171. Adye, *A Treatise on Courts-martial:* 60–61 "The crimes that are cognizable by court-martial, as repugnant to military discipline, are pointed out by the mutiny act and articles of war . . . and as to other crimes which officers and soldiers being guilty of, are to be tried for by the ordinary course of law in like manner with other subjects: *Mutiny Act* Article 62,"

172. See further, Norman Davies, *The Isles, a History* (Papermac, 2000): 350–56. The war clearly went for longer than 100 years.

173. See Sir Thomas Edlyne Tomlins, *The Law-Dictionary, Explaining the Rise, Progress, and Present State of the British Law: Defining and Interpreting the Terms or Words of Art, and Comprising Also Copious Information on the Subjects of Trade and Government* (Oxford University, 4 ed, 1835), Courts—Martial I. II; See also Squibb, *High Court of Chivalry:* 20 "Armies were raised in the Middle Ages by 'indentures' in which Commanders contracted with the Crown to provide specified numbers of troops and in return subcontracted their obligations to smaller men. By the beginning of the Hundred Years War indentured troops had practically replaced the old feudal force based upon tenure by knight service."

174. David B. Ralston (ed), *Soldiers and States. Civil-Military Relations in Modern Europe, Studies in History and Politics* (D.C. Heath and Company, 1966): 18.

175. See Colonel H. C. B. Rodgers, *Battles and Generals of the Civil Wars*, (Seeley Service & Co. Ltd, 1968): 207–209 "The New Model Army consisted of 22,000 full-time professional rather than militia soldiers. A professional officer corps was established and the officers were prohibited from holding seats in either the Houses of Lords or Commons. This was to encourage their separation from the political or religious factions among the Parliamentarians."

176. S. E. Finer, *The Man on Horseback. The Role of the Military in Politics* (Penguin Books Ltd, 2nd revised ed, 1976): 23.

177. *Petition of Right 1627* (UK) 3 Chas 1 c 1.

178. *Mutiny Act* 1689, 1 Wm. 81 Mary, Ch. 5 Pt. VI.

179. See *The Armed Forces Act* (UK) 2006; Wiener, *Civilians under Military Justice*: No Mutiny Act was in force 1698–1702 during times of peace, 8.

180. Robinson, "For Christ's Sake.

181. Geoffrey Robinson, *For Christ's Sake: End Sexual Abuse in the Catholic Church . . . For Good* (Australia: Garratt Publishing, 2013).

182. McClellan, "Royal Commission": Transcript produced by DTI 24/08/2015 (156) 16046.

Chapter Six

Concerns and Consequences for the Continuation of Separate Societies

ISSUES FOR POWER RELATIONS IN DEMOCRACIES

A democracy is a society operating under the rule of law with voice given to its participants through regular free and fair elections.[1] Inherent in this is the right to express different views, to debate and question. The liberal notion of freedom from interference by the state, provided harm is not done to others, is also implicit. In a democracy, the military is located in the executive arm of government as part of the executive's tool of ultimate enforcement. Machiavelli in *The Art of War* noted the reciprocal relationship between the military and the social and political elements of a society. This, he argued, required the general populous to understand and engage in military matters, and if they did not, they could no longer control the military but it would come to control the people.[2] Observation of this has been referred to here as the militarization of the civilian domain.

A key aspect of democracies, as identified by Montesquieu,[3] is what has become known as the doctrine of the separation of powers. Montesquieu observed that the separation and independence of each of the three arms of government, namely the legislature, executive, and judiciary, provided the greatest chance for democracy to thrive. Key in this relationship is the independence of the judiciary. The judicial role is to resolve disputes between citizens, including organizations, and between citizens and their state, and in federal systems such as Australia and the US, between the various states and the federal government. In this regard, the Australian and US Constitutions acknowledge the separation of powers doctrine through the division of the chapters and articles in their respective constitutional layout: Ch I/Art I: The Legislature, Ch II/Art II: The Executive, and Ch III/Art III: the Judiciary.

The Australian High Court[4] and the US Supreme Court[5] have affirmed the doctrine as an inherent part of the system of governance in both countries.

Due to the blurring of the division between the legislature and the executive, with the Australian adoption of the British Westminster system of responsible government, the importance of maintaining the independence of the judiciary, in order to maintain democratic ideals such as the rule of law, is paramount. This was established early on by the High Court in the *R v. Kirby; Ex parte Boilermakers' Society of Australia* in 1956: "[t]he absurdity is manifest of supposing that the legislative powers conferred by s51 or elsewhere enabled the Parliament to confer original jurisdiction not covered by [the judicial powers] ss75 and 76."[6] However, where the line between the three arms of government sits is something the courts, as arbitrator, must decide, and it can vary, depending on the matter. As noted, the military, which is under the executive arm with some legislative control, is one area the courts have been absent from, due to their claiming ignorance in military subject matter and out of the need to respect the military necessity argument in chapter 1.

In the US, the understanding of the balance in the separation of powers is also contested ground. In *Morrison v. Olson,*[7] dissent existed on which arm of government the independent council, established under the *Ethics in Government Act*, was located. Rehnquist CJ for the majority, taking an agency view, indicated that ". . . we have never held that the Constitution requires that the three Branches of Government 'operate with absolute independence.'"[8] Justice Scalia, in dissent, saw it very differently, stating that ". . . without a secure structure of separated powers, our Bill of Rights would be worthless."[9] Rishikof speaks of the politically charged nature of institutional boundary intrusions, and argues that when constitutional prerogatives are spotlighted, the "struggle determines the notion of who can decide, as an institutional matter, what the 'right thing' to do is."[10]

A democracy supports individual freedom to pursue one's interests, bound only by the constraint of not harming others, whereas many interpret the military function as solely to be strong enough to protect the nation. This is the functional imperative, which ignores the vital support that is needed, based on the structural imperative, for both societal values being upheld, as well as for the constitutional structure of the democracy within which the military sits. The latter aspect means the superintendence by all three arms of governance,—the executive, legislature, and the courts—are required. Former High Court Justice Kirby clearly expressed this position:

> When it comes to a feature of the Constitution that is fundamental, defensive of the rule of law and protective of the rights of persons to have serious controversies about life, liberty and property settled conclusively by independent and impartial courts, this Court must be vigilant to uphold the constitutional provisions.[11]

The question becomes how these two entirely different systems—the military and the civilian-led democracy—with inherently opposing values, can work together. Turley suggests that "[b]y transferring criminal cases to the civilian system, the military would focus on maintaining its cultural values and practices through disciplinary actions while leaving criminal acts to the civilian authorities."[12] Instead, both the US Supreme Court and the Australian High Court have moved to a seemingly wholesale hand-over of the balance, in favor of the military system. Without the desire to maintain strong judicial superintendence, a number of decisions have given extraordinary powers to the executive and legislative arms through the use of the Constitutional defense power (US art II s2; Australia s51(vi)). Historically, this was the case in times of war when the leeway given to the use of the defense power was widened, but even then, still constrained. For instance, the High Court in *Communist Party v. The Commonwealth*[13] tested legislation that attempted to abolish the communist party in Australia using the defense power. The court limited the reach of the defense power to pass such legislation by reiterating that the government operated under the constitution, which presumed certain principles such as the rule of law.[14] However, now perhaps more than previously, under the guise of the so-called "war on terror," a seemingly interminable war, the highest civilian courts in both countries have been ready to recognize the changed circumstances, such that civil rights and liberties are in decline under the threat of terror.[15] In *Thomas v. Mowbray,*[16] the Australian High Court accepted the defense power s51 (vi) as supporting an interim control order restricting a person's activities, including freedom of movement and communication. The *Criminal Code* (Cth)[17] allowed these orders to be imposed ex parte with no arrest, trial, or conviction required. The majority allowed a broad reading of the defence power, enabling its application to internal threats in Australia.[18] It invoked a lament by Justice Kirby over the diminishing of cases such as the *Communist Party* case:

> I did not expect, during my service, I would see the *Communist Party Case* sidelined, minimised, doubted and even criticized and denigrated in this Court. . . . further evidence of the unfortunate surrender of the present court to demands for more and more governmental powers, federal and state, that exceed or offend the constitutional text and its abiding values.[19]

An additional consideration for the US and Australia is that both operate a federal system of government. A difficulty for federal systems is that the criminal law is largely state-based and can therefore vary across states. This federal or shared responsibility can enable cracks to develop, which both secret coteries and perpetrators can use to their advantage. As the Royal Commission suggested, the outcome of a criminal action should not be dependent on the institutional location in which the offence occurred. At least survivors and citizens of a state should receive one consistent approach, particularly where in Australia the *Convention of the Rights of the Child*[20] applies, requiring the interests of the child to be prioritized at all times.[21] Federal criminal law can happily apply to the military in an overarching manner. However, fragmentation of domains of law has enabled a creeping militarization of the primary civilian society.

MILITARIZATION OF THE CIVILIAN DOMAIN

The military in most Western democracies is said to operate under the control of the civilian authority. It is claimed the military can only properly comply with its duties if politically controlled, and to do this, it needs to be disciplined. However, that same claim often suggests that civilian control by the courts may disrupt the ability of the military to operate effectively—Argument 2 being military necessity.[22] This view of operating under political control means the sphere left to the military is the expertise required to conduct a combat operation, but the when and why is left up to the civilian political arms. However, control does not just encompass this narrow conception. It also concerns the discipline from the top of the pyramid to the bottom, and when it comes to discipline, courts and the law inevitably will have a role to play. An enforced separateness sustains the distance between the citizen and the soldier with little ability for the political control to be understood and scrutinized by the media and the citizens.

The US military started life as a highly political body and now operates under a self-imposed concept of civilian control. While this is the accepted standard, it could be suggested that the significant presence of veterans in politics, and civilian and private institutions that work with the military, provide a large footprint of influence in the operation of the primary civilian society. As powerful cliques, their ability to gate keep information can limit the ability to make good decisions on superintendence.[23] This influence, although subtle and largely hidden, may well account for the sustained perception that the military is under the civilian institutions' control. However, it has been observed by researchers dedicated to uncovering the military political interaction that there is often considerable influence ". . . on Capitol Hill. . . . High-level officers are capable of wielding sufficient pressure as a group to stymie major policy initiatives effectively. . . ."[24]

Kohn has described the civil-military relationship as unbalanced: "the American military has grown in influence to the point of being able to impose its own perspective on many policies and decisions."[25] As part of the military industrial complex, the influence is extensive, with most efforts directed to military evasion of policies that do not work for the military institutions interests, but also supporting policies beyond their sphere of operation where they do.[26] It is naive to suggest that the military should remain apolitical when the social and the political are intertwined completely in the modern military, particularly through the interactions of the elites.

The framers of the US Constitution were concerned to avoid militarization of the civilian sphere, as ancient societies such as the Romans and the Greek Spartans had experienced. Sparta practiced an inverted civilian and military society, one in which the military predominated and the civilian served a subsidiary purpose.[27] The notion of living in harsh circumstances to prepare for the toughness needed of a warrior, with the associated constraints and controls imposed, were ultimately the undoing of the Spartans and an abject lesson in the need to honor civilian society and its institutions.[28] Perhaps an apt lesson for today is that, in the Spartans case, surrendering freedoms for perceived security contributed to the demise of the society.[29] The Roman system varied over the span of the Roman Empire but much can be learned from its military inclinations to expansion and wealth generation through conflict, its separateness from the political system, and its elite professionalization, which created a class able to support cliques that fed the greed of various internal military coteries.[30] Ultimately, the introduction of foreign fighters and the increasing disconnection from the political system led to disintegration. The US experience with the world's largest military and its nearly continual war footing has generated wealth, by the adding of oil fields and access to valuable resources, which bring private gain for the moguls of the military industrial complex, but at a huge public cost.[31] Carrying a budget burden means that services for the civilian population are reduced as the expenditure on apparent military needs mount.

It is not suggested the US system is like the Roman military, as military members remain part of civil society, and although they may preference military social associations, they have civilian connections and interests. Another significant difference from the Roman model of separation is the operation of the constitutional system with shared governance observing a separation of powers acting as a check and balance on power. This three-way institutional governance apparatus places the military under the executive arm with some legislative control, particularly in regards to budget expenditure. However, the self-removal by the courts leaves the control system in a diminished state. The executive arm in the republic's presidential system in the US, as well as in the Australian two-way power separation, means powerful executives, in the form of the president, who wears the dual hat of commander in chief, and the prime minister, who is in command of the executive government through cabinet, which in turn advises the governor general as commander in chief, have immense power in their use of, and control over, the military coterie. The US system, established by the founders and influential in the Australian Constitution's development, remains clouded by a powerful executive and legislative authority that considers it has the ability to operate a separate criminal punishment system.[32]

The introduction of non-citizens and private military contractors (PMC) into the US and Australian military creates a further fracture in the ties to the civilian political society.[33] The use of PMCs is extensively written about,[34] and it is not the focus here other than to point to the Roman experience of this, which allegedly contributed to the demise of that empire.[35] As the Roman army became more separated, developing strong cliques and including non-Romans in its composition, the support for the citizens of the Roman Empire and their political system waned.[36] Lessons from Rome can still provide instruction today.

We see in a climate of the "#MeToo" movement that sex scandals across the board are able to bring not only powerful individuals down but also institutional reputations.[37] Sirco[38] describes two such notable events in Roman times. The first involved Appius Claudius and his infatuation with a betrothed plebeian girl named Verginia. In order to prevent Appius Claudius achieving his desire, Verginia's father, Verginius, killed his daughter and then called on the legions for support. The legions gave their support and a new government was elected with an assurance that the plebeian and the patricians would be subject to the law equally. Appius Claudius committed suicide and eight others had their property taken and were forced to leave Rome completely.[39] Sirico describes the downfall of the Tarquin line of kings as the second example, when a revolution resulted from the rape of the wife of a wealthy patrician by a son of Sextus Tarquinius. The consequences led to the demise of the monarchs and their replacement with the Republic Roman Empire.[40] The effect of ignoring the impact that even a single sexual incident can have is underestimated. Endless inquiries may stall things for a time but eventually, reckoning is demanded. Such historical lessons still confirm today that the three institutions of government need to work effectively if the issue is to be addressed at a fundamental level.

With the voluntary professional military, the nature of the coterie is even tighter, as the elite feelings of privilege demand even greater loyalty and investment in the norms of the society. Banner has suggested voluntary membership can mean "persons have '*willingly discard[ed]* their old selves in the hope of finding something better.'"[41] The consequences of continuing on the current road will diminish the military institution and does nothing for survivors or the primary society, especially when considering the following:

> More than 85,000 veterans were treated [in 2013] for injuries or illness stemming from sexual abuse in the military, and 4,000 sought disability benefits for crippling depression and PTSD. Compensation amounts for these claims vary, but some cases cost over $500,000 per victim over the course of a lifetime. In addition to medical costs, "one researcher has put the costs of sexual harassment to the U.S. Army at $250,000,000 a year in lost productivity, personnel replacement costs, transfers, and absenteeism." These financial costs do not include the costs on combat readiness and effectiveness. Sexual assault and harassment in the military is thus a high-cost, high-stakes problem that demands the careful attention of policy makers and military members alike.[42]

Kemp and Hudin suggest that ". . . the Commander-in-Chief requires that, in doubtful cases, the soldier's obligation is to follow the orders of the president . . . rather than the legislature or the courts."[43] This raises the question of the "proper institutional locus of military loyalty," given the doctrine of separation of powers and respective roles of the institutions of government. Is it for the military, the legislature, the people, or the judiciary to intervene? In reality, in current practice, the control of the military lies with the elites within government and the elites within the military. Decisions to use the military as a tool towards political strategies are decided by these elites with often very little public debate influencing the decision.[44]

The Federalists relied on the separation of powers to prevent abuse of power by the president as commander in chief.[45] The case of *Hamdan v Rumsfeld* [46] is a rare example where the US Supreme Court did preference individual human rights, and limited inherent executive powers based on the Constitution and an interpretation of its limits on power. Ruling that the Military Commissions for Guantanamo inmates were beyond power, this decision brought a rarely seen level of public debate.[47] Russett claims "that decisions on national security in Western democracies are 'insulated from popular control and knowledge.'"[48] Groves[49] further notes the uneasy relationship between military and civilian law, despite the orthodox legal doctrine that the military law is subject to the civilian law. He refers to the fact that

> [m]ilitary commanders have long maintained that the armed forces require considerable autonomy from the civilian legal system in order to maintain effective command and control . . ., [arguing that] . . . recourse to the civilian courts and civilian processes of law by service members has the potential to undermine military culture and fragment the command structure. . . .[50]

THE SEPARATE SOCIETY

As a tool of the executive, the military's separateness is confronted in this work, in particular in the area of criminal punishment. The repeating statements in both the US Supreme Court and the Australian High Court, which reflect values relating to an entirely different military and historical time, become self-sustaining with little genuine investigation, and they create a self-serving basis for military leaders to argue the maintenance of this separation. The claims may in effect damage the functional imperative of the military and the society in which it operates.[51]

Investigating the evidence that supports these special coteries' claims is pivotal. The military has expanded from the position it held at the time of the establishment of the US and Australian Constitutions when it operated out of specific dedicated functions pertaining to providing a fighting force, and it now operates as a secondary separate non-democratic oligarchic society. This US society provides a separate coterie for over one million citizens with bases in over 800 countries, and the Australian society has around 79,000 active and reserve members and around 60 Australian bases.[52] They duplicate many of the services provided in the primary civil society. Civilians are entitled to scrutinize the operation of these organizations within the respective democracies in which they operate, even if members of the military institution are discouraged from political activity.[53] An image of good governance portrayed by the military coterie glosses over the absence of the principles of democratic good. Turley comments that

> as its size and functions grew, the military simply replicated practices and values designed for the insular functions of combat effectiveness and used them to govern millions of citizens in virtually every aspect of their daily lives from garbage collection to criminal adjudication; [this] has created conflicts and discontinuities for service members who are caught between two fundamentally different cultures.[54]

The military in the US includes separate medical services, hospitals, prisons, drug-testing facilities, universities, and a discipline system. The latter, which is also the case in Australia, operates outside the court system that is provided as one of the three arms of governance for the primary group. It represents a significant difference between the two societies. Aspects of the civilian law would benefit the military if it utilized the civilian system to avoid not only the cost and distraction of duplication and institutional separateness, but also to aid with military members being integrated in the civilian system, thereby increasing the likelihood of shared understanding and values. The reach of military control into such broad governance areas as separated systems of health and criminal discipline goes beyond that envisioned by the framers of the Constitution in both the US and Australia.[55]

Keeping separate prison facilities for mostly drug and sex or other violent offenders would appear to serve little purpose other than to sustain the separate military society. In Australia, military members are in barracks-type detention facilities if custody is required for a short time. Any sentence between 14 days and two years can lead to detention at the Lamia Barracks, Holsworthy Defence Force Correctional Establishment; detention for longer periods is in civilian prisons.[56] Irrespective of receiving a custodial sentence, most are also discharged from the military. These factors around punishment influence aspects of workplace normative status.

The change in conduct of modern technological wars is far from the experience of WW II, yet the military discipline process has remained largely constant since shortly after that war in 1950, when the UCMJ was legislated in the US. World War II was fought with the whole of the society participating in the war effort. Changes in the manner of operation within militaries requires a fresh look at the arguments supporting hierarchical discipline. The "Revolution in Military Affairs" (RMA) brings a need to address what this means for the discipline system.[57] The new organizational approach is a more level networking structure, which is heavily dependent on new technologies and communication methods. The hierarchical organization was heavily reliant on the need for discipline and command control, which have underpinned the reasoning in many court cases for the exceptional position of the military vis-à-vis civilian society, but this is no longer the same, which in turn has consequences for the social and organizational nature of the military coterie:

> Since the results of networked technologies are likely to have their greatest impact on the sociology of military organizations, the greatest challenges to be faced are likely to be cultural, in the form of introducing changes in thinking and behavior. Australian military innovation is likely to be defined by its human ability to respond to technology's impact on organizational structure. Accordingly, in order to achieve success, Australian defence planners will be compelled to look closely at personnel policies and human resource questions if they are to manage a transformation from an industrial-age force towards an information-age, networked force.[58]

The military coterie supports a collectivism over individualism that is quite opposite to a democracy. Much of the legal process in dealing with punishment in the military follows the principles of the civilian system of criminal law, in a civilianization that may appease soldiers and some civilians. However, some within the military show concern that this attempt at social respectability may actually place military functional aspects at risk, highlighting the tension between the different values of a legal system in a democracy and a punishment system in an oligarchic society.[59] The military discipline system is not only distinctly different in key aspects, but it blurs the boundary between crime and workplace discipline. This is a blurred distinction between crimes like rape and murder, for which the civilian courts are designed, and disobedience, which is concerned with order, or a code of conduct. All exist on a seamless line that the commander is largely free to determine where on the line a matter shall be dealt with—courts-martial or administrative discipline. This is in stark contrast to a democratic system under the rule of law. The military coterie becomes a rule by men and as such, it is wholly dependent on good men being good leaders. Military leaders focus on the military, which is their job, and their philosophy is that while laws, not men, rule a democracy, the military is instead ruled by one man: "[a]n army is a collection of armed men obliged to *obey one man.* Every enactment, every change of rules which impairs the principle weakens the army, impairs its value, and defeats the very object of its existence."[60]

Many see civil-military control as an aspect of governance by the executive and to a more limited extent the legislature. Few consider the court has a role in this, including the majority in the civilian highest courts in Australia and the US. This elite political-military level of civil-military interaction concerns itself largely with funding, and purchases of armaments. To a lesser extent, concern with discipline relies on the internal workings of the coterie. However, as this work has noted, when the abuse and sexual assault scandals come into the public domain, greater interest peaks for a period.

CIVILIAN COURTS

The civil courts have effectively closed the door to military members. As Kohn correctly observes: "[t]he federal judiciary possesses wide jurisdiction over the armed forces even if judges and justices chose not to exercise that jurisdiction for many decades after the Constitution went into effect, and then to forfeit much of that jurisdiction during the Chief Justiceship of William Rehnquist."[61] Janowitz[62] proposes that the military can influence policy by inappropriately dominating the civil domain. The Supreme Court facilitates this, when it removes itself from effective oversight and the important balance of civilian institutional control of the military, and it can occur when

> [u]nanticipated militarism develops from a lack of effective traditions and practices for controlling the military establishment, as well as from a failure

> of civilian political leaders to act relevantly and consistently. . . . In such cases "a vacuum is created, which not only encourages an extension of the tasks and power of military leadership but actually compels such trends."[63]

Root and branch change of the whole system of military discipline is required. Patchwork changes that see minor incremental, often ill-considered and hastily developed adjustments miss the implications of not providing a holistic approach. The Australian Military Court is a prime example of unnecessary cost and upheaval that has failed. Spasmodic change tends to lead to suspicion about the benefits of any new initiatives.[64]

Cases such as *Feres v. United States*[65] in 1950 saw the Supreme Court take an unambiguous statute, the *Federal Tort Claims Act* 1946 (FTCA), and judicially rewrite it by holding that actions under the FTCA could not be brought where the injuries arose "out of or are in the course of activity incident to service."[66] This is prohibitive when it comes to a service member being entitled to sue for tortious damage. At best, it leaves uncertainty, where each factual event has to be potentially determined case by case,[67] as to whether the matter is incident to service, or at worst there is a total bar on any military members ever making a claim. Judge Ferguson, in dissent in *Costo and Graham v. United States*,[68] a case subsequently considering *Feres*, argues cogently that the ". . . blind adherence has proved virtually unworkable, a result that only underscores the wisdom of our founding fathers and the fragile complexities of our system of government. . . . [L]iberty can have nothing to fear from the judiciary alone, but would have everything to fear from its union with either of the other departments."[69] Ferguson J goes on to state:

> I am left to conclude that the only conceivable reason for the Court to engage in re-writing of such a momentous statute [the FTCA] was that it believed that Congress had not given enough protection to the government against the men and women in the armed forces. It is curious that the Court thought that it had to protect the government against those persons whose sole duty was to protect the government.[70]

The majority in *Costo and Graham* felt reluctantly compelled by the rules of precedent to apply *Feres* but urged the Supreme Court to revisit the *Feres* doctrine.[71] The point of absurdity of *Feres* was reached when in *Costo and Graham* it was evident that military persons on the rafting trip that lost their lives were barred from claiming damages, whereas the civilians in exactly the same raft could claim for the negligent actions of the civilian raft operator. That this serves no logical purpose was apparent: "I cannot find a rational basis for the court to engage in such line-drawing on the basis of an 'incident to service' test."[72]

Unfortunately, the Supreme Court has remained resistant to the many lower courts' urgings and in 2011 again refused a petition for a writ for *certiorari,* in the case of *Witt v. United States.*[73] This case concerned a classic medical negligence in which any civilian would be likely to recover damages. Witt, an airman, was admitted to the David Grant USAF Medical Centre for an appendectomy. Post-operation, a military nurse intubated Witt incorrectly causing air to fill his stomach rather than his lungs. This resulted in Witt suffering a brain injury and his eventual death three months later. His widow was prohibited from making a claim under the FTCA. The Supreme Court absenting the tort law protection has now seen a claim that there appears to be a higher incidence of medical malpractice within the military.[74] Perhaps the day will arrive when the Supreme Court will see that to continue its current position, as regards the equal protection rights of military members and the constitutional separation of powers, is to contribute to the unhappy state of military scandals.

One of the few judges with a military enlistment, Rehnquist, guided the deference provided by the US Supreme Court. *Parker v. Levy*[75] was a case in which Levy, a doctor in the Vietnam War,[76] sought to challenge his convictions under article 133—"conduct unbecoming an officer and a gentleman"—and article 134—"all disorders and neglects to the prejudice of good order and discipline in the armed forces"—on the basis that these two general articles were vague and thus void as a violation of the First amendment. Rehnquist J (elevated to Chief Justice in 1986) took an *obiter* statement by Justice Jackson in an earlier case of *Orloff v. Willoughby*,[77] that "the military constitutes a specialized community *governed by a separate discipline* from that of the civilian,"[78] and thereby developed the broad position that still operates today. The Supreme Court has adopted Rehnquist's statement as its clarion call in matters military: ". . . the military is, by necessity, a *specialized society, separate from civilian society* [and] a *society apart from civilian society.*"[79] This reconfiguration of Justice Jackson's words has resulted in providing foundational support for a *separate society*, rather than just acknowledging that there existed a *separate disciplinary system.*[80] It has contributed to the creation of a highly separated coterie.

The public are disengaged from an all-volunteer professional military and it is only the media, as the fourth arm of democracy, that keep the public informed, largely when scandals erupt, when large military purchases are made, or when the country is about to engage in conflict.[81] The secret coterie owns the soldier, as *Stanley v. United States*[82] most clearly demonstrates. In *Stanley*, the Supreme Court reasoned that

> it is irrelevant to a "special factors" analysis whether the laws currently on the books afford Stanley, or any other particular serviceman, an "adequate" federal

> remedy for his injuries . . . *congressionally uninvited intrusion into military affairs by the judiciary is inappropriate.* [83]

These cases fly in the face of claims of military protection of its members. Relying on superintendence by "good men" as leaders, those in the military legal or medical areas should also be subject to their external professional bodies' discipline, and also to the same system of discipline as ordinary military members. The secret coterie asks its members to adhere to its own internal self-discipline. The need for instant obedience, contained in Argument 3, is one of the main propositions underpinning these discipline claims. However, this claim would seem to fall flat when it is apparent that abuse, including sexual abuse, remains a problem for the military, apparently unable to ensure an instant obedience by a disciplined force.

Judges who focus on military necessity and the need for obedience as justification for absenting their adjudication in a matter leave unaddressed the issue of civilian control and in a democracy, in particular, the protection of fundamental rights of the individual. CJ Rehnquist, as one of only three Chief Justices of the Supreme Court to have experienced military service, stands out from his judicial colleagues in his reverence for military concerns.[84] The courts draw on a bevy of excuses to stay out of military disputes. These include suggesting that courts have a deficiency in knowledge of the subject area, or that "policy" and "political" concerns mean the courts should avoid these controversial areas. However, it is clear that courts are capable and prepared to adjudicate in many areas in which they are not subject area experts, as they interpret and apply the law, which is something at which they are *the* experts. Human rights also pushes courts to address matters in areas they may otherwise be reluctant to enter.[85]

Dissenting judges differ because they have a greater concern for the structural imperative, by balancing the rights of an individual under a democracy with the functional military necessity arguments.[86] The court, as one of three vital civilian governance institutions, has focused almost solely on the functional imperative without understanding the vital underpinning given by the structural imperative to support civil-military relations.

An aspect of the rule of law that equalizes all, by giving uniform ability to access important institutions of governance, is replaced by the hierarchal discipline of military persons. Having voice in a democracy enables gradual changes for adjustments and improvements as society advances. This system enables discourse and reflection, engagement and acceptance, even when the majority preference is against an individual's desires. A rigid hierarchical system, such as the military, will only significantly change through rupture. However, this is often avoided by overlays of policy and procedures drowning in complexity, which nevertheless create enough of a perception of change to placate members and outsiders, such as politicians. This does not make for a flexible nor quick and responsive organization as the military claims to be.

VALUES RIGHTS AND PERCEPTIONS

Militaries of democratic states are often involved in joint operations and exercises. International human rights, such as the *Convention for the Protection of Human Rights and Fundamental Freedoms* (*ECHR*),[87] have brought changes to European states' militaries, particularly as regards the use of civilian courts for criminal matters and the methods of operation of their discipline systems. This tends to have a trickle-down effect, as soldiers become more aware of their rights and of how other states' military institutions treat their members. That the European Court of Human Rights in Strasbourg has nevertheless concluded that the operation of a system of military discipline parallel to the civilian justice system is permissible and legitimate is based on the case law of common law that countries such as the US and Australia adhere to, but in which the highest civilian courts have followed a flawed argument.[88] Bronnit and Nolan note that there are

> continuing international human rights obligations to ensure that any determination of guilt must follow from a process that is fair. Australia is obligated to ensure that its ADF members receive a fair trial as guaranteed by the *International Covenant on Civil and Political Rights*. It is surely fairness and legitimacy, rather than merely military effectiveness that should now be the touchstone guiding our response to the High Court's decision and the modernization of the military justice system.[89]

This concern with rights includes internal behavior towards members of a military as well as rights of those on both sides of a conflict. Ethical and moral decline involving sexual and other abuse is a form of power abuse. It raises the question as noted previously, if military members can treat other members in abusive ways, how can they guarantee observance of the Geneva Conventions and laws of war when dealing with the enemy? Working on the premise that an organization is only as good as its members are happy would seem to indicate there is a way to go in coteries that rely on repression of speaking about *la brutta figura* while not having the same freedom and rights available as their civilian counterparts. In organizations based on hierarchy and rank, those at the base of the pyramid often have no structural opportunities for representation of their interests. The commanding officer is the controlling figure, the one who is to look after "his" men and women.

Civilian's participation in political debate, unions,[90] and access to the civilian courts to protect their interests and to counter powerful forces is removed when they become part of the military coterie. It has been a recommendation in the European states that they follow suit of some states who have military unions, and that "states should permit all members of the armed forces to join either a professional association or a trade union representing their interests."[91] Interestingly, in some European states military members have long been given voice through unions or associations. This seems to work and ensures members' complaints can be addressed in a timely way. However, the concept of military unions is likely to be an anathema to common law countries and their military, such as the US and Australia.

Access, training, information availability, and other barriers make this a far harder process for military members wanting to engage in the political communication space.[92] Such a tight hierarchical structure not only restricts communication with the primary group, namely civil society, but it curtails communication within the secretive structure. Complaints often stay at the unit level, as issues are preferably resolved at the level at which they arise. Sending negative communication upward is not likely to be welcome or reflect favorably on an officer. Tailhook and other sexual abuse cases are examples of having to go to a higher level, or externally to the media as a whistle-blower, in an attempt to avoid this repression.

Over 1.3 million military members of this subset of the US primary citizenship group are dependent on the right actions by an elite management imbued with a belief in *la bella figura*, which places reputation in priority over rights of the individual. The officers in command face a divided loyalty between the reputation of the organization, their own self-interests, and those under their command. As the case examples illustrate, external control is only provoked when the media pushes the legislator's interest to respond or make comment. Military members live partially within a democracy, but mostly within a hierarchical oligarchy, in which the institution, in the US at least, applies capital criminal punishment, without recourse to the democratic protections for the primary societal group available under the Constitution.

Those military members on death row in the US facing capital punishment provide an example of distinguishing factors, yet they rarely see their sentence executed. Of the five members currently facing execution, three are white and two are African American. This number compares with around 2,843 of the civilian population on death row. Such contradictory figures may support an argument against the claim that the military operates a harsher discipline system to ensure the members carry out the more difficult role of a soldier.[93] Three states, Texas, Missouri, and Georgia, account for the vast majority of executions, but the military has not completed a sentence of execution in the last 10 years. Overall, 19 states in the US have abolished capital punishment, and another 4 have governor-imposed moratoriums on the death penalty, so military members coming from these states would now appear to be subjected to a criminal punishment regime they do not face in their primary home-state society.[94]

The reality remains that no matter how much control the military coterie may impose on its members, their coexistence in the primary society still affects their values and expectations. The separate coterie runs a clear risk of developing values that are non-aligned to the primary society. When addressing values, a better understanding of how an individual's internal value system works, and whether it is, or even can be, attuned to the organizational values, is required.[95] The plethora of values expressed in various service domains and the ADF do not accommodate each other, leave alone that an individual can only hold approximately seven values in a hierarchical structure. Otherwise, competing values will cause internal dissonance. Devos et al. have found clear differentiation in values and levels of institutional trust, noting

> there is a tension between values that emphasize independent thought and action and favor change and those that stress self-restriction, stability, and preservation of customs and traditions. . . . There is also conflict between values that favor pursuit of one's own relative success and dominance over others and those that stress acceptance of others as equals and concern for their welfare. . . . Religious individuals and right-wing supporters display a relatively strong motivation to preserve traditions, the *status quo*, and certainty in relationships with others—values with a strong affinity to trust in institutions.[96]

Sexual abuse is one area where value differences may be evident in the responses. The requirements for changes in the military discipline system to more closely align with civilian practices in regards to survivors, including the taking and giving of evidence in criminal matters, their support and counselling needs, and generally the level of unacceptability of such conduct, move it ever closer to a replication that begs the question of why there is a need for two systems. If Sherman[97] and other military leaders who suggest that adopting civilian processes and values weakens the functional imperative are to be believed, the military should not be taking notice of the demands for reform in the area of sexual abuse and discipline. Certainly, their beliefs support the resistance that has led to slowed changes.

The law is a high-value system in the civilian arena and a representation of the cultural mores that can contest the value system of the military, in which hierarchical command obedience for the service of combat readiness prevails. The military culture, with its dominant focus on combat readiness, may feel that cultural values emanating from the law, which place emphasis on equality and fairness, are a threat to be avoided.[98]

The decisions by the highest military appellate court CAAF demonstrate the tension created when serving two masters: military values, and the principles of law that exist in a democratic system. CAAF has had to exercise its jurisdiction along a fine line in a manner that negotiates these tensions. The military does value due process and honor, but within an internal system dependent on individual leadership. The justification for maintaining a criminal enforcement system creates an added burden that is a constant distraction from the core function of the military—to train a fighting force. Leaving the criminal punishment to the very capable civilian system would alleviate some of this burden.

Janowitz, unlike Huntington, has suggested an integration of social values in which civilian values took precedent. This speaks to the first aspect of the structural imperative. Soldiers need to have an affinity with the people whom they are placing their lives on the line to defend. An all-volunteer military force, which comprises non-citizens and private military contractors, is likely to become removed from the citizenry. This work supports the Janowitzian contention, but goes further by attending to the second aspect of the structural imperative, namely that the constitutional superintendence of the military is vital and requires involvement by the three governance institutions provided for in the Constitution. This aspect of the structural imperative is failing due, in particular, to the stance taken by the courts when observing an overweening deference. Taking the criminal prosecution of members back into the fold of the civil courts, and the highest civil court actively adjudicating on soldier's rights in a holistic way, will ensure that the functional imperative is supported.[99]

CRIMINAL OFFENDING

Moving areas of military governance, such as the criminal punishment system, into the civilian criminal law system will not undermine the functional imperative to provide a strong fighting force. The ability to refer matters to the civilian system for criminal investigation and punishment, along with the complimentary operation of workplace discipline such as administrative punishments, is threat enough for the commanding officer to maintain control and influence over the troops. The operation of other life-and-death professions, such as the police and firefighters, under the civilian system, has not shown a diminished responsiveness when they are called upon to perform their job. The actions of police, rescue workers, and firefighters in the bombing of the World Trade Centre and the 2017 Las Vegas shootings, as well as other examples, have repeatedly shown an ability to continue to do heroic jobs despite facing death or injury. This shows that commitment is not dependent on any special punishment threat.[100] Professional roles carry an expectation of professionalism in performance, which equally applies to a volunteer professional military. Failures should result in workplace discipline, or if they tip over into criminal conduct, a prosecution within the criminal system.

Criminal offences exist as part of the civilian society's agreement that such behavior fits a category that is offensive to the whole community. Placing a barrier, or an extra step by which coteries such as churches and military can filter the behavior for their own purposes, standards, or values, weakens the ability of the system to ensure a level of conduct acceptable to the whole of society. The interests of the coterie are not necessarily aligned with the primary community values. This has played out in regards to the treatment of same-sex preference and adultery in different ways within the military. The courts-martial system asserts the separate governance by the military of its members; it does not clarify how this achieves greater obedience. As with any workplace discipline system, the threat of reprimand, reduction in rank, and even discharge as the result of a successful criminal conviction, or even in some cases where this is not so but where the lesser discipline is considered necessary, it remains a large deterrent with significant costs to an individual who is disobedient.[101] Society pays for its justice system and has a right to transparency and participation; criminal law is public law that exists in the interest of the whole of society.

The countervailing benefits of using the civilian courts are manifold. Not only will the structural imperative be strengthened by supporting closer alignment to the civilian values of the population the military is in place to defend, but most importantly, it strengthens the system of civilian governance by upholding a clear rule of law. Furthermore, it underpins support for the functional imperative. In an all-volunteer professional force, individuals will work at their best where they feel valued and they can participate in a safe and supportive work environment. Loyalty is encouraged by a respectful work environment rather than a fearful and threatening one.[102] The research on what sustains good workers has much to offer the outmoded value system of a coterie that is dependent on fear and the philosophy of *la bella figura.*

The dominance of the rhetoric of providing security for the primary civilian system is in reality turned on its head if the functional imperative for strong security comes at the cost of diminishing the very system it was intended to protect. The democratic system is threatened by a militarization from within.[103] European and other military experiences around the world show that the availability of a strong and functional military is not dependent on the existence of a separate military coterie.[104]

The US and Australian military have not produced solid empirical evidence to support their assertions in this respect, which have become largely repeated myths attaining the semblance of a mantra. There is little evidence that the goals of a criminal system, such as punishment and deterrence, are satisfied, yet there is a clear historical continuation of abuse, including sexual abuse, which appears systemic in its regularity, despite efforts to try to clean this up.[105] One is left wondering whether a military person is more deterred by threatened prosecution within the military or within the civilian system. Research on this question appears to be non-existent.

The determination of which system applies is entirely based on the Supreme Court's implementation of the deceptively simple "status test," or in Australia the "service test," which has in practice effectively devolved to become a status test.[106] The status test was again an invention of Rehnquist CJ in *Solorio v. US.*[107] Although the Australian High Court claims to follow the earlier service test enunciated in the Supreme Court's *O'Callahan v. Parker*,[108] namely that a matter must have a connection to the members' service before it falls under military jurisdiction, this has effectively been eroded to become a status test.[109] The military practice of using status as the test to determine whether a civilian or a military police investigation, and a civilian or military punishment system apply is arbitrary. The reality of determining which system is appropriate can be far from certain and is problematic, as cases such as *Hennis, Nazario, Green*, and *White* demonstrate.

Nazario and *Green*, described in chapter three, were both military members, tried in the US civilian system for crimes committed on the battlefront. The infamous Mahmudiyah killings represent a criminal event that gave rise to multiple offences in a war zone, yet different processes and treatment were applied.[110] Steven Green faced a civilian criminal trial on charges attracting the death penalty.[111] Green was convicted for the rape of a 14 year old and the killing of her and her family. The jury, however, did not reach a unanimous decision on the death penalty, so Green was sentenced to five consecutive life sentences with no parole to be served in a civilian prison.[112] He ended up taking his own life while serving his sentence in 2014.[113] Green's co-offenders received lighter sentences. Despite receiving significant sentences, all three military co-offenders' sentences were capped by the Convening Authority, making them eligible for parole, which in the case of Spielman and Cortez was after 10 years and for Barker after 20 years.[114] All three also received a dishonorable discharge. Spielman was sentenced to 110 years in prison.[115] Cortez pleaded guilty in a court-martial to rape, conspiracy to rape, and four counts of murder as part of a plea deal to avoid the death penalty, and he was sentenced to 100 years in prison. Barker negotiated a plea deal, which included giving evidence against the other soldiers, to avoid facing the death penalty, despite the fact he was the one who suggested the victims and the sexual attack.[116] He was sentenced to 90 years. All three are serving their sentences at the Department of Defense's only maximum-security prison at Fort Leavenworth, Kansas. It highlights the inequality that is possible by continuing the two parallel systems.

A civilian jury acquitted Sergeant Nazario for his part in killing two Iraqi detainees while in combat. During the second battle of Fallujah, in November 1994, subordinates were effectively ordered to kill two captive Iraqis.[117] The incident occurred in the heat of battle. During a house-clearing operation in which a US soldier had died, four Iraqis in possession of weapons were detained.[118] Nazario was advised by his commander to "take care of them," so they could continue with the operation.[119] Nazario had been separated from the military for three years before a criminal complaint was filed. This meant he could no longer be subject to military discipline due to his civilian status, despite the fact that this incident fell squarely within the argument as to why military discipline is required.[120] However, both *Green* and *Nazario* demonstrate the ability of the civilian system to apply and reach outcomes that follow the law notwithstanding the crimes occurred in another jurisdiction and during conflict.

It is not surprising that Green argued for a military process given the lighter punishment received by his four co-conspirators, who were still soldiers of the 502 Infantry Regiment when charged and dealt with by court-martial. He challenged the convictions, claiming he should have been dealt with in the military system and contending that the *MEJA* was unconstitutional because it "violates the separation-of-powers principle and the non-delegation doctrine, equal protection, and due process."[121] The argument was that Congress had delegated to the executive "power to define crimes, punishments, and adjudicative procedures" and "unconstitutionally enhanced the Executive power to prosecute."[122] The court rejected this. While avoiding the constitutional question, the Circuit Federal court acknowledged that the UMCJ does provide the executive with discretion to prosecute a military member who is not subject to the UMCJ. However, no discretion as to the forum is provided, it being within the civilian court system.[123] On the equal-protection argument, Green contended that there was nothing to distinguish him from his co-offenders in relation to the crime, and that he should therefore have been subject to the same discipline system as his co-conspirators. The arbitrariness of the status test applied and the Court of Appeal was satisfied that at the time the charge was laid, which was the relevant time to consider, Green was no longer a part of the military.[124]

If Green and the military punishment of his co-offenders is any representation, then the far greater sentence Green received in the civilian system diminishes the claim that military punishment is necessary to enforce greater obedience because it is harsher. Green did not have the indulgence of a convening authority intervention. Putting the convening authority option together with the practice of dealing with serious matters at the lower administrative penalty range means that it is questionable just how much harsher military punishment actually is, and therefore what degree of deterrence is operating as a factor in military punishment.[125] Again, this discussion has to be considered against the backdrop of the level of impunity that can operate in a hierarchical secret coterie, where rules are applied by men and not by a rule of law.

The matter of *Hennis*,[126] in juxtaposition to the above cases in which crimes occurred in a foreign war and were tried in a US civilian court, a criminal offence of murder on US soil, while the alleged perpetrator was a civilian at the time of first arrest, was ultimately tried in a court-martial. This shows the apparent absurdity and arguably the lost way of military discipline when these two systems operate side by side. *Hennis* involved the murder of a woman and her two daughters on US territory. At the time of the offence, Hennis, the alleged offender, was in the military. The complexity, with a capital offence and death penalty involved, has seen the case cross from civilian to military jurisdiction and matters remaining unresolved over many years. Hennis was retired from the military when first charged and tried in the civilian court of North Carolina for three murders and a rape, and he was convicted and sentenced to death in 1986. The North Carolina Supreme Court reversed this because the trial court had erred when permitting the prosecution to present macabre photographs of the crime scene and autopsy at the trial.[127] After his acquittal, Hennis re-enlisted in the military but had retired again in July 2004. By 2005, advancements in DNA evidence testing resulted in the re-testing of semen as part of cold case investigations. A match was allegedly found and Hennis was recalled to active duty in order to enable charging him with the three murders under the UCMJ. On March 17, 2010, he was tried by court-martial, convicted, and sentenced to death.[128] Hennis' acquittal at his second state trial and the Double Jeopardy Clause were irrelevant. This was firstly on the grounds that the federal jurisdiction is separate from the state of North Carolina, and second that army regulations provide that a person who is subject to the UCMJ and who has been tried in a civilian court "*may*, but ordinarily will not," be tried by court-martial.[129] The jurisdiction of the UCMJ article 2(4) also permits application to: "[r]etired members of a regular component of the armed forces who are entitled to pay."[130] The problem of retired military members highlights the blurring of jurisdiction, which the status test contributes to, and this then extends the reach of the coterie's criminal punishment regime to thousands more civilians who happen to be veterans.[131]

Differences in the two systems can bring perceptions of unequal treatment. Such perceptions operate unfairly both ways, as indicated by the cases of *Green* and *Hennis*. In addition, all those civilians subject to criminal convictions may feel they are treated differently from this separate cohort of the same community, particularly those on death row. The argument that justifies the benefits of separate discipline, when dissected, is frail and certainly does not justify the costs. Moving criminal punishment into the civilian courts, to which military members are already subject, would address the uniform treatment of survivors and perpetrators in abuse and sexual assault matters and integrate the values of both groups as regards acceptable and unacceptable conduct.[132] The military does not articulate well why this should be different.

Rape is inherently a criminal rather than a military offence, although violence being an aspect of rape and other assaults is also part of wars' destructive activities. Coletti draws on Brownmiller's theory of the intertwined nature of rape and war as aspects of a warrior culture in which "the dehumanization and violent power over another"[133] provide a distress outlet, much like drugs and alcohol. Including women in this environment means this loss of ethical morality has to be addressed. It drew condemnation when an Australian, female captain reportedly raised the possibility of sex workers, or sex toys, being permissible on the front line to relieve stress and loneliness.[134]

The need for strict obedience in combat scenarios is undermined by many considerations, such as resources for punishment in battle zone situations; that the majority of offending is unrelated to strict combat obedience; that military populations can be operating largely in peacetime where civilian courts are open and available; and that enforcement for breaches is seemingly not at a standard that justifies the claim for stricter obedience. Improving the interaction between military members and civilian institutions overcomes the barriers, as noted, by the reduced cost of oversight, and an increased level of understanding between the two.

The end of conscription bought with it a disengagement by citizens in military matters. This is not a healthy thing when it is the citizen who votes for the politicians who in turn determine the laws and conditions that impinge on military members, and the executive that decides how the military will be used. Having civilian juries is not the anathema the military claim it to be. Explaining the context surrounding any criminal activity is something a jury must take into account in any crime, to enable an understanding of the mental state of the perpetrator. Expert evidence can be called in a civilian trial, and the ability to explain operations in a manner that civilians can understand is a good thing. Juries serve the purpose of ensuring elite legal jargon does not become the norm in criminal law, by requiring explanations in simple laypersons' terms. Military fears that they will be judged harshly in their actions, because of a lack of understanding by civilian juries of the level of stress and pressure they work under, are allayed when it is apparent that juries may have a tendency to weigh this highly in favor of the military when making their determinations. This was likely the case in *Nazario*'s acquittal described previously.

Juries are considered capable of determining allegations of criminal negligence by doctors who may be working in high-pressured, high-stress environments, with the jury not knowledgeable at the level of the surgeons' lived experience, but this is not a reason that they cannot make an informed decision. A civilian jury hearing a military matter will bring an integration and greater cohesiveness between the primary and secondary community, thereby increasing the understanding of values and the contexts in which both operate. The use of adultery in the US military, which is no longer a criminal offence in the civilian domain in Australia and most US states, to deal with matters that perhaps more appropriately fall under other criminal offending is but one example. Having these matters tried in the civilian courts also demands the military to be able to communicate in a manner that is understood in order to enable an exchange of ideas between both groups.[135]

Dealing with criminal offending in the civilian courts enables the transparency associated with media reporting. While this may threaten the reputation, or *la bella figura*, of the military, it should not be an overriding concern in a democracy. Reporting by the media is essential for the public to remain engaged and have an understanding of the issues facing this societal group. Such an institution with high public expenditure, but also a specialist organization that is lawfully able to apply violence to other combatants, is one that has to have consideration of transparency in meeting civilian demands of superintendence. Media reporting, which is possible in civilian court matters, enables political and legal discourse, which maintains the system with a currency of values, keeping it fresh.[136] One can hear the cries of outrage at such a suggestion, and certainly secret coteries will resist such suggestions just as many elite managers and controllers of an entity or group are prone to resist perceived intrusion in their realm.[137] This does not mean that it should not happen, and it is perhaps an even greater justification for the operation of a more transparent criminal justice system.

Contrary to military claims, a greater alignment does not threaten the functional military imperative but strengthens it by enabling the military to focus, in a concentrated and less distracted manner, on its core duties. Providing a criminal justice system was never intended to be one of its core duties. However, this is quite the opposite of the current understanding of the military and the highest civil courts, as they ignore the operation of the structural imperative. The more engagement and interaction between the military and civil society, the greater the awareness and understanding between civilians and military members. Janowitz's assertion supports the notion that "the military's first duty is to society, and if society changed and altered its strategic goals, the military must adapt to them,"[138] and arguably so should the courts.

Such a development for instance, may help overcome levels of depression and the estrangement evidenced within the military.[139] It would make soldiers feel part of the society they defend and facilitate finding a greater commitment to the state and its citizens. Civilian values, as they change, are reflected through the mechanism of the civil jury system, reinforcing the currently accepted standards of behavior as they evolve, and keeping the system relevant. This approach would also aid the theory of civil-military control by supporting all three governance institutions in overseeing the reach of the separate coterie, rather than actively ceding power to it. The struggle with addressing sexual abuse would no longer have the potential to damage the military, as it would be the civilian system's responsibility to address through the criminal justice punishment and the protection of survivors' rights.

ON OBEDIENCE

The military relies on three main tools to ensure obedience to the law: 1) the criminal domestic law and the Geneva Conventions, as incorporated in the domestic law, which in turn are absorbed into the military internal discipline system, 2) workplace conditions such as pay and levels of respect, this latter also being relevant to 3) the normative status accorded military members as a profession. Abuse and sexual assault affect all three areas.

In regards to the first tool, it is contended that the civilian system is required to enforce the criminal law to support the military's structural and functional imperative. The coercive threat to disobedience is not undermined if the soldier is subject to both workplace administrative discipline and the civilian criminal justice system.

Secondly, workplace conditions that create a feeling of safety are a priority. The military discipline system has not established evidence of how it can provide this. Instead, the evidence points to a failure, with rates of hazing and sexual assault generally higher, but certainly not substantially less, than in the civilian system. Survivors being able to report abuse to an independent civilian investigative process, designed to give the best protection to both the survivor and the perpetrators rights, would give greater support to this workplace aspect. Moreover, the military could still maintain its carrot-and-stick incentives through awards, honors, promotions, and workplace administrative discipline, such as reducing rank or issuing letters of reprimand.

The current heavy reliance on administrative-level punishments to avoid all the downsides of the courts-martial system diminishes respect for criminal law, as it is evaded by the enforcement of lesser penalties, such as the offence of adultery in the US instead of more serious offences such as rape. If people with violent propensities are already drawn to the military and the system then imposes a less onerous regime of detection and punishment, it becomes a haven for violent behavior outside the acceptable norms of civil society and diminishes the safety of the workplace. It also threatens the civil society when, as part of the administrative discipline, a dishonorable discharge means that the perpetrator sometimes goes back to the primary society without this group being made aware of the full extent of the danger.

Devin Kelley had been held in a mental health facility before being court-martialed in 2012 for a violent assault on family, resulting in his imprisonment for twelve months. Then, in 2014, he was discharged for bad conduct. Despite this, the air force had not entered the information in the federal register,[140] and he was able to purchase a weapon and proceeded to kill 26 and wound another 20 civilians while in their church, in one of the worse massacres in Texas.[141] This comes to mind as just one situation where the primary group had no genuine notice of the extent of the potential danger this member represented.[142]

The third tool enabling military obedience to the law concerns the engagement with the normative attraction that comes from being in the military profession, and it lends itself to elitism and status as part of the warrior class, through membership of the coterie. This is perceived by many in the military as the respect given by the primary civilian group for the protection offered by the military, and evidenced by ticker tape parades and honoring the memory of soldiers through special national days, such as Anzac Day in Australia. Unfortunately, normative status has not been in a healthy state, probably ever since the Vietnam War. Soldiers' experiences upon return from combat, in both the US and Australia, have often been less than they would like. Homelessness, suicide, drug and alcohol consumption, and PTSD have become significant problems. Correlations can be drawn between dishonorable discharge, suicide, homelessness, and further offending, due to the stigma attached, which also affects job and education opportunities.[143]

The structural imperatives are very important for military personnel. With such high incidents of mental distress, the provisions for insanity pleas become important. Lai[144] has written about the significant difference between the US civilian courts procedures for assessing sanity and the military's. He highlights the power of the convening authority in deciding competence prior to referring a matter to court-marital as an aspect of authority exercised in a potentially arbitrary and less than transparent manner.[145] The Australian Returned and Services League has shown this by its objection to the Military Court of Australia legislation that proposed the removal of juries.[146] Such different treatment increases the sense of alienation from the primary citizenry. This is explained in the Australian Defence Association's premier journal:

> Many Australians are completely disengaged from their defence force on a day-to-day basis. . . . Many simply ignore our current wars altogether, do not regard them as important, or see them as being fought by someone else and not by Australia or themselves in any personal, community or citizenship sense. Other Australians are conscious that we are at war but actively deny that the we involved includes them.[147]

Soldiers in countries such as the UK, where they have made efforts to address the civil-military covenant, have also identified the resulting isolation felt and the consequences for the morale of military members:

> Just imagine that you are a British soldier returning from a tour of duty in Iraq or Afghanistan. As you arrive back in Britain, you feel a mixture of relief, exhaustion and pride in your service. Yet your return seems at best to be a matter of supreme indifference to the public. There are no crowds at the airport, nor any large parades. You are expected to disappear quietly from view. . . . Increasingly, it seems that we soldiers serve a nation that considers us an embarrassment that simply doesn't want to know about us.[148]

Social and cultural norms will prevail in any group but in secret coteries the philosophy of *la bella figura* is dominant. This will exist irrespective of any extended system of criminal punishment, as the cultural norms of the group exert considerable control over the group's behavior.[149] The military and the courts seem keen to ignore this when presenting justifications for the military to maintain its separate system of criminal punishment. Controlling all aspects of a military member's life is not essential to extract the level of obedience needed to perform functionally. The next chapter looks more closely at the control achieved, and how mechanisms other than the criminal law are important for functionality at the leadership and group levels.

NOTES

1. See, The Charter of Paris for a New Europe adopted by the Conference on Security and Cooperation in Europe in 1990 cited in "American Society of International Law" *International Legal Materials* (1991): 190.

2. John Sloan, "Machiavelli on War" http://www.xenophon-mil.org/milhist/renaissance/machessy.htm Machiavelli "saw that warfare was no longer going to be the exclusive affair of a specialized class of warrior who fought over largely private interests, but the central activity of the then developing state and hence the concern of its rulers and indeed of all its inhabitants."

3. Baron Montesquieu (1689–1755) 1784, *Spirit of the Laws*. 1989 Eds. Anne M. Cohler, Basia Carolyn Miller, and Harold Samuel Stone (Cambridge University Press, 1989).

4. *R v. Kirby; Ex parte Boilermakers' Society of Australia* (1956) 94 CLR 254: a foundational decision confirming the separation of judicial and executive powers of the Commonwealth of Australia.

5. See e.g., *Youngstown Sheet & Tube Co. v. Sawyer*, 343 U.S. 579 (1952)—limiting the power of the president; *Bowsher v. Synar*, 478 U.S. 714 (1986) division of power between the executive and legislature; *United States v. Nixon* 418 U.S. 683 (1974) limiting executive privilege; *Zivotofsky v. Kerry*, 576 U.S. ___ (2015) outlines the checks on executive power.

6. *R v. Kirby*; *Ex parte Boilermakers' Society of Australia* (1956) 94 CLR 254, 274 (Dixon C.J., McTiernan, Fullagar, and Kitto JJ); see also *Australian Communist Party v. The Commonwealth Case* (1951) 83 CLR 1. This case declared the *Communist Party Dissolution Act* 1950 unconstitutional and invalid based on Parliament's inability to exercise the defence power in the manner attempted during peacetime.

7. *Morrison v. Olson, 487* U.S. 654 (1988). Charles Kesler, "What Separation of Powers Means for Constitutional Government" *First Principles Series* 17 (2007): 1 https://www.heritage.org/political-process/report/what-separation-powers-means-constitutional-government.

8. 487 U.S. 654, 694–95 (1988) (Rehnquist CJ).

9. 487 U.S. 654, 697 (1988) (Scalia J); *Mistretta v. U.S.* 488 U.S. 361 (1989) (Scalia J) in dissent again.

10. Harvey Rishikof, "Institutional Ethics Drawing Lines for Militant Democracies" *Joint Force Quarterly* 54 (2009): 48, 49.

11. *White v. Director of Military Prosecution* [2007] HCA 29, [190] (Kirby J).

12. Jonathan Turley, "The Military Pocket Republic" *Northwestern University Law Review* 97 (2002): 1, 120.

13. *Australian Communist Party* (1951) 83 CLR 1.

14. (1951) 83 CLR 1, [193] (Dixon J). See further, Andrew Sykes, "The 'Rule Of Law' as an Australian Constitutionalist Promise" *Murdoch University Electronic Journal of Law* 9 no. 1 (2002): 1; Lisa Burton Crawford, *The Rule of Law and the Australian Constitution* (Federation Press, 2017).

15. See e.g., Anne Twomey, "Review of High Court Constitutional Cases 2007" *UNSW Law Journal* 31 no. 1 (2007): 215; Kesler, "What Separation of Powers."

16. *Thomas v. Mowbray* [2007] HCA 33.

17. *Criminal Code* (Cth) Division 104.

18. *Thomas* [2007] HCA 33 (Gleeson CJ) [7], (Gummow and Crennan JJ) [145], (Hayne J) [435], (Callinan J) [585], (Heydon J) [649]; But *cf* (Gummow and Crennan JJ) the decision was confined to consideration of *interim* detention orders only [111].

19. *Thomas* [2007] HCA 33 [386] (Kirby J).

20. *Convention on the Rights of the Child* Adopted and opened for signature, ratification, and accession by General Assembly resolution 44/25 November 20, 1989 entry into force September 2, 1990. The United States is the only United Nations member that is not a party to the UN Convention on the Rights of the Child (UN-CRC), although it has signed the convention.

21. See The *National Framework for Protecting Australia's Children 2009–2020* Australian Government, Department of Social Services–outlines the roles of each level of government, and the non-government and private sectors https://www.dss.gov.au/our-responsibilities/families-and-children/publications-articles/protecting-children-is-everyones-business.

22. Christopher W. Behan, "Don't Tug on Superman's Cape: In Defense of Convening Authority Selection and Appointment of Court-Martial Panel Members" *Military Law Review* 176 (2003): 190, 238 "The very survival of the nation is at stake. Therefore, the consequences of judicial error concerning the effect of a practice on military effectiveness are particularly serious."

23. Turley, "The Military Pocket": 108 "In this way, both factional interests and informational distortions may undermine governance decisions of the military"; Richard Kohn, "The Erosion of Civilian Control of the Military in the United States Today" *Naval War College Review* 55 no. 3 (2002): 9.

24. Turley, "The Military Pocket": 85–86.

25. Kohn, "Erosion of Civilian": 9.

26. Gregory Hooks and Brian McQueen, "American Exceptionalism Revisited: The Military-Industrial Complex, Racial Tension, and the Underdeveloped Welfare State" *American Sociological Review* 75 (2010): 185; Richard H. Kohn, "First Priorities in Military Professionalism" *Orbis* 57 no. 3 (2013): 380.

27. Turley, "The Military Pocket": 105–6 "Accordingly, Spartans subjugated every familial or individual want to the collective good."

28. Ibid., 103.

29. Cullen Murphy, *The New Rome? The Fall of an Empire and the Fate of America* (Scribe Publications Ltd, 2007).

30. Benedict Kingsbury and Benjamin Straumann, *The Roman Foundations of the Law of Nations: Alberico Gentili and the Justice of Empire* (Oxford University Press, 2010).

31. Joseph Stiglitz and Linda J. Bilmes, *The Three Trillion Dollar War: The True Cost of the Iraq Conflict* (W W Norton, 2008).

32. Turley, "The Military Pocket": 111; Robert French, "The Courts and Parliament" (Paper presented at the Supreme Court of Queensland Seminar, Brisbane, August 4, 2012).

33. Currently or previously serving members from foreign countries may apply to serve in the Australian military https://www.defencejobs.gov.au/joining/can-i-join/citizenship.

34. See e.g., P. W. Singer, *Corporate Warriors: The Rise of the Privatized Military Industry* (Cornell University Press, 2008); James Brown, *Privateers in Australia's*

Conflict and Disaster Zones, Civil-Military Occasional Papers (Australian Government, 2015).

35. Louis J. Sirico, "The Federalist and the Lessons of Rome" *Mississippi Law Journal* 75 (2006): 431; Murphy, *The New Rome?*

36. Turley, "The Military Pocket": 107 "The Roman citizens lacked this type of core identification with the political system and ultimately supported the sacrifice of democratic rights to a series of tyrants."

37. Christen A. Johnson and K. T. Hawbaker, "#MeToo: A Timeline of Events" *Chicago Tribune*, March 19, 2018 http://www.chicagotribune.com/lifestyles/ct-me-too-timeline-20171208-htmlstory.html; Stephanie Zacharek, Eliana Dockterman, and Haley Sweetland Edwards, "'Silence Breakers' Named Time Magazine's Person of the Year," *Time*, 2017 http://time.com/time-person-of-the-year-2017-silence-breakers/.

38. Sirico, "The Federalist."

39. Ibid., 466.

40. Ibid., 468.

41. Banner, "Institutional Sexual Assault": 137.

42. Julie Dickerson, "A Compensation System for Military Victims of Sexual Assault and Harassment" *Military Law Review* 222 (2014): 211, 230 (footnotes omitted).

43. Kenneth W. Kemp and Charles Hudlin, "Civil Supremacy over the Military: Its Nature and Limits" *Armed Forces & Society* 19 no. 1 (1992): 7, 10.

44. Malcolm Mackerras, "Australia" *European Journal of Political Research* 43 no. 7–8 (2004): 927 "While much civil disagreement was expressed in 2003 the U.S. decision to go to war in Iraq had little impact other than to encourage Bush to obtain the approval of Congress, unlike past practise in the U.S. that had seen Presidents take unilateral decisions to go to war—Vietnam and Korea. Howard took the matter to the Australian Parliament only after he had made the decision to join the Coalition of the willing."

45. David Luban, "On the Commander in Chief Power" *Southern California Law Review* 81 (2008): 477, 519.

46. 548 U.S. 557 (2006).

47. Matthew Happold, "Hamdan v. Rumsfeld and the Law of War" *Human Rights Law Review* 7 no. 2 (2007): 418.

48. Bruce Russett, *Controlling the Sword: The Democratic Governance of National Security* (Cambridge Mass Harvard University Press, 1990): 148, in Percy Allum, *State and Society in Western Europe* (Polity Press Cambridge, 1995): 511.

49. Matthew Groves, "The Civilianisation of Australian Military Law" *University of New South Wales Law Journal* 28 (2005): 364.

50. Groves, "The Civilianisation": 364–65 (footnotes omitted).

51. Turley, "The Military Pocket": 96.

52. David Vine, "Military Bases, American —Foreign Countries" *Digital Research Archive*, 2017 https://dra.american.edu/islandora/object/auislandora%3A55685. The US has approximately 324 bases on US soil. https://militarybases.com/by-state/;

approximately 800 in other countries; Australian Military Strength, Global Firepower, 2018 https://www.globalfirepower.com/country-military-strength-detail.asp?country_id=australia; Nautilus Institute for Security and Sustainability http://www.defence.gov.au/Publications/Reviews/ADFPosture/docs/base_map.pdf. and bases overseas approximate estimate as at 2014, 59: https://nautilus.org/publications/books/australian-forces-abroad/australian-bases-abroad/ Australia approximately 45 bases on Australian soil.

53. See e.g., Constantine P. Danopoulos (ed), *Military Disengagement from Politics* (Routledge, 1988).

54. Turley, "The Military Pocket": 97–98.

55. Ibid., 95; See Pauline Collins, *Civil-Military "Legal" Relations: Where to from Here? The Civilian Courts and the Military in the United Kingdom, United States and Australia* (Leiden: Brill Nijhoff, 2018).

56. Ewa Kretowicz, "Detention Rates Falling in Armed Force" *The Canberra Times*, July 21, 2013 http://www.canberratimes.com.au/act-news/detention-rates-falling-in-armed-forces-20130720-2qbkh.html.

57. Ken Silverstein, *Private Warriors* (Verso, 2000): 17.

58. David Schmidtchen, *The Rise of the Strategic Private. Technology, Control and Change in a Network-Enabled Military Land Warfare Studies Centre*, (2006): 15.

59. Behan, "Don't Tug on Superman's Cape."

60. William T. Sherman, Commanding General of the Army from 1869 to 1883, before a congressional committee in 1879, cited in Edward F. Sherman, "The Civilianization of Military Law" *Maine Law Review* 22 (1970): 3, 4–5.

61. Richard H. Kohn, "Comment on Professor Yoo, Administration of War" *Duke Law Journal* 58 no. 8 (2009): 2313, 2314.

62. Morris Janowitz, *Sociology and the Military Establishment* (Russel Sage Foundation, 1959).

63. Ibid., 97.

64. Lord Levene et al., "Defence Reform; an Independent Report into the Structure and Management of the Ministry of Defence" Defence Reform Steering Group, 2011: 79 [7] "Some past attempts at reform have, for understandable reasons, focused on elements of a process or organization, rather than the system as a whole, which has sometimes resulted in displacing problems and / or not identifying the root cause"; See also, Stella Cernak, "Sexual Assault and Rape in the Military: The Invisible Victims of International Gender Crimes at the Front Lines" *Michigan Journal of Gender & Law* 22 (2015): 207.

65. 340 U.S. 135 (1950); *Brown*, 348 U.S. 112, 75 S.Ct. 141; *Shearer,* 473 U.S. 57, 105 S.Ct. 3039; See also, Michael Rust, "Expansion of the Feres Doctrine" *Emory Law Journal* 32 (1983): 237.

66. *Feres v. U.S.,* 340 U.S. 135 (1950); but *cf Levin v. U.S.*, 568 U.S. 2013; 11-1351 (2013) regarding medical battery.

67. *Martinelli v. United States Department of the Army*, 812 F.2d 872 (3d Cir. 1987), but *cf Jorden v. National Guard* 799 F.2d 99 (3d Cir.1986), where *Feres* was taken as an absolute bar on tort actions by military members against the government.

68. *Costo v. United States,* 248 F.3d 863, (9th Cir. 2001).

69. 248 F.3d 863, 876 (9th Cir. 2001) (Ferguson J citing The Federalist No. 78 (Alexander Hamilton)).

70. 248 F.3d 863, 875 (9th Cir. 2001).

71. 248 F.3d 863, 876 (9th Cir. 2001) (Judge McKeown) "As we noted at the outset, we apply the Feres doctrine here without relish . . . in determining this suit to be barred, we join the many panels of this Court that have criticized the inequitable extension of this doctrine to a range of situations that seem far removed from the doctrine's original purposes. See, e.g., *McAllister*, 942 F.2d at 1480; *Persons*, 925 F.2d at 299; *Atkinson*, 825 F.2d at 206; *Monaco v. United States*, 661 F.2d 129, 134 (9th Cir. 1981)."

72. 248 F.3d 863, 876 (9th Cir. 2001) (Ferguson J), *petition for cert. filed*, ___ U.S. ___, 122 S. Ct. 808, 151 L. Ed. 2d 693 (2001); See further *Jackson,* 110 F.3d at 1487; *Dreier,* 106 F.3d at 848; *Bon v. United States,* 802 F.2d 1092, 1094 (9th Cir.1986); See Barry Kellman, "Judicial Abdication of Military Tort Accountability: But Who Is to Guard the Guards Themselves?" *Duke Law Journal* (1989): 1597.

73. *Witt v. United States*, 2009 U.S. Dist. (E.D. Cal. Feb. 9, 2009); *Witt v. United States*, 131 S. Ct. 3058 denied June 27, 2011. See also, *United States v. Shearer* 473 U.S. 52, 105 S.Ct. 3039, 87 L.Ed.2d 38 (1985), reversing 723 F.2d 1102 (3d Cir.1984).

74. Turley, "The Military Pocket": 4.

75. *Parker v. Levy,* 417 US 733 (1974). See further, Robert Sherrill, *Military Justice Is to Justice as Military Music Is to Music* (Harper & Row, 1969); Robert Batey, "Parker v. Levy: A Primer in Judicial Persuasion" *Journal of Legal Education* 49 (1999): 97; Robert Strassfeld, "The Vietnam War on Trial: The Court-Martial of Dr. Howard B. Levy" *Wisconsin Law Review* (1994): 839.

76. See, for a discussion of the facts of this case, Sherrill, "*Military Justice*": 98–158.

77. *Orloff* 345 US 83 (1953).

78. 345 US 83, 94 (Jackson J) (emphasis added).

79. *Parker* 417 US 733, 744 (1974) (Rehnquist J) (emphasis added).

80. See further, Diane H. Mazur, "Rehnquist's Vietnam: Constitutional Separatism and the Stealth Advance of Martial Law" *Indiana Law Journal* 77 (2002): 701, 740–48 for a discussion of the impact of CJ Rehnquist's judgment in *Parker v. Levy*; Thomas Dienes, "When the First Amendment Is Not Preferred: The Military and Other 'Special Contexts'" *University of Cincinnati Law Review* 56 (1988): 779; Stephanie A Levin, "The Deference That Is Due: Rethinking the Jurisprudence of Judicial Deference to the Military" *Villanova Law Review* 35 (1990): 1009; Michael Gilbert, "The Military and the Federal Judiciary: An Unexplored Part of the Civil-Military Relations Triangle" *United States Air Force Academy Journal of Legal Studies* 8 (1997–1998): 197; But *cf* James M. Hirschhorn, "The Separate Community: Military Uniqueness and Servicemen's Constitutional Rights" *North Carolina Law Review* 62 (1983–1984): 177.

81. Pippa Norris, *Driving Democracy: Do Power-Sharing Institutions Work?* (Cambridge University Press, 2008) Chapter 8 "The Fourth Estate": 186–206.

82. 483 US 669 (1987).

83. *Stanley,* 483 US 669, 671, 683 (1987) (Scalia J) (emphasis added).

84. Andrew Cohen, "None of the Supreme Court Justices Has Battle Experience" *The Atlantic*, August 13, 2012 https://www.theatlantic.com/national/archive/2012/08/none-of-the-supreme-court-justices-has-battle-experience/260973/ "William Rehnquist (1972–2005) was a sergeant in the Army Air Corps stationed in North Africa as a weather observer."

85. See e.g., *Rasul v. Bush* 542 U.S. 466 (2004); *Hamdan v. Rumsfeld* 548 U.S. 557 (2006); *Boumediene v. Bush* 553 U.S. 723 (2008).

86. See Collins, *Civil-military "Legal" Relations*; *Goldman* 475 US 503, 515 (1986) (Brennan J); *Brown v. Glines* 444 US 348, 368–9 (Brennan J) (1980).

87. *The Convention for the Protection of Human Rights and Fundamental Freedoms*, short title the *European Convention* on *Human Rights*, opened for signature in Rome on November 4, 1950, and came into force in 1953.

88. *Morris v. United Kingdom* (Application Number 38784/97 dated 26 February 2002); *Cooper v. Findlay* [2003] ECtHR Grand Chamber.

89. Simon Bronitt and Mark Nolan, "Our Sights Must Be Set on Justice" *The Age*, August 28, 2009 [19].

90. Robert Smol, "Why We Should Unionize the Military" *National Post*, May 20, 2015 nationalpost.com/opinion/robert-smol-why-we-should-unionize-the-military; "Military Unions and Associations" in Ian Leigh et al. (eds), *Handboook on Human Rights and Fundamental Freedoms of Armed Forces Personnel* (OSCE Office for Democratic Institutions and Human Rights (ODIHR), 2008): 65.

91. Leigh "Military Unions": 73. Paul Verschuur, "Redefining What Makes a Good Soldier: Dutch Army Steps to a Different Drum" *Associated Press*, April 23, 1998 http://articles.latimes.com/1989-04-23/news/mn-1763_1_senior-noncommissioned-officer-soldiers-air-force.

92. Turley, "The Military Pocket"; Eugene Fidell, "A World-Wide Perspective on Change in Military Justice" *The Air Force Law Review* 48 (2000): 195.

93. US Death Penalty Information Center https://deathpenaltyinfo.org/.

94. Ibid.

95. Erik D. Masick, "Moral Injury and Preventative Law: A Framework for the Future" *Military Law Review* 224 (2016): 223.

96. Thierry Devos et al., "Conflicts among Human Values and Trust in Institutions" *British Journal of Social Psychology* 41(2002): 484, 491–92. See also Milton Rokeach, *The Nature of Human Values* (The Free Press, 1973); Shalom H. Schwartz and Florencia M. Sortheix, "Values and Subjective Well-Being" in *Handbook of Well-Being* edited by E. Diener, S. Oishi, and L. Tay (Salt Lake City, UT: DEF Publishers, 2018).

97. Turley, "The Military Pocket": 98–99.

98. Ibid., 100.

99. Collins, *Civil-Military "Legal" Relations*.

100. Turley, "The Military Pocket": 127–28.

101. Ibid., 129.

102. Jacob K. Eskildsen and Mikkel L. Nussler, "The Managerial Drivers of Employee Satisfaction and Loyalty" *Total Quality Management* 11 no. 4–6 (2000): 581; Alam Sageer, Sameena Rafat, and Puja Agarwal, "Identification of Variables Affecting Employee Satisfaction and Their Impact on the Organization" *Journal of Business and Management* 5 no. 1 (2012): 32; Robert J. Sternberg and Todd I. Lubart, *Defying the Crowd. Cultivating Creativity in a Culture of Conformity* (The Free Press, 1995); The Defence Committee, "Pathway to Change: Evolving Defence Culture A Strategy for Cultural Change and Reinforcement" (Department of Defence, 2012) www.defence.gov.au/pathwaytochange/; Michael I. Spak and Alice M. McCart, "Effect of Military Culture on Responding to Sexual Harassment: The Warrior Mystique" *Nebraska Law Review* 83 no. 1 (2004): 79.

103. Collins, *Civil-Military Legal Relations*; Richard G. Fox and Jodie E. Lydeker, "The Militarisation of Australia's Federal Criminal Justice System" *Criminal Law Journal* 25 (2008): 287.

104. George Nolte and Heike Krieger, "European Military Law Systems: General Comparative Report" in George Nolte (ed), *European Military Law Systems* (De Gruyter Recht, 2003): 19.

105. Turley, "The Military Pocket": 128.

106. Collins, *Civil-Military "Legal" Relations*: 264.

107. 107 S. Ct 2924 (1987).

108. 395 US 258 (1969).

109. *Re Colonel Aird; Ex parte Alpert* (2004) 220 CLR 308; *White v. Director of Military Prosecutions* [2007] HCA 29; *Williams v. Chief of Army* [2016] ADFDAT 3 [50]-[51] (Tracey and Hiley JJ).

110. See Jim Frederick, *Black Hearts: One Platoon's Descent into Madness in Iraq's Triangle of Death* (Harmony Books, 2010); See also Brian De Palma's film *Redacted* 2007, which is influenced by the events at Mahmudiyah.

111. *Green* 654 F.3d 637 (6th Cir. 2011).

112. Defendant Green, Crim. No 5:06- CR-5-R document 282 filed 9/4/2009 http://www.kywd.uscourts.gov/3-06-00230/pdf/entry287.pdf. *Green* 654 F.3d 637 (6th Cir. 2011) 2.

113. Steve Almasy, "Former Soldier at Center of Murder of Iraqi Family Dies after Suicide Attempt" *CNN*, February 19, 2014 https://edition.cnn.com/2014/02/18/us/soldier-steven-green-suicide/index.html.

114. *Green* 654 F.3d 637 (6th Cir. 2011) 7; See further, Norbert Basil MacLean, "Separate and Unequal Military Justice," *Los Angeles Times*, September 10, 2008 http://www.latimes.com/opinion/la-oew-maclean10-2008sep10-story.html.

115. Green was convicted of rape, conspiracy to commit rape, housebreaking with intent to rape, and four counts of felony murder. He had pleaded guilty earlier to lesser charges of conspiracy, obstructing justice, arson, wrongfully touching a corpse, and drinking.

116. See *Green* 654 F.3d 637 (6th Cir. 2011), (Martin J), 3.

117. *United States v. Nazario*, No. ED CR 07-127-SGL, (C.D. Cal 2007): Defense argued "[T]he political branches of government are accorded a particularly

high degree of deference in the area of military affairs. . . . Mr. Nazario's case, on the other hand, is *not* an ordinary charge of manslaughter, which a lay civilian jury could consider. Instead, this case is an examination of combat action, and to allow the application of MEJA to that circumstance flies in the face of legislative intent . . ." (citation omitted); See Johnny Dwyer, "Former Marine Jose Nazario Acquitted of All Charges in Fallujah Killings: Would Have Been First American Serviceman Convicted in Civilian Court for Battlefield Crimes" *LA Weekly News*, December 31, 2008 http://www.laweekly.com/authors/johnny-dwyer-2127170.

118. *Nazario*, No. ED CR 07-127-SGL, (C.D. Cal 2007): 3.

119. *Nazario*, No. ED CR 07-127-SGL, (C.D. Cal 2007): 3–4.

120. See further, James Hartney, "A Call for Change: The Military Extraterritorial Jurisdiction Act" *Gonzaga Journal of International Law* 13 (2010): 2.

121. *Green* 654 F.3d 637, 641 (6th Cir. 2011) (Martin J).

122. *Green* 654 F.3d 637, 650 (6th Cir. 2011) (Martin J).

123. *Green* 654 F.3d 637, 650 (6th Cir. 2011) (Martin J).

124. *Green* 654 F.3d 637, 652 (6th Cir. 2011) (Martin J) ". . . because Green appears to raise an equal protection claim based on the government's charging decision, he must prove that he was similarly situated to his co-conspirators at the charging stage."

125. Turley, "The Military Pocket": 129.

126. *State v. Hennis*, 323 N.C. 279, 372 S.E.2d 523 (N.C. 1988); *Hennis v. Hemlick*, No. 10-6400 (4th Cir. Apr. 1, 2010).

127. *Hennis*, 323 N.C. 279, 372 S.E.2d 523 (N.C. 1988) (Mitchell, J and Meyer, J., filed a dissenting opinion).

128. Dwight Sullivan, "Top 10 Military Justice Stories of 2010: The Reconviction and Death Sentence of MSGT Timothy Hennis (Ret.)" *Nimj blog*, January 2, 2011 http://www.caaflog.com/2011/01/02/top-10-military-justice-stories-of-2010 "This is the first death sentence adjudged by a court-martial since 2005 and only the 16th under the current military death penalty procedures, promulgated by President Reagan in 1984."

129. See e.g., *Moore v. Illinois*, 55 US 13, 20 (1852); See further, Nicholas Schmidle, "Three Trials for Murder. In the Name of Justice, Did the Military Sidestep Double Jeopardy?" *New Yorker*, November 14, 2011 https://www.newyorker.com/magazine/2011/11/14/three-trials-for-murder; Robert D. Merrill, "The Military's Dilution of Double Jeopardy: Why United States v. Easton Should Be Overturned" *Military Law Review* 219 (2014): 176.

130. UCMJ s 802(4); Sullivan, "Top 10": 150: Hennis' counsel tried to stop the court-martial on jurisdictional grounds but the US district court denied habeas relief on abstention grounds; *Hennis v. Hemlick*, No. 5:-09-HC-2169-BO (E.D.N.C. Mar. 16, 2010). His appeal to the Fourth Circuit seeking an injunction to stop the court-martial was denied: *Hennis v. Hemlick*, No. 10-6400 (4th Cir. Apr. 1, 2010): ". . . federal courts are not at liberty to presume that the decision of the [military courts] would be otherwise than is required by the fundamental law of the land. . . . Consequently, comity generally requires that a service member first exhaust all available military remedies before seeking federal court intervention into pending court-martial proceedings."

131. See *Green* 654 F.3d 637 (6th Cir. 2011), (Martin J) 13–14 describes the difficulties in determining discharge—"Because of the lack of decided cases in our sister circuits, we have sought guidance from decisions of the US CMA. It has held that 'Although UCMJ does not define the point in time when discharge occurs, courts look to 10 U.S.C. ss 1168(a) and 1169 to determine the requirements to effectuate a discharge.' . . . Courts have read sections 1168(a) and 1169 as requiring that three elements, known as the *King* elements, be satisfied to accomplish an early discharge: (1) a delivery of a valid discharge certificate; (2) a final accounting of pay; and (3) the undergoing of a 'clearing' process as required under appropriate service regulations to separate the member from military service." (citations omitted).

132. Turley, "The Military Pocket": 128 ". . . service members are already subject to civilian criminal law authority. The suggested change would only make this integration complete and create a more clear line between the military and civilian authorities."

133. Leslie J. Coletti, "In Search of a New Culture: The Sexual Violence against U.S. Military Women by Their Fellow Soldiers, 1978–Present" *Dietrich College of Humanities and Social Sciences Thesis* (2010) http://repository.cmu.edu/cgi/view content.cgi?article=1049&context=hsshonors: 1, 38.

134. "Army Captain Calls for Prostitutes to Be Sent to Front Line to Relieve Soldiers' Stress: Report" *Yahoo7 News*, December 4, 2017 https://au.news.yahoo .com/a/38133843/australian-army-captain-says-sex-workers-could-help-soldiers/.

135. Turley, "The Military Pocket": 108.

136. Ibid., 109 "The use of civilian courts reduces these practical barriers for the media in reporting on cases and controversies in the military. . . ."; Michael Kramer and Michael Schmitt, "Lawyers on Horseback? Thoughts on Judge Advocates and Civil-Military Relations" *University of California and Los Angeles Law Review* 55 (2008): 1407.

137. Turley, "The Military Pocket": 109 "This may not be entirely welcomed by the management of the military system any more than corporate officers welcomed the increased involvement of stockholders under modern corporate law"; Gustav Eyler, "Gangs in the Military" *The Yale Law Journal* 118 (2009): 696.

138. Lindsay Cohn, "The Evolution of the Civil-Military 'Gap' Debate" *Paper prepared for the TISS project on the Gap between the Military and Civilian Society* (1999): 5.

139. See Hayden Cooper, "Combat Stress Strikes Australian Soldiers" *Broadcast: transcript available* November 4, 2012 http://www.abc.net.au/7.30/content/2012/ s3475312.htm.

140. Gun Ban for Individuals Convicted of a Misdemeanor Crime of Domestic Violence 1996, Pub.L. 104–208, 18 U.S.C. § 922(g) (9) known as the "Lautenberg law."

141. Sebastian Murdock, "Texas Church Shooter Escaped from Behavioral Health Facility In 2012" *Huffington Post*, November 8, 2017 http://www.huffington post.com.au/entry/texas-church-shooter-escaped-from-behavioral-health-facility _us_5a01fd4ce4b06ff32c93dd0d.

142. Melissa Jeltsen, "Air Force Failed to Enter Church Shooter's Domestic Violence Record in U.S. Database" *Huffington Post*, November 8, 2017 http://

www.huffingtonpost.com.au/entry/texas-church-shooting-domestic-violence-record_us_5a00d8c0e4b066c2c039ace8; See further for issues in registering sex offenders in the military—*United States v. Kebodeaux*, June 24, 2013 Supreme Court of the US No. 12–418.

143. AISRP, "Suicidal Behavior and Ideation among Military Personnel: Australian and International Trends" *Technical Report*, July 2016, 18–19; Sara Darehshori, "Dispatches: US Navy to Protect Soldiers with Mental Health Conditions" June 3, 2016 https://www.hrw.org/news/2016/06/03/dispatches-us-navy-protect-soldiers-mental-health-conditions; Thomas W. Britt et al., "Morale as a Moderator of the Combat Exposure-PTSD Symptom Relationship" *Journal of Traumatic Stress* 26 (2013): 94.

144. David C. Lai, "Military Justice Incompetence over Competency Discriminations" *Military Law Review* 224 (2016): 48.

145. Manual for Courts-martial, United States R.C.M., 706(b) (1) and (2) (2012).

146. "Military Court of Australia Bill 2010, A Submission by the Returned & Services League of Australia" 2010 https://sitedesq.sportstg.com/assets/console/document/documents/MCABill2010.pdf: 1; Justin Whealing, "The Fight for Military Justice" *Lawyers Weekly*, November 16, 2010 http://www.lawyersweekly.com.au/blogs/special_reports/archive/2010/11/16/the-fight-for-military-justice.aspx.

147. Editorial, "Disengagement, Deficient Debate and Defeat" *Defender*, Autumn, 2007: 1.

148. Colonel Jorge Mendonca, "If We No Longer Respect Our Fighting Men and Women, the Future of Britain Itself Is in Peril," *Daily Mail*, October 3, 2007; Bryan D. Watson, "A Look Down the Slippery Slope" *Air & Space Power Journal* 22 no. 1 (2008): 93; Thomas E. Ricks, "The Widening Gap between Military and Society" *The Atlantic*, July 1997 https://www.theatlantic.com/magazine/archive/1997/07/the-widening-gap-between-military-and-society/306158/.

149. Turley, "The Military Pocket": 122, 126.

Chapter Seven

Reform Necessary for Respect and Discipline

COMMAND RESPONSIBILITY

Much of the emphasis during scandals is placed on the leadership and command responsibility for behavior. Commanding officers have a very onerous series of obligations placed on them. Somewhat like a feudal lord, they are responsible for the lives of those under them, for their discipline and justice, to represent their needs higher up the chain, and to ensure they are always combat ready. A more subtle influence and concern is that commanding officers are also subject to work reviews and will themselves desire promotion up the ranks.[1] These diverse and countering demands require attendance that is influenced by an individual's value system. Value systems are hierarchical in operation,[2] and it is likely that considerations of personal advancement and combat readiness are high on a commanding officer's value system, with altruism further down. As Turley declares, "the use of the COC system by officers to play an active representative role in governance is fraught with difficulties and conflicts of interest."[3] This system fails further when a commander or someone higher in rank uses their power to abuse those under them in rank.

The smooth operation of teams and ensuring a highly functioning group for combat readiness is dependent on the team's leadership and team dynamics. As the military coterie becomes so large and pervasive, lessons can be drawn from the church on the significance of the local group or teams. It is the functionality at this level that ensures tasks are completed, and respect plays a significant role in this.

LEADERSHIP

Literature on leadership explains the military hierarchy as a system that fosters many of the following factors: a collective as opposed to individual outlook, avoidance of uncertainty, and a power distance between those high in rank and those low in rank. Collectivism lessens the importance of individual needs and concerns over those of the group. The emphasis is on loyalty and cooperation to ensure the group's survival. Members are indistinguishable and difference is discouraged. In and outgroup behavior is encouraged to build the group's cohesiveness. The first thing a cadet experiences is a haircut and wearing a uniform. They learn that standing out in the crowd is definitely an undesirable attribute to be quickly avoided, and the idea of being a "grey person," one who does not attract attention, prevails. Any attention attracted to oneself can be perceived as potentially inviting bullying.[4]

Command obedience becomes a focus and this is centered on leadership ideals. Dependent more on moral obligation felt to a leader and loyalty to the group than on the threat of discipline, one suppresses one's personal interests.[5] Notwithstanding this ideal, discipline is a tool through which ambiguous application by those higher ranked enables fear to operate as a controlling factor. By ensuring the lower ranks feel uncertainty they are enticed to look to their commanders for guidance.[6] This creates a dependency that helps locate the focus of power on those perceived as higher ranked and it encourages conformism. Security and comfort is found in routines and rituals. Hofstede[7] describes power distance as being effective in enabling greater acceptance by the lowly ranked of power differentials, where low education or disparity in social class exists. This can support tyrannical or "dark" leaders who arise when collectivism, uncertainty avoidance, and high power distance prevail.[8] In the churches, a bishop has influence over the priests, and a ranked system prevails, demanding loyalty in both directions between the bishop and the priests.[9] Any institution that relies on secret coteries led by individuals, and that emphasizes collective behavior, needs strong superintendence by accountable bodies and by the checks and balances offered by the three arms of government in democratic societies.

A collective drive to uniformity risks that the collective behavior is not always the "right" behavior. Ongoing sex scandals evince such a possibility. The requirement to report to your chain of command is problematic because they can sometimes be the perpetrator, or a friend of the perpetrator, or be afraid they will not get a promotion if they expose the matter. A 2011 US Army survey of leadership indicated that around 12 percent of leaders were not on a path to higher-level leadership, nor did they match expectations of leadership.[10] This included toxic or counterproductive commanders who put themselves first, are considered to be callus and overly controlling through micromanaging, or display poor judgment in making decisions. In 2014, this statistic showed that counterproductive leaders tend to be in the lower ranks of NCOs, at the platoon sergeant or squad leader levels. While the ratings were in the lower percentile, they remained consistent across 2010–2014.[11] The notion of rule by fear is not the only way to maintain control and is often one of the more ineffective ways to induce cohesive teamwork. Team and group research demonstrates that a team works best when trust is high and communication is transparent.[12]

A military coterie of the size established in the US will find it only natural that consolidation of the power structure will be sought. Law and governance institutions that threaten that power will be replaced with bodies that enhance the power. Just as the civilian courts have stepped back and the mythical reasons for this deference are propagated, the system is replaced with the military's enlarged internal discipline system. These beliefs become entrenched and accepted as "situation normal": "[t]hey do this by replacing constructive institutions with those designed to enhance central control; by eliminating rivals and dissidents; by manipulating the media and exploiting educational systems, using propaganda to legitimize the process. The new policies soon become ingrained in the culture."[13] For instance, the refrain is often that civilian control means civil society holds the commanders responsible for the actions of those under them. The mechanisms for accountability are fragile and often only the media operate as an arm of democracy, ready to hold the military to account. Still, the number of commanders who have resigned because of their subordinates' actions are limited indeed.

Behan rightly notes that "[c]areers, lives, and international relations between nations can all be affected by the discipline or indiscipline of individual service members."[14] However, while he suggests it is unfair to place this responsibility on a commander, he then paradoxically uses this to justify the need to give the commander authority over the punishment system, suggesting it would otherwise be unsustainable. This is where unconscious bias and flawed thinking creeps in. As argued in this work, governance through utilizing a secondary punishment system that mostly replicates the civilian criminal justice system, except that it is overseen by individuals as opposed to a rule of law governance structure, is not required at this level to ensure commander obedience. It is not convincingly explained why administrative workplace discipline and the threat of referral of activity to the civilian system for criminal investigation and enforcement is not enough. Even in combat, a person can be stood down and removed to their home country while an investigation is carried out. Such an investigation can be conducted either by specialist military police, as currently is the case, or even better, by a specially trained and equipped section of the civilian police force. The Senate Inquiry into the Effectiveness of the Military Justice System in Australia recommended the Australian federal police for this role.[15]

Behan adopts a circularity of argument by using the words "lawful control," suggesting that a commander "[t]hrough his role in sending cases to courts-martial and selecting panel members . . . is able to exert *lawful control* over the military justice system."[16] This so-called "lawful control" comes through a historical acceptance of a system by the courts that is no longer a justified interpretation of the Constitution. It is one that abrogates the role of the civilian courts as a check and balance of the democratic system. Leaving the commander to determine what conduct will be dealt with at which level, administrative or criminal, is unacceptable. It empowers an entirely arbitrary system dependent not on the rule of law, or even the whim of one man, but on many different individuals. The reality is that while most commanders hold the integrity, honor, and trustworthiness that is expected of them, some do not. A system in which this possibility exists is a system that is unreliable and decreases the functional imperative of the military. Just as described in the Australian Royal Commission into Institutional Response to Child Sexual Abuse, when the loyalty and command influence breaks down through lack of respect, there is a tendency for the lower ranks, such as the priest, or the soldier, to disengage and focus solely on their unit level, be it the local parish or the military unit level, thereby fragmenting the unified institution. Something said to be vital to a functional military.[17] It has been acknowledged

> that the obligation not to engage in or tolerate sexually harassing behavior is not a regulatory issue but a values and leadership issue. Sexual harassment and assault are values issues because they are fundamentally at odds with the obligation of men and women in uniform to treat all with dignity and respect.[18]

There should really be no surprises in the scandals that arise when secret coteries are left to deal with criminal behavior of members outside the public justice system. If legal processes such as the criminal law, refined over centuries, are tampered with and left in the hands of those most interested in protecting their own and their institutional reputation, hidden, non-public processes and lack of accountability will see conflict of interest and bias come to the fore. It is what one would expect when leaders are trying to satisfy two masters. Inevitability, it leads to achieving that which is sought to be avoided—the shattering of the institution's reputation. This includes the lives of those involved and the society as a whole, as its institutions are diminished and its citizens are abused, leaving them broken and unable to contribute, as one would hope they could in a healthy society. One survivor most poignantly described this pain; discovering he had cancer shortly before giving evidence in the Australian Royal Commission into Institutional Response to Child Sexual Abuse, he thought

> That's the best news I've ever had in my whole life. The pain will stop. That's the effect that you have all your life from these events. It doesn't go away. It holds you. All you hope for is death, just to stop the pain.[19]

For secret coteries such as the military and the church, embellished with the philosophy of *la bella figura*, respect is a value often referred to, but seemingly little understood. The next section engages in a deeper exploration of how respect operates.

THE VALUE—RESPECT

As a value asserted both in military and civilian society, respect seems to be a term used loosely with little comprehension of its full significance. Bringing the military into the civilian criminal justice system can only strengthen a genuine two-way understanding of respect and improve the civil-military relationship. Noted in this work are the ritual practices that are prevalent in groups that rely on ensuring obedience to power and dependence on the collective. These have included behaviors involved in initiation rituals, often termed hazing or bastardisation, as part of a breaking down of one's individualism through bullying and humiliation.[20]

The military system is reliant on groups across the three areas of army, navy, and air force, and within each structure supports a coterie system. This also includes the smaller but powerful area of JAGS and military legal personnel. The divisions limit the range of career progression. Cliques develop and demand protection, including where possible expansion of these domains of interest to ensure power, status, and careers can be developed.[21] As was found in relation to the church abuse cases, priests tended to be interested in supporting each other and disbelieving any allegations that threatened them or their fellow priests.[22] This protective denial keeps *la brutta figura* hidden. Each coterie will do all it can to sustain its justification for existence, particularly as the unwieldy expansion of the military results in loss of definitional clarity of its main role. Smaller groups become the sustaining force, but as they are constrained within the oligarchic structure, they start to compete with each other internally. This risks a breakdown in the collective as group interests come to dominate. However, the emphasis on small groups and teams, operating as the cohesive units within the overarching institutional structure in the military, is an essential part of its fabric.

The Australian Defence Force has as one of its three core values "teamwork," the other two being courage and initiative. In response to the Jedi Council scandal, then Chief of Defence Morrison felt a need for "respect" to be added as a value to the existing trio of values. Morrison spoke of respect at both the personal and institutional level. In relation to the personal, he described it as

> respect for who you are; for your self-discipline; for the standards of your personal behavior; for respect you show to your mates and their respect for you—an expert in close combat; physically and mentally tough; compassionate and courageous; committed to learning and working for the team; a believer in trust, in loyalty and Country.[23]

Of key importance, respect is served best when it operates on a two-way basis. A deep reflexive understanding of ethics and morality enables an understanding of the difference between one's own values and others', including the values of the military organization.[24] This calls for an understanding of the reciprocity required for respect to flourish. An individual can identify when respect has been violated and the consequences can have lasting implications.

Kant, as one of the foremost philosophers enmeshed in dissecting "respect," provides a starting point for understanding "respect."[25] Kant was often seen as a pacifist; however, his work is now being considered for the insight it provides into conflicts involving human rights and cultural sensitivities.[26] Kant argued that all human beings be accorded a degree of respect because of the inherent "humanness" or intrinsic nature of the human being.[27] This applied, according to Kant, even when individuals could be said to be unworthy or unmeritorious.[28] This respect is described as a "basic respect"[29] or "recognition respect."[30] However, Kant's work has been interpreted in different ways. For instance, what is the meaning of the term "human person"? Are there categories of "humans" that would allow some to fall outside basic respect? Such an analysis leads to an unwinding of the basic Kantian precept, because once the meaning of "human beings" can be restricted, it devalues the concept entirely by creating potential for an ingroup and outgroup. In this scenario, one would not even have to consider questions of merit, or "appraisal respect," as the "human being" would no longer fall within the concept. Such outgroups (non-belonging), then risk becoming the demonized "non-human."[31] However, the concept is to be understood objectively and not subjectively. Respect for another is accorded to the individual as a human being. As Kant intones: "I cannot deny all respect to the vicious man as a human being: I cannot withdraw at least the respect that belongs to him in his quality as a human being, even though by his deeds he makes himself unworthy of it."[32]

This raises the question of "respect worthiness," and the respect due to someone who may not act morally, which invites consideration of the concept of dignity.[33] It can lead to the danger of who is deciding what moral action is, leaving open the possibility of categorizing a "human" as being beyond respect worthiness. However, "appraisal respect"[34] applies a duty to oneself to act with dignity by showing one holds standards of excellence, achievable through "agreement with the autonomy of the rational being."[35] Hay[36] argues that Kant's concept requires a successful "exercise" of the capacity for moral rational behavior, not merely the "capacity" for such actions.[37] Autonomy arises from this morality of action. Massey refers to Kant's reference to "reverence," linking the concept to the act of being moral, as opposed to the mere capacity for rational moral action that attracts basic respect.[38] While the latter is due to even a terribly immoral human, the former is reverence due to "those who actually act in accord with the [moral] law."[39]

Morality is objectively determined by the capacity for the choice to be universalized.[40] For instance, a soldier in war can kill an enemy combatant in order to defend their life or country as it can be universalized to all combatants having equal rights to kill in such circumstances, following the rules of international humanitarian law.[41] These rules of war have moral status. On this basis, universalizing means "I cannot kill on the battlefield" if the other can no longer kill—a soldier when *hors de combat* should be treated with respect, as a human being, with dignity. Likewise, when it comes to sexual offences, there is no universal right to exert sexual power or dominance over another; quite the contrary, a universalized morality demands that one is free from assault. Respect requires treatment of yourself and the other, never as a means to an end but always as the end in and of itself.[42] In turn, Kant attaches dignity to this autonomy or personality. Hay describes dignified personality as

> end in itself-hood—is what imposes an obligation to respect someone; . . . dignity—is what gives someone unconditional and incomparable value. One is an end in herself in virtue of her humanity; one has dignity in virtue of her personality. Humanity is our rational nature—our capacity to set and pursue ends on the basis of reason and independently of our desires. Personality, on the other hand, is not the mere capacity to set and pursue ends on the basis of reason; personality is, rather, the successful exercise of this capacity. We achieve personality, then, only when we manage to act morally: when our free wills set and pursue ends that are in accordance with the laws of morality.[43]

Hay argues that dignity, according to Kant, also links to the duty individuals hold to respect their own humanity. If one fails to respect oneself, thus losing dignity, this will affect "appraisal respect," as personality (the capacity to act in accord with the laws of morality) constrains behavior in regard to "appraisal respect."[44] This does not alter "basic or recognition respect," which applies to humanness and the capacity to be rational.

Some deny that humanness provides sufficient grounds to treat all people with equal respect. These arguments tend to mix deference, or a hierarchical quality of merit, with "appraisal respect" in order to demand "respect" worthiness. For instance, being inculcated into performing in a meritorious way within the military organization is often given far greater emphasis than learning, at a deep level, the meaning of important values such as respect. This was evidenced in Connor and McDermott's observation that ". . . cadets face the anxiety of ensuring they are 'performing' their new identity correctly (cadets would regularly discuss their presentation of self, such as correct marching style, saluting and uniform)."[45]

Dean clarifies that in a Kantian world, a claim for worthiness in the actual individual human is not called for. When approached from the perspective of pure reason, which he argues is Kant's project, one not embedded in empirical experience, the worthiness of individuals is irrelevant to the claim of rational and morally perfected ideal humans.[46] In Kant's theory, the appropriate respect is due to the perfected human as rationally conceived and not actual humans, who may often fail these ideal standards of rationality and morality. The benefit of such reasoning is to provide an objective moral end, "equally valid for all rational beings,"[47] as a benchmark by which the morals of individual humans can be gauged. This enables empirical observation of how much an individual's actions deviate from the ideal of rational humanity. This is a process Kant refers to as "moral anthropology."[48] Kant left this project for others but suggested that where a human abuses their actual ability to apply practical reasoning, empirically it would be wrong to disrespect such an individual as it would deny ". . . that (they) could never be improved, and this is not consistent with the idea of a human being, who as such (as a moral being) can never lose entirely (their) predisposition to the good."[49]

Contestations around the meaning of respect aside, Kant claims that the main goal is for human beings to aspire to the perfect idea of humanity. This is clearly different to the concept of *la bella figura,* which is concerned with putting the best image forward. Kant states that

> [we] shall often have to take as our object the particular nature of human beings, which is cognized only by experience, in order to show in it what can be inferred from universal moral principles. But this will in no way detract from the purity of these principles or cast doubt on their *a priori* source.[50]

Most understand that this basic humanity attracts negative duties such as not abusing, denigrating, or harming other human beings. Actions involved in hazing and bastardisation rituals or sexual abuse come to mind. Cureton describes these actions as follows:

> [W]e disrespect someone in this more familiar way when we mock him for his religious convictions, degrade him by forcing him to engage in compromising acts, embarrass him by making him prostrate himself before us, and address him with racist epithets that tell him he is a despised animal in our eyes.[51]

It is thus not a simplistic case of respect given out of merit, regard, or deference for a person or their position in a class or hierarchical sense that may be mistaken as respect in a coterie based on rank. Learning to respect the military hierarchy and salute and dress in a certain manner is more the behavior of an acolyte, a very superficial understanding of respect. In aiming for a climate that drives an environment of right behavior for professional soldiers, leadership must instill the value of respect to include, at minimum, a basic or recognition respect for humanness. Leadership that cultivates and rewards right decision-making, even when under adverse pressure, is required.[52] Part of the challenge lies in Kant's exhortations not to engage in "fault finding and mockery"[53] or "demand that others think little of themselves in comparison with us."[54] The latter is challenging in an environment based on a warrior culture, power distance, and ranking. Hazing, as a typical practice, is an example of absence of respect that can lead to PTSD, suicide, and mental health breakdown.

Respecting the Other

Empathy plays a significant role in respect. Former Lieutenant General Morrison acknowledged its importance by noting that ". . . if militaries are required, as they continually are, to protect threatened societies from violence, their capacity for empathy and their respect for the diversity intrinsic to those societies can only make them more effective, not less."[55] Treating others as you would have them treat you, and showing an ability to feel and respond to others' emotions and experience, are essential elements of empathy. The cognitive aspect of respect requires a thinking well of others. Empathy runs alongside an emotional component that requires feeling well towards another. Demanding this of a collective, in which "in" and "out" group behavior and ambiguity are tools used to cement the collective coterie, could be considered as a very contradictory and almost impossible task.

Loss of self-esteem arises when one feels disrespected or "belittled." The strong belief in *la bella figura* within a coterie means that expectations in this area are likely to be heightened or supersensitive. When a perceived disrespect occurs, the individual can respond in a corresponding manner that can escalate to the level of overt violence.[56] Thus, an integration in the civilian criminal justice system would bring synchronicity and overcome the risks associated with isolation of cliques and groups.

Reinforcing respect requires a deep communicative ability. Dialogue in which no one leads, but each interacts, is essential and more readily possible in the primary democratic civilian society. Regular assessment of others' perceptions of an individual's ability in this area is useful feedback to the individual. Here personal narrative, knowing the story of how empathy and respect are "felt" and "shown," is vital and storytelling can be useful as a training tool. It is important that it is not only ingroup- but also outgroup-focused, as respect also requires consideration of the "other" or outgroup. Inability to empathize and to demonstrate respectful actions to another can give rise to emotions of shame within the other, eliciting a sense of unfairness that denies pride and a feeling of belonging. Studies show that the social isolation and alienation that can accompany a denial of respect is closely aligned with violent responses, such as emotional opportunistic lashing out, or PTSD.[57]

The Kantian view suggests that for humans to be happy, they need the help of others and cannot hope for a universal law that permits refusal to help others.[58] This demands avoidance of narcissistic traits and egotism, giving rise to an inflated view of oneself, often at the expense of others, which can arise from aspects such as position, title, or belonging to a select group. Such a propensity exists in the hierarchical command structure of an elite secret coterie. To suggest others should think less of themselves, based on one's claim to superiority, can cause loss of respect on both sides of the transaction:

> I am rationally disposed to regard it as my responsibility, not anyone else's, to value myself as a person with dignity . . . so I cannot accept a principle that says I owe it to anyone other than myself to acquire self-respect.[59]

Self-Respect

Concepts of peace, justice, and fairness are inextricably linked with self-respect and the concept of self.[60] Studies in crime and restorative justice show the fundamental importance of respect and equality of treatment.[61] Sherman notes that in punishment theory, the value of respect, along with redemption, have had far more success than the notion of "shaming."[62] Ethics is the domain in which respect and self-respect are determined. Law cannot enforce this value.

It is often said, in cases of torture and war crimes for instance, that it was the actions of a few bad apples, singling out perpetrators as sociopaths or psychopaths.[63] However, the investigation of the Abu Ghraib scandal discovered that none of the convicted soldiers had sociopathic personalities, but instead worked in a conforming dysfunctional and toxic employment environment: "[a]ll the reports refer to dysfunction regarding the doctrine of command responsibility, and to poisoned command climates, social climates and climates of social opinion."[64]

In a conforming systemic culture, a barrel of bad apples can arise through contamination, due to the propensity for others to be influenced by "bad apples." Lieutenant General Morrison painfully noted that

> the tribal culture through which we sought to build small teams capable of enduring combat had become distorted, misinterpreted and abused. . . . I had already concluded that the "bad apple" theory was a comforting self-delusion . . . cultural problems are just that: they are systemic and ingrained not the work of a few rogues.[65]

The literature on group behavior demonstrates that in the reduced likelihood of group exclusion, such as secret coteries where military members are protected from outside interference, even one bad apple can contaminate others more readily.[66] In this regard, self-respect through adhering to one's personality by taking moral action is less enabled. Operational necessity demands a highly rigid and conforming group, which may satisfy collective belonging needs. Personal autonomy, or individuality requirements, which enable maintenance of self-esteem, are more likely to be challenged in these coteries. It is not surprising that a group, trained to be highly conforming when given direction, whether by civilian or military leadership, can have damning aftereffects. The statement by Dick Cheney, at the time of the Iraq conflict, that "[w]e've got to spend time in the shadows . . . it is going to be vital for us to use any means at our disposal . . . to achieve our objective," demonstrates this.[67] This dark leadership of a collective brings the ethical and psychological dimensions of being a human into focus in the legal world of rights and duties.

Respect in the Military

As noted, empathy and compassion are key components in an individual's psychological makeup, as they are predictors of actions that convey respect.[68] Unfortunately, modern war has required that training of soldiers must help them overcome the inherent human tendencies to abhor killing and violence. As Grossman observes: "[t]he history of warfare can be seen as a history of increasingly more effective mechanisms for enabling and conditioning men to overcome their innate resistance to killing their fellow human beings."[69]

During World War II, many soldiers fired over, rather than at, their opponents, displaying an abhorrence to killing others, even when outgroup members, and in times of hostile conflict.[70] In World War I the famous Christmas

Truce incident,[71] in which soldiers of the opposing forces came together for Christmas Eve and shared each other's company, singing and eating together, is an example of rational moral citizen-soldiers acting with dignity in doing a job that requires otherwise abhorrent behavior. Their actions in killing each other was objectively justifiable as acceptable because it was legally legitimated universally as conduct enabled according to the rules of war. These rules include, for instance, acknowledging that where combatants are wounded they are *hors de combat*—effectively off the battlefield and so can no longer be subjected to harm.[72]

Empathy and respect is made more difficult when considering the changes in training required to overcome the tendency for soldiers to fire over the heads of enemy combatants.[73] Training to kill inherently requires some dehumanizing of the enemy "other," and this can only impact on the empathetic human ability of those involved. This paradox for the modern military member may have implications for PTSD and other adverse health effects.[74]

Dr. Steven Scally, an experienced regimental medical doctor in the Australian military, has explained the process as a

> deeply entrenched process of indoctrination, which occurs at a programmatic level of both the higher and lower centres of the brain. These processes are deeply burnt into the survival and alert centers of the soldier's brain. Without this programming, they would not be able to carry out what it takes to be a soldier. Ask any infantry soldier: "The role of the infantry soldier is to seek out and close with the enemy, to kill or capture him, to seize and hold ground, to repel attack, by day or by night, regardless of season, weather or terrain." All servicemen and women are inculcated with this type of mindset. This ethos does not translate to civilian life. There are thousands of currently serving personnel and (ex-serving) "civilians" who are still operating with this mindset. Being very basally programmed within the brain, this conditioning is something that cannot be switched off at the cortical level. Hyper-alertness and hyper-vigilance are strongly associated with this programming. . . . Many veterans struggle to live their lives with an acculturation and programmed mindset that is not at all compatible with post-service life.[75]

The activities described in this work largely relate to member-on-member behavior and abuse within the secret coterie. As has been noted, how such immorality works on the battlefield, when soldiers are dealing with enemy combatants and civilians, remains unknown. The law of armed conflict provides a legal regime that is meant to control this behavior, and as stated by a German soldier following these rules, it is like a code: "[y]ou fight by the rules to keep your humanity."[76] In war we hear of both honorable conduct[77] and dishonorable conduct.[78] The modern wars in Afghanistan and Iraq have bought their share of extraordinary allegations of soldiers failing the code and behaving badly.[79]

Respect underpins rules that outlaw torture, ensuring its universalized immorality. In this relation, the incidents of torture by soldiers in the Abu Ghraib scandal in the US provide an example of the loss of moral stature governments experience, particularly if leadership has authorized, condoned, or failed to investigate such actions properly.[80] Tarrant, Branscombe, Warner, and Weston[81] studied whether torture perpetrated by members of a national in-group is considered morally more acceptable by the in-group. Testing the group response to inter-group harm, because social identity theory indicates that group members want to see their group in a positive manner,[82] highlights that in-group members find that errant behavior causes an uncomfortable dissonance they seek to overcome.[83] In seeking to reduce the dissonance felt, attitudes change to more closely align with the deviant behavior, and often denial or minimizing of the harm (it was a few errant "bad apples") subsequently occurs. This can include distancing the perpetrators from the in-group, justifying it morally, or seeking to morally exclude the survivor as a "human" not owed empathy and respect, thus effectively blaming the survivor and denying them "appraisal respect." Many sexual abuse survivors describe this feeling of isolation, as if they are worthless outsiders.[84] Tarrant et al. found that

> participants believed that the torture was more morally justified when it was perpetrated by members of the ingroup . . . participants experienced lower levels of empathy for the torture survivor, blamed the survivor more, and perceived the perpetrators as more prototypical of their national group. . . .[85]

Bandura[86] has described the attempts made to provide a moral justification for such conduct in situations of collective in-group violence or immoral behavior towards an out-group or minority. These include euphemistic labelling (e.g. illegal enemy combatants, collateral damage regarding civilian deaths); diffusion—everyone is doing it so no one person is responsible; or displacement (I was following orders). Such processes are resorted to by humans in ensuring their social identity and worldview is undiminished by the behavior. These various techniques assist with overcoming the cognitive dissonance experienced by suspending normal emotional and cognitive responses to inherent values, such as avoiding killing or harming another. Comments made during the naval online photo sex scandals can be evoked here.[87] Secretary of Defense James Mattis, a retired marine general, has referred to the values and the actions of perpetrators of assault as showing a "[l]ack of respect for the dignity and humanity of fellow members of the Department of Defense [which] is unacceptable and counter to unit cohesion."[88] However, none of his speech addresses the survivors. It focuses on claims that perpetrators would be removed from the navy, and that, by implication, they would be good enough for civilian society, which in itself evinces disrespect.

The discussion of respect from a Kantian position draws attention to the very nature of a hierarchical command, in which one is to be unquestionably obedient and ready to kill when required, which in turn challenges inherent human values. Certainly instilling values and attitudes of respect and empathy, more easily aligned with civilian over military requirements, becomes a difficult and delicate task in this context. However, the military organization is presented with a dilemma when experiencing the importance of these demands, which is foregrounded when required to engage in winning hearts and minds in order to win the long-term battle, or when dealing with internal abusive treatment of members of the organization. Incorporating discipline within the one civilian criminal justice system provides some clues on how these dilemmas may be addressed.

The impact of abuse and sexual assault conflicts with demands for self-respect and justice. If the military's discipline does not work, it cannot recruit desirable people. This in turn destroys team cohesiveness, which is the fundamental determinative of the functional and structural imperatives. Embracing a holistic change, rather than engaging in reactive measures and multiple inquiries, is demanded from the military, the legislature, the executive, and the courts. Who comprises the military membership, and the persons attracted to join, are factors relevant to the composition and creation of the secondary society.

CULTURE CONCERNED WITH VIOLENCE

A link between pre-military experience of violence and abuse is suggested by some research that indicates those with child sexual abuse experience are likely to join the military and are at greater risk of experiencing abuse within the military.[89] The research has not delved into why survivors may be attracted to join the military, but Turchik and Wilson speculate that it could be to escape and start afresh, or alternatively to find a place to release aggression.[90] Certainly, research into the general population has linked childhood antisocial behavior to later antisocial and criminal behavior.[91] Studies have also found a connection between self-reported pre-deployment aggression as being strongly linked to post-deployment aggression over factors such as combat exposure.[92]

The US central civilian organization, the Center for Disease Control and Prevention (CDC), has presented research that links survivors of violence as more likely to have experienced differing forms of violence, and that survivors are at risk of perpetrating violence. Similarly, people who carry out violent actions are more likely to commit other forms of violence.[93] The attraction of a significant number of members who may have a prehistory of violence to a profession that engages in violence may well indicate a secondary society with a cultural propensity for aggression and violence. If this is so, it would be all the more reason for the civilian criminal justice system to be applied, to maintain order in society generally and to reinforce the primary society's values to remove any possible impunity. One may behave like a good warrior on the battlefield but this does not necessarily signify good behavior more generally, as the case studies show. Releasing a person, who may have experienced pre-military violence and then military violence back into the civilian population, without any attempt at reform of their behavior or integration with civilian values, leaves a civil society unprotected. The horrific incidence of the largest massacre of civilians in Texas by Devin Kelley is just one example.

There is an absence of research into the connection between military service and post-military offending. However, a UK study, one of the first of its kind, which used a large randomized trial of current and ex serving military members to investigate linkages with criminal records, found that 17 percent had a criminal record in their lifetime and violent offending (11 percent) was the most prevalent offending type.[94] A US study using self-report for antisocial behaviors, criminal justice involvement, and substance abuse, compared the civilian population with military members, including reservists and separated or retired members. This study found that "military members were more prone to lifetime arrests and overall substance misuse."[95] However, it was also noted that further research is needed as the results highlighted a connection with those who were discharged, often at an early stage of their career.[96]

While bad behavior may exist irrespective of military service participation, research has found that pre-military antisocial behavior implicated negative military behavioral consequences in those sent to Iraq.[97] This research also showed a strong independent association with severe alcohol intake, angry outbursts, aggressiveness, and risk-taking behavior.[98] Other studies have shown a close correlation between pre-military antisocial behavior or experience of violence and abuse with later violence and abuse. For instance, exposure to family or other violence can model "dominant and gendered scripts for how they are expected to be in the world."[99] This correlation has been stronger than between combat exposure and tendency to violence.[100] Certainly, combat exposure remains significantly associated, but the experience of violence pre-military is a factor that requires greater consideration for the intake of military members. MacManus et al. showed a connection in their study between pre-military violence, ongoing violence, and post-deployment violence. They have also conducted meta-analysis research of all relevant studies, finding that aggressive behavior was prevalent among serving and formerly serving members.[101] The process for dealing with this behavior while members are in the military, and before returning them to civilian society, needs a great deal more thought.[102] As many from disadvantaged and violent social backgrounds find purpose and meaning within the rule-controlled military coterie, any screening would have to be a sensitive process. Regardless however, this evidence provides an added reason for military members to remain subject to the civilian criminal enforcement and value system so as not to provide a protective or reinforcing haven in the coterie.

Another aspect to be addressed specifically is sexual violence, and whether the military as an institution is attractive to pedophiles and other sex offenders. Fifteen-year-old boys were recruited into all three-service areas through to the 1980s in Australia. It has been identified that large power differentials, combined with demands for trust, present a toxic combination that "professional sex offenders" can exploit.[103] Use of alcohol, mental wellness levels such as psychosis or impulse disorders, and severe stress can negatively affect perpetrators' resistance to offending.[104] The DLA Piper report in Australia stated that

> it is a well-known fact that "some people, who wished to have sexual access to boys, sought out positions in orphanages, schools, churches and similar institutions where they could have power over, and access to, children. . . ." There was no reason to think that such people would not have targeted relevant parts of the ADF.[105]

REFLECTIONS

Without insight into how to manage this behavior, a military coterie may inadvertently sustain such behavior by leaving it unaddressed. Belief in *la bella figura* supports feelings of elitism and pride in one's warrior attributes, which includes the ability to be aggressive and violent, but denial of *la brutta figura* permits the disavowal of one's personal immoral conduct.

To avoid the consequences that may arise from the loss of respect the military may attract when criminal and other abusive behavior occurs, there is a need for both increased provision of appropriate individual education and a display of respect through leadership by avoiding actual or perceived cover-ups. While the discipline and criminal laws would appear to cover the range of behaviors to be addressed, the difference is in their application. In a military coterie, it is subject to human decisions by other officers that may have opposing considerations that factor into their thinking. In the civilian realm, such behavior usually attracts wider reporting and discussion within the community in which the law officers enforce the law. While civilian police may exercise discretion, it is publicly documented and accountability is thus more readily possible. That the military can lack this accountability is noted by Brown, who has questioned the Australian military by stating that "[i]t is worth considering why the [ADF] is not able to implement its own policies, nor comply with the law when it comes to transparency."[106]

Education is essential to making fundamental changes so all individuals operating in their respective domains can clearly see the implications of their actions.[107] For civilian roll back of military creep, and for greater civilian control, the lack of general, but also legal, education around civil-military relations requires redress. Many writers decry the lack of law school engagement with military issues.[108] Perhaps the senior civilian courts deference has contributed to this gap. Connor and McDermott found that civilian values were outranked by military values when teaching a homogenous group of mostly white males, often with a military parent.[109] Danielsson and Weibull have described teaching values and sociology to military members as a challenging experience.[110] Cox has cautioned that "commanders make a mistake assuming that once inculcated, every unit forever retains good organizational values. Values need constant reinforcement. . . ."[111] Broderick has discussed the introduction of a Healthy Relationships and Sexual Ethics Program for cadets in the ADFA as a necessary aspect of intended cultural change: "the Advice examines the need for ongoing reform and oversight by building on relevant cultural reforms already implemented at ADFA and across the ADF."[112]

Behaviors left unaddressed by piecemeal actions, in regard to both perpetrators and survivors, have consequences for recruiting military members. Now retired Lieutenant General Morrison acknowledged the damage that potential scandals have, stating: "[o]ur fragile contract with the Nation was ruptured. Questions were asked as to whether we continued to reflect the very best values of Australia."[113] The damage if this is not achieved, he noted, widened to the dwindling population from which recruits can be gained. The taxpayers carry the financial burden for training military members, and this becomes a lost investment when they resign or leave the force early. Australia reportedly has around 69 percent of all recruits across the ADF leave before completing their training.[114] It becomes a further cost when they return to the civilian community and engage in violent behavior, particularly if this is without proper warning or the protection of the primary civilian group. The law sets out the standards of behavior expected and acceptable to the whole of society, and this is enhanced when coteries are brought within the same system, which then improves the whole of society's acceptance and understanding of these mores.

Oddly, awareness around abuse and perpetrators' behaviors such as grooming is only really beginning to take hold in the community. Institutions have shown this lack of awareness, and disbelief in the possibility of the abhorrent stories that survivors tell. Lack of understanding of how the legal system operates, the duties on citizens, the duty of care of an institution, and the structure, and principles on which our democratic societies operate abound. Chapter five and six have described the difficulties when institutions, and particularly those who operate secret coteries, do not communicate across their areas of operation, or even within their own institutional boundaries where the protection of the reputation of the coterie's brand is the primary concern.[115]

The need to align methods of recording offences with the outcomes would be obviated if one criminal justice system prevailed. Currently the different approaches prevent any clear comparison of the primary and secondary societies. Even synchronizing current survey instruments, definitions, and statistical data collection would enable some useful comparative data. Although this has been called for repeatedly and for a long time, it remains outstanding. If one system prevailed, no comparison would be needed and instead the money spent could be diverted towards improving the overall situation.

The issues with command leadership have been addressed, in the form of an identified need to focus on a deeper understanding of the meaning of respect. If understood at this level, command control can be reinforced without the need for elaborate discipline systems that incorporate the whole of the criminal law. Team leadership and morale, along with awareness of the psychological types attracted to becoming a military member, can provide significant support in addressing issues of obedience and improving mental health outcomes.[116]

This work has shown that separate coteries, becoming more separated from the primary society, when given protected domains in which different treatment may apply, see a number of justifications arise that ultimately may support bad behaviors such as sexual offending.[117] This can be the masculine warrior culture in the military, the elite church cultures attracting certain types of offenders and youth cultures of promiscuity, and drug taking on university campuses. The problem becomes a fragmentation of domains when each institution protects its reputation as demanded by the ubiquitous *la bella figura*, undermining the rule of law as established by the criminal law that operates holistically for all. These various coteries in their isolation go to seemingly extraordinary lengths to hide *la brutta figura* often through a costly plethora of inquiries, which suggests they are attempting to fix intractable problems but finding genuine change evasive. Indeed, as Justice Black once warned, a failure to contain the operation of military discipline would lead to a type of military rule,[118] or, as described in this work, a militarization of the primary society.

The requirement needed for change is an entirely different approach that acknowledges societies where the change has already occurred without the sky falling in. Once the transformation to the civilian criminal law has been made, this new approach will create the elusive cultural changes so long sought. As Lorsch and McTague observe

> . . . culture isn't something you "fix." Rather . . . cultural change is what you get after you've put new processes or structures in place . . . like reworking an outdated strategy or business model. The culture evolves as you do that important work . . . it makes intuitive sense to look at culture as an outcome—not a cause or a fix.[119]

The consequences of the militarization of the civilian domain would likely make the framers of the US Constitution turn in their graves. Although Madison and Hamilton had opposing visions for the structure governing the US,[120] neither would imagine the strength acquired by the president under the two-party system, as head of both state and party, as well as commander in chief of a vast standing military.[121] The advancement of the separate military coterie, and the interpretation by the Supreme Court of the separation of powers that enables it, has resulted in an inexorable militarization. Arguments, as outlined in the beginning of this work, that justify the operation of a separate society with its own military discipline, have a demonstrable impact on the rights of soldiers and survivors of soldiers' actions within the US and Australia. The Westmoreland Committee in 1971,[122] established to investigate the effectiveness of the military punishment system at the commander level, noted the following:

> The protection of individual human rights is more than ever a central issue within our society today. An effective system of military justice, therefore, must provide of necessity practical checks and balances to assure protection of the rights of individuals. It must prevent abuses of punitive powers, and it should promote the confidence of military personnel and the general public in its overall fairness.[123]

Unfortunately, speaking from within the military coterie, General Westmoreland's committee presented a solution that lacked a broader consideration of the structural integrity of constitutional governance and the role of the military within that space. His committee's solutions were designed to free up a swift and effective punishment regime for commanders. To do this, the courts-martial system, encumbered by law and legal protections, was considered inept for the military mission. The refusal to engage with civilians and acknowledge the Supreme Court's position in *O'Callahan v.*

Parker facilitated a clear confirmation bias in identifying the issues. As such, the committee failed to deliver a solution,[124] just as the Powell Report,[125] and the many that followed since, have been ineffective in addressing the fundamental underlying issues because they focus on the narrow picture from a skewed perspective. The US constitutional power contained in Article 1, section 8 cl. 14 "[t]o make Rules for the Government and Regulation of the land and naval Forces," and the court's interpretation that this can be entirely separate from Article III, do not logically follow. The legislative power enables Congress to raise and support armies, provide and maintain a navy, and provide for organizing and disciplining them. It does not follow that the discipline system means incorporating the whole of the civilian criminal law to be administered internally by the military. Conversely, it does not preclude the legislature from subjecting military members to the ordinary criminal law while also having a normal code of conduct, which is administered, like many other professions, within workplace laws.

The implications of the civilian courts in this militarization process are exposed. Relevant inquires and case examples demonstrate the concerns and the possibility for improvement in outcomes. The refrain by the military, that a state ". . . can't simply abolish its entire military justice system and rely upon civilian courts and existing civilian criminal laws to handle misconduct committed by military members,"[126] is not a claim that is supported by the evidence, as revisiting the justifications demonstrates.

The many thousands of articles written on military discipline make it clear that groupthink has developed. They invariably start with a common, almost biblical recitation of the beginnings of military law and its *raison d' être*, repeating the standard arguments set out in chapter 1 for its existence. Many take a particular position, as the pendulum swings narrowly between greater rights for military personnel in the discipline process and greater protections for survivors of military personnel from perpetrators. This all occurs in a climate in which a hands-off approach is taken by the legislator and the courts, and change appears slowly and rarely, as resistance and obfuscation are strong. This work's contribution is to take the standard justifications for a separate military discipline system and, instead of repeating them as a mantra, put them under a spotlight. The findings and claims may be uncomfortable for many, and they are most likely going to be rejected initially, as it takes time for such thinking to become acceptable. The suggested changes are not that command should not be involved, which is often an objection to change, but rather that they should be involved through an entirely new vision that still supports their power and authority as commanders, but in a more regular manner.

The Senate Inquiry into the Effectiveness of Australia's Military Justice System, now well over a decade old, made some very pertinent observations. These included that in 2005 the military discipline system in Australia had not seen a wholesale review, despite enormous changes in civilian justice. As with the US, almost continual inquiries meant that changes were piecemeal, lacked cohesiveness, and were often resisted or reactive only.[127] It was noted that despite attempts by the ADF to fix issues, the issues remained ongoing and thus were evidence to support the need for a wholesale "watershed" change.[128] The inquiry went on to claim that the importance of having good military discipline, "which currently they do not,"[129] affected not only members and the institution but also the public. Unfortunately, some of the changes made subsequent to the inquiry never followed the recommendations fully, and thus led to the unhappy result, post the High Court's decision in *Lane v. Morrison,*[130] of returning military discipline effectively to the pre-2005 inquiry climate.

This work has argued none of the four justifications outlined at the beginning of the work withstand probing. The historical development of the military shows a process of resistance to change, made often reluctantly in response, in some cases to the courts, in others to the legislature or the media, but mostly to persons who have been affected by the consequences of the application of the discipline system. It is evident that change will occur only when unhappy soldiers demand it from within,[131] or from without, usually in the aftermath of a scandal that highlights the system's failures.[132] This is rendered more important by the ". . . absence of unions, lack of legislative oversight, limited media interest in non-sex scandal military-legal matters, and a lack of sustained academic interest."[133] All of this perpetuates the hands-off separate society, making the military an inscrutable area of operation within the state. The important role the media has to play in maintaining the democratic agreement as regards the civil-military relationship is clear. As Fidell states, ". . . the media could serve as an effective agent of change by raising the level of public understanding."[134] However, the media's effectiveness is under threat from the Trump government's attacks and the erosion of confidence through its "fake" news claims. Hansen draws attention to the fact that

> . . . much of the criticism does not focus on individual cases or specific examples of injustice within the military justice system. Rather, the assumption is that if these processes differ and seem less protective of individual rights than the protections which exist in the civilian system, then military justice is inherently unfair and must be brought in line with the civilian system. Other reformers gauge the fairness of a particular respective military justice system by focusing on how authority is divided within the system.[135]

As Banner aptly suggests:

> Sexual assaults within the military or university systems, however, are not only the product of discrete institutional cultures but a larger-socio legal environment that, increasingly, is distrustful of expansion of rights. This larger rights-antagonistic environment is exacerbated in the context of sexual assault, where, when such crime occurs; deeply held beliefs in mythologies come up against entrenched support of long-standing and deeply entrenched institutional ideals.[136]

Hansen identifies two camps, the human rights and the separation of powers reformers that have largely converged in their claim for reform. While both provide support for change, this work addresses the challenge outlined by Banner and goes beyond. It seeks to argue that the very foundational arguments and institutional ideals supporting the continuation of the current system are fundamentally not only unsupported but that they damage the civil-military relationship and the military enterprise itself. The military claim for legitimacy rests in large part on civilian courts sustaining a certain approach to interpreting the Constitution and history. If this is absent, the military "has a far greater problem in establishing that it is legitimate as a form of governance . . . while rejecting most of the practices and principles that define good and just government."[137]

Simply, it is argued that the military should focus on its core duties and that separateness of certain systems, such as the criminal punishment system, has no justification beyond sustaining the perpetuation of a secondary coterie within the primary civilian political system. Integration into the civilian system would improve the ability for the military to focus on its core training and service in protection of the state, without the distraction of many inquiries and the damage that abuse does to members and the whole of society. This adjustment would be a reflection of the changes made by many militaries around the world and would give both civilian and military personnel an equality of treatment in accordance with the precepts of the rule of law. Both would receive an equal standard of law enforcement and this would assist in reducing any perceived gap in the civil-military relationship, and improve both the standing of the military and the understanding of the civilian society. Turley aptly notes that

> [s]ervice members are already part of the general society as neighbors, church members, and through other social functions, but they remain artificially segregated from the most influential social institutions. Courts play a significant social role that reinforces collective values and self-definition for citizens.[138]

It is not proposed that the military is an overall danger or indeed an abusive institution. Much of the institution works extremely well, but this is predominately reliant on good people doing the right thing. Questions arise however, around the fundamentals and the justifications for maintenance of such a separate society, as well as the arguments sustaining separate governance functions, such as the individual criminal punishment system. Inevitably, the risks to the political structure has to be reflected on in this discussion. The military operating as a separate and secretive coterie has the potential, whether it realizes it or not, to consume the society from within, much like a Trojan parasite. This is critical, and the dissonant voices come from a place that have the best interests of the military and society in mind. The discussion needs to be open to all members of society to ensure balance and representation, as the suggestions aim for improvement, not only in the military's capability to deliver functionally, but also to deliver structurally.

The latter can be improved in two ways, firstly in its concern for the individual experience of military members and its operation within the democratic society in a sustainable manner.[139] Secondly, the conservative court decisions that look to old histories of the military, with corresponding tendencies to give *carte blanche* power to the military in the exercise of its disciplinary control, need to change.

Greater integration with the primary civilian group will increase engagement with the wealth of research on the role of teams, groups, cliques, violence, and respect, and enable a single point for transparent engagement with these challenging societal concerns. This avoids leaving the military coterie to risk failure as it becomes more isolated in its struggles to grapple with internal one-on-one membership abuse, let alone breach of the laws of war as a result of errant behavior being insufficiently checked.

CONCLUSION

The military institution sits within the primary society, which it is established to protect. Both societies are changing, evolving, and growing, and the military as a conservative traditional and often closed institution, changes at a varied, but often snail's pace. A tension arises between the values expressed in the civilian society and the military society. It is a symbiotic relationship with institutional isomorphism, resulting in influences flowing in both directions. The risk is that civil-military relations and the three organs of government trying to honor an appropriate separation of powers, while operating in a unitary manner designed to constrain the flow from the military into the civilian society, may no longer be able to contain the military. If this is the case then a militarization spills into the primary society.

The refrain that the "emperor is wearing no clothes" is clearly applicable when we all participate in failing to heed the cries of the lone voices of individuals presenting a reality none are prepared to face. Taking an elite and exceptional stance ignores the power of public demand for change, along with the individuals within the system calling for respect and recognition of their rights. Brooker aptly warns that scholars' writings often present an early warning, and that it is important to be open to diverse and dissenting voices in order to address the issues.[140] While the civil domain is far from perfect, it presents an equality in treatment that is fundamental and supportive of democratic values. The saving of the public purse in bringing military criminal offending within the civilian criminal law system would provide funds to enable greater advancements in improving the one system for all citizens.

As history demonstrates, if ever the military are to be put back in the box and operate as intended by the constitutional founders in both the US and Australia, this will depend on the power of individuals with intelligence, talent, far-sightedness, and determination, operating effectively within the institutions of the courts, executive, legislatures, and the military to make these changes.[141] Ideally, they would work in unison, but such a happy coincidence is unfortunately rare. Nevertheless, the role of institutions, such as the courts and civilian society, can ensure that the values of the primary society are upheld, as "institutional change does not occur spontaneously but as a result of these coercive and mimetic factors."[142]

At this stage, it would appear that the military coterie has a strong and pervasive influence as a separate society, with its own values that seep into the civilian society within which it sits. Throughout history, sexual abuse has often been the undoing of empires and institutions if it is ignored and unaddressed. Rome provides salient lessons, where sexual actions by individuals have resulted in revolutionary changes. Learning from history and placing individual human rights and needs at the pinnacle means legal demands on institutions may ultimately provide a force for change in the secret coteries. This is required in a democracy that upholds the civil-military relationship and seeks to ensure effective discipline and criminal punishment, as the rule of law demands, on an equal basis for all citizens irrespective of status.

NOTES

1. Jonathan Turley, "The Military Pocket Republic" *Northwestern University Law Review* 97 (2002): 1, 92.
2. Milton Rokeach, *The Nature of Human Values* (The Free Press, 1973).
3. Turley, "The Military Pocket": 93.
4. Ibid., 93; J. Connor and V. McDermott, "Service Teaching and Sociological Critique: Lessons from a Military Academy" *Journal of Sociology* 49 no. 4 (2013): 501, 505.

5. Anthony J. Ghiotto, "Back to the Future with the Uniform Code of Military Justice: The Need to Recalibrate the Relationship between the Military Justice System, Due Process, and Good Order and Discipline" *North Dakota Law Review* 90 (2014): 485, 521–22.

6. Robert Sherrill, *Military Justice Is to Justice as Military Music Is to Music* (Harper & Row, 1969).

7. Geert Hofstede, *Cultures and Organizations: Software of the Mind* (McGraw-Hill, 1991).

8. Fred Luthans, Suzanne J. Peterson, and Lelina Ibrayeva, "The Potential for the 'Dark Side' of Leadership in Post-Communist Countries" *Journal of World Business* 33 no. 2 (1998): 185, 188 a dark leader will demand unconditional loyalty; Art Padilla, Robert Hogan, and Robert B. Kaiser, "The Toxic Triangle: Destructive Leaders, Susceptible Followers, and Conducive Environments" *The Leadership Quarterly* 18 (2007): 176, 186.

9. Peter McClellan, Robert Fitzgerald, and Helen Milroy, "Royal Commission into Institutional Responses to Child Sexual Abuse" (December 15, 2017) https://www.childabuseroyalcommission.gov.au/final-report: Transcript produced by DTI 24/08/2015 (156) 16027.

10. Ryan Riley et al., "Annual Survey of Army Leadership (Casal): Military Leader Findings" (Center for Army Leadership, May 20, 2011): 17, 23, 53.

11. Ryan Riley, Josh Hatfield, and Tyler E. Freeman, "2014 Annual Survey of Army Leadership (Casal): Military Leader Findings"(Center for Army Leadership, June 2015) http://www.dtic.mil/dtic/tr/fulltext/u2/1000497.pdf: vii, 57, 60; Walter F. Ulmer Jr, "Toxic Leadership. What Are We Talking About?" *Army* (June 2012): 47.

12. Dean Lusher, Peter Kremer, and Garry Robins, "Cooperative and Competitive Structures of Trust Relations in Teams" *Small Group Research* 45 no. 1 (2014): 3; John E. Box, "Toxic Leadership in the Military Profession" (2012) *Masters Thesis: Master of Strategic Studies Degree* http://www.au.af.mil/au/awc/awcgate/army-usawc/box_toxic_leadership.pdf.

13. Padilla et al., "The Toxic Triangle": 186. See further, Hofstede, *Cultures and Organizations*; R. Hogan, *Personality and the Fate of Organizations* (Erlbaum, 2006).

14. Christopher W. Behan, "Don't Tug on Superman's Cape: In Defense of Convening Authority Selection and Appointment of Court-Martial Panel Members" *Military Law Review* 176 (2003): 190, 231.

15. Defence and Trade References Committee, The Senate Foreign Affairs, "The Effectiveness of Australia's Military Justice System" (June 2005): Recommendation 2, 3.121 "The committee recommends that the investigation of all suspected criminal activity committed outside Australia be conducted by the Australian Federal Police."

16. Behan, "Don't Tug on Superman's Cape": 293.

17. McClellan, "Royal Commission" Transcript produced by DTI 24/08/2015 (156) 16028: "Disengagement with things diocesan, with things the bishop was doing and simply concentrating on one's own parish and looking after that; so that the diocese became separate parishes rather than any unified body."

18. Gerald L. Hoewing et al., "The Report of the Defense Task Force of Sexual Harassment and Violence at the Military Service Academies" (Department of Defense, June 2005): 10.

19. McClellan, "Royal Commission" Case study 3, North Coast Children's Home: 14.

20. Ben Wadham, "Crossing the Line: Why the Royal Commission Examined Initiation Rituals and Defence Abuse" *The Conversation* (July 1, 2016).

21. Turley, "The Military Pocket": 86.

22. McClellan, "Royal Commission" Transcript produced by DTI 24/08/2015 (156) 16028: ". . . they did tend to be pro-priest . . . and to disbelieve a lot of the accusations."

23. David Morrison "Respect—The Fourth Value Remarks" Speech Townsville (2013): 5.

24. See e.g., Rokeach, *The Nature of Human*; See also, E. Wortel and J. Bosch "Strengthening Moral Competence: A 'Train the Trainer' Course on Military Ethics" *Journal of Military Ethics* 10 no. 1 (2011): 17; Erik D. Masick, "Moral Injury and Preventative Law: A Framework for the Future" *Military Law Review* 224 (2016): 223.

25. Immanuel Kant, *Ethics of Virtue*, ed. Monika Betzler (Berlin: Walter de Gruyter, 2008), 175–200.

26. B. Orend, "Kant's Ethics of War and Peace" *Journal of Military Ethics* 3 no. 2 (2004): 161; Marcus Shulzke, "Kant's Categorical Imperative, the Value of Respect, and the Treatment of Women" *Journal of Military Ethics* 11 no. 1 (2012): 26.

27. See S. J. Massey, "Kant on Self-Respect" *Journal on the History of Philosophy* 21 no. 1 (1983): 57; See also, *The Universal Declaration of Human Rights*, United Nations http://www.un.org/en/documents/udhr/.

28. Kant, *Ethics of Virtue*.

29. T. Hill Jr., *Respect, Pluralism, and Justice* (Oxford University Press, 2000): 59.

30. S. Darwell, "Two Kinds of Respect" *Ethics* (1977): 88. See also, S. Darwell, *The Second Person Standpoint* (Cambridge, MA: Harvard University Press, 2006).

31. See e.g., *Yolngu in Milirrpum v. Nabalco Pty Ltd* (1971) 17 FLR 141, 201 (Blackburn J) ". . . uncivilized inhabitants in a primitive state of society" (Grove Island land rights). See also, Schulzke, "Kant's Categorical": 29.

32. Immanuel Kant, *The Metaphysics of Morals* M. Gregor, trans, (Cambridge University Press Royal Prussian Academy, 1991): 6, 463.

33. See e.g., O. Sensen, *Kant on Human Dignity* (Berlin: Walter de Gruyter, 2011).

34. See Darwell, "Two Kinds."

35. O. Sensen (ed), *Kant on Moral Autonomy* (Cambridge University Press, 2013): 51.

36. C. Hay, "Respect-Worthiness and Dignity" *Dialogue* 51 no. 4 (2012): 587.

37. Ibid., 593.

38. Massey, "Kant on Self-respect": 59.

39. Ibid., 64.

40. Hay, "Respect-Worthiness": 603.

41. See Orend, "Kant's Ethics."

42. Kant, *The Metaphysics of Morals*: 4, 429.

43. Hay, "Respect-Worthiness": 594.

44. Ibid., 596. See Kant, *The Metaphysics of Morals*: 4: 429: "'Act in such a way that you treat humanity, whether in your own person or in any other person, always at the same time as an end, never merely as a means' this is known as Kant's 'Humanity Formula.'"

45. Connor and McDermott, "Service Teaching": 509.

46. Richard Dean, "Respect for the Unworthy" *Pacific Philosophical Quarterly* 95 no. 3 (2014): 293, 310–311; ". . . this reading of Kant does not leave room to say that the reason real humans ought to be respected is that they possess perfected humanity, since many real humans obviously fall short of ideal rationality and morality."

47. Kant, *The Metaphysics of Morals*: 4, 427.

48. Immanuel Kant, *Critique of Practical Reason* M. Gregor, trans Cambridge, (Cambridge University Press, 1996): 5, 127; Kant, *The Metaphysics of Morals*: 6, 217, 468–69.

49. Kant, *The Metaphysics of Morals*: 6, 464.

50. Ibid., 6, 217.

51. A Cureton, "From Self-Respect to Respect for Others" *Pacific Philosophical Quarterly* 94 (2013): 166, 170.

52. See e.g., R. F. Foley and D. A. Goudreau, "Consideration of Others" *Military Review* 76 no. 1 (1996): 25, 28; Tom Ayres, "Haditha: A Case Study in Response to War Crimes" in David Lovell (ed) *Investigating Operational Incidents in a Military Context: Law Justice, Politics* (Brill Nijhoff, 2014): 87, 96–97.

53. Kant, *The Metaphysics of Morals*: 6, 465.

54. Ibid., 6, 466.

55. D Morrison, Chief of the Australian Army, Address to the Closing Plenary Session at the Global Summit to End Sexual Violence in Conflict, London, UK June 13, 2014: 3.

56. See e.g., A. Long, "'Green on Blue': Insider Attacks in Afghanistan" *Global Politics and Strategy* 55 no. 3 (2013): 167.

57. Masick, "Moral Injury."

58. Kant, *The Metaphysics of Morals*: 6, 393; See further, Cureton "From Self-Respect": 171.

59. Cureton, "From Self-Respect": 179. See Kant, *The Metaphysics of Morals*: 6, 462.

60. See e.g., J. Rawls, *A Theory of Justice* (Cambridge, MA: Harvard University Press, 1971): 3; See further, A. Sen, *The Idea of Justice* (Penguin Books, 2009).

61. R. Paternoster, B. Brame, R. Bachman and L. W. Sherman, "Do Fair Procedures Matter? The Effect of Procedural Justice on Spouse Assault" *Law and Society Review* 31 (1997): 163; Mark Austin Walters, *Hate Crime and Restorative Justice. Exploring Causes, Repairing Harms* (Oxford University Press, 2014); Alex Edney-Browne, "Embodiment and Affect in a Digital Age Understanding Mental Illness among Military Drone Personnel" *Journal of Contemporary Philosophy* 1 (2017): 18; Presenter: Natasha Mitchell and Guest: Brandon Bryant, "Drone Warfare and the Psyche: An Insider Speaks" *Radio National Broadcast*, 2017 http://www.abc.net.au/radionational/programs/sciencefriction/drone-warfare-and-the-psyche-an-insider-speaks/8817340.

62. Sherman, "Do Fair Procedures Matter?": 15.

63. The Schlesinger Report: An Investigation of Abu Ghraib (Cosimo Reports, 2005). See also, G. Gibson "Abu Ghraib Prison Investigation: 'Animal House on the Night Shift'" *Baltimore Sun*, August 25, 2004.

64. S. Mestrovic and R. Romero, "Poisoned Social Climate, Collective Responsibility, and the Abuse at Abu Ghraib—Or, the Establishment of 'Rule That Is a Lack of Rule'" *International Journal of Law and Psychiatry* 35 (2012): 62, 68; See further, C. Levin and J. McCain, "Senate Armed Services Committee Inquiry into the Treatment of Detainees in US Custody" http://levin.senate.cov/newsroom/release.cfm?id=305735.

65. David Morrison, Speech to the Australian Human Resource Research Institute Conference on Diversity, November 16, 2012.

66. N. Kerr, A. Rumble, E. Park, J. Outwerkerk, C. Parks, M. Gallucci, and P. van Lange, "How Many Bad Apples Does It Take to Spoil the Whole Barrel? Social Exclusion and Toleration for Bad Apples" *Journal of Experimental Social Psychology* 45 (2009): 603, 611.

67. D. Fromkin, 2005, "Cheney's 'Dark Side' Is Showing" *Washington Post blog* cited in Adam Lankford, "Promoting Aggression and Violence at Abu Ghraib: The US Military's Transformation of Ordinary People into Torturers" *Aggression and Violent Behaviour* 14 (2009): 388, 392.

68. F. B. M. De Waal, "Putting the Altruism Back into Altruism: The Evolution of Empathy" *Annual Review of Psychology* 59 (2008): 279.

69. E. Grossman, *On Killing: The Psychological Cost of Learning to Kill in War and Society* (Boston: Little Brown and Co., 1995): 13; Ghiotto, "Back to the Future."

70. D. L. Smith, *The Most Dangerous Animal: Human Nature and the Origins of War* (New York: St. Martin's Press, 2007).

71. Grossman, *On Killing*: 12.

72. See e.g., *Hague Regulations* art 23(c); *Geneva Conventions* common art 3; *Protocol Additional to the Geneva Convention* (Protocol I), art 41 (1).

73. Grossman, *On Killing*.

74. Hayden Cooper, "Combat Stress Strikes Australian Soldiers" *ABC Broadcast: transcript available* November 4, 2012 http://www.abc.net.au/7.30/content/2012/s3475312.htm; Mitchell, "Drone Warfare"; Thomas W. Britt et al., "Morale as a Moderator of the Combat Exposure-PTSD Symptom Relationship" *Journal of Traumatic Stress* 26 (2013): 94.

75. Gallacher et al, "The Constant Battle: Suicide by Veterans" (Foreign Affairs, Defence and Trade References Committee, August 2017) https://www.aph.gov.au/Parliamentary_Business/Committees/Senate/Foreign_Affairs_Defence_and_Trade/VeteranSuicide/Report: Submission 59, 3.

76. Marcia Reyes Steward, "A Higher Call: An Incredible True Story of Combat and Chivalry in the War-Torn Skies of World War II" *Army Lawyer* (December 2014): 20, 22.

77. Stephen Harding, "The Last Battle: When U.S. and German Soldiers Joined Forces" in the *Waning Hours of World War II in Europe* (Da Capo Press, 2013); Phil Nordyke, *Four Stars of Valor: The Combat History of the 505th Parachute Infantry*

Regiment in World War II (Zenith Press, 2006); Patrick. K. O'Donnell, *Into the Rising Sun: World War II's Pacific Veterans Reveal the Heart of Combat (*2002).

78. Thomas Wayde Pittman and Matthew Heaphy, "Does the United States Really Prosecute Its Service Members for War Crimes? Implications for Complementarity before the International Criminal Court" *Leiden Journal of International Law* 21 (2008): 165; Paul Maley, "Defence Consultant Uncovered Culture of Drugs, Sex, Crime" *The Australian*, June 9, 2018 https://www.theaustralian.com.au/national-affairs/defence/defence-consultant-uncovered-culture-of-drugs-sex-crime/news-story/46d1a90ea53473e14cd1709936461397.

79. Jonathan Haynes, "Marines Charged with Murder over Afghanistan Death" *The Guardian* (London), Sunday October 14, 2012 http://www.guardian.co.uk/world/2012/oct/14/marines-charged-murder-afghanistan; *ABC Televsion*, "Former Commando 'Can't Atone' for Special Forces Raid that Killed Afghan Children" *Australian Story*, May 23, 2016 http://www.abc.net.au/news/2016-05-23/soldier's-story-exposes-serious-flaws-in-deadly-adf-raid/7435548; Nick McKenzie, Chris Masters, and David Wroe, "Secretive and Elite SAS Soldiers Grilled about Alleged War Crimes" *Canberra Times*, June 8, 2018 https://www.canberratimes.com.au/politics/federal/secretive-and-elite-sas-soldiers-grilled-about-alleged-war-crimes-20180608-p4zkau.html.

80. J. Mayer, *The Dark Side: The Inside Story of How the War on Terror Turned into a War on American Ideals* (New York: Anchor, 2009); Nick Davies, "Iraq War Logs: Secret Order That Let US Ignore Abuse. Mistreatment of Helpless Prisoners by Iraqi Security Forces Included Beatings, Burning, Electrocution and Rape" *guardian.co.uk*, October 22, 2010.

81. M. Tarrant, N. Branscombe, R. Warner, and D. Weston, "Social Identity and Perceptions of Torture: Is Moral When We Do It" *Journal of Experimental Social Psychology* 48 (2012): 513.

82. H. Tajfel and J. C. Turner, "An Integrative Theory of Intergroup Conflict" in W. G. Austin and S. Worchel (eds) *The Social Psychology of Intergroup Relations* (Monterey, CA: Brooks Cole, 1979): 33.

83. Mitchell, "Drone Warfare."

84. Spak, "Effect of Military Culture."

85. Tarrant et al., "Social Identity": 516. See further, Rachel Kerr, "The UK in Basra and the Death of Baha Mousa" in David Lovell (ed) *Investigating Operational Incidents in a Military Context: Law Justice, Politics* (Brill Nijhoff, 2014): 71, 72.

86. A. Bandura, "Moral Disengagement in the Perpetration of Inhumanities" *Personality and Social Psychology Review* 3 (1999): 193; A. Bandura, "Selective Moral Disengagement in the Exercise of Moral Agency" *Journal of Moral Education* 31, (2002): 101.

87. See chapter 3.

88. Erik Ortiz, "Pentagon Chief James Mattis Calls Marines' Photo Scandal 'Unacceptable'" *NBC.News*, January 12, 2017 https://www.nbcnews.com/news/us-news/pentagon-chief-james-mattis-calls-marines-photo-scandal-unacceptable-n732011.

89. B. S. Coyle, D. L. Wolan, and A. S. Van Horn, "The Prevalence of Physical and Sexual Abuse in Women Veterans Seeking Care at a Veterans Affairs Medical Center"

Military Medicine 161 (1996): 588–93 in Jessica A. Turchik and Susan M. Wilson, "Sexual Assault in the U.S. Military: A Review of the Literature and Recommendations for the Future" *Aggression and Violent Behavior* 15 no. 4 (2010): 267, 270: female veterans indicating experience of child sexual abuse at a rate of 27 percent; Lex L. Merrill et al., "Childhood Abuse and Premilitary Sexual Assault in Male Navy Recruits" *Journal of Consulting and Clinical Psychology* 69 no. 2 (2001): 252.

90. Turchik et al., "Sexual Assault": 270.

91. Deirdre MacManus et al., "Aggressive and Violent Behavior among Military Personnel Deployed to Iraq and Afghanistan: Prevalence and Link with Deployment and Combat Exposure" *Epidemiology Review* 37 (2015): 205: found that "pre-military violent offending . . . was the strongest risk factor for post deployment violent offending."

92. MacManus et al., "Aggressive and Violent."

93. CDC and the Prevention Institute, *Connecting the Dots: An Overview of the Links among Multiple Forms of Violence* (July 2014) cited in Brenda S. Farrell et al., "Sexual Violence. Actions Needed to Improve DoD's Efforts to Address the Continuum of Unwanted Sexual Behaviors" (US Government Accountability Office, 2017) https://www.gao.gov/assets/690/689086.pdf: 13.

94. MacManus et al., "Aggressive and Violent."

95. David L Snowden et al., "Military Service and Crime: New Evidence" *Social Psychiatry and Psychiatric Epidemiology* 52 no. 5 (2017): 605

96. Ibid., 612.

97. Deirdre MacManus et al., "Impact of Pre-Enlistment Antisocial Behaviour on Behavioural Outcomes among UK Military Personnel" *Social Psychiatry and Psychiatric Epidemiology* 47 no. 8 (2012): 1353.

98. Ibid.

99. McClellan, "Royal Commission" Final Report Vol 2 Nature and Cause: 154.

100. Cynthia Gimbel and Alan Booth, "Why Does Military Combat Experience Adversely Affect Marital Relations?" *Journal of Marriage and Family* 56 no. 3 (1994): 691 Vietnam veterans pre-war antisocial behavior was a stronger predictor of veteran violence than combat exposure; MacManus et al., "Aggressive and Violent": 209.

101. MacManus et al., "Aggressive and Violent": 204.

102. Casey T. Taft et al., "Examining the Correlates of Aggression among Male and Female Vietnam Veterans" *Violence and Victims* 24 no. 5 (2009): 639; C. R Brewin et al., "Objective Predictors of Delayed-Onset Post-Traumatic Stress Disorder Occurring after Military Discharge" *Psychological Medicine* 42 no. 10 (2012): 1 "Those with post-discharge PTSD had significantly more disciplinary offences, specifically absence without leave, disobedience, and dishonesty, than the no-PTSD group, and this excess of offences was present before any exposure to trauma."; MacManus et al., "Aggressive and Violent": 209 ". . . the seductions of screening for vulnerability mean that it is something that is proposed from time to time for various reasons, even if there is still a lack of any robust evidence base to support it."

103. McClellan, "Royal Commission" Final Report Vol 2 Nature and Cause: 131 "The experiences shared by survivors in public hearings and private sessions tell us that it is difficult for children to identify, resist and disclose sexual abuse by 'professional perpetrators' who are in positions of authority and hold power over them."

104. McClellan, "Royal Commission" Final Report Vol 2 Nature and Cause: 142, 145.

105. Gary Rumble, Melanie McKean, and Dennis Pearce, "Report of the Review of Allegations of Sexual and Other Abuse in Defence. Facing the Problems of the Past" *DLA Piper Review* (October 2011) Volume 1, Executive Summary, xxix http://www.defence.gov.au/foi/docs/disclosures/224_1112_Document.pdf.

106. James Brown, "A Disconnect between Policy and Practice: Defence Transparency in Australia" *Security Challenges* 11 no. 1 (2015): 29, 33.

107. Mick Ryan, "A Study of Army's Education, Training and Doctrine Needs for the Future" *The Ryan Review*, edited by Commonwealth of Australia, April 21, 2016 https://www.army.gov.au/sites/g/files/net1846/f/2016_05_dgt_theryanreview_web.pdf.

108. See Eugene R. Fidell, "Military Justice Instruction in Civilian Law Schools" *Journal of Legal Education* 60 no. 3 (2011): 472, 474 ". . . the vast majority of schools still do not offer courses in military law."

109. Connor and McDermott, "Service Teaching": 505.

110. E. Danielsson and A. Weibull, "Sociology at Military Academies. The Swedish Case" *Armed Forces and Society* 35 no. 1 (2008): 91.

111. Jeniffer G. H. Cox, "Proposing a New Strategy for Army Ethics Training" *Military Law Review* 224 (2016): 541, 578.

112. Elizabeth Broderick, "Advice to the Minister for Defence the Hon. Kevin Andrews" (Australian Human Rights Commission, June 24, 2015): 5.

113. Morrison, "Chief of Army Message": 4.

114. P. J. Hoglin and N. Barton, "First-Term Attrition of Military Personnel in the Australian Defence Force" *Armed Forces and Society* 4 no. 1 (2015): 43, 60.

115. McClellan, "Royal Commission Interium Report (Attorney-General's Department, 2014): 174.

116. Thomas W. Britt et al., "Morale as a Moderator": 94.

117. Danielle Rogowski, "Quis Custodiet Ipsos Custodies? The Current State of Sexual Assault Reform within the U.S. Military and the Need for the Use of a Formal Decision Making Process in Further Reform" *Seattle University Law Review* 38 (2015): 1139.

118. *Reid v. Covert,* 354 U.S. 1, 26–27 (1957) (Black J).

119. Lorsch, "Culture Is Not": 98.

120. Max Farrand (ed.), *The Records of the Federal Convention of 1787* (Volume 1, Yale University Press).

121. Luban, "On the Commander."

122. S. H. Matheson, "The Committee for Evaluation of the Effectiveness of the Administration of Military Justice" June 1, 1971 https://www.loc.gov/rr/frd/Military_Law/pdf/Report_General-Westmoreland.pdf.

123. William C. Westmoreland, "Military Justice—a Commander's Viewpoint" *American Criminal Law Review* 10 (1971): 5, 8 cited in Bozarth, "Strange Bedfellows": 1016.

124. Brooker, "Improving Uniform": 27–28.

125. Herbert B. Powell, "Committee on the Uniform Code of Military Justice, Good Order and Discipline in the Army" (United States Department of Defense, January 18, 1960) https://www.loc.gov/rr/frd/Military_Law/pdf/Powell_report.pdf.

126. William A. Moorman, "Fifty Years of Military Justice: Does the Uniform Code of Military Justice Need to Be Changed?" *The Air Force Law Review* 48 (2000): 185.

127. The Senate Foreign Affairs, "The Effectiveness of Australia's Military Justice System": 108–112.

128. Ibid., 107, 122.

129. Ibid., 108.

130. [2009] 239 CLR 230.

131. The resistance is discussed in Jonathan Lurie, *Military Justice in America. The U.S. Court of Appeals for the Armed Forces, 1775–1980* (University Press of Kansas, 1998); James T. Hill, "Achieving Transparency in the Military Panel Selection Process with the Preselection Method" *Military Law Review* 205 (2010): 117; Paul Cornish and Andrew M. Dorman, "Breaking the Mould: The United Kingdom Strategic Defence Review 2010" *International Affairs* 86 no. 2 (2010): 395.

132. See Rosenblatt, "Non-Deployable: The Court-martial System in Combat from 2001 to 2009" *Creighton Law Review* 44 (2011): 1045.

133. "Military Unions and Associations" in Ian Leigh et al. (eds), *Handboook on Human Rights and Fundamental Freedoms of Armed Forces Personnel* (OSCE Office for Democratic Institutions and Human Rights (ODIHR), 2008): 65.

134. Eugene Fidell, "Country Reports" (Paper presented at the Continuity and Change in Militay Justice, London, December 12, 1998): 8.

135. Victor Hansen, "The Impact of Military Justice Reforms on the Law of Armed Conflict: How to Avoid Unintended Consequences" *Michigan State International Law Review* 21 (2013): 229, 231.

136. Banner, "Institutional Sexual": 171–72.

137. Turley, "The Military Pocket": 98.

138. Ibid., 109.

139. Ibid., 94: Turley refers to the claim made by Madison that "a flawed system could be entirely composed of the world's greatest philosophers, but still produce dysfunctional results."

140. Brooker, "Improving Uniform": 119–20.

141. Defence and Trade References Committee, The Senate Foreign Affairs, "The effectiveness of Australia's military justice system" (June 2005): This Inquiry has possibly been the most wide ranging, honest and frank assessment of military discipline; See *White* [2007] HCA 29 (19 June 2007), Kirby J [116] "Some transitional inconvenience would, of course, arise. But this Court, as the only body with the power and duty to do so, would establish the correct constitutional principle. It would uphold the language and design of the Constitution, read in its entirety. Better to do so belatedly than to persist with a 'defence of the indefensible.'"

142. Banner, "Institutional Sexual Assault": 165–66; see also Brasch, *More Martial than Court.*

Reference List

Abadee, Brigadier Hon A. R. "A Study into Judicial System under the DFDA." 1997.

"A Complete List of the 35 Basic Military Training Instructors Court-Martialed in the Lackland Air Force Base Sex Scandal." July 29, 2016. https://militaryjusticeforall.com/2016/07/29/a-complete-list-of-the-35-basic-military-training-instructors-court-martialed-in-lackland-air-force-base-sex-scandal/.

Adye, Stephen Payne. *A Treatise on Courts-martial, to Which Is Added an Essay on Military Punishments and Rewards*. (3 ed. London: J Murray, 1786).

Alleman, Lindsy Nicole. "Who Is in Charge, and Who Should Be? The Disciplinary Role of the Commander in Military Justice Systems." *Duke Journal of Comparative & International Law* 16 (2006): 169–92.

Allen, John. *All the Pope's Men: The Inside Story of How the Vatican Really Thinks*. (New York: Doubleday, 2004).

Almasy, Steve. "Former Soldier at Center of Murder of Iraqi Family Dies after Suicide Attempt." *CNN*, February 19, 2014. https://edition.cnn.com/2014/02/18/us/soldier-steven-green-suicide/index.html.

Alvarez, Devon M. "Death by Hazing: Should There Be a Federal Law against Fraternity and Sorority Hazing?" *Journal of Multidisciplinary Research* 7, no. 2 (2015): 43–75.

Arizmendi, Clint. "A Culture of Reviews." *Australian Defence Force Journal* 192 (2013): 81–89.

"Army Captain Calls for Prostitutes to Be Sent to Front Line to Relieve Soldiers' Stress: Report." *Yahoo7 News*, December 4, 2017. https://au.news.yahoo.com/a/38133843/australian-army-captain-says-sex-workers-could-help-soldiers/.

Army White Paper. *The Profession of Arms*, December 8, 2010.

Australian Defence Force. "Annual Report." (Department of Defence, 2014–2015).

Australian Defence Force, "Annual Report." (Department of Defence, 2015–2016).

Australian Government. "Processes to Support Victims of Abuse in Defence." *Australian Government Response to the Foreign Affairs, Defence and Trade References Committee Report*. Canberra: 2015.

———. "Response to the Foreign Affairs, Defence and Trade Committee Report the Constant Battle: Suicide by Veterans." Canberra: 2017.

Australian Human Rights Commission. "Pathway to Change: Collaboration for Cultural Reform in Defence, Women at ADFA: Measures to Promote Gender Equality and Assessment of Their Adequacy." Department of Defence, 2014.

Bagot, Kathy. "Administrative Accountability in Prisons." *Australian Journal of Administrative Law* 9 (2002): 143–59.

Baker, James E. "Is Military Justice Sentencing on the March? Should It Be? And If So, Where Should It Head? Court-Martial Sentencing Process, Practice, and Issues." *Federal Sentencing Reporter* 27, no. 2 (2014): 72–87.

Baldor, Lolita C. "Two-Star General Demoted after Affair." *The Associated Press*, December 16, 2016. http://www.armytimes.com/news/your-army/2016/12/16/two-star-general-demoted-after-affair/.

Baldor, Lolita C., and Jeffrey A. Sinclair. "U.S. Army General, Charged with Forcible Sodomy, Adultery," *Huffington Post*, November 26, 2012.

Banner, Francine. "Institutional Sexual Assault and the Rights/Trust Dilemma." *Cardozo Public Law, Policy and Ethics Journal* 13 (2014): 97–172.

Barrouquere, Brett. "Steven Green Spared Death Penalty for Iraqi Rape, Murders." *Huffington Post*, May 21, 2009.

Bastick, Megan. "Integrating a Gender Perspective into Internal Oversight within Armed Forces." Geneva: DCAF, OSCE, OSCE/ODIHR, 2014. http://www.osce.org/odihr/118325?download=true.

Batey, Robert. "Parker v. Levy: A Primer in Judicial Persuasion." *Journal of Legal Education* 49 (1999): 97–125.

Beck, Robert L. *Inside the Tailhook Scandal: A Naval Aviator's Story*. (Meadville PA: Fulton Books Inc, 2016).

Becker, Elizabeth. "Army Demotes Retired NATO Commander Who Admitted Affairs with Wives of Subordinates." *New York Times*, September 3, 1999.

Behan, Christopher W. "Don't Tug on Superman's Cape: In Defense of Convening Authority Selection and Appointment of Court-Martial Panel Members." *Military Law Review* 176 (2003): 190–308.

Bentley, Amelia. "Ex-Naval Officer Faces Child Sex Trial." *Brisbane Times*, July 26, 2011.

Bernard, G. W. *The King's Reformation: Henry VIII and the Remaking of the English Church*. (Yale University Press), 2005.

Bernstein, Anita, and Paul Fanning. "Heirs of Leonardo: Cultural Obstacles to Strict Products Liability in Italy." *Vanderbilt Journal of Transnational Law* 27 (1994): 1–32.

Biesecker, Michael. "Army General Fined, Reprimanded in Sex Case."*Daily News*, March 20, 2014. http://www.military.com/daily-news/2014/03/20/army-general-fined-reprimanded-in-sex-case.html.

Bigler, Bradford D. "Rebalancing Military Sentencing: An Argument to Restore Utilitarian Principles within the Courtroom." *Military Law Review* 225 (2017): 1–34.

Bingham, Clara. "Code of Dishonor." *Vanity Fair*, December 2003. http://www.vanityfair.com/news/2003/12/airforce200312.

Blackwell, Eoin. "Former SAS Trooper Evan Donaldson Declines $1 Million Settlement Offer from Defence." *The Huffington Post*, June 16, 2016.

Blasek, Roman. "Perception of Security Risks by the Population of the Czech Republic." *The Journal of Slavic Military Studies* 11, no. 3 (1998): 89–96.

Blinder, Alan. "General in Sex Case to Retire with a 2-Rank Demotion Jeffrey Sinclair to Receive Benefits, but at Lower Level." *New York Times*, June 21, 2014, A15.

Blok, Anne-Claire. "Sexual Violence in the U.S. Military." *The Avon Global Center for Women and Justice at Cornell Law School, Cornell Law School's Global Gender Justice Clinic, Service Women's Action Council*: Human Rights Council, 2015.

Bloom, Sarah. "No Vengeance for 'Revenge Porn' Victims: Unraveling Why This Latest Female-Centric, Intimate-Partner Offense Is Still Legal, and Why We Should Criminalize It." *Fordham Urban Law Journal* 42, no. 1 (2016): 234–89.

Bojan, Mark E. "Bad Paper: Reforming the Army Reprimand Process." *Military Law Review* 224 (2016): 1150–210.

Borch, Frederic L. "Lore of the Corps "I Want That Man Shot": A War Crime in Vietnam?" *Army Lawyer*, September (2014): 1–4.

———. "The History of 'Don't Ask, Don't Tell' in the Army: How We Got to It and Why It Is What It Is." *Military Law Review* 203 (2010): 189–206.

———. *Judge Advocates in Combat. Army Lawyers in Military Operations from Vietnam to Haiti*. Office of the Judge Advocate General Washington, D.C: U.S. Government Printing Office, 2001.

Box, John E. "Toxic Leadership in the Military Profession."*Masters Thesis: Master of Strategic Studies Degree* (2012). http://www.au.af.mil/au/awc/awcgate/army-usawc/box_toxic_leadership.pdf.

Bozarth, Graci. "Strange Bedfellows: The Military, the University, and Sexual Assault." *University of Missouri-Kansas City Law Review* 84 (2016): 1003–32.

Bracknell, Butch. "The U.S. And the International Criminal Court: An Unfinished Debate." *Los Angeles Times*, May 26, 2011.

Brady, Heidi L. "Justice Is No Longer Blind: How the Effort to Eradicate Sexual Assault in the Military Unbalanced the Military Justice System." *University of Illinois Law Review* (2016): 193–250.

Brasch, Jacoba. *More Martial than Court: From Exceptionalism to Fair Trial Convergence in Australian Courts-Martial*. Thesis Publication, University of New South Wales, 2011.

Bremer, Paul. "Coalition Provisional Authority Order Number 17 (Revised)." (2004).

Brennan, Thomas James. "Hundreds of Marines Investigated for Sharing Photos of Naked Colleagues." *The War Horse*, March 4, 2017. https://www.revealnews.org/blog/hundreds-of-marines-investigated-for-sharing-photos-of-naked-colleagues/.

Brenner, Hannah, Kathleen Darcy, and Sheryl Kubiak. "Sexual Violence as an Occupational Hazard and Condition of Confinement in the Closed Institutional Systems of the Military and Detention." *Pepperdine Law Review* 44, no. 81 (2017): 881–956.

Brenner, Samuel. 'I Am a Bit Sickened': Examining Archetypes of Congressional War Crimes Oversight after My Lai and Abu Ghraib." *Military Law Review* 204, (2010): 1–93.

Brennerbecka, Dru. "Assessing Guidelines and Disparity in Military Sentencing: Vive La Difference!" *Federal Sentencing Reporter* 27, no. 2 (2014): 108–20.

Brewin, C. R., B. Andrews, J. Hejdenberg, and L. Stewart. "Objective Predictors of Delayed-Onset Post-Traumatic Stress Disorder Occurring after Military Discharge." *Psychological Medicine* 42, no. 10 (2012): 1–8.

Brissenden, Michael. "HMAS Leeuwin: Navy Chief Says Defence Turned a Blind Eye to 'Sickening' Abuse against Young Sailors." *ABC News*, June 18, 2014. http://www.abc.net.au/news/2014-06-18/navy-chief-says-defence-turned-blind-eye-to-hmas-leeuwin-abuse/5533766.

Brissenden, Michael, and Alex McDonald. "Former Deputy Commandant Warned Australian Defence Force Academy Not the Best Way to Train Next Generation of Officers." *Four Corners ABC*, June 10, 2014. http://www.abc.net.au/news/2014-06-09/former-deputy-commandant-issued-warning-on-adfa/5510658.

Brissett, Wilson. "Air Force Academy Questioned for Response to Sexual Assault." *Airforce Magazine*, December 14, 2017. http://www.airforcemag.com/Features/Pages/2017/December%202017/Air-Force-Academy-Questioned-for-Response-to-Sexual-Assault.aspx.

Britt, Thomas W., Amy B. Adler, Paul D. Bliese, and DeWayne Moore. "Morale as a Moderator of the Combat Exposure-PTSD Symptom Relationship." *Journal of Traumatic Stress* 26 (2013): 94–101.

Broderick, Elizabeth. "Advice to the Minister for Defence the Hon. Kevin Andrews." Sydney: Australian Human Rights Commission, 2015.

———. Report "Cultural Renewal at the University of Sydney Residential Colleges" (Elizabeth Broderick & Co., 2017).

———. "Report on the Review into the Treatment of Women at the Australian Defence Force Academy." Australian Human Rights Commission, 2011.

———. "Report on the Review into the Treatment of Women at the Australian Defence Force, Phase Two of the Review into the Treatment of Women in the Australian Defence Force." Australian Human Rights Commission, 2012.

Bronitt, Simon, and Mark Nolan. "Our Sights Must Be Set on Justice." *The Age*, Opinion Page, August 28, 2009.

Brook, Tom Vanden. "Army Demotes 'Swinging General' after Investigation into Affairs, Lifestyle." *USA TODAY*, December 16, 2016. https://www.usatoday.com/story/news/politics/2016/12/16/army-demotes-swinging-general-david-haight/95493058/.

———. "Disgraced Army General Fired after 'Inappropriate' Relationship with Young Woman on Staff." *USA TODAY*, June 23, 2017. https://www.usatoday.com/story/news/politics/2017/06/23/disgraced-army-general-fired-after-inappropriate-relationship/422902001/.

Brooker, John W. "Improving Uniform Code of Military Justice Reform." *Military Law Review* 222 (2014): 1–128.

Broussard, Jeremy D. "Restoring Balance to the Scales: Higher Panel Quorums and Voting Requirement in Light of Article 60 Restrictions." *Army Lawyer* (2016): 5–15.

Brown, Gary. "Homosexuality and the Australian Defence Force: The Issues." Parliamentary Research Service. Canberra: Department of Parliamentary Library, 1992.

Brown, James. "A Disconnect between Policy and Practice: Defence Transparency in Australia." *Security Challenges* 11, no. 1 (2015): 29–38.

———. *Privateers in Australia's Conflict and Disaster Zones*. Civil-Military Occasional Papers. Australian Civil-Military Centre. (Australian Government, 2015).

Browne, Kingsley R. "Military Sex Scandals from Tailhook to the Present: The Cure Can Be Worse Than the Disease." *Duke Journal of Gender Law & Policy* 14 (2007): 749–89.

Browne, Rachel. "Church Laws Deliberately Misused to Cover Up Sex Claims: Royal Commission." *Sydney Morning Herald*, February 9, 2017.

Buckingham, Antony. "A Brief History of Australian Military Law." Australian MP History Website, June 16, 2018. http://home.iprimus.com.au/buckomp/BriefHistAustralianMilLaw.htm.

Bunn, Sherilyn A. "Straight Talk: The Implications of Repealing 'Don't Ask, Don't Tell' Preserving Aspects of the Current Policy." *Military Law Review*, no. 203 (2010): 207–83.

Burgess, Rebecca. "Veterans in the 115th Congress." *AEIdeas*, November 18, 2016. http://www.aei.org/publication/veterans-in-the-115th-congress/.

Burris, Matthew. "Thinking Slow about Sexual Assault in the Military." *Buffalo Journal of Gender, Law & Social Policy* 23 (2014–2015): 21–72.

Burton-Bradley, Robert. "ADA Says Women Not Suited for Land Combat Because of Rape Risk." *News Ltd*, April 13, 2011.

Byrne, Elizabeth. "ADFA Cadet Found Not Guilty of Raping Woman after Night out in Canberra." *ABC News*, July 5, 2017.

Cahill, Desmond, and Peter Wilkinson. "Child Sexual Abuse in the Catholic Church: An Interpretive Review of the Literature and Public Inquiry Reports." *Centre for Global Research, School of Global, Urban and Social Studies*, August 2017. https://www.rmit.edu.au/content/dam/rmit/documents/news/church-abuse/child-sex-abuse-and-the-catholic-church.pdf.

Carpenter, Zoë. "20 Years Ago, an Army Veteran Reported a Sexual Assault. She's Still Waiting for Justice." *The Nation*, February 24, 2014. https://www.thenation.com/article/nearly-two-decades-after-speaking-veteran-waits-sexual-assault-reform/.

Carson, Julie K., and Brad R. Carson. "The Historical Roots and Future Directions for Military Law and Policies on Rape and Sexual Assault." *Military Psychology* (2017): 1–14.

Carter, Kevin W. "Fraternization." *Military Law Review* 113 (1986): 61–136.

Caruço, Rodrigo M. "Treating Members of the Military at Least as Well as Inmates and Students: Determining When Military Necessity Requires Infringing upon Constitutional Rights in Cases before the Court of Appeals for the Armed Forces." *The University of Memphis Law Review* 46 (2015): 61–134.

Castle, Stephen. "Pervasive Abuse Found in Belgian Church." *New York Times*, September 11, 2010, 8A.

Castro, Marin R. “Sexual Assault in the Military.” *Statutory Enforcement Report*, edited by U.S. Commission on Civil Rights, 1–228. Washington: United States Commission on Civil Rights, 2013.

Cauterucci, Christina. “The Military’s Nude-Photo Sharing Scandal Is Worse Than We Thought.” *Slate.com*, March 15, 2017. http://www.slate.com/blogs/xx_factor/2017/03/15/the_military_s_nude_photo_sharing_scandal_is_getting_worse.html.

Cerel, Julie, John R. Jordan, and Paul R. Duberstein. “The Impact of Suicide on the Family.” *The Journal of Crisis Intervention and Suicide Prevention* 29, no. 1 (2008): 38–44.

Cernak, Stella. “Sexual Assault and Rape in the Military: The Invisible Victims of International Gender Crimes at the Front Lines.” *Michigan Journal of Gender & Law* 22 (2015): 207–41.

Chamallas, Martha. “The New Gender Panic: Reflections on Sex Scandals and the Military.” *Minnesota Law Review* 83 (1998): 305–75.

Chema, J. Richard. “Arresting ‘Tailhook’: The Prosecution of Sexual Harassment in the Military.” *Military Law Review* 140, Spring (1993): 1–64.

Cheney, Christopher Robert. *From Becket to Langton: English Church Government, 1170–1213*. (Manchester University Press, 1956).

Choa, Jonathan. “Civilians, Service-Members, and the Death Penalty: The Failure of Article 25a to Require Twelve-Member Panels in Capital Trials for Non-Military Crimes.” *Fordham Law Review* 70 (2002): 2065–107.

Christenson, Sig. “After Killings, Pentagon Added Thousands of Dishonorable Discharge Cases to FBI Database.” *San Antonio Express-News*, February 12, 2018.

———. “Changes Driven by Lackland Scandal Not Complete.” *San Antonio Express News*, September 9, 2014.

———. “Ex-Lackland Instructor Dead in Apparent Suicide.” *mySAnantonio.com*, September 2, 2014. http://www.mysanantonio.com/news/local/military/article/.

Churches, Steven. “The Shield of the Crown in England and Australia: The Need for Statutory Interpretation that Applies the Principle of Legality.” *Public Law Review* 22 (2011): 182–201.

Cohen, Andrew. “None of the Supreme Court Justices Has Battle Experience.” *The Atlantic*, August 13, 2012.

Cohen, Zachary. “Navy, Marines Prohibit Sharing Nude Photos without Consent.” *CNN.com* April 19, 2017.

Cohn, Lindsay. “The Evolution of the Civil-Military ‘Gap’ Debate.” *Paper prepared for the TISS project on the Gap between the Military and Civilian Society* (1999).

Coletti, Leslie J. “In Search of a New Culture: The Sexual Violence against U.S. Military Women by Their Fellow Soldiers, 1978–Present.” *Dietrich College of Humanities and Social Sciences Thesis* (2010): 1–62. http://repository.cmu.edu/cgi/viewcontent.cgi?article=1049&context=hsshonors.

Collins, Pauline. *Civil-Military “Legal” Relations: Where to From Here? The Civilian Courts and the Military in the United Kingdom, United States and Australia.* International Humanitarian Law Series, 51 (Leiden: Brill Nijhoff, 2018).

Commonwealth. "Defence Force Disciplinary Code: Report of the 1973 Working Party." 1974.

Commonwealth and Defence Force Ombudsman. "Managment of Disciplinary Complaints. Submission by the Commonwealth and Defence Force Ombudsman." *IGADF Review*, 2011.

Connor, James, and Vanessa McDermott. "Service Teaching and Sociological Critique: Lessons from a Military Academy." *Journal of Sociology* 49, no. 4 (2013): 501–14.

Conte, Alex. "ICJ Welcomes UN Expert Report on Military Tribunals." *ICJ Press Release* October 29, 2013. https://www.icj.org/icj-welcomes-un-expert-report-on-military-tribunals/.

Cooper, Hayden. "Combat Stress Strikes Australian Soldiers." *Broadcast: transcript available. ABC*, April 11, 2012. http://www.abc.net.au/7.30/content/2012/s3475312.htm.

———. "Officer Breaks Ranks to Condemn ADF's 'Neglect' of Abuse Victims." *7:30 Report ABC*, March 8, 2013 http://www.abc.net.au/news/2013-03-07/army-officer-says-adf-fails-abuse-victims/4558834.

Cooper, Norman G. "Gustavus Adolphus and Military Justice." *Military Law Review* 92 (1981): 129–37.

Cornall, Robert. "Defence Abuse Response Taskforce Final Report." *Defence Abuse Response Taskforce*: Commonwealth of Australia, 2016.

Cornish, Paul, and Andrew M. Dorman. "Breaking the Mould: The United Kingdom Strategic Defence Review 2010." *International Affairs* 86, no. 2 (2010): 395–410.

Cox, Jeniffer G. H. "Proposing a New Strategy for Army Ethics Training." *Military Law Review* 224 (2016): 541–89.

Crawford, Lisa Burton. *The Rule of Law and the Australian Constitution*. (Federation Press, 2017).

Cullen, Simon. "Sexual Predators May Have Targeted Military: Report." *ABC News*, 10 July, 2012. http://www.abc.net.au/news/2012-07-10/government-releases-report-into-adf-sex-abuse/4121056.

———. "Smith Delivers Apology for Defence Force Abuse." *ABC News*, November 26, 2012.

Cumming, Charles S. "The English High Court of Admiralty." *Tulane Maritime Law Journal* 17 (1993): 209–56.

Cunliffe, Mark, Geoffrey Brown, and Gerard Fogarty, "Re-Thinking Systems of Inquiry, Investigation, Review and Audit in Defence. Annex G Specialist Roles and Processes." *Stage B Report for Secretary and CDF*, 2014.

Dahm, J. Michael. "Innocent until Investigated." *Proceedings Magazine* 142, no. 4 April, 2016.

Dalton, Colleen. "The Sexual Assault Crisis in the United States Air Force Academy." *Cardozo Women's Law Journal* 1 (2005): 177–202.

Danielsson, E., and A. Weibull. "Sociology at Military Academies. The Swedish Case." *Armed Forces and Society* 35, no. 1 (2008): 91–105.

Danopoulos, Constantine P., ed. *Military Disengagement from Politics*. (New York: Routledge, 1988).

Darehshori, Sara. "Booted. Lack of Recourse for Wrongfully Discharged US Military Rape Survivors." Human Rights Watch, May 19, 2016.

———. "Dispatches: US Navy to Protect Soldiers with Mental Health Conditions." Human Rights Watch, June 3, 2016.

———. "Embattled. Retaliation against Sexual Assault Survivors in the US Military." Human Rights Watch Report, May 18, (2015).

Davidson, Michael J. "Court-Martialing Cadets." *Capital University Law Review* 36 (2008): 635–73.

Davies, Nick. "Iraq War Logs: Secret Order That Let US Ignore Abuse. Mistreatment of Helpless Prisoners by Iraqi Security Forces Included Beatings, Burning, Electrocution and Rape." *Guardian.co.uk*, October 22, 2010.

Davies, Norman. *The Isles, a History*. (London: Papermac, 2000).

Davis, Lisa, Amanda Grifka, Kristin Williams, and Margaret Coffey. "Workplace and Gender Relations Survey of Active Duty Members." Office of People Analytics (OPA), Alexandria, VA: Defense Research, Surveys, and Statistics Center, 2016.

Dawe, Tim, and David Connery. "Army-Police Interoperability: Collective Contributions to Future Land Power." *Australian Army Land Power Forum* (2017). https://www.army.gov.au/our-future/blog/amphibious-joint-interagency/army-police-interoperability-collective-contributions.

Decaux, Emmanuel. "Draft Principles Governing the Administration of Justice through Military Tribunals." In *Special Rapporteur of the Sub-Commission on the Promotion and Protection of Human Rights*: Commission on Human Rights Sixty-second session, U.N. Doc. E/CN.4/2006/58 (January 13, 2006).

Defence Committee, "Pathway to Change: Evolving Defence Culture a Strategy for Cultural Change and Reinforcement." Commonwealth of Australia: (Department of Defence, 2012) www.defence.gov.au/pathwaytochange/.

Defence and Trade Senate Standing Committee on Foreign Affairs, "Sexual Harassment in the Australian Defence Force" (August 1994) .

Department of Defence, "Annual Report." 1–244. Canberra: Australian Government, 2016–2017.

———. "Government Response to the Senate Foreign Affairs, Defence and Trade References Committee 'Report on the Effectiveness of Australia's Military Justice System.'" Canberra, 2005.

———. "Sexual Misconduct Prevention and Response Office Supplementary Report 2016–17 a Supplement to the Defence Annual Report 2016–17." 1–13. Canberra: SEMPRO, 2016–2017.

———. "Memorandum of Understanding between the Australian Directors of Public Prosecution and the Director of Military Prosecution," May 22, 2007, Annex B in McDade, Lyn "Director of Military Prosecutions Annual Report for the Period 12 June 2006 to 31 December 2007" (Commonwealth of Australia, 2008: 1–59).

Department of Defense, "US Department of Defense Sexual Assault Prevention and Response Program." http://www.sapr.mil/.

———. "Report to the President of the United States on Sexual Assault Prevention and Response" 2014.

DeVille, Adam. "Kenosis vs. La Bella Figura." *The Canadian Journal of Orthodox Christianity* 2, no. 3 (2007): 94–106.

Devine, Miranda. "It's Not Too Late to Say Sorry, David Morrison. Many are still waiting to hear a few simple words." *The Daily Telegraph*, October 22, 2016.

———. "Mardi Gras: Why Were Aussie Soliders Allowed to March?" *The Queensland Times*, March 6, 2017.

Devlin, Dave. "Joint Service Police Group Launched." *News. Navy*, June 17, 2017. http://news.navy.gov.au/en/Jun2017/Events/3794/Joint-Service-Police-Group-launched.htm#.WnKXv2iCzIU.

Devos, Theirry, Dario Spini, and Shalom H. Schwartz. "Conflicts among Human Values and Trust in Institutions." *British Journal of Social Psychology* 41 (2002): 481–94.

Dickerson, Julie. "A Compensation System for Military Victims of Sexual Assault and Harassment." *Military Law Review* 222 (2014): 211–70.

Dienes, Thomas. "When the First Amendment Is not Preferred: The Military and Other 'Special Contexts.'" *University of Cincinnati Law Review* 56 (1988): 779–843.

Dominguez, Michael L., Roger A. Brady, and John Speigel. "Report Concerning the Assessment of USAF Sexual Assault Prevention and Response." Office of the Assistant Secretary of the Air Force (Manpower and Reserve Affairs), Department of Air Force, 2004, 1–96.

Dorney, Girard. "Australia Investigates Horrific Abuse of Over 200 Teenage Boys at Navy Base." *Vice News*, July 21, 2014. https://news.vice.com/article/australia-investigates-horrific-abuse-of-over-200-teenage-boys-at-navy-base.

"DPP Quits over Promotion 'Misjudgment.'" *ABC News*, May 15, 2011.

Draper, Michelle. "A Royal Australian Navy Sailor Has Broken Down after Being Found Guilty of Raping a Female Defence Force Colleague." *The Sydney Morning Herald*, August 10, 2011.

Draper, Robert. "The Military's Rough Justice on Sexual Assault." *New York Times*, November 26, 2014.

Drew, Jonathan. "Bergdahl Lawyers: Trump's Criticism Prevents Fair Trial." *The Navy Times*, January 20, 2017. https://www.navytimes.com/news/your-army/2017/01/20/bergdahl-lawyers-trump-s-criticism-prevents-fair-trial/.

Dudziak, Mary L. "Law, Power, and 'Rumors of War': Robert Jackson Confronts Law and Security after Nuremberg." *University of Southern California Legal Studies Working Paper Series* Paper 88 (2012).

Dumas, Daisy. "Woman of the Year Is ADFA Skype Sex Scandal Cadet." *Sydney Morning Herald*, December 16, 2013.

Duncan, Ian. "Midshipmen and Cadets Testify before Congressional Panel about Sexual Assault and Retaliation." *The Baltimore Sun*, May 2, 2017.

Duxbury, Alison. "The Curious Case of the Australian Military Court." *Oxford University Commonwealth Law Journal* Winter (2010): 155–84.

Dwyer, Johnny. "Former Marine Jose Nazario Acquitted of All Charges in Fallujah Killings: Would Have Been First American Serviceman Convicted in Civilian Court for Battlefield Crimes." *LA Weekly News*, December 31, 2008.

Earley, Geoff. "Review of the Management of Incidents and Complaints in Defence Including Civil and Military Jurisdiction." Commonwealth of Australia: Department of Defence, 2011.

———. "Review of the Management of Incidents and Complaints in Defence Including Civil and Military Jurisdiction." Commonwealth of Australia: Department of Defence, Audit Phase Second Report February 25, 2014.

Editorial. "Disengagement, Deficient Debate and Defeat." *Defender*, Autumn 2007: 1.

Edney-Browne, Alex. "Embodiment and Affect in a Digital Age Understanding Mental Illness among Military Drone Personnel." *Journal of Contemporary Philosophy*, no. 1 (2017): 18–33.

Edwards, Michael. "Robert Langdon: Last Western Prisoner Held in Afghanistan Pardoned, Flown Home to Australia." *ABC News*, August 10, 2016.

Effron Andrew S, "Report of the Military Justice Review Group. Part I UCMJ Recommendations." December 22, 2015: 1–1300.

Eggleston, Alan. "Report of the DLA Piper Review and the Government's Response." Foreign Affairs, Defence and Trade References Committee, 2013.

Ellison, Jesse. "Judge Dismisses 'Epidemic' of Rape in Military Case." *The Daily Beast*, December 13, 2011.

Embrey, Ellen P., Kenneth A. Arnold, Cynthia Bingham, James Cockerill, Susan G. Dunlow, Terri J. Rau, Jenice Staniford, and Jayme M. Sutton. "Task Force Report on Care for Victims of Sexual Assualt." US Department of Defense, 2004: 1–99.

Eskildsen, Jacob K., and Mikkel L. Nussler. "The Managerial Drivers of Employee Satisfaction and Loyalty." *Total Quality Management* 11, no. 4–6 (2000): 581–88.

Eyler, Gustav. "Gangs in the Military." *The Yale Law Journal* 118 (2009): 696–742.

Farrell, Brenda S. "Whistleblower Protection: DoD Has Improved Oversight for Reprisal Investigations but Can Take Additional Actions to Standardize Process and Reporting." *Report to Congressional Requesters*: United States Government Accountability Office, 2016.

———. "Whistleblower Protection DoD Needs to Enhance Oversight of Military Whistleblower Reprisal Investigations." *Report to Congressional Requesters*: United States Government Accountability Office, 2015.

Farrell, Brenda S., Thomas Gosling, Isabel Band, Matthew Bond, Vincent Buquicchio, Caroline DeCelles, Mae Jones, Kirsten Lauber, and Brian Pegram. "Sexual Violence. Actions Needed to Improve DoD's Efforts to Address the Continuum of Unwanted Sexual Behaviors." Defense Capabilities and Management Director, United States Government Accountability Office, 2017: 48.

Farrell, Theo. *Norms of War: Cultural Belief and Modern Conflict*. (Boulder, CO: Lynne Rienner, 2005).

Felsman, Janine P. "'To Support and Defend' against Sexual Misconduct: Calling on Future Military Leaders to Bridge the Cultural Divide." *Ohio State Journal of Criminal Law* 11, no. 1 (2014): 353–87.

Fidell, Eugene. "Criminal Prosecution of Civilian Contractors by Military Courts." *South Texas Law Review* 50 (2009): 845–57.

———. "A World-Wide Perspective on Change in Military Justice." *The Air Force Law Review* 48 (2000): 195–209.

———. "Military Justice Instruction in Civilian Law Schools." *Journal of Legal Education* 60, no. 3 (2011): 472–79.

Filippini, Leonardo, and Karina Tchrian. "Argentina's New Military Justice System—a Review of Law 26394 (El Nuevo Sistema De Justicia Militar Argentino—Comentario a La Ley 26394)." *Derecho Penal y Criminología* 91 (2010): 103–35.

Finer, Samuel E. *The Man on Horseback. The Role of the Military in Politics*. (2nd revised ed., Hammondsworth: Penguin Books Ltd, 1976).

Fleming, Bruce. "Mishandling Sexual Assault, and Other Military Problems." *Society* 52, no. 6 (2015): 521–26.

Foley, Tony. "Institutional Responses to Child Sexual Abuse: How a Moral Conversation with Its Lawyers Might Contribute to Cultural Change in a Faith-Based Institution." *Legal Ethics* 18, no. 2 (2015): 164–81.

"Former Commando 'Can't Atone' for Special Forces Raid that Killed Afghan Children." Australian Story, ABC. Television, May 23, 2016.

Foster, Kevin. *Don't Mention the War: The Australian Defence Force, the Media and the Afghan Conflict* (Melbourne: Monash University Publishing, 2013).

———. "Looking for Failure? Why the ADF Hates the Australian Media." *The Conversation*, August 13, 2013.

Fowler, T. K., J. Bunting, M. J. Nardotti, A. M. Carpenter, J. W. Ripley, L. L. Miller, and Sally L. Satel. "Panel to Review Sexual Misconduct Allegations at the U.S. Air Force Academy." Arlington: Senate Armed Services Committee, House Armed Services Committee, Secretary of Defense September 22, 2003: 1–107.

Fox, Richard G., and Jodie E. Lydeker. "The Militarisation of Australia's Federal Criminal Justice System." *Criminal Law Journal* 25 (2008): 287–303.

Luthans Fred, Suzanne J. Peterson, and Lelina Ibrayeva. "The Potential for the 'Dark Side' of Leadership in Post-Communist Countries." *Journal of World Business* 33, no. 2 (1998): 185–201.

Frederick, Jim. *Black Hearts: One Platoon's Descent into Madness in Iraq's Triangle of Death*. (Harmony Books, 2010).

Freiderich, Kent. "Strange Bedfellows: The American Public and Its Military in the Aftermath of September 11th." Edited by Dr Marybeth Ulrich Project Advisor, 43. Pennsylvania: U.S. Army War College Carlisle Barracks, 2003.

French, Robert. "The Courts and Parliament." Paper presented at the Supreme Court of Queensland Seminar, Brisbane, August 4, 2012.

———. "The Executive Power." Paper presented at the Inaugural George Winterton Lecture, Sydney Law School, The University of Sydney, February 18, 2010.

Friesen, Lana. "Certainty of Punishment versus Severity of Punishment: An Experimental Investigation." *Southern Economic Journal* 79, no. 2 (2012): 399–421.

Frystak, Marek. "Pre-Trial Proceedings in the Czech Republic." *Jurisprudence* 3, no. 121 (2010): 251–67.

Funnell, Nina, and Anna Hush. "The Red Zone Report. An Investigation into Sexual Violence and Hazing in Australian University Residential Colleges." End Rape on Campus (EROC) Australia, 2018.

Futterman, Craig B., H. Melissa Mather, and Melanie Miles. "The Use of Statistical Evidence to Address Police Supervisory and Disciplinary Practices: The Chicago

Police Department's Broken System." *DePaul Journal for Social Justice* 1, no. 2 (2008): 251–92.

Gageler, Stephen. "Deference." *Australian Journal of Administrative Law* 22 (2015): 151–56.

Gallacher, Alex. "Processes to Support Victims of Abuse in Defence." Commonwealth of Australia. Canberra: Senate, Foreign Affairs, Defence and Trade References Committee, 2014.

———. "The Constant Battle: Suicide by Veterans." Commonwealth of Australia. Canberra: Senate, Foreign Affairs, Defence and Trade References Committee, 2017.

———. "Matters Raised by NSW Police Strike Force CIVET." Commonwealth of Australia. Canberra: Senate, Foreign Affairs, Defence and Trade References Committee, 2017.

———. "Operation of the Australian Defence Force's Resistance to Interrogation Training." Commonwealth of Australia. Canberra: Senate, Foreign Affairs, Defence and Trade References Committee, 2017.

Gardiner, Stephanie. "'Jedi Council' Sex Ring Leader Hastings Fredrickson Sentenced to 15 Months." *The Sydney Morning Herald*, February 9, 2015.

Ghiotto, Anthony J. "Back to the Future with the Uniform Code of Military Justice: The Need to Recalibrate the Relationship between the Military Justice System, Due Process, and Good Order and Discipline." *North Dakota Law Review* 90 (2014): 485–543.

Gierke, H. F. "Sparky." "The Use of Article III Case Law in Military Jurisprudence." *Army Lawyer*, August (2005): 25–39.

Gilbert, Michael. "The Military and the Federal Judiciary: An Unexplored Part of the Civil-Military Relations Triangle." *United States Air Force Academy Journal of Legal Studies* 8 (1997–1998): 197–235.

Gillibrand, Kirsten E., et al. "The Relationships between Military Sexual Assault, Post-Traumatic Stress Disorder and Suicide, and on Department of Defense and Department of Veterans Affairs Medical Treatment and Management of Victims of Sexual Trauma." *One Hundred Thirteenth Congress Second Session, Hearing before the Subcommittee on Personnel of the Committee on Armed Services United States Senate*, February 26, 2014: 1–116.

Gimbel, Cynthia, and Alan Booth. "Why Does Military Combat Experience Adversely Affect Marital Relations?" *Journal of Marriage and Family* 56, no. 3 (1994): 691–703.

Glantz, David M. "Military Training and Education Challenges in Poland, the Czech Republic, and Hungary." *The Journal of Slavic Military Studies* 11, no. 3 (1998): 1–55.

Goldberg, Matthew. "Death and Injury Rates of U.S. Military Personnel in Iraq." *Military Medicine* 175 (2010): 220–36.

González-Ramírez, Andrea. "The Navy & the Marines Have Made Revenge Porn Illegal—Here's Why." *Refinery29.com*, April 20, 2017.

Goodman, Ellen. "'Great and Sustained Discipline' Required." *The Spokesman-Review*, May 2, 1997.

Graham, Bradley, and Josh White. "Top Pentagon Leaders Faulted in Prison Abuse Oversight by Rumsfeld and Others Inadequate, Panel Says." *Washington Post*, August 25, 2004.

Graney, David W. *Rogue Institution: Vigilante Injustice, Lawlessness, and Disorder at the Air Force Academy*. (Tuscon, Arizona: Wheatmark Inc, 2010).

Greene, Andrew, and Dylan Welch. "Police Say Defence Failed to Cooperate with Jedi Council Sex Scandal Investigation." *ABC.net.au*, November 23, 2016.

Grey, Bronwen. "Review into Harassment and Sexual Offences at the Australian Defence Force Academy." Australian Defence Force, 1998.

Gribbin, Caitlyn. "Defence Abuse Response Taskforce Reverses Call for Royal Commission into Sex Abuse at ADFA." *ABC News*, September 2, 2016.

Gross, Jane. "Sergeant Major Gets One-Step Demotion but No Time in Jail." *New York Times*, March 17, 1998.

Grossman, Dave. *On Killing: The Psychological Cost of Learning to Kill in War and Society*. (Back Bay Books, 2009).

Groves, Matthew. "The Civilianisation of Australian Military Law." *University of New South Wales Law Journal* 28, no. 2 (2005): 364–95.

———. "The Purpose and Scope of Prison Discipline." *Criminal Law Journal* 26 (2002): 10–28.

Grummitt, David. "The Court, War and Noble Power in England, c. 1475–1558." In *The Court as a Stage: England and the Low Countries in the Later Middle Ages*, edited by Antheun Janse and Steven Gunn, (Woodbridge: Boydell Press, 2006): 145–55.

Gyles, Rodger. "HMAS Success Commission of Inquiry Allegations of Unacceptable Behaviour and the Management Thereof." Department of Defence, 2011: 170.1

Hagan, William R. "Overlooked Textbooks Jettison Some Durable Military Law Legends." *Military Law Review* 113 (1986): 163–202.

Hale, John Rigby. *War and Society in Renaissance Europe, 1450–1620.* (Fontana History of European War and Society, Leicester University Press, in association with Fontana Paperbacks, 1985).

Hansen, Victor. "The Impact of Military Justice Reforms on the Law of Armed Conflict: How to Avoid Unintended Consequences." *Michigan State International Law Review* 21 (2013): 229–72.

Hanson, Eric. "Know Your Ground: The Military Justice Terrain of Afghanistan." *Army Lawyer*, November (2009): 36–44.

Happold, Matthew. "Hamdan v. Rumsfeld and the Law of War." *Human Rights Law Review* 7, no. 2 (2007): 418–31.

Hart, Anthony, David Lane, and Geraldine Doherty. "Historical Institutional Abuse in Northern Ireland between 1922 and 1995." United Kingdom, 2017.

Hawley, Samantha. "Defunct Military Court Leaves Defence in Chaos." *ABC Radio–PM*, September 27, 2009.

Haynes, Jonathan. "Marines Charged with Murder over Afghanistan Death." *The Guardian*, October 14, 2012.

Healy, Melissa. "Pentagon Blasts Tailhook Probe, Two Admirals Resign." *Los Angeles Times*, September 25, 1992: 2.

Held, David. *Models of Democracy*. (2nd ed. Cambridge: Polity Press, 1996).

Hemphill, Holly, Bernice F Belcer, Margarethe Cammermeyer, Nancy Duff Campbell, Teresa S Christenson, Julia J Cleckley, and Jacqueline DiRosa. "Defence Advisory Committee on Women in the Services." 2013 Report: 1–185.

Heydon, D. "Judicial Activism and the Death of the Rule of Law." *Quadrant* 47, no. 1 (2003): 9–22.

Hill, James T. "Achieving Transparency in the Military Panel Selection Process with the Preselection Method." *Military Law Review* 205 (2010): 117–49.

Hillman, Elizabeth L. "Front and Center: Sexual Violence in U.S. Military Law." *Politics and Society* 37, no. 1 (2009): 101–29.

Hirschhorn, James M. "The Separate Community: Military Uniqueness and Servicemen's Constitutional Rights." *North Carolina Law Review* 62 (1983–1984): 177–254.

Hodný, Jirí, and Radim ŠTastný. "Bullying in the Army of the Czech Republic." *The Journal of Slavic Military Studies* 10, no. 1 (1997): 128–40.

Hoewing, Gerald L., Delilah D. Rumburg, Anita M. Carpenter, Sharon K. G. Dunbar, Gina S. Farrisee, Louis V. Iasiello, and Alford L. McMichael. "The Report of the Defense Task Force of Sexual Harassment and Violence at the Military Service Academies." Department of Defense, 2005: 1–46.

Hofstede, Geert. *Cultures and Organizations: Software of the Mind*. (New York: McGraw-Hill, 1991).

Hogan, Robert. *Personality and the Fate of Organizations*. (Hillsdale, NJ: Erlbaum, 2006).

Hoglin, P. J., and N. Barton. "First-Term Attrition of Military Personnel in the Australian Defence Force." *Armed Forces and Society* 4, no. 1 (2015): 43–68.

Hollywood, Dana Michael. "Creating a True Army of One: Four Proposals to Combat Sexual Harassment in Today's Army." *Harvard Journal of Law & Gender* 30 (2007): 151–202.

Holtzman, Elizabeth, Barbara S. Jones, Victor Stone, Thomas W. Taylor, and Patricia A. Tracey. "Statistical Data Regarding Military Adjudication of Sexual Assault Offenses for Fiscal Year 2015." *Report of the Judicial Proceedings Since Fiscal Year 2012 Amendments Panel*, Judicial Proceedings Panel, 2017: 1–116.

Hooks, Gregory, and Brian McQueen. "American Exceptionalism Revisited: The Military-Industrial Complex, Racial Tension, and the Underdeveloped Welfare State." *American Sociological Review* 75, no. 2 (2010): 185–204.

Hopkins, C. Quince. "Rank Matters but Should Marriage?: Adultery, Fraternization, and Honor in the Military." *UCLA Women's Law Journal* 9, no. 2 (1999): 177–262.

Hoyle, Lindsay. "Command Responsibility—a Legal Obligation to Deter Sexual Violence in the Military." *Boston College International & Comparative Law Review* 37 (2014): 353–88.

Huestis, Bradley. "Anatomy of a Random Court-Martial Panel." *Army Lawyer* (2006): 22–32.

Hunter, Mic. *Honor Betrayed: Sexual Abuse in America's Military*. (Barricade Books, 2007).

Ignatieff, Michael, ed. *American Exceptionalism and Human Rights*. (Princeton University Press, 2005).
Immel, Steven M. "Development, Adoption, and Implementation of Military Sentencing Guidelines." *Miltary Law Review* 165 (2000): 159–236.
Iorfino, Alexandra. "Military Justice: Whether a Systematic Overhaul of the Uniform Code of Military Justice Is Required to Combat the Sexual Assault 'Epidemic.'" *Chapman's Journal of Law & Policy* 20 (2014–2015): 45–60.
Irons, Peter. "'The Constitution Is Just a Scrap of Paper': Empire versus Democracy." *University of Cincinnati Law Review* 73 (2005): 1081–99.
Irwin, Latisha. "Justice in Enlisted Administrative Separations." *Military Law Review* 225 (2017): 35–83.
Janowitz, Morris J. *Sociology and the Military Establishment* (Russel Sage Foundation, 1959).
———. *The Professional Soldier: A Social and Political Portrait*. (Glencoe Illinois: Free Press, 1960).
Jay, Alexis, Ivor Frank, Malcolm Evans, and Drusilla Sharpling. "The Independent Inquiry into Child Sexual Abuse." England and Wales, 2015.
Jeltsen, Melissa. "Air Force Failed to Enter Church Shooter's Domestic Violence Record in U.S. Database." *Huffington Post*, November 8, 2017.
Johnson, Christen A., and K. T. Hawbaker. "#Metoo: A Timeline of Events." *Chicago Tribune*, March 19, 2018.
Johnson, Jeh Charles, and Carter F. Ham. "Report of the Comprehensive Review of the Issues Associated with a Repeal of 'Don't Ask, Don't Tell'" Department of Defense, 2010: 266.
Joinet, Louis. "Issue of the Administration of Justice through Military Tribunals." UN Sub-Commission on the Promotion and Protection of Human Rights 54th session, 2002.
Jolliffe, J E A. *The Constitutional History of Medieval England from the English Settlement to 1485*. (New York: W W Norton and Company Inc, 1961).
Jones, Andee. "Abuse in the Military: Running with a Pack of Wolves."*ABC News*, January 23, 2012.
Jones, Gary L. "Collaborative Policing: A Facilitated Approach to AFP/RACMP Inter-Agency Co-Operation." Army Australian website (2017). https://www.army.gov.au/our-future/blog/strategy/collaborative-policing-a-facilitated-approach-to-afpracmp-inter-agency-co.
"Judge Rapke's Report on Recruit's Charges: Connolly Admitted Bullying." *Navy News*, 1971: 6.
Kagawa, Takashi. "Soldier's First Offense: Article 15 or Summary Court-Martial?" *Army Lawyer*, January (2014): 33–36.
Kaiser, Andre. "Parliamentary Opposition in Westminster Democracies: Britian, Canada, Australia and New Zealand." *The Journal of Legislative Studies* 14, no. 1 (2008): 20–45.
Karen J. Terry, Margaret Leland Smith, Katarina Schuth, James R. Kelly, Brenda Vollman, and Christina Massey. "The Causes and Context of Sexual Abuse of Minors by Catholic Priests in the United States, 1950–2010." Edited by John Jay

College Research Team, 143. (Washington, DC: United States Conference of Catholic Bishops, 2011).

Kassebaum-Baker, Nancy, Richard Allen, John Dancy, Robert H. Forman, Donald R. Gardner, Marcelite J. Harris, Deval L. Patrick, et al. "Federal Advisory Committee on Gender-Integrated Training and Related Issues." (Washington, D.C. U.S. Dept. of Defense, 1997).

Keehn, Shelbi Nicole. "Striking a Balance between Victim and Commanding Officer: Why Current Military Sexual Assault Reform Goes Too Far." *Columbia Journal of Law and Social Problems* 48. No. 3 (2015): 461–500.

Keller, Jared. "At Least 30 Marines Face Courts-Martial in 'Marines United' Investigation." *Task & Purpose*, Lafayette Media Group, May 1, 2017.

Keller, Kirsten M., Miriam Matthews, Kimberly Curry Hall, William Marcellino, Jacqueline A. Mauro, and Nelson Lim. *Hazing in the U.S. Armed Forces: Recommendations for Hazing Prevention Policy and Practice*. RAND Corporation, 2015.

Kellman, Barry. "Judicial Abdication of Military Tort Accountability: But Who Is to Guard the Guards Themselves?" *Duke Law Journal* (1989): 1597–639.

Kelly, Jeremy. "Ex-Digger Robert William Langdon Gets Death Sentence in Afghanistan." *NewsCore*, January 27, 2010.

———. "Former Australian Soldier Robert William Langdon Spared Death Penalty." *The Australian*, January 6, 2011.

Kemp, Kenneth W., and Charles Hudlin. "Civil Supremacy over the Military: Its Nature and Limits." *Armed Forces & Society* 19, no. 1 (1992): 7–26.

Kesler, Charles. "What Separation of Powers Means for Constitutional Government." *First Principles Series*, no. 17 (2007): 1–11.

Khan, Irene Zubaida. "The Rule of Law and the Politics of Fear: Human Rights in the Twenty-First Century." *Buffalo Human Rights Law Review* 14 (2008): 1–13.

Kilborn, Peter T. "Sex Abuse Cases Sting Pentagon, but the Problem Has Deep Roots." *New York Times*, February 10, 1997.

Kime, Patricia. "DoD Spends $84m a Year on Viagra, Similar Meds." *The Military Times*, February 13, 2015.

———. "Tragedy and Injustice: The Heartbreaking Truth about Military Medical Malpractice." *Military Times*, July 10, 2016.

Kingsbury, Benedict, and Benjamin Straumann. *The Roman Foundations of the Law of Nations: Alberico Gentili and the Justice of Empire*. (Oxford: Oxford University Press, 2010).

Knaul, Gabriela. "Report of the Special Rapporteur on the Independence of Judges and Lawyers." United Nations General Assembly, 2013.

Knaus, Christopher. "Royal Commission Reveals Scale of Child Sexual Abuse in Anglican Church." *The Guardian*, March 17, 2017.

Knaus, Christopher, and Michael Inman. "ADFA Skype Scandal Cadets Sentenced, Avoid Jail." *The Canberra Times*, October 23, 2013.

Knies, Jennifer S. "Two Steps Forward, One Step Back: Why the New UCMJ's Rape Law Missed the Mark." *Army Lawyer* (August 2007): 1–45.

Kohn, Richard. "The Erosion of Civilian Control of the Military in the United States Today." *Naval War College Review* 55, no. 3 (2002): 9–59.

———. "How Democracies Control the Military." *Journal of Democracy* 8, no. 4 (1997): 140–53.

Kohn, Richard H. "Comment on Professor Yoo, Administration of War." *Duke Law Journal* 58, no. 8 (2009): 2313–19.

Kontos, Alexis P. "'Private' Security Guards: Privatized Force and State Responsibility under International Human Rights Law." *Non-State Actors and International Law* 4 (2001): 199–238.

Kopel, David B., Paul Gallant, and Joanne D. Eisen. "The Human Right of Self-Defense." *Brigham Young University Journal of Public Law* 22, no. 3 (2007): 43–178.

Koziol, Michael. "Former SAS Trooper Breaks Down Telling Senate Inquiry of Brother's Attempted Suicide." *The Sydney Morning Herald*, November 18, 2016.

Krebs, Ronald R. "One Nation under Arms? Military Participation Policy and the Politics of Identity." *Security Studies* 14, no. 3 (2005): 529–64.

Kretowicz, Ewa. "Detention Rates Falling in Armed Force." *The Canberra Times*, July 21, 2013.

Kríž, Zdenek. "Army and Politics in the Czech Republic Twenty Years after the Velvet Revolution." *Armed Forces & Society* 36, no. 4 (2010): 627–46.

Kujat, H. "The Role of the Military in a Democracy." *NATO Information Seminar*, July 2–3, 1998. http://www.nato.int/docu/speech/1998/s980702h.htm.

Laguerre-Wilkinson, Magalie, and Phil Hirschkorn. "Pentagon Battling Military Rape 'Epidemic'" *CBSnews.com*, January 28, 2013.

Lai, David C. "Military Justice Incompetence over Competency Discriminations." *Military Law Review* 224 (2016): 48–86.

Laird, Lorelei. "Military Lawyers Confront Changes as Sexual Assault Becomes Big News." *ABA Journal*, September 1, 2013.

Lambert, Anthony. "Mediating Crime, Mediating Culture: Nationality, Femininity, Corporeality and Territory in the Schapelle Corby Drugs Case." *Crime, Media, Culture* 4, no. 2 (2008): 237–55.

Lamothe, Dan. "For the First Time, the Marine Corps Plans to Have a Female Infantry Officer among Its Ranks." *Washinghton Post*, September 21, 2017.

Landsman, Stephan. "A Brief Survey of the Development of the Adversary System." *Ohio State Law Journal* 44 (1983): 713–39.

Langdon, Allison. "D Is for Disgrace Episode 1–3." *60 Minutes, Channel 9NOW*, March 4, 2018. https://www.9now.com.au/60-minutes/2018/episode-3.

Laporta, James S., and Rory Laverty. "Marines Keep Sharing Women's Nude Photos in Secret Groups after Getting Busted" *The Daily Beast*, March 10, 2017.

Larkin Paul J. Jr. "Revenge Porn, State Law, and Free Speech." *Loyola of Los Angeles Law Review* 48 (2014): 57–117.

Leigh, Ian, Hans Born, Cecilia Lazzarini, and Ian Clements. *Handbook on Human Rights and Fundamental Freedoms of Armed Forces Personnel*. (Warsaw: OSCE Office for Democratic Institutions and Human Rights (ODIHR), 2008).

Levene, Lord, David Allen, Bjorn Conway, John Day, Gerry Grimstone, Nick Houghton, George Iacobescu, Raymond McKeeve, and Baroness Noakes. "Defence Reform; an Independent Report into the Structure and Management of the Ministry of Defence." UK Defence Reform Steering Group, 2011.

Levin, Stephanie A. "The Deference That Is Due: Rethinking the Jurisprudence of Judicial Deference to the Military." *Villanova Law Review* 35 (1990): 1009–61.

Levin, Carl, and John McCain, "Senate Armed Services Committee Inquiry into the Treatment of Detainees in US Custody." 2008: 1–19.

Lewis, Michael W. "Drones and the Boundaries of the Battlefield." *Texas International Law Journal* 47, no. 2 (2012): 293–314.

Lewis, Neil A. "Ex-Sergeant Pleads Guilty to Having Sex with Trainees." *New York Times*, April 8, 1997.

Lichtman, Steven B. "The Justices and the Generals: A Critical Examination of the U.S. Supreme Court's Tradition of Deference to the Military, 1918–2004." *Maryland Law Review* 65 (2006): 907–65.

Light, Mark F. "The Navy's Moral Compass. Commanding Officers and Personal Misconduct." *Naval War College Review* 65, no. 3 (2012): 136–52.

Lineberry, Timothy W., and Stephen S. O'Connor. "Suicide in the US Army." *Mayo Clinic Proceedings* 87, no. 9 (2012): 871–78.

Lion, Patrick. "ADF Investigation Service Sent 'Insulting and Humiliating' Emails." *News Corp Australia Network*, June 21, 2013.

Lipari, Rachel N., Paul J. Cook, Lindsay M. Rock, and Kenneth Matos. "Gender Relations Survey of Active Duty Members." Defense Manpower Data Center Report No. 2007-022 Arlington, VA, 2006: 1–246.

Lisak, David, and Paul M. Miller. "Repeat Rape and Multiple Offending among Undetected Rapists." *Violence and Victims* 17, no. 1 (2002): 73–84.

Lohman, Alexandra. "Silence of the Lambs: Giving Voice to the Problem of Rape and Sexual Assault in the United States Armed Forces." *Northwestern Journal of Law & Social Policy* 10, no. 1 (2015): 230–79.

"The Long Term Perspective for Defence 2030." Prague: Ministry of Defence of the Czech Republic, 2015.

Lopez, German. "Trump: Allowing Transgender Military Service Would Hurt Combat Readiness. Actual Research: Nope." *Vox Media*, July 26, 2017.

Lorsch, Jay W., and Emily McTague. "Culture Is Not the Culprit." *Harvard Business Review*, April (2016): 96–105.

Luban, David. "On the Commander in Chief Power." *Southern California Law Review* 81 (2008): 477–569.

Ludwig, Dean C., and Clinton O. Longenecker. "The Bathsheba Syndrome: The Ethical Failure of Successful Leaders." *Journal of Business Ethics* (1993): 265–73.

Lurie, Jonathan. *Military Justice in America. The U.S. Court of Appeals for the Armed Forces, 1775–1980*. (University Press of Kansas, 1998).

Lusher, Dean, Peter Kremer, and Garry Robins. "Cooperative and Competitive Structures of Trust Relations in Teams." *Small Group Research* 45, no. 1 (2014): 3–36.

Lynch, Colman. "Indonesia's Use of Capital Punishment for Drug-Trafficking Crimes: Legal Obligations, Extralegal Factors, and the Bali Nine Case." *Columbia Human Rights Law Review* 40 (2008): 523–93.

Macdonald, Roderick A. Nathalie Des Rosiers, Gwen Boniface, Stephen Owen, and Alan Buchanan. "Restoring Dignity: Responding to Child Abuse in Canadian Institutions." Ottawa, Ontaria: Law Commission of Canada, 2010: 455.

MacDonnell, Timothy C. "Military Commissions and Courts-Martial: A Brief Discussion of the Constitutional and Jurisdictional Distinctions between the Two Courts." *Army Lawyer*, January (2015): 6–25.

Machiavelli, Niccolò. *The Art of War 1517–1520*. (Translated by Neal Wood. Indianapolis: Bobbs-Merrill, 1521).

Mackerras, Malcolm. *European Journal of Political Research* 43, no. 7–8 (December 6, 2004): 927–33.

MacKinnon, Catharine A. "Rape Redefined." *Harvard Law & Policy Review* 10 (2016): 431–77.

MacLean, Norbert Basil. "Separate and Unequal Military Justice." *Los Angeles Times*, September 10, 2008.

MacManus, Deirdre, Kimberlie Dean, Amy C. Iversen, Lisa Hull, Norman Jones, Tom Fahy, Simon Wessely, and Nicola T. Fear. "Impact of Pre-Enlistment Antisocial Behaviour on Behavioural Outcomes among UK Military Personnel." *Social Psychiatry and Psychiatric Epidemiology* 47, no. 8 (2012): 1353–58.

MacManus, Deirdre, Roberto Rona, Hannah Dickson, Greta Somaini, Nicola Fear, and Simon Wessely. "Aggressive and Violent Behavior among Military Personnel Deployed to Iraq and Afghanistan: Prevalence and Link with Deployment and Combat Exposure." *Epidemiologic Reviews* 37 (2015): 196–212.

Marquis, Jefferson P., Coreen Farris, Kimberly Curry Hall, Kristy N. Kamarck, Nelson Lim, Douglas Shontz, Paul S. Steinberg. "Improving Oversight and Coordination of Department of Defense Programs that Address Problematic Behaviors among Military Personnel." Santa Monica: RAND Corporation, 2017: 1–172.

Mascaro, Lisa. "Senate Rejects Stronger Military Sexual Assault Bill." *Los Angeles Times*, March 6, 2014.

Masick, Erik D. "Moral Injury and Preventative Law: A Framework for the Future." *Military Law Review* 224 (2016): 223–89.

Masterton, R. Peter. "Recent Developments in Military Justice." *Federal Lawyer* 63, no. 9 (2016): 8–19.

Matheson, S. H. "The Committee for Evaluation of the Effectiveness of the Administration of Military Justice." *Report to General William C. Westmoreland, Chief of Staff, U.S. Army*, 1971.

Mazur, Diane H. "Rehnquist's Vietnam: Constitutional Separatism and the Stealth Advance of Martial Law." *Indiana Law Journal* 77 (2002): 701–85.

Mazurek, Rostislav, and Vladimír Karaffa. "Doctrine of the Armed Forces of the Czech Republic." Vyškov: Ministry of Defence, Joint Forces Command, University of Defence and Training and Doctrine Directorate, 2004:145.

McClellan, Peter, Robert Fitzgerald, Robert Atkinson, Helen Milroy, Jennifer Coate, and Andrew Murray. "Interium Report." *Royal Commission into Institutional Responses to Child Sexual Abuse*. Barton, ACT: Attorney-General's Department, 2014: 1–344.

McClellan, Peter, Robert Fitzgerald, and Helen Milroy. "Report of Case Study No. 40. The Response of the Australian Defence Force to Allegations of Child Sexual Abuse." Commonwealth of Australia: *Royal Commission into Institutional Responses to Child Sexual Abuse*. Barton, ACT: Attorney-General's Department, 2017: 1–174.

———. "Royal Commission into Institutional Responses to Child Sexual Abuse." Commonwealth of Australia, Barton, ACT: Attorney-General's Department, 2017.

McClelland, J. "Starting from Scratch: The Military Discipline System of the East Timor Defence Force." *Journal of Conflict and Security Law* 7 (2002): 253–73.

McDade, Lyn. "Director of Military Prosecutions Annual Report for the Period 12 June 2006 to 31 December 2007." Commonwealth of Australia, 1–59.

McDonald, Alex. "'Jedi Council' Ringleader Hastings Fredrickson. Who Shared Photos of Sex Acts Facing Correction Order." *ABC News*, February 9, 2015.

McPhedran, Ian. "Senior Australian Defence Force Investigator Risked Execution When She Carried Heroin from Afghanistan to Dubai." *The Courier Mail*, May 29, 2012.

———. "Defence Sex Scandal: Cadet Secretly Filmed Liaison with Colleague," *Adelaide Advertiser*, April 6, 2011, 17.

Merrill, Lex L., Cynthia J. Thomsen, Steven R. Gold, and Joel S. Milner. "Childhood Abuse and Premilitary Sexual Assault in Male Navy Recruits." *Journal of Consulting and Clinical Psychology* 69, no. 2 (2001): 252–61.

Merrill, Robert D. "The Military's Dilution of Double Jeopardy: Why United States v. Easton Should Be Overturned." *Military Law Review* 219 (2014): 176–95.

"Military Academy Sexual Harassment Report Survivors of Sexual Assault and Harassment in Military Academies. "House Armed Services Subcommittee on Military Subcommittee on Military Personnel, 2017.

"Military Court of Australia Bill 2010 a Submission by the Returned & Services League of Australia." (2010): 1–18.

"Military Law—Justiciability—Eastern District of Virginia Dismisses Suit against Government for Military Sexual Assaults—*Baldwin v. Department of Defense* No. I:15-CV-OO424 (E.D. Va. Oct. 14, 2016)." *Harvard Law Review* 130 (2017): 2243–50.

"Military Sexual Assault Amendment Defeated in Defense Bill Markup " *Clip of Fiscal Year 2018 Defense Authorization Markup* Part 2 (2017). https://www.c-span.org/video/?c4675219/military-sexual-assault-amendment-defeated-defense-bill-markup.

"Military Unions and Associations." Ch. 9 *Handboook on Human Rights and Fundamental Freedoms of Armed Forces Personnel*, edited by Ian Leigh, Hans Born, Cecilia Lazzarini, and Ian Clements, 65–73. (Warsaw: OSCE Office for Democratic Institutions and Human Rights (ODIHR), 2008).

"Military Veterans in the Next Congress." *Los Angeles Times*, November 5, 2014.

Millar, Lisa. "Ireland Has Lessons for Australia Eight Years after Its Own Child Abuse Commission of Inquiry." *ABC News*, December 14, 2017.

Ministry of Defence of the Czech Republic, "White Paper on Defence." (Prague: Department of Communication and Promotion, 2011).

Mitchell, Andrew D. "Too Close for Comfort: Lane v. Morrison and Its effect on Australian Military Justice."*Public Law Review*, 2, no. 1 (2010): 9–13.

Mitchell, Natasha, and Brandon Bryant. "Drone Warfare and the Psyche: An Insider Speaks." *Radio National Broadcast*, August 19, 2017.

Montgomery, Nancy. "Emails Show General Warned against Reversing Wilkerson Verdict." *Stars and Stripes*, August 29, 2013.

Moorman, William A. "Fifty Years of Military Justice: Does the Uniform Code of Military Justice Need to Be Changed?" *The Air Force Law Review* 48 (2000): 185–94.

"More Nude Photos of Female Military Personnel Shared Online, 1 Year after Marines United Scandal." *RT News*, March 10, 2018.

Morral, Andrew R., Kristie L. Gore, and Terry L. Schell. "Sexual Assault and Sexual Harrasment—Top-Line Estimates for Active-Duty Service Members from the RAND Military Workplace Study in Andrew R. Morral, Kristie L. Gore, and Terry L. Schell, "Sexual Assault and Sexual Harrasment in the U.S. Military" (Santa Monica, CA: RAND Corporation, 2014).

Morrison, David. "Address to the Closing Plenary Session at the Global Summit to End Sexual Violence in Conflict." London, UK, June 13, 2014.

David Morrison "Respect—The Fourth Value Remarks." Speech, Townsville (2013).

Murdock, Sebastian. "Texas Church Shooter Escaped from Behavioral Health Facility in 2012." *Huffington Post*, November 8, 2017.

Murdough, Robert E. "Barracks, Dormitories, and Capitol Hill: Finding Justice in the Divergent Politics of Military and College Sexual Assault." *Military Law Review* 223, no. 2 (2015): 223–311.

Murphy, Cullen. *The New Rome? The Fall of an Empire and the Fate of America.* (Carlton North, Victoria: Scribe Publications Ltd, 2007).

Murphy, Yvonne, Ita Mangan, and Hugh O'Neill. "Commission of Investigation. Report into the Catholic Archdiocese of Dublin." Dublin, 2009.

Nagin, Daniel S., and Greg Pogarsky. "Time and Punishment: Delayed Consequences and Criminal Behavior." *Journal of Quantitative Criminology* 20, no. 4 (2004): 295–317.

Nelson, Daniel N. "Civil Armies, Civil Societies and NATO's Enlargement." *Armed Forces & Society* 25 (1998): 137–59.

Nelson, Teri Spahr *For Love of Country: Confronting Rape and Sexual Harassment in the U.S. Military*. (New York: Routledge, 2002).

Nevin, Jack, and Joshua R. Lorenz. "Neither a Model of Clarity nor a Model Statute: An Analysis of the History, Challenges, and Suggested Changes to the New Article 120." *The Air Force Law Review* 67 (2011): 269–91.

Newman, Richard J. "Upheaval at the Academy." *Air Force Magazine* (January 2004): 56–59.

Niskanen, William. *A Bureaucracy and Representative Government.* (Aldine-Atherton, 1971).

Nolte, George, and Heike Krieger. "European Military Law Systems: General Comparative Report." In *European Military Law Systems*, edited by George Nolte, 19–182. (Berlin: De Gruyter Recht, 2003).

Norris, Pippa. *Driving Democracy: Do Power-Sharing Institutions Work?* (Cambridge: (Cambridge University Press, 2008).

"Nude Photo Scandal Grows to 21 Felony Cases as Military Scours Web for Evidence." *CBS News*, May 5, 2017.

O'Connor, Phillip. "New Sex Scandals at Fort Leonard Wood." *St. Louis Post-Dispatch*, November 23, 2008.

Orme, C. W. "Beyond Compliance—Professionalism, Trust, Capability in the Australian Profession of Arms." *Report of the ADF Personal Conduct Review*, Commonwealth of Australia, Canberra: Department of Defense, 2011: 1–68.

Ortiz, Erik. "Pentagon Chief James Mattis Calls Marines' Photo Scandal 'Unacceptable.'" *NBC.News*, March 11, 2017.

Otto, Jean L., and Bryant J. Webber. "Mental Health Diagnoses and Counseling among Pilots of Remotely Piloted Aircraft in the United States Air Force." *Medicial Surveillance Monthly Report* 20, no. 3 (2013): 3–8.

OuYang, Elizabeth R. "Can Military Courts Deliver Justice to a Subordinate Hazed by Superiors?" *Asian American Policy Review* 23 (2012): 81–87.

Padilla, Art, Robert Hogan, and Robert B. Kaiser. "The Toxic Triangle: Destructive Leaders, Susceptible Followers, and Conducive Environments." *The Leadership Quarterly* 18 (2007): 176–94.

Padilla, Mary, and Kristin Williams. "Workplace and Gender Relations Survey of Reserve Component Members: Tabulations of Responses." Defense Manpower Data Center. Alexandria, VA: Human Resources Strategic Assessment Program, 2013.

Parsons, Elizabeth, and Vincenza Priola. "Agents for Change and Changed Agents: The Micro-politics of Change and Feminism in the Academy." *Gender, Work and Organization* 20, no. 5 (2013): 580–98.

Philbin, Tom, and Michael Philbin. *The Killer Book of Serial Killers*. (Sourcebooks, Inc., 2009).

Pipon, J. F., and J. K. Collier. *Manual of Military Law*. (3rd Revised ed. London: William H Allen, 1860).

Piquero, Alex R., Zenta Gomez-Smith, and Lynn Langton. "Discerning Unfairness Where Others May Not: Low Self-Control and Unfair Sanction Perceptions." *Criminology* 42 (2004): 699–733.

Pittman, Thomas Wayde, and Matthew Heaphy. "Does the United States Really Prosecute Its Service Members for War Crimes? Implications for Complementarity before the International Criminal Court." *Leiden Journal of International Law* 21 (2008): 165–83.

Pollock, Sir Frederick, and Frederic William Maitland. *The History of English Law. Before the Time of Edward I.* (2nd ed. Vol. I, Cambridge: Cambridge University Press, 1968).

Powell, Herbert B. "Committee on the Uniform Code of Military Justice, Good Order and Discipline in the Army." *Report to the Honourable Wilber M. Brucker, Secretary of the Army*, United States Department of Defense, 1960: 284.

Price, Terry L. "Explaining Ethical Failures of Leadership." *Leadership & Organization Development Journal* 21, no. 4 (2000): 177–84.

Quinn, Kathryn. "Sexual Harassment in the Australian Defence Force." Canberra: Commonwealth of Australia, 1996.

Ralston, David B., ed. *Soldiers and States. Civil-Military Relations in Modern Europe*. (Massachusetts Institute of Technology, Studies in History and Politics. Boston: D.C. Heath and Company, 1966).

Raz, Joseph. "The Rule of Law and Its Virtue." *Law Quarterly Review* 93 (1977): 193–211.

Reed, Robert, et al. "Sex Crimes and the UCMJ." *A Report for the Joint Service Committee on Military Justice*, Department of Defence, 2005: 1–826.

"Report on Internal Security and Public Order in the Czech Republic in 2015." Prague: Ministry of the Interior of the Czech Republic, Security Policy and Crime Prevention Department Analyses and Strategies Unit, 2016.

"Reporting Rape in 2013, Summary Reporting System (SRS) User Manual and Technical Specification." *Criminal Justice Information Services (CJIS) Division Uniform Crime Reporting (UCR) Program*, Law Enforcement Support Section, U.S. Department of Justice. Federal Bureau of Investigation, 2014: 1–20.

Riley, Ryan, Trevor Conrad, Josh Hatfield, and Heidi Keller-Glaze. "2011 Annual Survey of Army Leadership (Casal): Military Leader Findings." Fort Leavenworth: Center for Army Leadership, 2012, 20.

Riley, Ryan, Josh Hatfield, and Tyler E. Freeman. "2014 Annual Survey of Army Leadership (Casal): Military Leader Findings." Fort Leavenworth: Center for Army Leadership, 2015: 1–126.

Risen, James. "Attacked at 19 by an Air Force Trainer, and Speaking Out." *New York Times*, February 27, 2013.

Rishikof, Harvey. "Institutional Ethics Drawing Lines for Militant Democracies." *Joint Force Quarterly* 54 (2009): 48–54.

Roan, James B, and Cynthia Buxton. "The American Military Justice System in the New Millennium." *The Air Force Law Review* 52 (2002): 185–211.

Roberts-Smith, Len. "A Nettle Grasped Lightly: The Introduction of the Australian Military Court." Paper presented at the 2007 Judicial Conference, Washington, DC, May 17, 2007.

———. "Seventh Interim Report to the Attorney-General and the Minister for Defence." Defence Abuse Response Taskforce, 2014.

Robinson, Geoffrey. *For Christ's Sake: End Sexual Abuse in the Catholic Church . . . For Good.* (Australia: Garratt Publishing, 2013).

———. "For Christ's Sake: Confronting the Culture of Abuse within the Catholic Church." ABC, November 13, 2012, http://www.abc.net.au/religion/articles/2012/11/13/3632146.htm.

———. "Confronting Power and Sex in the Catholic Church: Reclaiming the Spirit of Jesus." *Sophia* 47, no. 2 (2008): 231–39.

Robinson, Shirleene. "Witch-Hunts and Surveillance: The Hidden Lives of Queer People in the Military." *The Conversation*, April 25, 2017. https://theconversation.com/witch-hunts-and-surveillance-the-hidden-lives-of-queer-people-in-the-military-76156.

Rock, Lindsay M., Rachel N. Lipari, Paul J. Cook, and Andrew D. Hale. "Workplace and Gender Relations Survey of Active Duty Members: Overview Report on Sexual Assault." Arlington, VA, 2010: 1–126.

Rogowski, Danielle. "Quis Custodiet Ipsos Custodies? The Current State of Sexual Assault Reform within the U.S. Military and the Need for the Use of a Formal Decision Making Process in Further Reform." *Seattle University Law Review* 38 (2015): 1139–173.

Rokeach, Milton. *The Nature of Human Values*. (New York: The Free Press, 1973).

Rosenblatt, Franklin D. "Non-Deployable: The Court-martial System in Combat from 2001 to 2009." *Creighton Law Review* 44 (2011): 1045–90.

Rosenthal, Marc Edward. "Where Is the Justice? The Sexual Assault Crisis Plaguing the Military and a Lack of Meaningful Justice." *University of Miami National Security & Armed Conflict Law Review* 41 (2013): 295–343.

Ross, James. "Black Letter Abuse: The US Legal Response to Torture Since 9/11." *International Review of the Red Cross* 89, no. 867 (2007): 561–90.

Rostker, Bernard D., Susan Hosek, and John D. Winkler. *Sexual Orientation and U.S. Military Personnel Policy: An Update of Rand's 1993 Study*. National Defense Research Institute and National Defense Research Institute Santa Monica: RAND Corporation, 2010.

Rough, Jill A., and David J. Armor. "Sexual Assault in the U.S. Military: Trends and Responses." *World Medical & Health Policy* 9, no. 2 (2017): 206–24.

Rowe, Peter. *The Impact of Human Rights Law on Armed Forces*. (Cambridge: Cambridge University Press, 2006).

———. "The Soldier as a Citizen in Uniform: A Reappraisal." *N.Z. Armed Forces Law Review* 7 (2007): 1–17.

Rumble, Gary, Melanie McKean, and Dennis Pearce. "Report of the Review of Allegations of Sexual and Other Abuse in Defence. Facing the Problems of the Past." DLA Piper Review (2011): 1567.

Rust, Michael. "Expansion of the Feres Doctrine." *Emory Law Journal* 32 (1983): 237–71.

Rustico, Greg. "Overcoming Overcorrection: Towards Holistic Military Sexual Assault Reform." *Virginia Law Review* 102 (2016): 2027–2074.

Ryan, Mick. "A Study of Army's Education, Training and Doctrine Needs for the Future." *The Ryan Review*, Commonwealth of Australia, 2016.

Ryan, Sean, Norah Gibbons, Fred Lowe, Marian Shanley, Edward Tempany, Anne McLoughlin, and Mary Fennessy. "The Commission to Inquire into Child Abuse." Dublin: Government of Ireland, 2009:2,500.

Sabur, Rozina. "Mass Grave of Up to 800 Children Found Underground at a Former Home for Unmarried Mothers and Their Babies in Ireland." *The Telegraph*, March 3, 2017.

Sageer, Alam, Sameena Rafat, and Puja Agarwal. "Identification of Variables Affecting Employee Satisfaction and Their Impact on the Organization." *Journal of Business and Management* 5, no. 1 (2012): 32–39.

Samuelsohn, Darren. "McCaskill's Sexual Assault Bill Passes." *Politico Pro*, October 3, 2014.

Sarvaš, Štefan. "The NATO Enlargement Debate in the Media and Civil-Military Relations in the Czech Republic and Slovakia." *European Security* 9, no. 1 (2000): 113–26.

Schaefer, Agnes Gereben, Radha Iyengar, Srikanth Kadiyala, Jennifer Kavanagh, Charles C. Engel, Kayla M. Williams, and Amii M. Kress. "Assessing the Implications of Allowing Transgender Personnel to Serve Openly." National Security Research Division, RAND Corporation, 2016: 1–112.

Schenck, Lisa M. "Informing the Debate About Sexual Assault in the Military Services: Is the Department of Defense Its Own Worst Enemy?" *Ohio State Journal of Criminal Law* 11 (2014): 579–671.

———. "'Just the Facts, Ma'am': How Military Appellate Courts Rely on Factual Sufficiency Review to Overturn Sexual Assault Cases When Victims Are 'Incapacitated'" *Southwestern Law Review* 45 (2016): 523–60.

Schlueter, David A. "American Military Justice: Responding to the Siren Songs for Reform." *The Air Force Law Review* 73 (2015): 193–232.

———. "The Military Justice Conundrum: Justice or Discipline?" *Military Law Review* 215 (2013): 1–74.

Schmid, Megan N. "This Court-Martial Hereby (Arbitrarily) Sentences You: Problems with Court Member Sentencing in the Military and Proposed Solutions." *The Air Force Law Review* 67 (2011): 245–68.

Schmidle, Nicholas. "Three Trials for Murder. In the Name of Justice, Did the Military Sidestep Double Jeopardy?" *New Yorker*, November 14, 2011.

Schmidt, Michael S., and Matt Apuzzo. "David Petraeus Is Sentenced to Probation in Leak Investigation." *New York Times*, April 23, 2015: A16.

Schmidtchen, David. *The Rise of the Strategic Private. Technology, Control and Change in a Network-Enabled Military*. The General Sir Brunenell White Series. Canberra: Commonwealth of Australia, Land Warfare Studies Centre, 2006.

Schmitt, Eric. "Judge Dismisses Tailhook Cases, Saying Admiral Tainted Inquiry" *New York Times*, February 9, 1994.

Schwartz, David Saul. "Making Intramilitary Tort Law More Civil: A Proposed Reform of the Feres Doctrine." *The Yale Law Journal* 95, no. 5 (1986): 992–1016.

Schwartz, Shalom H., and Florencia M. Sortheix. "Values and Subjective Well-Being," in *Handbook of Well-Being*, edited by E. Diener, S. Oishi, and L. Tay. (Salt Lake City, UT: DEF Publishers 2018).

Seidman, Guy I. "The Origins of Accountability: Everything I Know about the Sovereign's Immunity, I Learned from King Henry III." *Saint Louis University Law Journal* 49 (2005): 393–480.

Semple, Kirk. "Army Officer Reaches Deal in the Suicide of a Private." *New York Times*, 2012, A24.

Senate Foreign Affairs, Defence and Trade References Committee. "The Effectiveness of Australia's Military Justice System." Commonwealth of Australia. Canberra: Foreign Affairs, Defence and Trade References Committee, 2005.

Shadley, Robert D. *The Game: Unraveling a Military Sex Scandal*. (Beaver's Pond Press, 2013).

Shanker, Thom. "West Point Sergeant Pleads Guilty to Videotaping Female Cadets." *The Washington Post*, March 7, 2014: A18.

Sherman, Edward. "Legal Inadequacies and Doctrinal Restraints in Controlling the Military." *Indiana Law Journal* 49 (1974): 539–80.

———. "The Civilianization of Military Law." *Maine Law Review* 22 (1970): 3–103.

———. "Military Justice without Military Control." *The Yale Law Journal* 82, no. 7 (1973): 1398–425.

Sherrill, Robert. *Military Justice Is to Justice as Military Music Is to Music*. (New York: Harper & Row, 1969).

Shin, Annys. "Judge Finds Midshipman Not Guilty in Naval Academy Sex Assault Case." *The Washington Post*, March 20, 2014.

Siegfried, Richard S., Evelyn P. Foote, John P. McLaurin Ill, Claudia J. Kennedy, Larry R. Ellis, Ruby B. DeMesme, and Cynthia A. Pritchett. "The Secretary of the Army's Senior Review Panel Report on Sexual Harassment." U.S. Dept. of Defense, 1997: 1–91.

Silverstein, Ken. *Private Warriors*. (London: Verso, 2000).

Simms, Suzanne. "Revision of Article 60 and the Military Convening Authority's Clemency Power: An Alternative to the Enacted Legislation." *National Security Law Journal* 2, no. 2 (2014): 301–30.

Singer, P. W. *Corporate Warriors: The Rise of the Privatized Military Industry*. (London: Cornell University Press, 2008. Updated paperback ed).

Sirico, Louis J. "The Federalist and the Lessons of Rome." *Mississippi Law Journal* 75, no. 2 (2006): 431–94.

Sloan, John. "Machiavelli on War." http://www.xenophon-mil.org/milhist/renaissance/machessy.htm.

Smawley, George R. "Making Justice Flat: A Challenge to the View that Deploying Commanders Must Relinquish Command and General Court-Martial Convening Authority over Non-Deploying Forces." *Army Lawyer* (2013): 29–36.

Smith, Anne. "The Scottish Child Abuse Inquiry." (Edinburgh: Scottish Government, 2015).

Smith. Stephen "Paper Presented on the Defence Abuse Response Taskforce." *Press Release*, June 20, 2013. http://www.minister.defence.gov.au/2013/06/20/minister-for-defence-stephen-smith-paper-presented-on-the-defence-abuse-response-taskforce/.

Smol, Robert. "Why We Should Unionize the Military." *National Post*, May 20, 2015.

Snell, Angela. "The Absence of Justice: Private Military Contractors, Sexual Assault, and the U.S. Government's Policy of Indifference." *University of Illinois Law Review* (2011): 1125–163.

Snowden, David L., Sehun Oh, Christopher P. Salas-Wright, Michael G. Vaughn, and Erika King. "Military Service and Crime: New Evidence." *Social Psychiatry and Psychiatric Epidemiology* 52, no. 5 (2017): 605–15.

Social Research Centre, Melbourne. "Public Opinion towards Governance: Results from the Inaugural Anu Poll." (2008). publicpolicy.anu.edu.au/anupoll/.../2008-04-16_ANUpoll_governance_report.pdf

———. "Attitudes to Government and Government Services, 2011. http://csrm.cass.anu.edu.au/research/publications/attitudes-government-and-government-services.

Spak, Michael I., and Alice M. McCart. "Effect of Military Culture on Responding to Sexual Harassment: The Warrior Mystique." *Nebraska Law Review* 83, no. 1 (2004): 79–113.

Spak, Michael I., and Jonathan P. Tomes. "Sexual Harassment in the Military: Time for a Change of Forum." *Cleveland State Law Review* 47 (1999): 335–69.

Speier, Jackie. "Rep Speier Demands Protection for Military's Most Vulnerable; Introduces Legislation to Shield Trainees from Sexual Assault by Instructors." *Press Release*, January 28, 2013. https://speier.house.gov/media-center/press-releases/rep-speier-demands-protection-militarys-most-vulnerable-introduces.

———. "Reps Speier, Braley and Meehan Introduce Bipartisan Bill to Prevent Military Commanders from Overturning Convictions." *Press Release*, March 12, 2013. https://speier.house.gov/media-center/press-releases/reps-speier-braley-and-meehan-introduce-bipartisan-bill-prevent-military.

Spilman, Zachary D. "Not Helping: How Congressional Tinkering Harms Victims during the Post-Trial Phase of a Court-Martial." *Columbia Law Review* 114 (2014): Sidebar 70.

Squibb, G. D. *The High Court of Chivalry: A Study of the Civil Law in England.* (Oxford: Oxford University Press, 1959).

Stahlman, Shauna, Marjan Javanbakht, Susan Cochran, Alison B. Hamilton, Steven Shoptaw, and Pamina M. Gorbach. "Self-Reported STIS and Sexual Risk Behaviors in the U.S. Military: How Gender Influences Risk." *Sexually Transmitted Diseases* 41, no. 6 (2014): 359–64.

Steiger, Kay. "This Lawsuit Could Change How the Military Handles Sexual Assault." *Think Progress.org*, April 2, 2015. https://thinkprogress.org/this-lawsuit-could-change-how-the-military-handles-sexual-assault-b6d70f7e200c/.

Steinhauer, Jennifer. "Remark by Obama Complicates Military Sexual Assault Trials." *New York Times*, July 14, 2013: A1.

Stellios, James. "The Dismantling of the Australian Military Court: Lane v. Morrison." *The Australian Centre for Military Law and Justice*, no. 2 (2010): 3–6.

Stephens, Jeremy. "Factually Insufficient: A Response to the Military Justice Review Group's Appellate Review Proposal." *Army Lawyer* (2016): 32–38.

Sternberg, Robert J., and Todd I. Lubart. *Defying the Crowd. Cultivating Creativity in a Culture of Conformity*. (New York: The Free Press, 1995).

Steward, Marcia Reyes. "A Higher Call: An Incredible True Story of Combat and Chivalry in the War-Torn Skies of World War II." *Army Lawyer*, (December 2014): 20–23.

Stiglitz, Joseph, and Linda J. Bilmes. *The Three Trillion Dollar War: The True Cost of the Iraq Conflict*. (W W Norton, 2008).

Strassfeld, Robert. "The Vietnam War on Trial: The Court-Martial of Dr. Howard B. Levy." *Wisconsin Law Review* (1994): 839–963.

Street, Alexander. "Australian Military Justice and Chapter III Where to Next?" Paper presented at the APCML/CCSJoint Seminar, October 6, 2009.

———. "Submission No 2 of Alexander Street SC." *Inquiry into the Military Court of Australia Bill 2012 and Military Court of Australia (Transition Provisions and Consequential Amendments) Bill 2012*, July 11, 2012. http://www.aph.gov.au/DocumentStore.ashx?id=3846db08-d509-42cd-8c36-e3eb12fb9157.

Street, Sir Laurence, and Air Marshal Les Fischer. "Report of the Independent Review on the Health of the Reformed Military Justice System." Canberra, 2009.

Strosnider, Kim. "FBI Investigates Charges that Female Cadets at the Citadel Were Hazed." *Chronicle of Higher Education* 43, no. 18 (1997): A51.

Substance Abuse and Mental Health Services Administration (SAMHSA). "Veterans and Military Families." 2017. https://www.samhsa.gov/veterans-military-families.

Sullivan, Dwight. "Top 10 Military Justice Stories of 2010: The Reconviction and Death Sentence of MSGT Timothy Hennis (Ret.)." *Nimj blog*, January 2, 2011. http://www.caaflog.com/2011/01/02/top-10-military-justice-stories-of-2010.

Sykes, Andrew. "The 'Rule of Law' as an Australian Constitutionalist Promise." *Murdoch University Electronic Journal of Law* 9, no. 1 (2002): 1.

Taft, Casey T., Candice M. Monson, Claire L. Hebenstreit, Daniel W. King, and Lynda A. King. "Examining the Correlates of Aggression among Male and Female Vietnam Veterans." *Violence and Victims* 24, no. 5 (2009): 639–52.

Tapsell, Kieran. "Child Sexual Abuse and the City of Man: A Response to Philip Almond." *ABC Religion and Ethics*, no. October 23, 2017: Opinion. http://www.abc.net.au/religion/articles/2017/10/23/4754231.htm.

———. "On Abuse: Francis Yet to Make Critical Clerical Changes." *National Catholic Reporter*, July 28, 2017. https://www.ncronline.org/news/accountability/abuse-francis-yet-make-critical-clerical-changes.

———. "Sex Abuse and the Seal of the Confessional." *National Catholic Reporter*, August 18, 2017. https://www.ncronline.org/news/opinion/sex-abuse-and-seal-confessional.

Taylor, Marisa. "Senate Rejects Bill to Reform Sexual Assault Prosecution in the Military." *Aljazeera America*, June 17, 2015.

Terry, Karen, and Jennifer Tallon. "The Nature and Scope of Sexual Abuse of Minors by Catholic Priests and Deacons in the United States 1950–2002." The John Jay College of Criminal Justice; The City University of New York., Washington, D.C, The United States Conference of Catholic Bishops, 2004, 285.

Thompson, Mark. "'Don't Ask, Don't Tell' Turns 15." *Time*, January 28, 2008.

———. "Military Sexual Assault Victims Discharged after Filing Complaints." *Time*, May 18, 2016.

Thornton, Margaret. "Sexual Harrasment Losing Sight of Sex Discrimination." *Melbourne University Law Review* 26 (2002): 422–44.

Tomes, Jonathan P., and Michael I. Spak. "Practical Problems with Modifying the Military Justice System to Better Handle Sexual Assault Cases." *Wisconsin Journal of Law, Gender & Society* 29 (2014): 377–408.

Tomlins, Sir Thomas Edlyne. *The Law-Dictionary, Explaining the Rise, Progress, and Present State of the British Law: Defining and Interpreting the Terms or Words of Art, and Comprising Also Copious Information on the Subjects of Trade and Government*. Edited by J. and W. T. Clarke. 4 ed. Vol. 1: (Oxford University, 1835. Digitized September 18, 2006.)

Tracy, Carol E., Terry L. Fromson, Jennifer Gentile Long, and Charlene Whitman. "Rape and Sexual Assault in the Legal System." *Women's Law Project and AEquitas* (2013). http://jpp.whs.mil/Public/docs/04-Meetings/sub-20150507/03_Rape_SexAsslt_LegalSystem_WLP_AEQuitas_20120605.pdf.

Tsouras, Peter, ed. *Warriors' Words: A Dictionary of Military Quotations*. (London: Arms and Armour Press: A Cassell Imprint, 1994).

Turchik, Jessica A., and Susan M.Wilson. "Sexual Assault in the U.S. Military: A Review of the Literature and Recommendations for the Future." *Aggression and Violent Behavior* 15, no. 4 (2010): 267–77.

Turley, Jonathan. "The Military Pocket Republic." *Northwestern University Law Review* 97 (2002): 1–133.

Twomey, Anne. "Review of High Court Constitutional Cases 2007." *UNSW Law Journal* 31, no. 1 (2007): 215–37.

Tyrrell, Peter, and Diarmuid Whelan. *Founded on Fear* (Dublin Transworld Ireland, 2006).

Ulmer, Walter F. Jr. "Toxic Leadership. What Are We Talking About?" *Army* (June 2012): 47–52.

Usborne, David. "Soldiers, Sexual Abuse—and the Serial Killer: The US Military's Secret Sexual Assaults." *The Independent*, June 28, 2013.

Verschuur, Paul. "Redefining What Makes a Good Soldier: Dutch Army Steps to a Different Drum." *Associated Press*, April 23, 1998. http://articles.latimes.com/1989-04-23/news/mn-1763_1_senior-noncommissioned-officer-soldiers-air-force.

Vine, David. "Military Bases, American—Foreign Countries." *Digital Research Archive*, May 14, 2017. https://dra.american.edu/islandora/object/auislandora%3A55685.

Wadham, Ben. "Crossing the Line: Why the Royal Commission Examined Initiation Rituals and Defence Abuse." *The Conversation*, July 1, 2016.

Walker, Mary L. "The Report of the Working Group Concerning Deterrence of and Response to Incidents of Sexual Assault at the U.S. Air Force Academy." 2003.

Walters, Mark Austin. *Hate Crime and Restorative Justice. Exploring Causes, Repairing Harms*. (Oxford: Oxford University Press, 2014).

Warren, Samuel. *Blackstone's Commentaries Systematically Abridged and Adapted to the Existing State of the Law and Constitution*. (London: W Maxwell, Bell Yard, Lincoln's Inn., 1855).

Waters, Christopher. "Beyond Lawfare: Juridical Oversight of Western Militaries." *Alberta Law Review* 46 (2009): 855–911.

Watts, Larry L. "Reforming Civil-Military Relations in Post-Communist States: Civil Control vs. Democratic Control." *Journal of Political and Military Sociology* 30, no. 1 (2002): 51–70.

Weber, Jeremy Stone. "Sentence Appropriateness Relief in the Courts of Criminal Appeals." *The Air Force Law Review* 66 (2010): 79–133.

———. "The Disorderly, Undisciplined State of the 'Good Order and Discipline' Term." *Air War College* Thesis Publication, February 16, 2016.

Weiland, Richard. "Court-Martial Charges for Australian Commandos Dismissed." *nimjblog.org* (2011). http://www.nimjblog.org/2011/05/court-martial-charges-for-australian.html.

Welch, Dylan. "Fighting the Enemy Within." *The Sydney Morning Herald*, April 16, 2011.

Westmoreland, William C. "Military Justice—a Commander's Viewpoint." *American Criminal Law Review* 10 (1971): 5–8.

Westwood, Ian. "Australian Military Court Report." Canberra: Department of Defence, 2009.

Wexler, Ian. "A Comfortable SOFA: The Need for an Equitable Foreign Criminal Jurisdiction Agreement with Iraq." *Naval Law Review* 56 (2008): 43–86.

Whealing, Justin. "The Fight for Military Justice." *Lawyers Weekly*, November 16, 2010.

Whitlock, Craig. "Disgraced Army General, Jeffrey A. Sinclair, Receives Fine, No Jail Time." *The Washington Post*, March 20, 2014.

———. "Sordid Details Spill Out in Rare Court-Martial of a General." *The Washington Post*, August 14, 2013.

Whitlock, Craig, and Adam Goldman. "Pentagon Will Not Discipline Petraeus in Sex-and-Secrets Scandal." *The Washington Post*, January 30, 2016.

Wiener, Frederick Bernays. *Civilians under Military Justice. The British Practice Since 1689 Especially in North America.* (Chicago and London: The University of Chicago Press, 1967).

Willey, Harry. "Kelliher VC." *Digger History: An Unofficial History of the Australian and New Zealand Armed Forces* (2002). www.Keliher VC From Court Martial to VC.mht.

Williams, Andrew S. "Safeguarding the Commander's Authority to Review the Findings of a Court-Martial." *Brigham Young University Journal of Public Law* 28 (2014): 471–512.

Winkle, Elizabeth P. Van, Lindsay Rock, Margaret H. Coffey, and Maia Hurley. "2014 Survivor Experience Survey Report on Preliminary Results Fiscal Year 2014, Quarter 4." Defense Research Surveys, and Statistics Center, Alexandria, VA: Defense Manpower Data Center, 2014: 1–122.

Winkle, Elizabeth P. Van, Laura Severance, Lisa Davis, Amanda Grifka, Kristin Williams, and Margaret Coffey. "Workplace and Gender Relations Survey of Active Duty Members." Office of People Analytics (OPA), Alexandria, VA: Defense Research, Surveys, and Statistics Center, 2016: 1–506.

Woldoff, Rachel A., and Karen G. Weiss. "Stop Snitchin': Exploring Definitions of the Snitch and Implications for Urban Black Communities." *Journal of Criminal Justice & Popular Culture* 17 (2009): 184–223.

Wolf, Antenor Hallo de. "Modern Condottieri in Iraq: Privatizing War from the Perspective of International and Human Rights Law." *Indiana Journal of Global Legal Studies* 13 (2006): 315–56.

Woolf, Naomi. "Rape in the Military a Culture of Coverup" *The Guardian*, June 15, 2012.

Woodburn, Joanna, and Philippa McDonald. "Child Abuse Royal Commission: Former Navy Officer Says Abuse 'Surprised and Horrified' Him." *ABC News*, June 22, 2016.

Woods, Ann-Marie. "A More Searching Judicial Inquiry: The Justiciability of Intra-Military Sexual Assault Claims." *Boston College Law Review* 55 (2014): 1329–66.

Woodward, Margaret. "Developing America's Airmen: A Review of Air Force Enlisted Training." In *Commander Directed Investigation Report*, U.S Air Force, 2012: 1–156.

Wright, Jessica et al., "Annual Report on Sexual Harassment and Violence at the Military Service Academies Academic Program Year 2013–2014." Sexual Assault Prevention and Response Office, 2015.

Wroe, David, and Deborah Snow. "An Officer, If Not Quite a Gentleman." *The Sydney Morning Herald*, December 1, 2012.

Wyatt, Michael. *The Italian Encounter with Tudor England: A Cultural Politics of Translation*. (Cambridge University Press, 2012).

Zacharek, Stephanie, Eliana Dockterman, and Haley Sweetland Edwards. "'Silence Breakers' Named Time Magazine's Person of the Year." *Time*, December 6, 2017.

Zerach, Gadi. "Coping Strategies of Former Prisoners of War Mediate the Intergenerational Transmission of Post-traumatic Stress Symptoms." *Anxiety, Stress, & Coping* 31, no. 2 (2018): 175–87.

Zimmerman, Jean. *Tailspin: Women at War in the Wake of Tailhook*. (New York: Doubleday, 1995).

Zipfel, Tomas. "The Politics and Finance of Civil-Military Reform in the Czech Republic." *Journal of Communist Studies and Transition Politics* 17, no. 1 (2001): 96–112.

Zoroya, Gregg. "General Avoids Jail Time in Case Involving Affair with Subordinate." *USA Today*, March 20, 2014.

Index

About the Author

Pauline Collins is a Professor in the School of Law and Justice at the University of Southern Qld, Toowoomba, Australia. Pauline has researched and published widely on military discipline law and the civil-military relationship for over a decade. She is a member of the European Research Group on Military and Society, and the International Law Association, Australian Branch. Pauline teaches International Humanitarian Law and Dispute Resolution. Prior to joining the University of Southern Qld in 1995, Pauline worked in the Office of the Director of Public Prosecutions, South Australia, and in private practice.

www.ingramcontent.com/pod-product-compliance
Ingram Content Group UK Ltd.
Pitfield, Milton Keynes, MK11 3LW, UK
UKHW040155091026
15587UKWH00018B/274

9 781498 557047